A HALO PUBLISHING INTERNATIONAL ANTHOLOGY

SHATTERED SILENCE

STORIES OF LOSS AND HEALING

A HALO PUBLISHING INTERNATIONAL ANTHOLOGY

SHATTERED SILENCE

STORIES OF LOSS AND HEALING

Halo Publishing International
7550 WIH-10 #800, PMB 2069,
San Antonio, TX 78229

First Edition, April 2024
ISBN: 978-1-63765-600-6
Library of Congress Control Number: 2023924709

The information contained within this book is strictly for informational purposes. Unless otherwise indicated, all the names, characters, businesses, places, events and incidents in this book are either the product of the author's imagination or used in a fictitious manner. Any resemblance to actual persons, living or dead, or actual events is purely coincidental.

Halo Publishing International is a self-publishing company that publishes adult fiction and non-fiction, children's literature, self-help, spiritual, and faith-based books. We continually strive to help authors reach their publishing goals and provide many different services that help them do so. We do not publish books that are deemed to be politically, religiously, or socially disrespectful, or books that are sexually provocative, including erotica. Halo reserves the right to refuse publication of any manuscript if it is deemed not to be in line with our principles. Do you have a book idea you would like us to consider publishing? Please visit www.halopublishing.com for more information.

Acknowledgements

We extend our heartfelt gratitude to every individual
who has made a contribution to this book

Diane Lopes

Irene S. Roth

Angela Gilson

Anapaula Corral

Monica Septimio

Dave Grunenwald

Lisa Michelle Umina

Conrad M. Gonzales

Fran Walsh Ward, PhD

Dr. Carol Leibovich-Mankes

Contents

Our Authors

Introduction

Fran Walsh Ward, PhD

*G*rief is a relentless terrorist that abducts human beings and transforms them into zombie shadows of their former selves. Grief does not discriminate. It can overcome universally; or it can annihilate the body, mind, and spirit of an individual. Grief can ravage a community, a continent, or the whole world in one fell swoop. The invader's grasp is ubiquitous. No one is safe from the clutches of grief.

Although intertwined, grief and grieving are different. *Grief* is a natural *emotion* in reaction to experiencing loss. *Grieving* is the mourning *process* following the loss.

Usually manifesting first in physical form, such as crying, grief is felt in the solar plexus and migrates up the chest and through the brain to evoke memories and also a need for the bereaved to connect with others. Triggered by any kind of loss, grief can be the worst experience in a person's life.

***

This first chapter of the anthology *Shattered Silence: Stories of Loss and Healing* is a reflection of universal human conditions garnered along my path as a teacher, writer, peace advocate, and participant in rituals and practices of many faiths and cultures.

***

Grief is a thief. No person or culture can escape its criminal nature. It steals the breath. Lungs control the flow of energy in a body. Crying, convulsive gasps of despair, and holding in the breath decrease oxygen, the life force that fuels humans. Grief is emotion harbored in the lungs and large intestine. Emotional blockage from not letting go of grief can interfere with the in-and-out action of the lungs and with normal physical elimination functions, both of which leave a person feeling drained of energy.

Any kind of loss can trigger feelings of depression. Other common visible symptoms of grief are strong feelings of sadness or sorrow, lack of focus, inability to trust, loss of purpose in living, constant thoughts of what was lost, and denial of the loss.

Everyone thinks that his own grief and pain are the worst. The Holmes-Rahe Life Stress Inventory assigns numeric values to major life factors, but numbers cannot reflect the hurt inside. No one's grief should be marginalized (see the website stress.org for the inventory to score your own recent life stress). Our innate sense of compassion guides us to sympathize with all unspeakable losses that members of our family of man have suffered. We are *all* connected. The Stress Inventory rates the death of a spouse as the greatest life stressor (a divorce and a jail term rank equally high). Everywhere in the world, spouses are grieving lost loves. Half of all Americans report having lost a loved one in the last three years.

***

My dear friend is one of those suffering. She documented her husband's heartbreaking health decline. It is unimaginable how she mustered her strength to monitor his changes, administer treatments, comfort him, and post painful-to-read updates for our friends. Following his death, we sympathized as she mourned his loss, but we could not make her pain go away. No one could. Nothing can. She is adjusting to an empty world without him. Life will never be the same. She has memories, but she does not have him. We grieve for her and trust that she can cope. It will take time, patience, and forgoing expectations for her to move on without him; but the hope is that she can and she will.

I met a widow in a different situation in a taverna near Athens, Greece. Dressed in black, she was sitting at the exit by the cash register. She was the personification of sadness. Feeling grief for her lamented husband was the life she chose. Her grief, known as perpetual grief, indicates an inability or lack of desire to step forward and leave the past in the past. For someone experiencing inability to progress through the stages to approach healing, therapy can help.

***

Elizabeth Kübler-Ross, in 1969, proposed the death-adjustment pattern of five stages of grief: denial, anger, bargaining, depression, and acceptance. Since then, alternative paradigms for experiencing death and grief have been introduced stressing that the process is not necessarily linear and that stages can be experienced simultaneously and without time limits. "Shock and disbelief" have replaced the term denial, and "searching and yearning" attempt to explain one's new reality. Each person grieves in his own way in order to heal and be able to give and receive love.

***

The widow I met in Greece was not alone in the depths of her anguish. Her grief is magnified by 6,000 times in

Vrindavan, India, the City of Widows. Since the sixteenth century when a widow was expected to immolate herself on her husband's funeral pyre, women have escaped to Vrindavan. The horrific self-sacrificial practice is now outlawed, but draconian laws in India have not improved sufficiently to grant property rights to castaway widows to alleviate their homeless condition.

Many of these widows in India are illiterate and have been in arranged marriages since they were fourteen years old. Banished by the family of the deceased, they feel unworthy of love or life. Widowhood can mean disaster for forty million widows each year who have been purged from their husbands' patriarchal family homes. They flock to Vrindavan, India. Barefoot and wearing white saris to symbolize that all color has been leached from their lives, they swarm the dirt streets by the thousands and spend their remaining days praying, singing devotional songs in temples and ashrams, and begging from tourists visiting the holy city of the childhood home of the Hindu Lord Krishna, the god of compassion, protection, and love. These widows seek comfort in their faith.

***

In a family, there's another death that is universally tragic. The death of any child is catastrophic.

Grief takes life hostage when it abducts a child. The supreme artistic example of this can be seen in *La Pietà,* the masterpiece by Michelangelo, who is also known as the Divine One. This sculpture imbued one solid piece of marble with all the anguish of a mother who has lost her child. It is located in St. Peter's Basilica at the Vatican in Rome, and it depicts the Blessed Virgin Mary cradling the body of her slain son, Jesus Christ, following His descent from the cross. *La Pietà* is rich in meaning and emotion, and it is the only work of art Michelangelo ever signed.

The name of this sculpture is said to come from the Italian word for *pity* and the Latin word for *piety*. Emotion flows from the artist through the statue to the visitors in the Vatican who observe, kneel, weep, wail, and express personal and religious emotions towards Mother, Son, and mankind.

When I visited the Vatican (which is sacred but public), it felt as if it were an invasion of privacy to bear witness to the torment in one mother's torturous voice as it wrenched everyone's hearts and filled the cavernous space with woe.

I believe that the Holmes-Rahe Stress Inventory neglects to include the loss of a child as an unparalleled pain. Many individuals, speaking from personal experience, say that death of a child is the greatest pain imaginable.

Our hearts ache when we learn of the death of any child. Parents are inconsolable when a child is ripped away from childhood under any circumstances. Whether the cause was a medical condition, an accident, a natural disaster, or any other reason, the pain is universal. It is palpable. We feel it, and we empathize. When the death occurs under unnatural circumstances, grief is compounded.

Parents grieve equally, but male grief and female grief are often expressed differently. They are both intense, but women can often emote and express themselves. When a friend's toddler niece died of meningitis, her uncle expressed anger, hurt, suffering, anguish, and torment. Men are steam kettles that can bubble and boil over. There is no right way or wrong way for anyone to express emotion. When grief takes possession of a person, pressure must be released, or confusion can prevail, regardless of the cause of the loss.

***

Grieving can begin even while someone who will be mourned is still alive. Anticipatory grief is a reaction to an expected death. Caregivers can experience anticipatory grief for an individual with a terminal illness and might begin to envision life without that person. Someone can also experience grief following a job layoff (such as occurred during the coronavirus pandemic), a divorce, or a medical diagnosis.

***

I experienced anticipatory grief and grieving while I was in Vietnam. I visited a leprosy hospital near Ho Chi Minh City (formerly Saigon, the South Vietnamese capital during the Vietnam War). The hospital was filled with crying and grieving patients, parents, and visitors. A little-boy patient was lying on the floor in the corridor. He was blue—not from air temperature or lack of oxygen. His exposed skin was as bright a blue as that of members of the Blue Man Group performers. I did not express the shock that I felt when I saw him. When he waved his little hand at me, I smiled and waved back.

I was led from room to room by hospital personnel. I waved hello to every patient. I was happy to see patients of all ages smile and wave back. I don't know if all visitors to that hospital are taken to see the patients, but I felt that grief was suspended for a time during my unannounced visit as an ordinary American tourist.

Only after my visit did I read that leprosy (now called Hansen's disease) is still endemic in some areas of the world, including Southeast Asia. As I left the hospital, I asked why the boy was blue. He had been painted blue as his personal invitation to the Hindu Boy God, Lord Krishna (one of the most popular and revered Hindu deities, the god of protection, compassion, tenderness, and love, whose birthplace is Vrindavan, the City of Widows). Blue gods have a blue aura. Blue is the color that represents anything that is vast and beyond perception, like the ocean or the sky. So much seems to be beyond our perception, such as grieving and healing.

***

Natural disasters have also provided us common terrors, as well as opportunities for unification beyond our perception. Climate change has shown us a side of Mother Nature that we never imagined in our wildest dreams. The National Weather Service keeps track of Mother Nature's activity, but it does not have a crystal ball to predict it. It can warn us to prepare, and it can play Monday-morning quarterback to evaluate itself.

Some natural disasters have occurred on a grand, unimaginable scale. Because of media coverage, the world has been able to witness some crises before, during, and after they have taken place.

During Hurricane Katrina, observers wondered if they would have had the stamina, courage, and will to survive that some residents of New Orleans demonstrated by chopping holes in their roofs, climbing out, and exposing themselves to hurricane-force winds and rain, and waiting—not knowing if they would be spotted or rescued by an SAR (search and rescue) team or the volunteer, impromptu Cajun navy.

Not only Americans but also people around the world shared the experience. We called it collective grief. The pain from that natural disaster rippled far beyond Louisiana. Everyone empathized, felt the pain, and went through the same steps of mourning as the individuals in New Orleans. Mutual mourning unites the world and has followed significant events such as wars, natural disasters like the tsunamis in Japan and Indonesia, school shootings, terrorist attacks, mass shootings, coronavirus pandemic, and deaths of public figures.

Our lives are touched and changed when we experience the suffering simultaneously. We are comforted with mutual humanitarian empathy.

**

We can grieve collectively. We have all grieved individually. I have been on both sides of grief and grieving. I have grieved, but I never imagined that I would be mourning my own loss of health due to a childhood illness. My symptoms of grief transitioned into the mourning process once I received a terminal diagnosis.

Of all the stages of grief I experienced, depression was the most difficult.

Five years ago, heart damage caused by rheumatic fever caught up with me. The beginning of the end was in Petra where a Bedouin chief came to my aid when I experienced a cardiac episode. Soon after my return home from that trip, I couldn't breathe. I was rushed to the emergency room where they wrapped me in copper blankets and prepared me to be airlifted to the heart hospital in Norfolk.

There, they told me that there was nothing that they could do for me. I signed the DNR (Do Not Resuscitate) papers, and they arranged for my final days to be spent in hospice where I was engaged in grief, grieving and healing with other residents.

Friends and relatives in various stages of the grief came or called to grieve and to say goodbye, I did not have the strength to comfort them in their grief, and their telling me that I would be in a better place was never a comfort to me.

What was a comfort was a diversion so I didn't have to think about dying, I understood how important my visit to the leprosy hospital had been to provide a respite from grieving.

I welcomed members of my chapel who brought me an angel holding the message "BELIEVE!" I did believe! I might have been the only one who believed I was not dying. One friend did bring me a lipstick. It was such a symbol of hope to me; it made me think that I might go outside again someday. Friends could anticipate my passing; but in the midst of my grieving, I could still hope for a miracle, and a miracle occurred. A brilliant cardiologist, Albert A. Burton, MD, had a plan. It was the first glimmer of hope.

He arranged surgery for me at a medical college in Richmond, where a surgeon from India replaced my mitral valve with a titanium valve in an experimental surgery. During his post-surgery visit, he could see that I could already breathe effortlessly and that my health had improved!

Since the surgery, I can now walk and talk simultaneously —a first in my life. In a quiet room, I can hear the mechanical valve; it is a comforting sound. Two years later I am ready for more adventures.

I am grateful for my experiences and my personal process through the stages of grief. Leaving the past behind and stepping into the future is a sign of healing readiness.

When we leave the past behind and step into the future, we have been given another opportunity to fulfill our purpose, whatever it is. My purpose might be to share my experiences through my writing —just in case a reader can glean some message to apply personally.

***

Because it is an emotion, there is no cure to eliminate the horrors that the terrorist called grief inflicts. Grief can never be eliminated because emotions cannot be extinguished. There is no cure for emotion. Emotions are to be expressed, not cured or suppressed.

It hurts more than anything to lose someone, and there is no correct way to express that emotion. It is subjective —what anyone feels is true; and the way feelings are expressed is the correct way, the right way, and the true way for that individual. Allowing one's authentic self to emerge by expressing feelings is a major step on the road to recovery.

There is no cure for grieving because grieving itself is an act of healing. Grief is not easy. Grieving is not easy. Life is not easy. Life is not fair.

Grief cannot be cured, but a mourner can be healed. There is no shortcut or hack for healing; advancing through the grieving process is a way to take action to heal. It is a difficult process, but it is the only way to cheat the terrorist grief and reclaim a semblance of the life that existed before the pain of grief pillaged it. If you are grieving, you are not alone.

The steps to take in grieving are difficult, and people who grieve often develop physical symptoms from the stress. Forewarned is forearmed.

Taking care of oneself is vital to a mourner's health. Preparations are basic, but sometimes must be forced. Remembering to take care of one's responsibilities (especially to other individuals or pets) might seem daunting. Eating, bathing, dressing, and taking care of necessities are all steps towards recovery.

There is no shame in asking for help from friends and supporters who want to help but not infringe on your privacy. Tell them what you want or need, dismiss well-meaning but unsolicited advice.

If you are supporting someone who is grieving, be kind and gentle. Be positive.

From my own experience as a griever and a potential bereaved, a person's presence (physically or virtually) is welcomed. Just listen, a griever needs to talk. Feel honored if someone opens up, but do not force anyone to talk. Offer to bring groceries or a treat. Be patient and compassionate. Don't expect anyone to be gleeful.

Many are going through stages of grieving. I have witnessed people around the world in various stages of the process. The most encouraging was a double amputee in a wheelchair on a pig farm in Vietnam. When I met him, I apologized for America and said I really didn't understand the Vietnam War. He called it "the *American* War." He told me that he did not hate me or any Americans. His was the most forgiving and sweetest heart.

He made it. He has gone through his grieving steps and made it to the final one: acceptance. He has earned the reward of stepping into the future.

Now more than ever, we should all be aware that people are fragile and carry burdens of physical and emotional hurt and pain. We need to show compassion and understanding as we meet and greet others gently. We can neutralize the terrorist grief with our love, hope, and compassion.

In Memory
of Anasofia

The Healing Journey after Losing a Child

Anapaula Corral

*O*ur lives may be sometimes bittersweet, but they are also miraculous. Even if it's for a short period, every second you breathe counts. The same is true for our loved ones. Every moment shared with our loved ones is significant.

If we look—really look—what bits of holiness can we find today? I glance around me at this very moment, and I see the lovely branches of the palm trees outside my window. I see the photos of my family. I see my hands; I touch my body; I feel my warm breath as I inhale and exhale; I feel my heartbeat...

I may be sad when I miss my daughter, but today the gratitude for having her is greater than the sorrow. My heart is still capable of loving, forgiving, and coping.

Today, I see the cozy space that shelters me as I pen these thoughts. I feel protected, I feel at peace, and, somehow, I have managed to put back together my heart, which for many years was shattered and silent.

In the year 2006, my daughter passed away. The day she died was the saddest day in my life. I really don't know how I made it through that day. It was the worst, most sad day any human being could experience. There is no word that can describe the pain, the emptiness in my heart, and the sorrow.

Losing a child before their first birthday is an indescribable and heart-wrenching experience. It's more than the loss of a loved one; it's the shattering of dreams, hopes, and the future that parents envisioned for their child. The pain is profound, and the grief is overwhelming. In just one year, parents form a deep bond with their child; that time is filled with countless moments of joy, laughter, and love. When that journey is abruptly cut short, the emotional toll is immense. It's an enduring ache, a void that can never be fully filled.

For those who have experienced such a devastating loss, compassion and support are crucial as they navigate the complex emotional fallout and healing process. Grieving is a complicated and personal experience that varies from person to person. While it's not accurate to say that no one likes to grieve, many people may find the process challenging and uncomfortable.

Grieving involves confronting and processing intense emotions such as sadness, anger, and loss. Many people find it difficult to face these emotions and may try to avoid the pain associated with grieving. Grieving requires individuals to be vulnerable and open about their feelings. Some people may perceive vulnerability as a weakness or may fear being judged, either of which can lead to denying grief and avoiding the grieving process.

Social norms and expectations can influence how individuals express and cope with grief. Different cultures may have unique ways of dealing with grief. In some cultures, grieving openly is encouraged, while in others, it may be a more private and internal process. In those cultures or communities that discourage open displays of emotion, it may be challenging for individuals to grieve in a way that feels natural. This has been a major problem for many, and I do not agree with any of these.

Fear of the unknown amidst grieving can lead to an uncertain and unfamiliar journey. People may fear the unknown aspects of the grieving process, including how long it will last and what the outcome will be.

This fear may lead some individuals to resist or delay the grieving process.

In certain cultures or communities where there is a stigma associated with grief, individuals may fear judgment or criticism for expressing their grief openly, either of which can lead to the suppressing of their emotions.

Some individuals develop coping mechanisms, such as avoidance or distraction, to deal with difficult emotions. These coping strategies can hinder the natural grieving process, as individuals may not allow themselves the time and space to grieve.

The topic of losing a child is often considered taboo due to the intense emotional pain and societal discomfort surrounding it. Society tends to avoid discussing subjects that evoke deep grief, sadness, and vulnerability. Losing a child is a heartbreaking experience that challenges societal norms, and people may be hesitant to bring it up out of fear of causing additional pain or not knowing how to respond. Additionally, cultural and religious beliefs may contribute to the taboo nature of discussing child loss. Different cultures may have varying perspectives on grief, death, and appropriate ways to address such sensitive topics.

It's important to note that breaking the taboo around discussing child loss can be crucial for providing support and understanding to those who have experienced such a profound loss. Encouraging open conversations and fostering empathy can help create a more compassionate and supportive community for individuals dealing with grief. Everyone copes with grief differently, and there is no right or wrong way to grieve. Encouraging open conversations about grief, providing support, and fostering a compassionate environment can help individuals navigate the grieving process more effectively.

Death is often considered sad because it involves the permanent loss of someone or something we care about. It is a significant and inevitable part of the human experience, and the emotions associated with death, such as grief and sadness, are natural responses to the profound impact it has on individuals and communities. The sadness may stem from the sense of loss, the absence of the person or thing, and the realization that life is finite. People often mourn the memories, connections, and experiences that they shared with the deceased. Additionally, cultural and societal norms contribute to the perception of death as a somber and emotional event.

So, yes, losing any of your loved ones is sad, and the timing of that loss is uncertain. However, there are many things you can do to change your state of mind and slowly try to find emotional balance.

Stages that can help you put your heart back together after it has been shattered due to the loss of a child:

Aknowledging the Pain

Grieve is a verb, and if you ever experience losing a child—or if you know anyone who is going through this—you will find that each person's grief is unique, and the grieving process is nonlinear. You will be emotionally, physically, and psychologically impacted. Write a journal.

Finding the Power of Inner Work

Introspection and self-reflection. Counseling, sharing with similar groups, and keeping active.

Being Resilient and Recovering

Share uplifting stories while navigating grief. Highlight the common threads of strength, courage, and perseverance in these stories.

Using Support Systems

Talk about the significance of having a support system, including family, neighbors, friends, and professional help. Highlight the role of empathy and understanding in fostering healing.

Finding Meaning

Explore how individuals can find meaning in their grief, perhaps through advocacy, creative outlets, or community involvement. Discuss the concept of post-traumatic growth and how it can be a transformative force.

Embracing Joy

Share stories of individuals who have found moments of joy and happiness after their profound sorrow. Discuss the importance of allowing oneself to experience joy without guilt.

Knowing the Journey Is Ongoing

Summarize the transformative power of healing. Emphasize that the journey continues, and healing is an ongoing process.

***

I also have several thoughts that I would like to share. These are general notes I have written in all the years I have worked on putting my shattered heart back together. It is my hope they will inspire you to heal.

Evolving

Human life is a series of attachments, transitions, and losses. We explore; we connect; we love. We grow; we change; we lose.

Over and over on our journey through life, we experience hurt. We often equate the death of a loved one with the term "loss." But, really, it's just one kind of loss. Many other losses are deeply consequential as well, from health and financial problems to divorce, estranged relationships, abuse, betrayals, traumatic events, moves from beloved places, lost or broken dreams, and more. Even happy, appropriate transitions can be partly painful, such as leaving for college, getting married, and seeing children into adulthood.

All these significant losses can be deeply hurtful. When they arise, we naturally grieve inside. But most of us haven't learned that, just as with death, it's essential to mourn—or express our grief—over them. It is through mourning that we integrate all our losses along life's path. It is through mourning that we heal and learn to live well with ever-deeper joy and meaning.

Grieving and mourning our life losses take intention and commitment. The good news is that you can mourn while living a meaningful life.

Navigating the Duality of Life and Death

No matter how much we wish for a life of sunshine and smooth sailing, the world always finds a way of humbling us. We're young until we're not. We're healthy until we receive a devastating diagnosis. We're with those we love until they're taken from us. Forests burn while the birds sing. Life's beauty is inseparable from its fragility.

This "bothness"—the persistent, sometimes painful duality of life—is a cornerstone of emotional agility. You're experiencing bothness when a career change both thrills and terrifies you in equal measure. It's present when your child has disappointed you, and you love them all the same. Bothness exists in our capacity to welcome conflicting emotions—to feel joy at having known someone even as we grieve when they've passed on.

This bothness—the integration into your life of all emotions, even the challenging ones—is a litmus test of psychological health and well-being. It is the ability of an individual to recognize a difficult emotion or experience as being part of them without allowing it to define their identity or dictate their actions. Mixing or integration is when we refuse to classify our feelings as inherently good or bad, and instead accept them as part of the experience of being human.

The opposite of integration is segmentation or separation. Segmentation happens when we separate our lives into things we think about and things we do not think about, places we go and places we do not go, topics we discuss and those that are off-limits. It often rears its head during challenging times. If a couple ignores a source of conflict within their relationship, they drive a wedge between them, cordoning off that topic with a No Entry sign. When a leader perceives an employee feels an organizational change is negative, rather than a signal that the employee is invested in their job, it is an erosion of that employee's psychological safety in the workplace. But reliance on segmentation is unsustainable. It doesn't match our lived reality, in which life's darkest and most joyful moments, interwoven, create its beauty.

We see the rigidity of segmentation all around us, from our adherence to traditional professional hierarchies, to the way we talk to our children, to the harmful or divisive. We assume leaders have the answers, so we don't ask rookies for their perspectives. Instead of acknowledging that riding a bike without training wheels is both frightening and achievable, we tell our kids, "It's not that scary." And when a loved one tries to broach a topic that makes us anxious, we shut down instead of opening a dialogue and trying to achieve an understanding. But effective coping rarely involves turning away and shutting down. After all, how will we ever have truly meaningful conversations if we can't stand to face discomfort?

Bothness allows you to engage with people whose values depart from your own. It allows you to understand that a conversation with someone who thinks differently from you doesn't negate what you hold dear. Indeed, it is often the choice not to reach out and engage that is antithetical to your values. There is wisdom in bothness. We can move forward in hope and in fear, respecting the contradictions inside each one of us. Bothness gives us access to the full spectrum of life. Too often, we think that the world is a series of either/or decisions. Be bold. Choose both.

Living in the Present Moment
Living in the moment and cherishing time with loved ones is a crucial aspect of leading a fulfilling and meaningful

life. Here are some ways to describe the importance of this:

- Limited Time Frame: Life is finite, and time is a limited resource. Embracing the present allows us to fully experience and appreciate the moments we have with our loved ones. Recognizing the transient nature of time encourages us to make the most of each moment.

- Strong Connections: Living in the moment fosters deeper connections with those we care about. When we are fully present, we engage more authentically with others, which strengthens our relationships. These shared experiences create lasting memories that contribute to the forming of strong bonds.

- Mindfulness and Well-Being: Being present in the moment involves practicing mindfulness, which has been linked to improved mental and emotional well-being. It reduces stress, anxiety, and worry about the future or past. Cherishing time with loved ones in the present contributes to a more positive and peaceful state of mind.

- Absence of Regrets: Regret often stems from missed opportunities or neglecting the present. By cherishing moments with loved ones as they happen, we minimize the likelihood of regret later in life. It allows us to look back without wishing we had been more present in certain situations.

- Positive Atmosphere: Living in the moment contributes to a positive atmosphere in our relationships. It allows us to appreciate the small joys, express gratitude, and focus on the positives, which creates an uplifting environment for ourselves and our loved ones.

- Quality Over Quantity: It's not just about the amount of time spent with loved ones, but the quality of that time. Being present ensures that the time we share is meaningful and enjoyable, which leads to more enriching experiences.

- Balance in Priorities: In the hustle and bustle of life, it's easy to get caught up in various responsibilities. Living in the moment helps us strike a balance between work, personal pursuits, and time with loved ones. It reminds us of the importance of prioritizing relationships.

In summary, living in the moment and cherishing time with loved ones is a conscious choice that adds depth, joy, and fulfillment to our lives. It's about savoring the present, building lasting connections, and embracing the beauty of shared experiences.

Leaving a Family Legacy

The death of a child can drastically change the family legacy; the profound impact of losing a child has the potential to reshape the narrative and trajectory of the family's legacy. Traditionally, a family legacy might be seen as a continuation, through generations, of the values, traditions, and accomplishments that have been passed down. However, the death of a child introduces a tragic and unexpected element that can alter this narrative.

The child's legacy will be different if we choose to see it can also contribute to society and create a legacy of its own amidst the grief and the pain. Despite the heartbreak and pain, there is an opportunity to reinterpret the legacy left by the child. Instead of focusing solely on the loss, one can choose to recognize the potential for the child's impact on society and the positive legacy that can emerge from their memory.

- Shift in Perspective: A shift in perspective from viewing the child's legacy solely through the lens of loss and grief, to considering the positive contributions and impact the child had during their time.

- Contribution to Society: Even in the face of tragedy, the child's legacy can extend beyond the family unit. This could involve acknowledging the positive qualities, values, or actions of the child that may have had a broader impact on the community or society.

- Legacy of Positivity amidst Grief: Despite the grief and pain associated with the loss, there is an invitation to create a legacy that encompasses positivity and meaningful contributions. This could involve memorializing the child through acts of kindness, charity, or initiatives that honor their memory.

- Recognition of Individuality: Each person, including a child, has a unique impact on the world. By recognizing and celebrating the individuality of the child, one can create a legacy that reflects their personality, interests, and the positive aspects of their presence.

- Inspiration for Others: The acknowledgment of a child's potential contribution to society, even in a short life, can serve as inspiration for others. It may motivate individuals to make a positive impact and cherish the moments they have with their loved ones.

- Narrative of Hope: Amidst the grief, there is an opportunity to shape a narrative of hope, resilience, and positive change. It encourages the family to focus on the enduring impact the child and the potential for that impact to continue in meaningful ways.

- Legacy of Resilience: Families may find strength in creating a legacy of resilience. This could involve supporting each other, engaging in charitable activities in memory of the child, or participating in support groups to help others going through similar experiences.

- Remembrance and Honor: Families may choose to remember and honor the child in various ways, such as creating a memorial, establishing a scholarship fund, or participating in events that commemorate the child's life. These acts contribute to a positive legacy in the face of tragedy.

- Impact on Future Relationships: The loss of a child can impact how family members approach future relationships and life decisions. It may influence perspectives on parenting, priorities, and the importance of cherishing moments with loved ones.

The power of choosing to see the child's legacy, not just in terms of loss, but as an opportunity to contribute positively to society. It encourages a perspective that acknowledges the child's unique legacy and the potential for creating a lasting impact that goes beyond the immediate grief and pain.

***

In the face of profound loss, we embark on a journey of healing, a path marked by the echoes of cherished memories. While the pain of losing a family member may never fully subside, our ability to endure and find solace reveals the strength within us. Just as wounds may fade, the love and shared moments linger, guiding us towards a space where healing coexists with the enduring spirit of those we hold dear. In this tapestry of loss and healing, we discover the resilience to navigate life's complexities, knowing that the indomitable bond of love transcends the boundaries of time and space.

My deep wish for you is that you can pick up the pieces of your shattered heart and start your healing journey. You are not alone.

In Memory of
Arthur Frank King

My Great-Uncle Art

This Was His Life

Angela Gilson

*A*rthur Frank King was born on May 4, 1936, to Waldo T. King and Helen E. King in Vaugh, near Sedro-Woolley, in the state of Washington. Art always had a smile on his face and was ambitious. During high school, he bought, refurbished, and resold seventeen old cars, worked for the *Olympia Daily News*, managed a local drugstore, and still made time for varsity cheerleading. He graduated with honors from Olympia High in 1954.

That same year, he joined the United States Air Force, where he trained as an aircraft mechanic. Shortly after

Mexico. He loved taking them to the ocean. His favorite hobbies were working on his planes, old cars, hunting, and fishing.

My Uncle Art, he wasn't just an uncle; he was a grandpa to me. I will always remember him as a funny, kind, and caring man who walked my grandma down the aisle and gave her away to my grandfather. He was like a father figure to my aunt Louise's kids who had lost their father. He stepped up, was there for them, and helped when they needed him.

I will always remember the trip we took to the jelly-bean factory, the funny poses we made at the beach, the sand castles we built, the ocean as we walked together in the water, and the pancakes at dinnertime when he and my grandma visited us. I remember his voice and will carry his warm hugs with me for the rest of my life.

I remember the time when Uncle Art and Aunt Kathy came to our home in California from Texas; Uncle Art and my dad put down wood floors and kitchen tiles in our home. They also built my mom an entertainment center. I learned a lot from watching him and my dad work together. Uncle Art also taught me about his RV and how it worked.

When we were at the dinner table, and I was really hungry and couldn't wait to eat, he noticed. So he took a couple of bites, and so did I. Then he went, "Shh," with a smile on his face. After that, everyone at the table said grace before the meal. I loved when Uncle Art said the grace.

Uncle Art was always devoted to his family, friends, and faith. He was a charter member of Grace Bible Church, where he participated in many leadership roles, deacon council, small groups, and men's group. He engaged in the community, the local VFW, and participated in a variety of service groups. His missionary spirit led him to support Gideons International and personally visit with the children of VivaKids.

Last time I saw Uncle Art was after work when they visited us. I had to get my last picture with him because, not long after that, a few months later, he passed away. We all knew he was sick in the beginning, so I said my goodbyes over the phone while my dad visited him. I told him he was like a grandpa to me. He choked up and almost started crying.

That day, he passed away. I was in college, and my dad texted me. My dad barely texts or calls, so at that moment, I knew Uncle Art had died. I cried silently in my dorm room. My boyfriend at the time had to pick me up off the floor. He asked what happened. I told him my Uncle Art had passed. He asked if my parents had told me, but I said no. I just knew he had passed. It breaks my heart till this day that I couldn't be there with him in person to give him one last hug.

That night, I remember as if it were yesterday. I woke from a nightmare at 4:30 a.m. I usually go for walks when I'm upset. Little did I know I wanted to go home, so I walked home that night, which turned out to be around a three-hour walk.

I didn't get home until around seven, right at sunrise. I didn't have a key; I had left it in my dorm. So I rang the doorbell. My parents were surprised that I was there at the front door. I went into my room, and they both followed me. My parents had sad faces. My dad sat next to me on my bed, and my mom was on the brink of tears.

They told me Uncle Art had passed away. I told them I already knew. They looked surprised and asked how I knew. I told my dad he never texts me, so that's how I knew. My dad, who doesn't show emotions, told me it was okay to cry because he wasn't just an uncle to us; he was a dad and a grandpa. My parents didn't want to tell me until class was over, but I already knew he had passed without them even telling me.

I remember, before school started, I got from Aunt Kathy a beautiful sea-turtle necklace, which I still have. Whenever I miss Uncle Art, I grab the sea turtle in my hands and remember him and his warm hug. I think just having that beautiful necklace helps me through it. I also pray to him and for his soul to find peace because he is no longer in pain.

At age eighty-three, Uncle Art passed away peacefully in his sleep on November 4, 2019, in Canyon Lake, Texas, from diabetes, which is what he suffered from for a long time. He is survived by his wife, Kathleen King; son, Jerry King, and wife, Beverly Luce; granddaughter, Caitlin King; brother, Alan King; sister, Joanne, and husband, Bill Brotten; and by a bounty of other family, in-laws, nieces, and nephews. He was preceded in death by his oldest son, Steven King, and brother, Douglas King. Uncle Art was buried on Friday, November 15, at Fort Sam Houston National Cemetery.

While I was grieving the loss of my uncle, I wanted to be alone most of the time. When I was alone, I coped by listening to music. That's how I express my emotions and let them out.

My Uncle Art will live within us. What my dad learned from his uncle, he is teaching me. We will always have the memories of dinners and places we visited. At the time of his death, I was already seeing a counselor, so we both talked about that night; the counselor said that I had a manic episode.

As a family, we talk about the loss of Uncle Art, but my dad keeps telling me that he was sick for a long time. But he had an amazing, long life and was surround by loved ones when he passed.

It Pays to Just Listen

Conrad M. Gonzales

$\mathcal{A}$ fter retiring from the San Antonio Fire Department in 1998 as a firefighter and paramedic, I often wondered if there would ever be another moment that I needed to put my paramedic skills to use. Would it be saving someone from choking? Applying a tourniquet? Saving a drowning victim? Or just saving a life by telling someone to make sure they buckle up? I thought to myself, *I hope not.*

Well, three weeks prior to writing this piece, I did, in fact, perform the abdominal thrusts on my mom as she started to choke while we were having lunch! That's the two, and sometimes three, jobs. He kept repeating that he did not deserve going through this torture and that he couldn't take it anymore.

We were on the phone for over twenty minutes when I offered to drive over to his house so we could sit down and talk. He refused my offer. He said there wasn't anything I could do for him. I asked him to just let me come over there, and I promised him that I would not call the police or EMS. He finally agreed. He gave me his street address, and as I told him thank you, I mentioned that I knew exactly where the street was because I used to work at the fire station a few miles north of where he lived.

I asked him, before hanging up, if he had any weapons, such as a gun or knife, on him or nearby. He said he did not. I told him that I trusted him, and I didn't want him to hurt me or try to kill me because I had children and people who cared about me. And if he tried to do something, I would die fighting him. He reassured me that he did not have any weapons at all. I informed him that I would be there in twenty minutes and asked him to please trust me. He responded by telling me that he trusted me and would wait. I got in my car and was on the highway in less than three minutes.

On my way to Robert's house, I was thinking about that call I went on as a paramedic, the one with the gentleman who was holding a knife to his own throat.

I asked myself, *Should I be doing this? Am I risking my life for someone I don't even know? Should I call the police or EMS?* I thought that it was actually my job back then, but here, now, was a human being who needed some help.

To this day, I have no idea how and why he called me at the office. Had I met him before? Had our paths crossed at some time? Had he attended any of my classes? At this point, it didn't matter. He needed someone to talk to. I needed to listen, and we needed to trust each other.

As I turned onto his street, I remember Robert's description of the house. It was an older one-story home with a white picket fence around the yard and red rose-bushes in front of the house. With the yard beautifully manicured, it was easy to spot. I stopped the car, stepped out, and started to cross the street and head toward the porch. I was looking around to see if there was a gun or rifle poking out a window or door. This, I learned from friends who were police officers. They would tell me to be observant "because you never know." So I looked to see if doors were made out of wood or steel, and I checked for alternative means of escape. Unfortunately, the only exit point I saw, should I need one, was the front door.

I knocked on the door. There was no answer. I knocked again and quietly yelled that it was Conrad. Then I heard footsteps on what sounded like a wooden floor. It sounded as if he was wearing boots. He opened the door slowly as he peeked around it; I could only see half of his face. He asked if there was anyone else with me. I assured him, just as I told him, that no one came with me. He opened the door and let me in. Yep, he was wearing boots, and I was correct—wooden floors.

I thanked him for letting me in as we walked slowly into the living room. I could see why he was devastated. The house was empty except for the dining room table and four chairs. He was right. She took everything in the house, even the refrigerator.

As we sat down at the table, Robert began to cry as he continued telling me how "messed up" it was for his wife to leave him without even a single notion or warning that she was tired of being his wife and that she wanted out of the relationship. There was a note on the dining room table. He grabbed it and showed it to me. He told me to read it.

In the note, Robert's wife described how the last few years were intolerable, and she just didn't love him anymore. "You're never home," the note read. He described how his wife had always wanted to "keep up with the neighbors" who bought better homes, cars, and went on vacations. Robert then explained that his plan was to work two, maybe three, jobs to please her and try to live the same lifestyle as the neighbors.

I asked Robert how long they'd been married.

"We've been married for nine years. Next week would have been ten."

I applauded him for doing what he could to make his wife happy, but told him, sometimes, that doesn't help. Working your butt off can lead to distress and increase the likelihood of heart disease, high blood pressure, and other ailments. He mentioned that he had high blood pressure, and his family had a history of diabetes. He'd been to the doctor a few weeks earlier and was told that he needed to be compliant in taking his medication as prescribed. I asked him if he was, and he responded by telling me that he "was and then wasn't."

I told him that he really needed to take care of himself if he wanted to see his kids. That struck a nerve. He started crying again and stated that she wasn't going to let him see the kids. I reassured him that he would see his kids again, but that it would take time, patience, perseverance, and a lot of prayers. I told him that, once, I didn't get to see my son for a year, and that hurt. But the courts finally decided in my favor and gave me joint custody, which was out of the norm back in those days.

As Robert finally calmed down, I came to the decision that I had to talk to him about his plan to kill himself. He said he was going to hang himself in the garage, where no one would find him. I asked him where he worked. He refused to say. I explained to him that, no matter

He looked at me and said, "Thank you."

I replied, "No, thank you for calling me and trusting me to be here with you."

We both turned around and stepped out of the garage. As I was walking behind him, I turned around to close the garage door. As I was doing that, I looked up to see where the rope had hung from the rafter. I took a deep breath and thought, *Thank you, Lord.*

I followed Robert and walked into the house. I had the bag in my hand. We walked to the dining room table and sat down again. As we did, the doorbell rang. I asked him if he was expecting anyone or if he had called anyone else.

He said no. He then asked me if I had called anyone. I reminded him that I promised not to call anyone or have anyone follow me. He got up, walked to the door, and stopped before opening it. He yelled to see who it was.

It was his sister. She had stopped by to check on him, as she had tried calling him earlier in the day. She was on her way home from work and had stopped to see how he was doing. She knew that he'd been having problems at home.

As she stepped in, she saw me sitting at the table. I stood up and introduced myself. Robert then told her that I was a friend who was visiting. It felt good that Robert now considered me a friend. Robert told her that I had come by, as he needed someone to talk to about his troubles.

Robert's sister looked around and noticed that all the furniture was gone. She seemed to be getting ready to ask Robert what happened, but he stopped her and said that everything was all right and that his wife had moved out. He then continued to tell her that he was fine and "my" friend Conrad was there to help. She turned and looked at me to thank me. She told me that she'd been trying to get someone to speak to Robert, but to no avail. I told her that things happen for a reason and that I was glad to be there for him. As she sat down at the table, I felt that it was time to leave Robert and his sister so they could talk.

Robert actually looked at me and said, "Thank you, Conrad. I got this."

I returned his gaze and said, "I know you do." I proceeded to the door; Robert walked with me and opened the door for me.

His sister then asked me as she looked down at the floor, "Sir, is this your bag?"

I told her, "Yes, thank you! I almost forgot it."

Little did she know what was in the bag and what had happened minutes before she arrived. She was reaching down for it when I told her not to worry; I would get it.

I picked the bag up, turned around, told Robert to call me anytime, and reminded him that he had my number. Then, we gave each other a big hug as he whispered, "Thank you, sir. You saved my life."

I responded, "We both did," as I stepped out the door and looked back at Robert as he closed the door. We gave each other a thumbs-up.

I walked to my car, opened the trunk, put the bag inside, and closed the trunk. I walked around and opened the car door, got in, started the car, and put on my seat belt. I turned to the left and looked over at Robert's house. It was dusk. Through the curtains, I could see the lights on in the dining room where Robert and I had sat. Now, there were two shadows, Robert and his sister. I took a deep breath, put my car in gear, and drove off.

As I was pulling out of the neighborhood, I had this feeling of relief, happiness, and exhaustion...emotional exhaustion. I felt drained as if I'd just gotten off work after a twenty-four-hour shift in EMS. I felt as though I were a tire with a slow leak, its pressure dropping so low the tire would soon be flat.

I called my supervisor at work. Something I hated doing while driving. I told her I would not be returning to work, as it was close to five o'clock. She asked me if I was all right. I told her I was just a little tired and going home to rest a bit and would see her the next day. She inquired about my whereabouts since I left without notifying her. I apologized and told her I had an emergency to tend to. I assured her everything was okay.

While driving, I was lost in my thoughts and thinking about Robert. Before I knew it, I was pulling into my driveway. I pulled up to my garage and stopped right in front of it. I reached for the remote to open the garage door but halted. I quickly remembered that my garage had exposed rafters. At that moment, I didn't really want to be reminded of what transpired at Robert's house.

I parked in the driveway, turned the car off, and stepped out of it. I then opened the trunk and took the bag out. I walked over to the garbage can, lifted the lid, and threw the bag into the garbage can. As the bag dropped in, I looked at it and said a quick prayer, "Thank you, Lord, for being there for me and for Robert." I then closed the lid and walked inside the house.

As I walked through my kitchen, I thought about Robert and how he must have felt as he walked into an empty house and found his wife and kids gone. I know it had to have been tough on him. He must have felt devastated and robbed of his life without his wife and children.

Emotionally drained, I walked into my bedroom and sat on the bed. I was grateful that I had a bed on which to sleep. I thought about Robert not having a bed, so I called him. The phone rang, and he answered. I asked him if he was okay, and he said he was fine and staying the night at his sister's house. I was relieved and assured him that I would be available if he needed anything.

He said, "Thanks, Conrad. I'm good now."

We hung up. I took off my shoes and shirt and laid my head on the pillow. I looked up at a picture of Jesus Christ, which was hanging on the wall. "I am with you every day," the caption read.

"Yes, He is. He was today."

Lying there, I remembered an important thing from my days in EMS. Whenever you come across a patient who is thinking about taking their own life, you have to be patient. Developing trust between you, as a paramedic, and your patient is tantamount to creating a positive outcome. Practicing patience, remaining calm, and, most important, listening play major roles in the end result.

Fast-forward to the year 2023—I spoke to Robert's sister and asked how he was doing. She said he was doing fine. He actually reunited with his wife not long after the incident; they have been together now for almost twenty years. She said they still have their ups and downs but have vowed to stay together. I told her to tell Robert hello for me and that I think about him and his family. For this piece, his sister said he declined to provide a photo of himself, as he wishes to remain anonymous. I told her that I understood, and we left it at that. I'm glad he's still with us.

One of many important characteristics of a first responder is the ability to listen. That day, Robert reached out, as he needed someone to talk to and someone to listen. I just happened to answer the phone when he called; ironically, the administrative assistant was on her break, and I just happened to answer the phone for her. It wasn't a coincidence; it was a "God-incidence."

One trait that my parents ingrained in me was the ability to let others talk and to lend an ear. I learned that characteristic at a very young age and carried it into my profession as a firefighter and paramedic. Witnessing countless injuries and deaths allowed me to learn and listen to those who were suffering from injuries or who had lost their loved ones. There were many times as a paramedic that I'd place my hand on someone's shoulder and quietly tell them, "I'm sorry for your loss. I'm here for you." They talked, grieved, and cried. And I listened.

Anger, denial, bargaining—these are some of the responses I witnessed when a spouse, child, brother, sister, mother, or father died. We were usually the first on the scene. This is why we're called first responders. We're the first to respond to those in need of assistance during a life-threatening crisis. That is our job. That is what I teach future EMTs and paramedics—how to respond in a crisis.

So how do we respond in a crisis? We respond to distress with eustress. Extreme anxiety, pain, and sorrow describe distress. Positivity and the ability to respond and cope in a positive and beneficial manner describe eustress. We must focus on reacting with eustress, as this will enhance the likelihood of a better outcome. Easier said than done, I've been told. Yes, but it *can* be done. All we have to do is reach out to someone and…listen.

In November of 2014, I wrote the following poem during a difficult time in my life as I was thinking that there IS light in the darkness. Hence the title, "The Lighter Side of Darkness." It is about finding positivity when grief and turmoil abound. I hope this poem keeps you healthy, safe, and sound.

"The Lighter Side of Darkness"

There are times in life when we suffer pain and sorrow,
and there seems as if there will be no tomorrow.
Pain is inflicted on our hearts and on our minds,
and solutions to despair may be impossible to seek or find.

There are times in life when tears will flow,
and when they stop, no one really knows.
Life will seem to be shadowed and obscured,
and in vain, we search for reasons and a cure.

There are times in life when darkness seems to take over,
and no one seems to be there to lean on or cry on their shoulder.
We never know when our time shall arrive,
so we must take charge of our feelings and our lives.

Darkness is a shadow cast upon our light.
What can we do to make things right?
Darkness is temporary only if we want it to be.
So we must make a change to live forever happily.

We must move from the shadow of darkness and seek the light.
We seek in ourselves peace and the God of Might.
The Lord allows us to see darkness to learn about love,
And pain is an ingredient of strength from above.

*In Memory
of "Sticks"*

Friendship and Grief

Dave Grunenwald

$\mathcal{A}$ s I prepared to write, I asked my pastor, "Does humor play a role when grieving—for example, pulling a prank on a dying friend? What I am about to tell you occurred, but I am wondering if it is okay to write about it?"

He answered, "Grief and humor often go together. The word *funeral* starts with the word *fun*."

Sometimes, laughter is the best medicine. This is a story that combines grief and humor.

a common basement two floors below. It would have been funny, except it scared my younger sister when she returned from the basement after doing laundry. She was upset; so much so, she called Mom, who came home from work.

Returning shortly thereafter to witness my mother and sister sitting on the *living room couch in the dining room,* I asked, "Why is the couch in here?"

Mom simply said, "Your friends are at it again."

Of course, my mother believed it was the Hunk's doing, but told him she forgave him, knowing he was often the target of our pranks. For years, he reminded Mom he had not rearranged the furniture, but she took her belief to the grave.

I did not have the heart to tell her he was not the culprit. Sticks and the Stud had gotten off the hook.

About a year or so later, looking around the living room, for the first time I realized they had also rearranged the pictures on the walls; they were still hanging in the wrong places.

Loss of a Good Friend

Many of us knew grief at an early age from losing a family member—in my case, my father when I was five and my sister seven. Loss of a family member can be a devastating event in one's life. As you grow, you come to realize that death is a part of life as you learn to accept and live with it. Such acceptance makes you stronger.

Remember, though, when we were young, we thought sixty was old!

Later in life, I lost my beloved spouse of forty years and several siblings. My friends have had similar experiences. Death of a family member saddens you, often leaving a scar that lasts a lifetime. You come to expect the eventual loss of parents and grandparents, and other family members as well, though it is always difficult to deal with.

Losing a lifelong friend in the prime of his life is different than losing a family member. Not more painful or sadder. Different.

By the time you reach your fifties, and have a spouse and kids, and a house and mortgage, it is different. You settle into midlife, raise children, see them leave the roost or head off to college, as you and your spouse become empty nesters, plan to travel, and enjoy life as you slow down.

Then, one day, one of these dear friends gets sick.

We learned Sticks had cancer when departing for a golf trip; at the last minute, we found out he would not be

Toilet Papering Houses

When we were younger, toilet papering each other's houses was a regular thing, and it became something of a game as we critiqued the quality of each other's work. Did the perpetrator cover the tops of the trees, not just the low branches? Did the toilet paper go over the roof of the house, not just hang from the edges? Was there an artistic quality to the layout?

Once, we took turns papering a house while the others judged, Olympics style, using cards with numbers one through ten. We always had fun, and as you can see, we took toilet papering seriously. Okay, okay, I made up the judging part; though, looking back, it seems as if it would have been a clever idea.

Sticks was known for the quality of his work. He acted whenever he came back to Youngstown to visit family. He papered a house and then left evidence behind, such as an article of clothing, intending to implicate someone else. As if we could not figure out it was Sticks'.

Sticks' efforts were legendary; so much so, we all promised him one day we would fly to Las Vegas and paper his house. He did not seem worried, figuring it would never happen; we were not sure either.

For that reason, one toilet-papering job stands above the rest.

Then Cancer Strikes

Sticks, along with his wife and kids, was dealing with this dreaded disease in ways we could not even imagine. The cancer was mangling his otherwise-healthy body. I remember when I asked him once what treatments the doctors prescribed.

He said, "I asked the doctors to try everything—I mean everything—radiation, chemotherapy, even things that were in a clinical-testing phase or existed in *science fiction*" (his words, not mine). He knew the score.

It was not the first time in our lives that we dealt with death. However, this was one of us, a great friend, a member of life's foundation. At times, we did not know what to think or how to act.

We came to learn how hard it is to deal with the illness of a great friend, and how helpless you feel when he lives a great distance away. We all wanted to be helpful to his wife and kids. I am sure we were in our own ways, though finding it hard at times. At this point, the rest of us had remained in the area, and we saw each other or talked on the phone regularly. You remember, the waning days of snail mail and landlines.

During the last year of Sticks' life, I was regularly traveling for business out west, therefore able to visit him once or twice a month. I saw him more in the last year of his

We proceeded to paper the backyard and rear of the house. It was a large house on a golf course in a newer section of Las Vegas, north of the Strip. What we were about to do was not something the neighbors were accustomed to seeing. We figured he would be in big trouble with the homeowners association; Sticks had received just that day a notice because his exterior garage light had burned out. This was a bit different.

We all sat on the back patio, talking and laughing, as we clandestinely took turns papering the back of the house and yard, including trees and bushes; you could see the mountains in the background. We decided to skip the front of the house, as setting up our dying friend to answer to the HOA was not part of the plan.

Sticks was unaware, as we were careful not to talk close to him; we assumed it is true that when you lose your eyesight, it sharpens your hearing. This was a smart guy; he might get suspicious if he thought we were up to something.

In the end, it was an amateurish quality of work, as we did not want to make too big of a scene. We were there because we loved him, not to earn an Olympics score of ten. Upon completion, we posed with Sticks, enabling his daughter to get just the right photo as we were about to let the cat out of the bag.

The Stud answered when the Kid called. He handed the phone to Sticks. The Kid told Sticks he was sorry for not joining us, but that he had enjoyed the photos the Stud had texted him (yes, texting photos was now possible), that he thought Sticks' home was beautiful, especially the view out the back towards the mountains. However, the Kid explained, he had never seen decorations quite like Sticks'.

Sticks asked, "What do you mean?"

The Kid said, "Your decorations, they are unique." When Sticks again asked the Kid what he meant, the Kid answered, "Ask the Stud."

Upon doing so, the Stud handed Sticks a roll of toilet paper.

Sticks then said, "Let me see if I have this right. I am blind and dying, and you guys toilet papered my house?"

"Yes, of course," we answered, reminding him we promised to do so one day.

The photo his daughter took at that moment has a place of honor in each of our homes.

Moments later, Sticks' sprinkler system, which was on an automatic timer, came on. We were not used to such high technology; we marveled at it as we watched the water soak the bushes and trees adorned by the toilet paper. Surprised, we quickly retrieved the toilet paper, not needing to keep quiet as the gig was up.

If only for a short while, I am quite sure Sticks felt normal. I know we did.

Goodbye, Old Friend

Sticks died a brief time thereafter. Many attended the celebration of life and demonstrated their love for Sticks. Friends and family from Youngstown, Las Vegas, and elsewhere were there.

We all attended his celebration of life in Las Vegas; both a sad and happy occasion not to be missed. We met a few of his local friends whom we had heard about over the years. The Stud and the Voice spoke, outlining the top-ten memories from our friendships. What do you suppose was at the top of the list?

When I was married, I had a photo taken of the six of us standing in a semicircle, each holding a raised shot glass, about to make a toast. Twenty-five years later, at Sticks' funeral, we recreated the photo, his son standing in for him. And at my daughter's wedding, fifteen years after that, the photo features Sticks' wife in his place. Enduring symbols of how much these friendships mean to all of us.

We gathered back at the house afterwards. Walking out to the nearby golf tee, carrying his ashes with us, we took turns hitting golf balls left-handed (a few of us, not well) and reminiscing. You guessed it, Sticks played golf left-handed.

After the gathering, the Hunk got up to leave and head to the airport. As we all said our goodbyes, he looked for his shoes but could not find them. He asked if anyone had seen his shoes.

Of course, we knew by the look on his face he already knew the answer as someone yelled out, "Check the freezer."

Epilogue

At the time, we all knew this was the end of a chapter and the start of a new one. We also knew the story of Sticks and these friendships would last forever. So they have.

My daughters and I had dinner with Sticks' wife recently in Las Vegas. We spent the time reminiscing and telling stories that get better over time. Yes, of course, his wife was wearing the Tiffany-style refrigerator-light-bulb necklace.

Sticks' wife has papered a few houses in Youngstown over the years following Sticks' passing. In fact, a few years ago, I papered the Kid's house after she encouraged me to do so, having spoken to her earlier in the day.

We all remain close friends. I trust we always will. In fact, the Voice helped conspire to hide my shoes in the Stud's freezer just last year when a good friend and I visited. Old traditions die hard.

To Dad—Jack Lopes. A father, an uncle,
a brother, a son, a smart businessman, a mentor,
a friend, an author, a beacon, a rock. My rock.

Losing Dad

Diane Lopes

*I*t was a Friday evening in late spring. The kind of day that was unusually warm and gave glimpses of the summer months ahead. I was deep in thought, contemplating what to make the kids for dinner or whether to order takeout. My phone on the table startled me when it rang; I looked and saw it was Dad calling. It was odd for him to call on a Friday evening but I always welcomed our conversations.

When I picked up, his voice was strained, shaky, but direct. "I need to go to the hospital. Please come over."

My feet hit the floor, I grabbed the keys, and I was out the door in minutes. I called my brother as I drove, my heart racing; I felt a warm flush come over my body. For Dad to call and say this, I knew it was serious. This was the man who, years earlier, left a message on my voicemail saying he "had a heart flutter" and "would be away a few days to take care of it." He was in Florida; I was in Connecticut. The heart flutter was a heart attack, and he was in the hospital having bypass surgery.

Dad was upstairs in bed when I arrived at his place. By the look on his face, I knew he was in agonizing pain. His usual beautiful olive complexion was pale gray. He couldn't get up or even move. I called 911 as my brother arrived.

The emergency-response team quickly got Dad onto a special chair to take him down the stairs and out the door to the ambulance. The pained look on his face was one I had never seen, nor will I ever forget it. In the years since, I have tried to erase that image from my memory to no avail.

I followed the ambulance to the hospital emergency room. My knuckles went white from my tight grip on the steering wheel, and I had to force myself to remember to breathe.

At the hospital, they determined Dad was in septic shock and needed to be transported immediately to a larger hospital. Dad had perforated diverticulitis and was very sick. The next few days were a blur as my brother and I rotated going to the hospital, talking to doctors, and determining the plan for surgery, treatment, rehab, and recovery. We almost lost him, but true to Dad's style, with grit and tenacity, he bounced back. Like a cat, he had nine lives. I had lost count, but at this point, he was probably down to six lives. This wasn't the first time Dad had a medical crisis that gave us a scare and made us think we'd lose him.

Dad was in the hospital for about two weeks following major intestinal surgery. He did not do well with anesthesia and had episodes of hallucinations that were terrifying. He also wasn't a good patient. Always a strong, independent man, Dad didn't like others caring for him. I love him dearly, but *belligerent* may be the right word for how he conducted himself. It pained me to see him like that because I knew him so well, but I also knew he needed to be in the hospital to heal and recover. At this point, I began to realize that things would never be the same.

Dad was discharged to a skilled-nursing facility. It was expected he'd be there for several weeks. He was now using a wheelchair, and he'd need extensive physical therapy to get back on his feet. Dad was a gregarious man, and his affability was infectious, but he also valued his privacy. To say he hated the facility is an understatement. He had a roommate and had to share a bathroom.

He would cocoon himself by pulling the curtain all the way around his bed tightly. It reminded me of the tents we'd make as kids with sheets and couch cushions—a bittersweet memory, as I had pangs of regret for not appreciating those carefree days as much as I missed them now.

Dad constantly asked to be discharged, saying he didn't need to be there. He said everyone there was "old and almost dead"; he saw himself as young and vibrant, so did I. It broke my heart, but also made me laugh a bit. Dad never looked or acted his age, and he could be a stubborn guy. It was that stubborn side that had him resisting all physical therapy. Again, he was borderline belligerent, but in the most respectful way toward the staff. A natural flirt, Dad loved to tease the staff and have fun. These were sparks of his old self. He once introduced one of his aides to me as my future stepmother.

Unfortunately, Dad never got back on his feet and the wheelchair became a permanent fixture in our lives. When he was discharged from the skilled-nursing facility, we had to move him into an apartment that was all on one level and wheelchair accessible. He couldn't go back to his condo as the bedroom and bathroom were on the second floor, and laundry was in the basement. He loved that condo, and it broke me to tell him he couldn't go back there.

Dad was at the apartment for only six days. We hired visiting nurses and personal aides, but Dad got pneumonia and went back into the hospital. After another lengthy inpatient stay, he was discharged again to the skilled-nursing facility. I knew in my heart that he would not be able to leave the facility this time. He was there to stay.

For as far back as I can remember, Dad forgot words or used the wrong ones. He used to buy me wine coolers and called them Broccoli & Jaymes (instead of Bartles & Jaymes). He always forgot peoples' names, and I had to remind him; we did it stealthily as I whispered in his ear. I thought this was the normal aging process, even though it probably started when he was in his fifties, the age I am now.

In the facility, Dad's memory deteriorated rapidly; he forgot significant life events, and his short-term memories escaped him. He often blamed it on his hearing aids, saying he couldn't hear what people were saying. This became a frustrating circle of dialogue—his hearing aids "not functioning." My brother and I got his hearing aids cleaned and adjusted, we repeatedly replaced the batteries, but he still claimed he couldn't hear. It was frustrating for all of us, but even worse, it was heartbreaking. In a desperate attempt to help him hear the correct words, we bought him brand-new hearing aids, which were customized following extensive hearing tests. Nothing helped. Dad continued to say he didn't hear the words. In reality, he heard the words; he just no longer understood them.

Slowly, day by day, Dad faded away. He would occasionally surprise us with a random story that he'd remember. He'd look at his high school yearbook and remember stories about his classmates, but the short-term memories vanished as they happened. Dad was often frustrated and angry, moods that I rarely had seen him display in the past. I knew he didn't want to be in the facility with no autonomy or independence. The wheelchair was a blessing and a curse as it kept him mobile but trapped at the same time.

I remember a conversation Dad and I had twenty-plus years prior. He said if he ever got to the point that he needed to live in a facility, he did not want to continue living. He agonized over the fact that he had to move his own beloved mother into one of those nursing homes, and he hated every minute of it. He never wanted that for himself or for us to have to force him into one. At that dinner table so many years before, during the conversation we had over a great dinner and bottle of white wine, he told me he'd rather be dead than live in that situation. He asked me to shoot him if it ever came to that. Yes, shoot him. We laughed, but then he got serious; apparently, he had a plan. He'd get a gun and keep it in a desk drawer for me to use if necessary. He told me that he knew I had it in me to fulfill this final request.

I didn't know if I should be honored or horrified. Shoot him!? Certainly, that wasn't something I could do, legally or emotionally. Seeing him in that facility and knowing his wishes, my heart broke more and more with each visit. There he was, in a facility and in that wheelchair, exactly like his own mother. I felt as if I had let him down.

Dementia and aphasia took Dad from us. It seemed gradual, increasing over many years, but also it felt as if it had occurred in the blink of an eye. Physically, he was there, but mentally he wasn't. I found myself torn between gratitude that he was physically with me and guilt knowing that he didn't want to live that way, but there was nothing I could do. I also realized that my grief had begun long before his death, while he was still present on this earth.

As an adult, I've spent a good amount of time reflecting on my childhood and my relationship with my Dad. When I was very young, Dad traveled extensively for work. His job provided him with a window to the world, literally and figuratively. I was too young to understand where he was specifically; I just knew that he wasn't home, and I missed him. When he returned from those trips, he always brought me a surprise, usually a stuffed animal. They would spark my imagination as to where Dad had been.

Once, it was a stuffed dog dressed as an English bobby, what the British call their police officers. I imagined Dad walking the cobblestone streets of London, searching for the perfect toy store to get me this most treasured gift. There was also a stuffed husky. I imagined Dad had gotten him in a snowy, mountainous country. One where people wore big, furry coats, boots up to their knees, and scarves wrapped around their red faces. As much as I hated him being away from home, I loved his return with these magical gifts. These stories filled my head for days and weeks, until Dad left on his next trip.

When I went to college, Dad moved to Florida for a new job opportunity. He seemed to love his new job, he loved Florida, and he met an amazing woman who joined our lives for decades to come. He was the happiest I had ever seen him. I was happy that he was happy. I felt that I had matured to the point that I could see a genuine ease and joy in him. Maybe he had moments of joy before that, but I don't think he was completely consumed with a sense of peace in his life until he moved to Florida.

We traveled back and forth and had wonderful visits and adventures. Dad and I always called our times together "shenanigans." Dad and I always had an unspoken connection. We'd make eye contact and just start laughing. Sometimes, it was at other people's expense, such as a person in the grocery store arguing with the butcher about the cut of meat (why was she so angry over pot roast?), or the time his employees went on strike and made a dummy of his likeness and hung it from a tree. I suggested we buy the strikers coffee and doughnuts because they were walking in circles in the frigid weather. These were people I had met many times at Dad's office and at company picnics. I didn't understand what "going on strike" meant. I just knew that I liked many of the people striking; they were always kind to me. Dad appreciated them and their right to strike as well, so he happily granted my request, and we bought them the coffee and doughnuts. It wasn't until my adult life that I realized how odd that must have seemed to these striking employees. Then again, they knew Dad and that he truly respected and supported them, so maybe they weren't surprised.

With Dad in Florida and me in Connecticut, we talked every Sunday morning. Sometimes, we talked for hours. He was eager and excited to hear about my new job after college and the progression in my career. I had started in an entry-level job at a big insurance company and received several promotions in my first couple of years. Dad was my career guide, mentor, advisor, and biggest fan. We bonded in an entirely new way. And new shenanigans. We laughed about my silly work stories and my dealings with customers, peers, and managers. And he shared more and more work-related stories with me.

Many stories were about those trips he used to take all over the world. It was fascinating to replace my childhood imaginary versions of his travels with reality. And reality was far beyond anything I could have imagined.

He told me stories of Turkey, Haiti, Israel, Germany, and other Eastern European countries. The people he met, the endeavors he took on, the work he did supporting under-served communities across the world. He was truly an impressive man.

I began traveling for work, which felt like a full-circle moments, as I was traveling as he had. On my trips, I got to know the airport gift shops. They had all the things a weary traveler needed. I had gotten married and had two daughters at this point, so I would buy them trinkets and toys in these shops. One day I had a realization. Did Dad buy all those stuffed animals in airport gift shops? My thoughts of him searching for hours for the perfect shop on cobblestone streets lined with gas lanterns to find me the perfect gift burst like a bubble. Poof!!

With the clarity of adult understanding, I felt mixed emotions, but mostly I chuckled to myself. It's amazing that parents can do something so simple, yet thoughtful, to brighten their child's day. It helped me understand Dad more, and I appreciated that he even thought of a gift when he was most likely tired and in a rush to catch a flight home. He could have easily passed by the gift ship without a second thought, but he didn't.

Dad passed away in the overnight hours of October 8, 2022. I left the nursing facility before dawn and headed home. The predawn darkness perfectly hid my tears and allowed me an escape from reality. Somehow, the sun rising didn't feel right. How could a new day dawn without my Dad on this earth. I raced home to crawl into bed before the light could shine on the sad reality that life goes on even after one amazing life ends.

In the days following Dad's passing, I found myself becoming puzzled, even annoyed, at seeing people going about their daily lives. They were grocery shopping, doing yard work, attending sporting events, jogging—things I didn't pay attention to before Dad died, but now they seemed out of place. The sun came up, and it set...again and again. But now my world had stopped, and I felt as if everyone else's world should stop too. Didn't they realize we lost the greatest man who walked the earth? I know; this sounds overdramatic, but it's how I felt.

I was also overwhelmed with a feeling of guilt. I didn't spend enough time with him. How did I not realize that one day he would be gone? I was upset with myself for taking for granted that he was always there. When my basement flooded, he came with a wet vac and spent hours dumping the water outside. When we got a puppy who needed daily walks, he was there. When I had a terrible kidney infection and needed to go to the emergency room, he drove me and sat with me for thirteen hours in the waiting room. When my kids had a sports game or a dance recital, he was there cheering them on.

He was unassuming, so very proud, and so very present. Now, he was gone. I would never again see him in the distance, waving with his whole body so that I could see him—the way he did when picking me up at the airport and when he arrived anywhere. As a teenager, it embarrassed me. His right arm extended fully above his head; stretching to see over the crowd and exuberantly waving. As an adult, it was a welcome sight that brought me comfort and peace. A sight that I will miss for the rest of my life.

In Memory of Malka Susana Lina
and Lloyd Joel Mankes

Echoes of Love

Navigating Grief, Finding Resilience,
Happiness, and Renewed Hope

Dr. Carol Leibovich-Mankes,
DrOT, OTR/L, PLCC, GC-C

Introduction

I view my life as a narrative, similar to a storybook. Every chapter, some of which I'll be sharing in the next few pages, has been filled with blessings, challenges, experiences, relationships, and pivotal events that have shaped the person I am today. Upon contemplation, I noticed that recurrent themes of grief and loss—steered by faith and encountered with resilience, hope, and the pursuit of happiness—are part of my journey. These repeating occurrences have taught me the importance of embracing vulnerability and finding strength in adversity. They have also deepened my appreciation for the power of resilience and the ability to overcome obstacles, which ultimately leads to personal growth, transformation, and healing.

My life story not only encompasses moments of joy and valuable lessons but also confronts the harsh realities of financial instability, immigration, divorce, infertility, shuttered dreams, and loss. All of these have led to a shared journey akin to a grief process. I had to navigate the emotional complexities, uncertainties, and adjustments associated with each unique struggle.

In the face of these numerous challenges, I've consistently chosen not to give up. Instead, I've opted to transform life's difficulties into opportunities. Recognizing that I cannot entirely control the past, present, and future, as those aspects lie in God's hands, however, I can control my daily approach. I have turned every challenge into an opportunity to initiate new chapters filled with hope and gratitude. Embracing a mindset of resilience and adaptability, I have learned to uncover silver linings in every situation, regardless of its difficulty. Through persistent effort and self-reflection, I have navigated life's storms and emerged with increased strength, compassion, and determination to seize the fullest potential of every moment.

In sharing these chapters of my life, I intend to guide and empower each reader to navigate grief and loss with resilience and hope. Grief and loss can be catalysts for growth, healing, and empowerment as we recognize that we have the power to shape our stories despite the challenges we encounter. By embracing our emotions and finding healthy coping mechanisms, we can transform our pain into strength and find meaning in despair. It is through these shared experiences that we inspire others to embrace their journeys of healing and discover the resilience within themselves.

Life-Altering Events Inducing Facets of Grief and Loss

Grief across Borders: Navigating the Immigration Journey and Parents' Divorce

At the age of twelve, a pivotal chapter unfolded in my life and marked my initial encounter with the journey of grief. This grief was intricately tied to the act of leaving my homeland, Israel, and embarking on the journey of emigration to the USA, which was a significant, profound, and transformative shift. Emigrating to a new country can be likened to a grief process, as it involves bidding farewell to the familiar, navigating uncertainties, and adapting to an entirely different way of life.

Navigating adolescence is inherently challenging; coupling that with the complexities of adapting to a new country, learning a different language, and assimilating into a foreign culture made the journey monumentally difficult. The familiar landscapes of Israel gave way to the unfamiliar streets of a new land. The language, Hebrew, I used to hear every day was replaced by English, a language that was initially unfamiliar and intimidating.

This relocation wasn't merely about adjusting to a new culture; it introduced a different kind of uncertainty—the constant worry of deportation. The sense of security and familiarity to which I was accustomed suddenly vanished. In their place were constant instability and continuous awareness of being an immigrant. The toll on my family was profound.

Navigating a new life strained my parents' marriage to the point of dissolution. The once-unified family structure unraveled, and when faced with challenges beyond what they'd anticipated, my parents decided to part ways. The dissolution of our family unit was life-altering. Grief, a constant companion, settled in as I grappled with the loss of what I had known. Family dinners, shared laughter, and unity gave way to solitude. The dynamics I previously took for granted were replaced by a fragmented reality, and the feeling of loss was deep.

But even though this chapter was transformative and painful, it gave me a deeper understanding of myself. Through the pain and grief, I discovered strength within me that I never knew existed. As I navigated this new reality, I learned to rely on my resilience and adaptability.

It was a bittersweet realization that sometimes growth comes from the most challenging circumstances.

Fertility's Trials: A Journey of Resilience, Grief, and Joy

Moving forward in life, the next significant chapter further developed my relationship with grief, as it unfolded after my high school sweetheart, Lloyd Mankes, and I began our married life armed with dreams and aspirations. I pursued a doctorate in occupational therapy, while he dedicated himself to law school. Together, we were scripting the story of our shared future.

As we embraced the prospect of expanding our family, an unexpected and arduous challenge awaited—a five-year struggle with infertility—which introduced an element of grief into our marriage. The emotional toll of infertility resonated daily, impacting not only our well-being but also the dynamics of our relationship. We confronted the stark reality of unfulfilled dreams and the persistent ache of longing for a child. Each failed attempt brought a layer of grief intertwined with the uncertainty of whether our dreams would ever materialize, which added emotional weight to our journey.

After numerous attempts, various infertility treatments, and significant financial investment, hope prevailed, and our prayers were answered. The arrival of our beautiful daughter, Arielle, brought immeasurable joy and marked the end of our infertility journey. It seemed as if life was finally aligning with our dreams. We had the family and stability we had wished for, and we were anticipating a future characterized by ease and tranquility.

Amid the challenges and emotional turbulence, we discovered resilience and strength. We learned to lean on each other for support and acknowledge that our shared journey through infertility was shaping us in ways we hadn't anticipated. The grief became a poignant presence, a reminder of the profound desire for a family and the resilience required to confront the unexpected twists on our path.

Grief amid Learning Differences

The subsequent significant chapter in my life unfolded when the birth of my daughter brought forth another dimension of grief—this time linked to navigating the intricacies of her learning differences. Like most parents, we had high hopes for our child's future, ones that followed the typical paths defined by social norms and milestones.

Despite the joy of having a healthy girl, we swiftly realized that our daughter's unique journey required an adjustment of those expectations. The conventional narrative of academic benchmarks and standard achievements had to shift and make room for a new definition of success—one that embraced individual strengths, celebrated small victories, and cultivated an environment that nurtured personal growth.

This process of adjustment wasn't without its challenges; it necessitated a recalibration of dreams and the cultivation of resilience in the face of societal pressures. In this journey, grief and loss weren't end points, but rather an ongoing process while adapting to new narratives and appreciating the inherent worth and beauty of neurodiversity. Through the lens of grief, we discovered that adjusting expectations wasn't a concession, but a powerful act of embracing the uniqueness of our daughter's path. This realization prompted a thorough exploration of her unique strengths and challenges.

Navigating the educational landscape transformed into an adventure of its own. We found ourselves passionately advocating for her needs, working collaboratively with teachers, and delving into innovative approaches to learning. Observing her resilience and determination in the face of challenges has been a source of profound humility and inspiration. This experience became a transformative chapter that not only reshaped our understanding of parenthood but also illuminated the strength derived from navigating uncharted territories with an open heart and an unwavering commitment to our child's well-being and happiness.

This journey of acceptance and growth has imparted the importance of celebrating small victories and finding joy in the present moment, rather than dwelling on what could have been. Ultimately, embracing reality has enriched our lives and allowed us to see the world through a new lens filled with compassion, understanding, and endless possibilities for our daughter's future.

Navigating the Depths of Grief: Confronting Dual Losses

My previous struggles were nothing compared to what awaited me in the next chapter, which was characterized by grief due to a devastating loss. This time, grief revealed itself in its truest, most agonizing form. In 2016, both my mother and husband were simultaneously diagnosed with cancer. This marked the beginning of a challenging period in which I found myself rushing from one hospital to another, tirelessly fighting for their lives.

While balancing this intense emotional struggle, I had to make critical decisions while maintaining a full-time job and attempting to provide a sense of normalcy for my daughter. Tragically, in just three weeks, both my mother and husband succumbed to cancer. It felt as though an unbearable weight had been placed on my shoulders, and the simultaneous departure of these two pillars in my life propelled me into a tumultuous whirlwind of emotions—grief, anger, and confusion. Each crashing wave threatened to engulf me with overwhelming force.

Grieving one loss would have been formidable, but facing the dual void seemed insurmountable.

Initially, the path through grief appeared shrouded in impenetrable darkness, each step a strenuous struggle, and the weight of sorrow threatened to pull me into its abyss. I found myself a single mom and a widow at forty-three. What was I to do? After overcoming numerous challenges in the past, it was difficult to fathom that I now faced a task that appeared to be as daunting as climbing Mount Everest.

Yet, within this darkness, I could perceive the outlines of resilience. Thinking back to the mountains I had previously climbed, I was confident that I could do it again because of my tenacity and faith in God. I came to understand that grief doesn't follow a straight path; it's more like a roller coaster with unexpected twists and turns. Grief requires both patience and courage. Upon reaching this realization, I made a conscious choice to ride out the tumultuous waves of grief and confront the pain head-on.

After making this choice, I sought to cultivate inner strength, foster perseverance, and nurture a sense of hope not only for myself, but also for my daughter, to guide us toward a brighter future. I decided once again that my new, unexplainable circumstances were not going to define me. I made a conscious decision to gather all my strength and life lessons and fight like a lion.

While grieving for my mom and husband, I needed to rebuild both my life and that of my daughter. I had to build a solid new foundation and find a new livelihood (being now the sole provider), be a solo mom, and move forward the best I could. I chose to be a warrior, not a victim.

Embarking on this healing journey, I solemnly dedicated myself to honoring the cherished memories of my beloved mother and husband; both left indelible imprints on my life. I reminded myself that their purpose while alive was to ensure my success and happiness, and I committed to keeping their flame alive. Their absence served as a constant reminder of the strength and resilience they had instilled in me. Embracing their legacy, I channeled the enduring flame of their love into fuel for my determination to create a brighter future for both my daughter and me.

Navigating Grief: Embracing Divine Timing and Enduring Love

As the seventh anniversary of the profound loss of my mom and husband approaches, the chance to share my experiences through writing this chapter has emerged. This serendipitous moment aligns with a day meant to honor what would have been my mother's birthday, December 12, and the week leading up to what would have been my wedding anniversary, December 17.

The timing of this unexpected opportunity adds a profound layer to the beliefs and convictions that have guided me throughout my life and assisted me in navigating the journey of grief. I've always held the steadfast belief that life unfolds as it's meant for each of us—not to bring a person down, but to build that person up. The secret is to be open and aware enough to accept the signs from above. Central to my journey has always been a steadfast belief in God's divine plan and the conviction that my life unfolds with a purpose meticulously tailored for me. This conviction holds even in the face of circumstances as incomprehensible as the ones I have encountered.

Embracing this belief led me to recognize that the fulfillment of both my daughter's and my distinct destinies necessitates not only acknowledging and contemplating our experiences but also striving to understand the profound lessons presented by the dear people we lost. Anchored in unwavering faith, this journey is a testament to the resilience of the human spirit, the power of belief, and the enduring impact of love, even in the shadow of profound loss.

Through this journey, I have come to understand that our loved ones never truly leave us, but instead they continue to guide and inspire us from beyond. Their presence is felt in the smallest of moments as they remind us to cherish every breath and embrace the beauty of life. This realization has given me the strength to carry on, knowing that their love will forever be a part of my daughter's and my unique paths.

Loss of My Loved Ones
Loss of a Mother: Malka Susana Lina

My mother, Malka Susana Lina, was born in Buenos Aires, Argentina, in 1952. She was a pillar of love characterized by the spirit of giving, unconditional affection, unwavering trust, and unparalleled support. Despite life's challenges, her legacy endures in the valuable lessons she passed on and the well of inspiration she provided. Her journey, from childhood dreams in Argentina to her role as a devoted mother in the USA, unfolded with threads of resilience, determination, and sacrifice.

At the age of ten, my mom moved with her family to Israel; she carried aspirations of becoming an artist and eventually emigrating to the USA to work for Disney. She attended a prestigious art school in Israel and secured a scholarship to study in France. However, life took her in a different direction. At nineteen, she embraced marriage and motherhood, and she eventually became a loving mother to my two brothers and me.

A courageous step at the age of thirty-two led my mom to uproot her family and move to the USA, pursuing the American dream and her longtime dream of being an accomplished artist. Despite the challenges that punctuated her life, my mom's journey was a testament to her resilience, determination, and the sacrifices she made for the well-being of our family. Her story mirrored the optimistic immigrant narrative filled with hopes and dreams and the persistent pursuit of a better life for her family. A woman of tenacity and ambition, she became a cornerstone of hard work, epitomizing the immigrant spirit. My mom's experience in the United States was characterized by her holding various jobs as she tirelessly pursued a dream she had nurtured since childhood. As always, her path took twists and turns, but she was determined to reach her lifelong goals.

As she navigated her journey, her entrepreneurial spirit blossomed and led her to establish a successful beauty salon that became more than just a business—it symbolized stability for our family for over two decades. However, my mom remained determined to fulfill her dream of becoming an artist.

Approximately five years before her untimely illness, she decided to retire and reignite her passion for the arts. During this period, she created stunning artwork that proudly adorns my living room today. Her creations spanned both traditional and nontraditional art, including three-dimensional pieces showcasing her innovative approach before it became widely popular. She was on the verge of redefining her life and achieving her goal when illness struck suddenly and claimed her.

Her absence, particularly on significant days like her birthday or Mother's Day, is a lasting burden. Those days heighten the longing, sorrow, and deep sense of missing her. Yet, amid grief, I've found comfort and strength in holding on to the vivid memories and reflecting on the precious times we shared. The process of recognizing and contemplating these experiences has been a poignant and transformative one. In recalling her laughter and the warmth of her embrace, I've discovered profound lessons that go beyond the confines of grief. It's a journey of understanding—not just the depth of loss but also the lasting impact that love and resilience can have on the human spirit.

My mom's legacy reaches far beyond her lifetime; it's an enduring influence that guides me. It embodies resilience, love, and the lasting impact of a mother's advice. This acknowledgment empowers me to face life's challenges with determination. Leveraging her entrepreneurial drive, I've crafted a successful legacy as a pediatric occupational therapist, parent coach, and grief counselor, embodying the spirit inherited from my mom. My recently released book is more than just a personal achievement; it stands as a powerful testament to my mother's unshakable belief in my abilities and my potential to reach great heights.

My mom's life serves as a poignant example of a journey intricately intertwined with a broader narrative of love, sacrifice, and the timeless pursuit of a better life.

It inspires my daughter and me to embrace these values and shape our choices for generations to come.

Loss of a Spouse: Lloyd Joel Mankes

My late husband, Lloyd Joel Mankes, was born in Florida, USA, in 1970, and he passed away at the tender age of forty-five as we celebrated twenty-one years of marriage. Our journey began in high school, and after four years of dating, we embarked on a journey filled with love and excitement to build a home together. We exchanged vows on December 17, 1995.

Despite being two very different people, we found inspiration in each other and pushed each other to reach our goals. Lloyd, a daring and tenacious spirit, lived life boldly. While he projected a tough exterior to those he met, his close friends knew him as a gentle, caring man always ready to go the extra mile for his loved ones. In 1998, he realized his childhood dream of becoming a criminal defense attorney, eventually becoming the president of the Broward Association of Criminal Defense Lawyers. His passion for advocacy was not just a profession but a commitment to justice and the well-being of his clients.

Throughout our twenty-five years together, we faced various challenges, including a five-year battle with infertility. Despite the difficulties, our resilience defied the odds. In 2006, the joyous occasion of fatherhood unfolded as Lloyd embraced the role of a dedicated and loving father to our daughter, Arielle. This new addition to our family brought immeasurable joy and added profound meaning to our lives. Lloyd's commitment as a father was truly remarkable, as he invested his heart and soul into cherishing Arielle. His purpose extended beyond the ordinary responsibilities of parenthood; he aimed to create a collection of beautiful memories that would resonate with warmth and love throughout Arielle's life. Every moment spent together became an opportunity for Lloyd to impart not just care but a sense of security, joy, and profound connection. Through his unwavering commitment, he shaped a legacy of love that left an indelible mark on Arielle's heart and enriched our family with a treasure trove of cherished moments; his legacy will endure.

Losing my spouse was a profound and life-altering experience that took me on a complex journey through a spectrum of intense emotions—from the deep ache of grief to the unsettling waves of loneliness that accompany the absence of a life partner. Beyond the emotional toll, this loss permeated every facet of my existence, touched on the practical aspects of daily life, and shook my fundamental sense of identity and purpose.

The loss of my spouse, combined with the simultaneous role of becoming a solo mom, thrust me into an alternate reality—a realm where the familiar was suddenly off-balance without the person who was always there. The weight of responsibilities became heavier as I attempted to navigate through a void of emptiness and shattered dreams. It's an inexplicable journey to become a solo parent, akin to entering uncharted territory with only memories of the past and crushing uncertainties about what lies ahead.

The impact was not confined only to me; it extended to my daughter. In the immediate aftermath of her father's passing, my daughter, age ten, confronted a whirlwind of emotions. As her mother, it fell upon me to deliver the heartbreaking news. I made a crucial decision to allow her to visit the hospital and bid farewell to her father. Though her dad was already in a deep coma, the belief persisted that he waited for her visit to finally let go. This decision aimed to offer some semblance of closure and prepare her for the devastating truth that followed.

The realization that her dad was no longer physically present brought forth a tidal wave of sorrow, anger, and frustration for my daughter. The unfairness of losing her father at such a tender age and the dreams and milestones they would never share stirred a fiery storm within me as her mother. Yet, amidst the pain, my unwavering promise as her mother was to stand by, comfort, and support her through this intricate and multifaceted process.

It's a delicate dance between mourning for myself and providing comfort to my daughter as she navigates her unique pain. This dance requires immense strength and resilience as we navigate the unpredictable waves of grief and strive to find meaning amid loss. It is a process that demands vulnerability, courage, and an intricate interplay of memory and healing. Each day brings new layers to this already complex experience.

Conclusion

This chapter, which unfolds as a narrative of my life, is a storybook filled with highs and lows in which grief and loss take center stage. However, amid the somber notes, an inner strength emerges, propelling me forward in the continued pursuit of happiness. My journey stands as a testament to human resilience, and it emphasizes the intentional choice to live joyfully despite the challenges.

Harnessing loss as a driving force for progress has become a crucial aspect of my understanding. I've grown to embrace the idea that progressing and finding happiness aren't betrayals of grief, but rather testaments to the complexity of our human experience.

Gratitude has become my compass; it guides me to be present in every moment and to celebrate life's small miracles. I am dedicated to the continual process of gaining insights from life experiences and lessons from loved ones I've lost. These have transformed me as I navigate through diverse situations and challenges.

Looking back on this journey, I see a story of love surpassing time and mortality. In the intertwined dance of grief and joy, my mother and late husband persist in their influence; they have extended beyond their physical presence to become enduring guides for my daughter and me. My aim is not merely to confront life's challenges, but to do so with the love and strength inherited from them. I will create a legacy of love, sacrifice, and pursuit of a better life.

To those grappling with grief and the healing process, I offer a reminder not to be too hard on yourselves. Grief is a journey, not a destination; it's ongoing and personal. No one can dictate what you should feel, when, or how. Yet I encourage readers to commit to finding resilience, renewed happiness, and, above all, a life that honors the enduring echoes of love.

In Memory of
Daria Switankowsky

Memories of My Late Mama

Irene S. Roth

I have so many memories of my mama, and I miss her so much. She passed away in March of 2011. And every March, before my birthday on the seventeenth, I recall how she used to call me to wish me a happy birthday and cry. She always cried on my birthday.

Now, many years after her death, I still cry on my birthday when I remember how emotional she was. There were always stories about how I was born during the St. Patrick's Day parade at two o'clock in the afternoon and how she was so happy to have me in her arms.

Then there were the stories of how I was famous when the hospital asked her if I could be in a baby-food commercial. She was so proud of that and always reminded me of how beautiful I was.

As I grew up, I felt very smothered by her love. At first, it was really wonderful to get all that attention. Because my mother had difficult pregnancies, I was an only child. She did try to have more children, but she kept miscarrying. In fact, I came after all these miscarriages. To be sure all would go well while she was carrying me, my mama had to quit her job and go on complete bed rest from the second trimester onwards to make sure that she didn't miscarry again.

Being an only child had a lot of perks, but also quite a few drawbacks. I had all the attention and love. My parents knew how to love and dote on me. So I got a lot of gifts at Christmas and on birthdays.

However, they didn't spoil me. They were able to say no, and when they said no, they meant it. My mama was the disciplinarian. There were times that her comments towards me were quite harsh. But despite being hurt, I always believed that she loved me. And she taught me a lot of valuable lessons during these times.

But not having any siblings or extended family made me very lonely at times. I remember sitting in my room and feeling so desperately alone. Also, because my mama was an immigrant and didn't speak English fluently, we didn't have a lot of people over to visit. She felt like an outsider, even among our neighbors.

Even when we went to church, she felt out of place and never reached out to any of the ladies there. They tried to be friendly towards her, and they all liked me a lot and called me a beautiful girl. But my mama was still very suspicious of them. So, again, I felt alone.

Our holidays were times of peace and quiet. There were just the three of us. I enjoyed the Christmas holidays, as my mama baked and cooked for a week before the big day. She baked her own bread, cakes, and shortbread cookies. I helped her. We used to put on Christmas carols while we cooked and baked. Sometimes, we'd sing along with them.

A few days before Christmas, we'd go to the delicatessen close to our home and pick up what seemed like a lot of deli meat and cherry strudel. I loved going to the delicatessen because it smelled so good. And everyone in the store seemed so happy and kind. It was certainly a time of great joy and jubilation. I couldn't wipe the smile off my face.

Then, my mama made all of her furniture covers and decorations for our home. We had a real Christmas tree.

The aromas of pine and spruce, depending on the year, wafted through the house. My tata always went to a tree farm close to where we lived and cut down his own tree. It was such a wonderful time of year. Many times, my mama and I accompanied him.

But I was still quite lonely. I started even feeling like a bit of a loner. I'd spend hours by myself in my room, reading, writing, and journaling. I'd even make my own crafts, sew homemade dolls, and make tiny furniture covers with my own small sewing machine.

I also loved crocheting. My mama always had a lot of different yarns to choose from. She taught me from a very early age how to knit and crochet. I started making some clothes for my Barbie and quickly progressed to making scarves for the Salvation Army. When I was sixteen, I started making socks for the homeless, as well as mitts and baby blankets.

So I had a lot of things to do. But I was still lonely. I craved having deep friendships with girls my own age. I wanted to be able to go out with people my own age. I even made up friends in my imagination so that I wouldn't feel so lonely.

Yet those years were some of the best times of my life; they formed the fabric of my life as it is now. Although

I have friends now, I still crave solitude. I am an introvert, and I love being on my own at least some of the time.

I really believe that if I hadn't spent so much time alone when I was a young girl and a teenager, I wouldn't be the writer or the person I am today. I also wouldn't have patience with my students and compassion to offer.

The other memory I have of my mama is her kindness. She was kind, not only towards me and my tata, but towards everyone she met. Even when my mama met strangers, she always reached out to them with an unquenchable love and kindness.

Because it was so easy for her to love people, her real estate career was next to none. People trusted her and loved her. And they bought property from her instead of the other ladies in the real estate company for which she worked.

I loved watching her close deals and seeing how people were so happy and content to be in her presence. Some even came back after their purchase with gifts and kind words. My mama was always grateful to have people like that in her life, even if it was only for a short time.

But through word of mouth, my mama was always busy selling homes. Families of previous buyers frequently sought her out. She was never idle, despite a few

growing up, I so wanted to be like her. Her face was always glowing and gorgeous. She dressed beautifully. Even when she stayed home, she put on a pretty blouse and a clean pair of slacks that matched her blouse. Her hair was always combed and styled. She just looked so beautiful.

Summer holidays were wonderful times too. I couldn't wait to get out of school so I could spend time with my mama. She knew how to rest, not just work.

We had a family cottage about 200 miles north of our home, in the eastern townships of Montreal, and we'd go there for weeks on end during the summer. The countryside around our cottage was so quiet. I remember taking my books and journals and just sitting or lying down on my lounger outside on nice days and doing nothing for hours. I loved these times and found them so deeply restorative.

My tata fished, and my mama fried the fish he caught. We ate fish a lot when we were at the cottage. But my mama also baked and cooked other things nonstop. That was one of the things we did together. I just loved to spend those times with my mama.

Cooking at the cottage was different. Our stove and oven weren't as powerful. But we still used them to cook and bake. And mama still made such wonderful pies and cakes. I always put on weight when we were at the cottage, despite the fact that I did a lot of walking.

But as August 1 approached, I started looking forward to going back to school. My mama always sewed me a new dress to wear the first day of the new school year. She'd start making it at the cottage, and then when we returned to the city around August 15, she'd put on the finishing touches.

Going back to school was always a wonderful time for me. I loved studying and doing well at school. I loved the library and was looking forward to meeting all my new teachers. But, more than that, there was something about just going to school that really appealed to me. I just loved to learn, to read, and to check out books from the library.

As I opened the door to my house when I came home from school, my mama ran to the door, gave me a great big hug, and kissed me. Aromas from my mama's cooking wafted through the house because she usually started prepping for dinner many hours before I came home. Sometimes, she used a Crock-Pot on the counter. It didn't matter what or how she was cooking, the house always smelled heavenly when I got home from school.

Then as I came into the kitchen, I usually saw a cake, some strudel, or some other delicious dessert on the counter. It was usually piping hot. Mama must have made it a half hour before she knew I would return from school. The house was so warm and inviting. It was such a wonderful time for me.

On any given night, I came home from school, got into my home clothes, and did my homework while my mama made supper. My mama always brought into my room a slice of homemade torte, strudel, or some of whatever she had made that afternoon so that I could continue studying until supper.

Then when it was time for supper, I ate my dinner with Mama and returned to my room to continue my homework or get into the comfy chair and read for an hour or two before going to bed. I had a lot of homework; this was back in the days when teachers believed in loading up the students with a lot to prepare for the next day. There were a lot of tests and quizzes too.

I'll never forget the day I heard that my grandmother passed away. I was twelve years old. I came home from school and knew right away something was very wrong. My mama's face was red, and her eyes were swollen, as if she had been crying for hours. She was sitting on the sofa, motionless. Typically, at that particular time of day, my mama would be running around doing so much to prepare for dinner. But that day was different.

As I came into the living room, I asked my mama if everything was okay. She said no. Then she told me that my grandmother had died the previous night.

I had never met my grandmother, as she lived in Kiev, but I had heard so much about her. My mama shared a story about her each week after Sunday dinner. When the Second World War broke out, my Mama was forced to leave her mama and her whole family. She never saw her mama again. So my grandmother's death really hit my mama hard.

As my mama sat crying, I wondered how I could help her commemorate and honor my grandmother's life from far away. We couldn't go back to Kiev. It was too late, and the funeral was the next day. As I sat beside my mama trying to comfort her, I wanted to create a space in our home that would both comfort my mama and honor my grandmother's life.

I didn't know how to talk to my mama about this because she was so upset. But as the days passed by, I decided to try to create a makeshift altar, one that was similar to the one my grandmother had in her home; I had seen it in the photos my mama shared with me over the years. I recalled there were always flowers, a few religious statues, a crucifix, incense, candles, and holy water.

Then, one day, while my mama was away, I started to assemble the items. I found in the basement a small table we weren't using. I cleaned it, put a pretty floral cloth over it, and placed a crucifix on it. I gathered a few candles and a bouquet of artificial flowers that were in a box in the basement. I also took one of the two statues I had of the Virgin Mary in my room and some incense, as well as some holy water I had in a small flask that I had brought home from church a while back.

Before my mama came home, I put all the items on the small table and arranged them in a circular fashion with the crucifix in the center. I also lit a few candles on either side of the crucifix and statue. It felt so real to me.

As I knelt to pray in front of this table, tears started flowing from my eyes. I knew in that moment my grandmother was watching over me as I prayed. I felt so connected to her. I prayed that my mama would feel some comfort in this sacred space, which was tucked into a corner of our living room.

When my mama came home, I greeted her at the door. I took her by the hand and led her to the small table in the corner of our living room.

She was visibly moved that I would create an altar to celebrate my grandmother's life. As she knelt in front of the little table, I joined her. We prayed for a few minutes in silence. And, somehow, the healing began. Right then, I felt connected to my mama and grandmother.

I've always believed that religion is a living component of our lives. Catholics certainly believe this when we are invited to live as disciples of God. This was one way for me to bring the living experience of religion into my home. I have continued to do that even now.

When my mama passed away in 2011, I was devastated. I had no idea how I was going to carry on. I had lost one of the most important and central people in my life. It was as if a part of me died with her. I wanted to create a way of honoring her life. So I thought about creating a home altar to honor her legacy and memory, just as I did when my mama's mother passed away.

I pondered for a while how I was going to accomplish creating this altar. Then I decided to plant a purple peony and create a makeshift altar in my backyard. My mama's favorite flowers were always purple peonies. She was also an avid lover of nature and found great comfort in communing with it. She always said that she saw God's handiwork in nature. She used to walk in the Botanical Gardens every day well into her eighties.

To honor my mother's life and who she truly was as a person, I devoted the left corner of my backyard to celebrating her life. I tilled the soil and added some fresh topsoil. That represented new beginnings for me. Just the process of creating this flower garden comforted me and helped me honor this wonderful lady whom I never want to forget.

Beside the purple peony, I made a cross from tree branches. Around the plant and cross, I planted a rose of Sharon bush and several hydrangea bushes. I also bought a small waterfall and placed that to the side of the bushes. This symbolized letting go, cleansing, and the continuous flow of energy and life. I wanted to create a space that reflected all things that my mama celebrated and drew energy from while she was alive. This way, I would be constantly reminded of her when I went into my backyard.

Over the years, this space has given me so much comfort. Every time I go into my backyard, I am still reminded of her in those beautiful purple peonies and the refreshing waterfall. I also put a small wooden chair beside it so I can sit down and say a few prayers.

But, more than that, I feel her presence somehow in that beautiful space. My mama would love it if she saw it. And this living symbol has helped me come to terms with her death. I realized that I didn't need to attend a church to get this feeling of completion and comfort or to honor her life.

My mama was one of the most wonderful people in my life. I look a lot like her, and I even act like her. I guess that shouldn't be surprising, given that I am her daughter and I spent so much time with her. But part of me feels connected with my mom, even now.

I miss her a lot, especially in the summer. But I have the makeshift memorial, and every summer I have beautiful flowers around it. It is a way of celebrating her, even now, a full decade since she passed away.

I love you, Mama, and I always will!
Your Doci!

This painting is a fragment of the dream that triggered my change through art. I named it Harvest.

Painting, Healing, and Having Faith

Let us inspire those who are afraid, not because we are brave, but because we have faith

Monica Septimio

Storyteller

I am the granddaughter of a wonderful woman. My paternal grandmother was a true Amazon, except she was five foot five and Northeastern Brazilian. She was brave; for example, when I saw her chopping off poisonous-snakes' heads with an axe, dropping her head to one side while the rest of her body writhed to the other. She was fearless. A super-artistic woman, she created, from scraps of cloth, beautiful blankets, rugs, and pillows of all the styles you can imagine. She was so ingenious that she went from raising chickens to pigs, from pigs to cows, and from cows to buying her own farm. No, it wasn't just her—my grandfather was the same way.

They could barely read. However, their wisdom and will-power made them reach beyond their dreams. Nothing was impossible for them; no problem impeded what they decided to do. My grandfather was a dreamer. When he told us something he was going to do, it usually seemed absurd to us. But even if it took a while, he carried out his project successfully.

From my grandparents, I learned how to love, to be obstinate, to be committed to fulfilling my dreams, and, of course, to tell stories. I believed that if I wanted something, and God did not object, I *would* accomplish whatever it was. In my teens, we installed electricity on my grandparents' farm. During my childhood, my family used kerosene lamps, so each morning my nostrils had to be cleaned, as they were undoubtedly black.

The most beautiful memories of my childhood are of my two grandparents. Before we went to sleep, my youngest aunt, who was four years older than I, sat with me as we listened to my grandparents' tales. It was like a ritual, and I couldn't wait until that magical moment when my grandmother told old wives' tales. At bedtime, she told us almost all the ancient fables in her own words. Today, I wonder how a semi-illiterate person knew so much about these stories, from the lying boy named Pinocchio, to the little girl who wore a red hood, to three little pigs building a house, and so on. But my favorite story was "Beauty and the Beast," followed closely by "Cinderella."

When I traveled, I pretended to be the characters in all those stories. When all the lights were off, and I was asleep, I dreamed of everything my grandmother told me. And for the stories that I didn't like the endings of, I invented my own happy endings. I have traveled in those tales narrated by my grandmother.

My grandmother also loved to tell the Brazilian folklore that was passed down from her ancestors. Some those stories scared me, and I imagined different conclusions—I always saved the day.

My grandfather told authentic and more elaborate chronicles of the past, narratives that he lived or heard about throughout his life. Some came from his genealogy, some stories were from the Bible, some were tales of saints who performed miracles, and some came from his own travels and exploits.

When I analyze this desire to tell stories, I realize that my initial spark to do the same came from those precious nights. If I struggled to sleep, I embarked on imaginary travels in the stories my grandparents had told. When I wanted to forget about some frustrations, I made up stories in my mind, which felt as if I were running away from reality when I was alone.

At my kindergarten graduation, I won my first book after learning to read. *The Legend of Alvorado* was about a wild white horse that helped other horses. As a teenager, I loved acting and found it easy to write plays. I didn't know how much I should do academically, but my creative ability to make up stories was very good. I also inherited from my mother her curiosity in exploring books and her love of writing.

With what seemed like suddenness, I grew up to the musicality of my father singing *vaquejada* (a sport typical of the Nordeste region of Brazil) tunes, which are musicalized tales about the fearless cowboys of Northeastern Brazil and the simplicity of life in that region. His deep, harmonious voice is still in my mind, helping me with the rhymes. That style of music is called *repente* or *aboio*—it's improvised, spontaneous music with unscripted rhymes created about a theme of the singers' choice. It's known for the fluid alignment of words in sentences and the passion in the message told as parables and metaphors. The cordel booklets—inexpensive leaflets that contain Brazilian folklore, poems, and songs—that came with us to Pará in Northeastern Brazil were a significant influence on my poetic side and on my desire to live a full and meaningful life.

Now, my proud father resurrects memories of his youthful adventures, suddenly enchanting friends with his smooth, rich voice when meeting. But I lost the other three. My grandparents lived full lives and died, leaving behind their beautiful story that marks their time here on earth; they are loved now as they were when alive. My mother rested in the Lord in 2020 due to complications after contracting COVID-19. She also reached her milestone before leaving us—she lived to see her daughters succeed and even her grandchildren achieve great goals. All four had notable lives, and all past hurts are forgiven, I choose to only remember the great examples of overcoming adversity, of wisdom, and of the love that they gave me. However, like my grandmother, I am only a storyteller, and my tale isn't about my four rocks.

Abandonment

This tale begins with the abandonment of a two-month-old child by his teenage mother when she felt preoccupied about being a minority and lacking experience. Living with her baby's father's parents' family and away from her own family, she freaked out and left her daughter in the care of her paternal grandparents. Her daughter's father was on a trip, and when he returned, he didn't find his then partner and mother of his daughter. At that moment, he went from thinking he had a family, to having a daughter without her mother.

Perhaps, this would be the moment when he began to take on the responsibility of a husband and family man. Who knows? Everything might have been different with a little more effort from this girl. But for one reason or another, in her despair, she left. Never knowing that her legacy she left behind for her baby was a future of emotional dysfunction and codependency.

Throughout her life, no matter how loved she was by her father, who played more of a brother's role in his daughter's life, she was completely centered on the shoulders of her grandparents, who loved her unconditionally. With all this zeal from her father and grandparents, that girl always felt that someone else must be the reason for her lack of happiness.

This is the first part of the story about my mother, my birth, and our misfortune. In my second month of life, my mother was insecure and unstable. She lived with my father in my paternal grandparents' house. According to her, my grandfather did not agree with this union. To make matters worse, some of my grandmother's relatives, out of great envy, wanted to take my mother's place.

With all the pressure and lack of support, she had to leave the house at the age of just nineteen. The arrangement was for her to settle down a little in life and then come back to get me. After four years she came back, and my grandparents didn't want to give me to her anymore. They had already fallen in love with the baby who was once given into their care by force. They ended up going to court to fight for custody of me. They won. My mother lost.

I didn't understand anything at the time. I just felt over the years the crater that abandonment makes. No matter the circumstances, those who have been abandoned suffer something that will cause a lot of damage. Most mothers don't leave their children because they don't love them or don't want the responsibility. Unfortunately, they leave because of something they think they can fix. Then, they come back hoping that the world stopped, and everything will be as it was when they left. But nothing stays the same. Every minute that passed, everything continued in motion, just like people's minds. What was once hard to find is now completely lost.

Unfortunately, for me, the first few months of a baby's life are when the bond between the mother and baby is created and formed for life. The misfortunes that both my mother and I suffered will be paid for over a lifetime. As much as I told my mom that I was okay and that I was where I had to be, as much as I had forgiven her for having to choose to leave me in a better place, she never stopped feeling pain.

I felt that pain when I made the same decision to leave my son behind, in my own country, to come to the United States. Before, I couldn't even approach the subject without getting hurt or angry, but once you're healed from a trauma, it doesn't hurt anymore. Yes, this is my tale.

Healing

The child does not stop loving his parents, but he stops loving himself, feeling unworthy of being loved, as if he were trash whom no one wants. The biggest problem with abandonment is the eternal feeling of emptiness. The eternal search to fill this void creates emotionally unstable people who are eternally needy and searching for a feeling that never fills them.

The worst period during this situation is adolescence. Adolescence for everyone is the most difficult time in their lives, as it is when they are searching for their own identities. Imagine, then, how difficult adolescence must be for those who no longer have any identity in the family with which they live.

My solution was a desire to be free from this void. And my healing came from my paintings, my therapy, and, of course, my God.

During my childhood, I had the stability of a family who loved me and of my mother who, whenever she could, came to visit me. She brought gifts and took me out with her as much as she could. Still, the early abandonment left ingrained consequences. How painful it is to be someone who was discarded from the life of the person who was the first to bond with you. I thought this was not a problem because I was loved from all sides—my grandparents, my father, and my uncles made sure that

I was protected and loved. Whenever my mother had the opportunity, she introduced me to members of her family too; some I am still in contact with. I thought the abandonment didn't negatively affect me, but unconsciously I developed a feeling that stayed with me for over forty years.

Not because it's my mother's fault, but because each chapter of life brings a sequence dependent on it, feelings that I had to identify and eliminate. But the biggest problem is, when these feelings become habits, they go unnoticed because they are old companions. Such habits acquired by small and large wounds in the soul, which were inflicted without treatment or attention, become chronic and affect your personality. These wounds cause you to act in ways that you think are just characteristic of you. My rebellion, resentment, envy of those who lived with both parents, desire to have a standard family, desire to have this emptiness filled, and desire to obtain what I think is missing—all these things seemed like common teenage angst. We all want what we don't have. But some only want what someone else has; once they get that or something similar, it no longer has any value.

Throughout my life, like a magnet, I have always been attracted to emotionally dependent people, to those like me, a codependent on a mission to "help." In this "help" I increasingly sank deeper into myself. I was forced to live the other person's life and to seek to achieve the dreams of the partner in question. I never allowed myself to have a dream of my own. In my last troubled, codependent relationship, which lasted fourteen years, it was clear from the beginning that he was not well. But the codependent goes through countless stages of denial to keep the object of codependency.

My ex-husband repeated the fallacy that "we must learn to be happy alone, because the company of others will be a matter of choice, not necessity." He said this to remind me that I was always a necessity to him. I was never his first choice. I was someone who helped him when no one was there, who picked him up when he was down. I wasn't someone he wanted and had chosen to grow old by his side. I was a necessity, the self-effacing codependent for the emotionally dependent.

I learned a lot from this, but I only put it into practice after almost fourteen years, after hearing him repeat it many times. Stupid people hide behind excuses to continue in their vicious cycle because both making decisions and making them happen are very painful. So I lived blindly because I refused to see what was clearly before my eyes. In this blindness, I insisted on guiding another person who was also blind, as they still had a shadow over their development and unconscious traumas from their childhood. Of course, it was already clear that this relationship was not going to work.

And so it happened, between betrayals and forgivenesses, which is what happens in the middle of a relationship like this; one acts by taking advantage of the codependent's unconditional commitment, and the other doesn't care about anything other than feeling good. These acts by an emotionally unbalanced person to feel good range from lying to supporting the codependent, and then temporary regret followed by another lie to the codependent who will certainly believe it. This cycle will repeat as long as it is allowed or until the emotionally unbalanced person finds another codependent who appears to be more attractive.

The codependent goes unnoticed because he is strong and always sees that the other remains emotionally weak while the codependent sinks, disappearing within himself. When the object of codependency is taken away by death or abandonment, the codependent no longer has anything, not even their own life, because they lived for the other. He dreamed other people's dreams; he never grew up because he was the shadow of the other person he made grow while the codependent stayed still.

Excessive dependence on others often leads to dysfunctional interpersonal relationships. The person on whom the codependent depends is a person who will forgive and blame the actions, not the person, for the harm that is inflicted, similar to the case of a mother whose son is addicted to drugs, is sick, or has some type of disorder.

A metaphor that I use in my painting groups is about the empty vase or container. Throughout our lives, we fill ourselves with knowledge, experiences, and traumas. Like a vase, we can be clean or stained. Like a vase, we can be broken. Like a vase, we can be full of both good and bad things. The vase must be maintained; the things that are acquired and that should not be retained must be cleaned away. Everything that could cause damage to the vase must be removed. But if this maintenance is not carried out, the items in the vase can rot and die, and the vase itself can be indelibly stained and damaged.

The codependent is a vessel that, due to lack of maintenance, always absorbs and compromises. Codependency is acquired not only by the current state of life, but by a series of factors that in the past overloaded the vessel. The codependent vessel is low in maintenance and therefore vulnerable to being what it is. This emotional deficiency is not caused by a single relationship. Codependency is a vessel that has become emotionally affected since childhood.

Codependency is a behavior that disguises itself and goes unnoticed, but it is a disorder of emotions. I needed to know that I had to seek help. Many end up putting up with everything to save their marriages or loved ones, until they end up getting sick too.

Change requires confrontation. Confrontation requires a decision. The decision, in turn, will only flow with attitudes.

Trauma causes unbalanced emotions. Unbalanced emotions end up making you look for wrong ways to get some personal satisfaction; it is a continuous silence that annuls you.

The probability of change is completely remote. There has to be some struggle forcing you into the unwanted transition of change. Otherwise, you would go into a deep, dark hole, and the more time that passes, the more decayed you would become.

The break is the same for many, but some have the resilience to be emotionally reborn. Others, unfortunately, will die. And be reborn.

Metamorphosis

On August 25, 2014, I dreamed that I was at my grandparents' house in my hometown. I was packing my personal things for a permanent move. So I started putting my things in boxes. They weren't just suitcases, but boxes for a big move. I came across a beautiful, shapely, thin wooden shelf.

In a dream, I saw a man wearing a cloak of peace, as if he was someone illustrious. Wherever he passed, people's faces changed to a singular expression—peace.

In the place where I lived as a child, he was sitting at a table. In his hand, a pen like a gold, it seemed of great value. He wrote on a blank sheet of paper. I couldn't read what he wrote, as it wasn't a language I knew; however, I could understand that he was giving me a mission to fulfill. When I was ready, he wrote an order.

I stopped in front of a wooden shelf, on it items had already been arranged in many organized boxes. I saw a lot of shoes on that shelf, shoes from my childhood that my innocent little feet had used. I recognized other shoes that I wore throughout my life and shoes that I still don't have, representing the dispersed past and a prepared future.

On the last shelf, there are sandals made with leather and blue beads, a spotlight on them from the lamp at the top of the shelf. I knew they were the most important thing I would wear, but, somehow, I knew my feet weren't ready to wear them. I knew that shoes mean preparation, and I was being prepared for a project that I still had no idea what it was.

I packed everything I needed to put in boxes. I took the paper from the man's hands. Even without seeing his face, his smile spread glory over me.

I woke up and went to work. When I arrived, I somehow needed to mark the dream. My stepdaughter had three colors of paint, two brushes, and two canvases left over from a school project. I started my first canvas and haven't stopped until today.

I had forgotten about all that. I didn't even imagine returning to my roots in my adult phase. I never dreamed of what I'm living now. For more than forty years, I never thought about being an artist, but my blood held my artistic heritage. I didn't know that my creative streak would influence my healing. However, God knew. He made my whole heritage clear through a dream. Activated art became healing!

Moreover, I didn't know how to do anything. I had to learn from scratch. The art worked to cure me. It branched out in countless directions and transformed my life, starting to put on a canvas my emotions, both those that make me feel inadequate and those that make me feel worthy, and especially my dreams.

For many long years, I remained motionless in the corner of the board, similar to a queen held by horses in a chess game. At forty-one years old, I was already in the middle of a game in which the queen is not expected to move. The game of chess seemed over, and God urged the queen to start a new round.

Art through painting, and then later through writing, took me out of the shadows and gave me an identity, made me look inside myself and analyze what should be balanced. I could only bring out through painting what was within my personal shadow, as if I poured it onto the canvas. I didn't understand what was happening. I didn't know the power of art as a cure; however, it was happening to me.

During this latent period, of which I now have much more understanding, I surrendered. Everything I did was an essential tool for healing my wounded soul, but I had no idea at the time; I just felt it. I needed a refuge to ease my pain, and painting was that refuge. I wasn't inspired by any artist or friends, nor did I get any tips from anyone. I never had the inclination to seek help from art. All of this really happened overnight and was a turning point in my life. Certainly, in my original form, I was created to be what I am today, but I was hidden and came to light in my moment of darkness.

Art has a power beyond our physical capabilities; it syncs with the subconscious. Art reveals what consciously would be impossible to express. Unconscious synergy and art make the projection of the unknown possible. Art, with its delicacy, takes not only the best, but also the worst of me and exposes it without causing pain. On the contrary, it helps, giving possibilities to clarify what cannot be said, but rather expressed through art.

Psychology and neuroscience would certainly say that it was all my psychic energy that strongly projected my artistic side in the midst of the crisis to save me. My subconscious brought the help I needed from my original form. In my faith, I am sure that what I experienced was a gift from my God to transform my life.

Convinced that what I experienced with art as a cure worked in practice, I decided to go back to college to learn the theory of what I experienced; it is still slow going. To me, God is the chief psychologist; He used my dreams to direct me. He instructed me how to get the message I dreamed of and helped me so much by guiding me towards what I was experiencing. After ten years of this death, mourning came, and the mourning expressed by paints and canvases, in turn, gave life to more than six hundred canvases, six books, coauthorship in three anthologies, and countless art exhibitions.

Loss breaks and can even kill. God transformed the silence of death into art and art into life. Since *Shattered Silence* transformed into artwork, it has inspired people both near and far, even in different countries.

We wait for miracles, forgetting that every day we are living in one.

In Memory of
Angelina Umina

Beyond Words

A Love-Letter Legacy
Written by My Grandmother

Lisa Michelle Umina

*M*y grandmother, Angelina, began a new chapter in her life shortly after I was born, when she moved to California to live with her sister Emma and settled into a small apartment. I'm not sure why she made this decision. She lived far away from her two sons and her four grandchildren, who were all in Cleveland. She nurtured her connection with distant loved ones by consistently sending heartfelt letters through the mail, a gesture that holds a unique significance in today's vastly changed landscape.

In retrospect, our geographical differences didn't weaken our bond. When I went to see my great-grandmother

Mary, she always planned a ritual. I used to sit at the dining room table with blue sheets of paper, pencil, and eraser she stored in her antique hutch. I remember it took me hours to write a two-page letter. Over the years, our written exchanges persisted, and a significant change unfolded when my grandmother returned to Cleveland following the passing of her mother.

In the quiet embrace of memories, I find myself drawn to the essence of my beloved grandmother, a guardian of love. As I begin to write our journey of words, it is not just a narrative about her, but a tribute to the unwavering love that formed the very fabric of who I am. My grandma had a particular way of expressing her love, a love that may have been difficult at times. Nonetheless, from time to time, she surprised me with a little trinket or sacred prayer book from the shrine where her charitable heart resided.

I know that there are numerous love tales, but the bond I shared with my grandma was special and meaningful. She stands out as a glowing exemplar of that distinct brand of affection when I reflect on those who imparted lessons about love. In the tapestry of my life, the threads woven with my grandmother stand out as vibrant and irreplaceable. Every visit to her home was an experience filled with love and warmth, her cozy home elevated by the little details. She added more than mere time to the hours we spent together; we had so many conversations about everything and anything.

She had an uncanny ability to look out for me. I recall a specific instance when my first book was featured in the newspaper, and she expressed her immense pride. Yet, amid her compliments, she insisted my front tooth was crooked, and I needed braces, especially if I intended to be in the newspapers or anywhere in public again promoting my book. It was her unique way of showing love, and I understood her underlying intention.

She had a remarkable way with words, I must say. Her affect and comments seemed harsh sometimes, but I could always tell that she didn't mean any harm. Some family members and her friends, however, found it difficult to interpret her remarks or sarcasm as well-intentioned. I often found myself in the position of apologizing on her behalf.

My grandmother's kitchen always smelled of garlic, even if she wasn't cooking. Even today, when I am cooking and I use garlic, I immediately think of her. Her lunches were more than just meals; they were carefully cooked and presented on pretty dishes, the table dressed with embroidered napkins.

Each visit, she brought me a present as a sign of her love. It may be a treasured memento from her life, a necklace that whispered stories from her past, or a thoughtfully selected item she knew would make me happy. These treasures were more than just gifts; they were physical representations of our relationship and acts of love.

Thinking back on such moments, with those gifts, I see that my grandma was teaching me how to make treasured memories out of the ordinary fabric of life. But even more than the delicious food and tangible presents, it was my grandmother's considerateness that enriched our experiences. What remains most vivid in my memory is her ability to transform everyday letters into treasured works of art, infusing them with a touch of artistry that made them genuinely extraordinary.

She adorned each handwritten card with gorgeous cutouts of tiny girls whirling in pastel-colored skirts and angels with golden wings. Her timeworn hands, with subtle grace, masterfully created each piece. Her artistic talent was also visible on the envelopes, which were adorned with these whimsical images that danced around the edges, setting the stage for the moving words that were inside. These precious scraps of paper developed a language all their own and conveyed tales of warmth, compassion, and affection.

Every envelope opened like a gift, unveiling a realm where love found expression through carefully selected words and charming paper cutouts, often sourced from magazines or newspapers. On the backs of the envelopes, she always added "S.W.A.B.K." *Sealed with a big kiss.*

Over the course of thirty-five years, the collection of letters grew, a tribute to a lifetime of shared memories.

Each cutout had meaning—a heart, a little girl, the Blessed Mother, angels. I can remember each one as if she wrote it yesterday. Even now, as I read those precious letters, the angels and young girls continue to remind me of the countless hours she spent making each letter or card.

When I made the big move to Mexico, it broke my heart that my weekly trips to my grandmother's house would turn into yearly visits, or sometimes twice a year. It never seemed as if it were enough time with her, and I couldn't stay long because she needed to lie down to rest in the afternoons. She had become more fragile each time I came to visit her.

My grandmother continued to write me when I moved to Mexico. She complained every time about the long Mexican address. I completely understand; it is a very long address, and the layout of the street address is different. I can honestly say I do not receive much mail here because of this, not to mention the turnaround time can take up to three to four months to receive a letter from anywhere in the world. God love her for trying. I could often see that she had attempted to address the missive correctly, but instead of organizing the lines properly, she scratched off some words and added others. I started to notice the cutouts were fewer and fewer.

The last letter that arrived, before she was too weak to write, was plain and simple—no ornate cutouts of angels or hearts. I opened the letter, and there it was, a master-piece of exhaustion. "Dearest Lisa," it began, "I had such a hard time writing your long address out on the envelope that I am too damn tired to write you a letter and sign it. I love you, Grandma." Now, most people would stash the envelope for a fresh start the next day, but not my grandmother. Oh no, this was her way of saying, "You live too damn far, and I'm just plain exhausted."

My grandma had strange habits and peculiarities, yet her love was a strong influence in my life. She had a way of contrasting her love of vivid words with the innate tenderness she displayed in her daily routines. She got up at four in the morning and spent her time saying rosaries and novenas in fervent prayer for her friends and family. Although her outward appearance suggested toughness, she concealed a tenderness that she rarely displayed. Few knew about her vulnerable side because she tended to guard her emotions well. My father used to talk about how hard she was on him, which I could see in action when we visited. Her stubborn walls baffled me, especially considering how obvious her love was for my father. I was confused by the contrast between her tough demeanor and her obvious affection for him.

A piece of my grandmother seemed to go with my father when he passed away. Her eyes lost their brightness. It was then that I realized, behind that thick wall of hers, a part of her died with him. That's when I started to wonder why some parents have a hard time showing their kids how much they truly love them. Yet, when it is their grandchildren, they do not have any reservations. My grandmother had her own way of showing love, but I wanted my father to see the tender side of her. I think he did when he saw his mother and me together.

The hardest part of saying goodbye to my grandma was the physical barrier that divided us in her last moments. I knew she didn't want me to see her fading, and she issued a "no visitors" order, permitting only medical workers to attend her. I am filled with an immense gratitude that words cannot fully capture for my cousin Nikki, who stealthily checked on her.

With his nurse's uniform on, Kyle managed to elude the nurses and set up a FaceTime call, which allowed me to be virtually present for those brief final moments with my grandma. I felt an intense pain upon her death, one that was comparable to losing the love of my life. The distance that stood between us at that critical moment added to the grief and intensified the anguish. I cannot fathom what I would have done if I couldn't say goodbye to her.

The influence of my grandma is still very much present and has braided itself into the core of who I am. Even though I didn't start the journey of parenthood myself, her love lessons have served as my compass, helping me navigate the complex world of relationships. My grandma

Angelina was a master of love; the smallest elements made up her symphony. She taught me the language of love, which is expressed in little, nuanced details, rather than in large, dramatic actions. For me, the art of love became a string of well-chosen phrases, memorable dinners, and unplanned gestures of love.

The value of expressing love in writing was one of the lessons that stuck with me the most. I picked up a pen and wrote some love notes to myself, motivated by the letters my grandmother had written me. These romantic letters developed into a link between hearts, an eternal communication that surpasses the transient quality of spoken words. The handwritten letter is a monument to the lasting power of concrete, unique gestures of love in this age of digital communication.

I also developed a love for cooking. The attention I give to the details in planning and preparing a meal has also become a way to show my affection for the people I love. More than just food, it is a way of expressing, "You matter, and this is my gift to you."

Thinking back on these teachings, I see that love is found in the little things, the nuanced details that come together to form a beautiful symphony of love. It's about the happiness of an unexpected gift, the scent of a well-prepared dinner, and the coziness of a handwritten note. These are the little things that make the ordinary remarkable.

My grandma showed me that love's beauty may be found in the small things, even in a world that is sometimes enthralled with spectacular displays. It is not the expensive presents or grandiose acts that leave an impression on the heart; rather, it's the small, everyday things that get ingrained in memories. Caring involves taking the time to attend to small details. It's crucial to show the people you care about that you've invested the effort in these thoughtful acts. Life is in the details, my grandmother used to tell me. It's in how we treat the individuals who are important to us. It's in the work we do to ensure they feel noticed, appreciated, and loved. We run the danger of missing a crucial piece in the intricate fabric of life when we ignore the little things.

All in all, my grandmother left me a love legacy presented in words that were precise. With this insight, I find myself navigating the currents of life and understanding that love is expressed not only by grandiose pronouncements, but also by the nuanced strokes of little, day-to-day deeds. The small things—the kind notes, the homemade meals, the unexpected gifts—are what accentuate the route of love and add significance to the experience. Ultimately, a timeless love story is woven from the small elements, the subtle intricacies.

I kept all my grandmother's letters in a wonderful handmade Mexican box. Periodically, I open the box, close my eyes, and take in the memories that each letter holds, each as it was given to me. Every line demonstrates her knowledge and sense of humor. The thing I adore the most is that each envelope opens to show me pages of her conversing with me as though we were having lunch in her kitchen.

I've been thinking about how important it is to honor my grandmother's great heart in my own deeds ever since she passed away. By being mindful of life's little details, I hope to uphold her legacy. I try to return the favor by showing my love through modest gestures and attentive details, just as her small acts of kindness moved me. The real grandeur of her character was revealed in her seemingly minor deeds. Making a phone call, sending a sincere text, or cooking a meal can all be considered small yet meaningful ways to show someone you care. I wish to continue her legacy by embracing the ability of little, meaningful gestures to remind others that they are appreciated, as I am aware of the enormous influence these acts had on me.

I notice that I often adopt her mannerisms in my everyday interactions with those around me. I'm aware that the small gestures I extend to others are aimed at making them feel valued and remembered. In our contemporary world, where communication is dominated by cell phones and text messages, genuine and thoughtful gestures seem to be scarce or nonexistent.

In emulating my grandmother's thoughtful acts, I strive to carry on her legacy of considering others in the smallest details. Her kindness has left an indelible mark on my approach to relationships and daily life. From the little gestures she made to ensure I felt special and cherished, I've learned the profound impact of thoughtfulness.

As I navigate the fast-paced world dominated by technology and fleeting interactions, I find solace in replicating her genuine care. Whether it's a handwritten note, a small gift, or a heartfelt gesture, I aim to uphold the tradition of making people feel seen and appreciated. In a society where personal connections often take a back seat to convenience, I draw inspiration from my grandmother's unwavering commitment to fostering meaningful relationships through the power of small, thoughtful actions.

My grandmother's influence continues to shape the way I engage with the world. I strive to perpetuate the warmth and connection she instilled in our relationship. I find purpose in upholding her legacy of genuine care and appreciation. Through simple yet meaningful gestures, I aim to make a positive impact on others, just as my grandmother did for me. In doing so, I hope to perpetuate a cycle of kindness and thoughtfulness that echoes her enduring spirit.

In the end, it's the little things, the details, that create a love story that transcends time.

About the Authors

https://franwalshward.com

The life of **Fran Walsh Ward, PhD**, has been an adventure. Like Ellyn (in her fantasy/ metaphysical series *Travels with Ellyn and Beyond the Drawbridge*, (written using the pen name Frances Ellen Walsh), she has traveled a spiritual path. Following her heart, she is an author, artist, and educator. Passionate about everything she does and everywhere she goes, she shares her joy of living and interacting with members of our global family who all complement each other. Peace and harmony are underlying currents of her existence. Grateful for her experiences, she eagerly anticipates her next chapters of life as they are revealed to her and as she has described them in her memoir *Soul Tattoos!*

Anapaula Corral is a loved and highly respected professional in her community. She was born in Mexico City and raised in Switzerland. She has an accomplished thirty-year career in the hospitality and residential industries. Her interest in writing her first book came from helping families and women who have lost a child. Writing was a healing and life-changing process for her. She intends to inspire other readers by writing more books on building strong and healthy communities and relations. She currently resides in Miami, Florida, with her boyfriend, Darryl, and their two dogs. She enjoys living life to the fullest and cherishes Anasofia's life every day.

Angela Gilson was born and raised in California. She published her first book in November 2022, at the age of twenty-three. The book is called *Sarabeth and Her New Best Friend*, which she dedicated to her rabbit, Hopper. She is a nature person who loves the outdoors and likes to travel.

Conrad M. Gonzales is a retired San Antonio firefighter and paramedic. He lives in San Antonio, Texas, USA. He is also a musician, performer, and songwriter, talents which he discovered later in life. He is the embodiment of the belief that "It is never too late to do great things to make a difference." Mr. Gonzales's passion has always been to provide safety education in order to save lives, especially those of children. To that end, he has been teaching safety to both children and adults for over forty years. He often says, "Children are our future, and I want to do whatever I can so that they live to see their future." You can listen to Captain Conrad, the Singing Firefighter on his social media channel.

Dave Grunenwald is a proud grandfather who was born, raised, and educated in Northeast Ohio. He has worn many hats in his professional life. Now "semi-retired", Dave has been an influential real-estate developer and attorney in Northeast Ohio for the last 30+ years. While he is still involved and active in that capacity, much of his time these days is spent wearing his DCGifts hat, creating the *Grandparent Merit Badges*™ series, and authoring a new series of children's story books.

Diane Lopes is a mother, daughter, sister, friend, corporate executive/leader, animal lover, and cancer fighter. Diane's father, Jack, became an author in his retirement which sparked Diane's desire to write. Diane's grief journey began when Jack started showing signs of dementia and aphasia. It was a years-long process that was difficult, agonizing, and sad, but sometimes funny as the shenanigans spark that was always there between the two, would peek out occasionally.

Diane has a children's book coming out soon called *Meet Jack Joybubbles*, a story about her family's rescue dog. Look for that coming soon from Halo Publishing International.

www.drcarolmankes.com
drcarolmankes@gmail.com

Dr. Carol Leibovich-Mankes, DrOT, OTR/L, PLCC, GC-C, was born in Israel to Argentinian parents and later emigrated to the USA. She is a multilingual professional fluent in English, Spanish, and Hebrew. With a career spanning twenty-five years, she serves as a pediatric occupational therapist and parent coach specializing in empowering kids (ages three to eighteen), parents, and teachers of exceptional children; she offers guidance on parenting, learning, handwriting, and other challenges they may face as life happens.

As an expert in her field, Dr. Leibovich-Mankes has faced personal challenges, including being a widow and a solo mom navigating through various losses and life transitions. Leveraging her experiences and professional expertise as an occupational therapist, certified life/ parent coach, and grief counselor, she has forged a path of healing. Dr. Leibovich-Mankes is dedicated to supporting others in similar circumstances, advocating for empowerment, and raising awareness about grief and loss. Through coaching, she encourages individuals to adopt a growth mindset and recognize that grief can manifest from different significant losses. These losses don't always encompass death but may also stem from loss of control, unexpected circumstances, and unique challenges posed by parenting exceptional children. These losses can greatly impact one's emotional well-being and ability to navigate life's challenges.

In addition to her clinical and coaching work, Dr. Leibovich-Mankes is the author of the book *On the Road to Handwriting Success: A Resource Guide for Therapists, Teachers, and Parents*. This comprehensive guide reflects her commitment to sharing knowledge and insights, in addition to offering practical support for individuals involved in the development of children's handwriting and learning skills.

With a heartfelt mission to inspire and empower others to face and overcome loss, pain, and shattered dreams, Dr. Leibovich-Mankes emphasizes the importance of understanding grief as a dynamic process applicable to various life experiences. Her goal is to ensure that society recognizes diverse forms of loss and grief, especially the emotional turmoil and myriad challenges that may be associated with raising an out-of-the-box child. Dr. Leibovich-Mankes stands ready to guide parents, siblings, teachers, caregivers, and, most of all, children toward a future filled with hope, laughter, and renewed vitality.

Irene S. Roth is a freelance writer and author. Ms. Roth was born in Montreal, but now lives in Ontario with her husband, Toby (cat), and Milo (dog). She writes self-help books for adults and the chronically ill. She uses her expertise in psychology and philosophy to educate people of all ages on how to live their most authentic and fulfilling lives. She also presents workshops for *Savvy Authors*.

Brazilian impressionist, artist, and author, **Monica Septimio** resides in Natick. She was healed and transformed by the power of art. Now, she pours her soul into art inspired by dreams, childhood, faith, and culture.

In 2015, during an obscure time of her life, after one dream she started painting. Self-taught, she delivers the message that art cures. She has impacted many who have attended her exhibitions. She is the author of four children's bilingual books and one for adult readers, *Joy*. She was a seminarian for four years at Community Preservation Committee in Framingham, Massachusetts. She studied philosophy for two years at the University of Philosophy of Maranhão, Rondon do Pará, Brazil. She is currently active in the Boston community and attends book fairs and conferences, in addition to exhibiting her paintings and promoting her literary pieces.

Award-Winning Author

Lisa Michelle Umina is the founder and CEO of Halo Publishing International, a company that has been in operation since 2002. She also established Hola Publishing Internacional as its sister company. Lisa, who is an award-winning author herself, provides coaching to fellow writers on publishing their own books and developing lucrative public speaking careers. She shares the tactics she has used to achieve success. Lisa is the author of the award-winning book "Milo and the Green Wagon," and the host of the "Award-Winning Authors" podcast.

YaleNewHavenHealth
Smilow Cancer Hospital

At Smilow Cancer Hospital, they offer the utmost in cancer care excellence. Their affiliation with Yale Cancer Center, the only National Cancer Institute (NCI)-designated comprehensive cancer center in Connecticut and one of only 56 Centers in the nation, means patients receive top-tier collaboration.

This partnership brings together esteemed scientists and physicians from Yale Cancer Center, Yale School of Medicine, and Smilow Cancer Hospital, ensuring optimal strategies for cancer prevention, detection, diagnosis, and treatment.

They provide 13 specialized cancer programs, each backed by teams of experts deeply versed in specific cancer types. Placing patients and their loved ones at the heart of their commitment, their approach prioritizes compassion and support throughout every individual's unique journey.

Halo Publishing International is a hybrid publishing company that combines the best aspects of traditional publishing and self-publishing. Our company aims to provide a flexible and affordable publishing options for authors who want more control over the publishing process while still receiving professional editing, design, and global distribution services. Halo Publishing International offers a wide range of publishing packages and services to suit different author needs and budgets, including editorial services, cover design, book formatting, printing, distribution, and marketing. With a focus on quality, integrity, and innovation, Halo Publishing International has helped numerous authors achieve their publishing goals and reach a wider audience.

OUR HISTORY
Halo Publishing International, our mission is to empower authors to share their stories worldwide. Since 2002, we have helped thousands of authors turn their ideas into published books that reach audiences globally. No matter the genre, whether it be science fiction, religious, children's literature, or an instruction manual, Halo Publishing International

is dedicated to providing the editorial support needed to make your book a success.

OUR MISSION

Halo Publishing International is a self-publishing company that publishes adult fiction and non-fiction, children's literature, self-help, spiritual, and faith-based books. We continually strive to help authors reach their publishing goals and provide many different services that help them do so.

We do not publish books that are deemed to be politically, religiously, or socially disrespectful, or books that are sexually provocative, including erotica.

Halo reserves the right to refuse publication of any manuscript if it is deemed not to be in line with our principles.

Follow us on our social media
HaloPublishingInternacional

To know more about Halo Publishing International please visit
www.halopublishing.com

Milton Keynes UK
Ingram Content Group UK Ltd.
UKHW020741190424
441445UK00013B/506

When you have tried everything

BEFRIEND YOUR
MIGRAINE

A book about migraine and about life

Maria Piema

CONTENTS

INTRODUCTION

This is the book I wish I had read when life was all about migraines, pain, anxiety and survival. I had tried all the medications and treatments that healthcare had to offer. Nothing helped and I did not want to live anymore. If I had read this book then, it would have given me hope for life and a direction forward when I no longer knew what to do with myself. I would have avoided detours, lost time and a strong feeling of loneliness.

Amongst other things, this book is about what helped me to no longer be afraid of living my life. To despite migraines, live a life I didn't think was possible, a life full of joy, love and creativity. A life where I can do whatever I want; work, exercise, travel, enjoy life, meet friends, create, evolve, discover and learn new things.

I won't make any promises of you becoming migraine-free, but with an open mind and a willingness to explore other ways to look at migraines and pain, I want you to feel hopeful of having a wonderful and fantastic life despite migraines.

For 25 years I suffered from migraines up to 20-25 days a month. Most of those days the pain was so terrible I ended up spending a lot of my time in dark rooms together with nausea and anxiety. It took courage, determination and self-love to let go of control and face the unknown. I finally decided that I actually wanted to participate in my life, and not just survive in a dark room. To choose life, quality of life, was the most important decision to make. I needed courage to go my own way. If I had listened to everyone who told me that there is nothing more to do, you have to live like this, you have to accept your situation, you will not be able to work etc., I would not be sitting here today. I needed self-love not to give up, to continue to encourage myself that I am valuable and in fact worthy of a fantastic life. To believe in myself when no one else did. That migraines are not my fault, but that I have a responsibility for what I do with my life. Having a migraine is not a punishment from hell for doing something wrong. I also needed self-love to understand that I don't have to achieve anything to be valuable, I don't have to compare myself with anyone else and I don't have to prove anything to anyone.

Today, when I look back on my life and what I have learnt so far from living with migraines, I feel gratitude. Migraine is a serious illness, but it also puts things at the forefront, we have to actively choose joy and life over suffering, otherwise the risk is that time just passes by and we miss out on all our dreams. When I finally realised that pain does not at all have to mean suffering, the door to freedom was opened. When I realised that all my suffering was something I did to myself, the realisation also came that I had a choice. I can't control my migraine, but I can decide for myself whether to choose the suffering, or the joy and love for life. Since the day I actively chose joy and love, my life turned for the better. Of course, I have highs and lows like everyone else, but nowadays I know that it's temporary and that it passes. I have opened the door to freedom and now there is no turning back.

During the years when I fumbled my way to better health and living, I at first felt extremely lonely, but I eventually found people who supported me. By support I don't mean those who wanted me to see "the reality", that migraines never go away and that I have to accept the pain, but the people who surrounded me in different ways and who through their attitude and love taught me that everything is possible. They taught me what acceptance really is, that I am not defined by my illness and that I can have the life I want.

THE STARTING POINT OF
THE BOOK

This book is written from the bottom of my heart, with love and compassion for all who suffer from migraines. It's written with the greatest understanding of what it's like to be affected by migraines. I know how it is. I know what it's like to lie in the dark, literally, but also in a darkness of hopelessness and despair. I know what it's like to feel completely powerless. I know what it's like to wake up in the morning and long for the evening when you can return to bed again. I know what it's like to be in so much pain that you believe something is going to break inside your head. I know how it feels when you think you're going to die, because you can't endure such pain and nausea. I know how it feels when you want to die because it feels like you have no life. I know what it's like to be depressed, to have anxiety and feel guilty. I know what it's like to have mood swings and blame everything and everyone, then regret it bitterly. I know what it's like to meet incompetent healthcare professionals. I know what it's like to sit and cry at the health centre week after week with a doctor who thinks you should just drink a glass of wine and relax. I know how it feels to take so much medicine that you have to be detoxified. I know what it's like not to be believed in. I know what it's like to feel alone in the world. I know what it's like to cry every single day and worry about your children and the future. I know what it's like to think you've done something wrong and migraines are the punishment from hell. I know how it feels when the days go by and you don't have the strength to participate. I know what it's like when all the loved ones meet and have fun and you can't take part. I know what it's like to be in a dark room on Christmas Eve. I know what it's like to have children and be annoyed and not be able to listen because my head hurts. I know what it's like to feel guilty. I know what it's like to try and make an effort to have a better life but nothing helps.

I also know what it's like to get out of the dark and start walking towards the light. I know that when I didn't give up on being worthy of a great life, the insights finally came. I know there are two steps forward and one back. I also know that if I can, so can you. I also know that if we help each other, it's easier. I know that who we are beneath all the layers of illness and pain can be brought out. I know we can find happiness, enjoyment and lust for life despite migraines. I know life is amazing. I know that love from fellow human beings can hold us up when we're in doubt. I also know that despite the hell migraines can bring, it can also be a turning point if we find the courage to take the step. I know we need to surround ourselves with positive forces that provides energy. I know that in order to have a better life, we must be prepared to change and evolve. And above all, I know that we are not our achievements and that we are not selfish when we take care of ourselves, on the contrary, when we get energy and feel better, we have the ability to spread joy wherever we go.

I also know that if we continue to do what we have done so far, the result will be the same as what we experience every day. To change a habitual pattern is always difficult, no matter what. It's even harder when your head hurts, but the rewards are even greater when we do.

TRIGGERS

A trigger is something that's often discussed when it comes to migraines.

It's usually various foods that cause migraines, the weather, hormones, stress and everything else between heaven and earth, and the advice from both healthcare and well-meaning fellow human beings is often to avoid your triggers and accept your limitations. If I had followed the advice to avoid my triggers and accept my limitations, I wouldn't have recovered at all. When I felt my worst, the migraines were triggered from pretty much everything. I woke up with migraines every single morning and the only way forward was to challenge my triggers two steps forward and one back. At the same time, it's important to remember that this doesn't mean that we should simply just go on and do everything we feel like doing without stopping. It means that we need to become aware of our triggers and acquire strategies on how we handle them. We have to challenge ourselves in a way that makes it possible to succeed, which means patience, confidence that things will get better and courage to let go of control.

Triggers from certain foods and beverages are common in many people. Refraining from foods and beverages that trigger migraines does not have to be a limitation in itself. There are endless of recipes to discover fantastic food that gives us the nutrition and energy our body needs. A lot of triggers are from unhealthy foods and additives that are not good for anyone. The problem is often about changing a habit and phasing out unhealthy food without giving up, even if it doesn't have an immediate noticeable effect on the migraine. Eating healthy becomes a piece of the puzzle for better health. Triggers from certain foods and drinks can also be about expectations from others, that we should eat what they offer, drink some alcohol with dinner and not bother with wanting other alternatives. Additionally, it's not uncommon for food and sweets to become an addiction, when our mood sways we often comfort eat to stun our emotions instead of facing them.

A common trigger for migraines is internal stress where a major contributing factor is our negative thoughts. Our negative thoughts are camouflaged as different things, but the bottom line is about loving oneself, feeling valuable and having a good self-esteem. It's about us all being worthy of a happy and fulfilling life, and we should *allow* ourselves to live life in full. Most of us know that all people are equally worth, that we are valuable whoever we are and that we are not defined by our achievements or the roles we take on throughout life. We also know that our differences are the contrasts that enriches us and help us grow. We all have our symptoms. Because we are social beings, we want to fit in and we often adapt to the external framework that tells us how we should be, what we should do and what we should not do. We listen to others around us more than we listen to our inner selves, we compare ourselves to others, which often means that we go against or even crush our own dreams and desires. Our longing is suppressed, and when we start feeling bad as a result, we blame ourselves for not being good enough, we convince ourselves that there is something wrong with us because we can't feel happy and satisfied, and we feel that we have to make an even bigger effort to fit in and to be like everyone else.

Performance anxiety is a major contributing factor to internal stress. We have to do something, be active, achieve, otherwise we are lazy, incompetent and unsuccessful, or something else that evokes a feeling of not being good enough as we are. We live in a society where experiences and baggage to handle and challenge, and the inner stress it causes gives different symptoms to different people. When we don't allow ourselves to live the life we deep down want and long for, everyone is somehow reminded of this through physical and / or mental achievement is seen as strength and success. Many of us also grew up receiving praise and attention, many times all in goodwill for what we have accomplished and because it's a virtue to make an effort. But what happens to us if we no longer can work or achieve things? Who are we if we can't work or, in our own eyes, contribute something to others?

Performance anxiety becomes a challenge for us who suffers from migraines. It's often difficult, if not impossible, to achieve things with an aching head and nausea. We get ourselves down because we don't have the strength / ability to perform, we feel worthless, we develop a bad conscience and everything becomes worse, the inner stress becomes more prominent. We strive to perform, we work even though we don't have the strength, we take care of others even though we don't have the strength, we do one thing or another even though we don't have the strength. And the migraine becomes increasingly worse, the tension in the body is growing and the inner struggle becomes harder. The thoughts of what we should do, what we should have done but didn't do and how unsuccessful we are wears us down. Performance anxiety can also affect us in our aim to feel better and appear when we make more of an effort to feel better. We try more medications and treatment methods, we try to exercise more and to avoid more, eat better and explore new discoveries. It often doesn't lead to more energy or less pain, but we simply go around in circles and we can't get out.

Since we've learnt that hard work is what's required to achieve success, it can be difficult to see that the solution may be to reduce performance requirements, and also drop them completely in certain contexts, so we simply stop making an effort instead. Learning to reduce certain performance requirements and completely let go of others can be a big challenge, but we can start with small steps, put an end to everyday life and think about what we really "have" to do and why. For whom do we have to achieve something? What happens if we ease our own demands? Many times, it's our own demands that are the most considerable, the people around us often have no issues with us going a bit easier on ourselves.

To *compare* ourselves to others is also about doubting ourselves and our worth. Each and every one of us is completely unique with different backgrounds and internal and external prerequisites. In whatever way we compare ourselves to others, it evokes inner stress because it doesn't go hand in hand with the fact that we are worthy just as we are. If we compare ourselves to others, we will diminish ourselves by, for example, noticing that we are on sick leave when others work and earn money. We barely have the energy walk around the house when others are exercising and running. We have to lie in a dark room when others go on excursions. If we compare ourselves to others and come to the conclusion that we are "better" than them, we also diminish ourselves because such a statement means that we must be or do something special to be good enough. None of this makes us feel better.

When we encounter someone who has succeeded in something that we ourselves long for or dream of, we can feel jealousy and irritation, which is expressed in negative thoughts and possibly negative expressions towards the other. This is never about the other person, but this is about us seeing and being reminded of where we are in relation to our dreams and our longing. We often look for excuses and explanations to why we find ourselves where we are, and why we have not come any further, which evokes a sense of failure as we put focus on the limitations.

It's only when we *don't have to* compare ourselves to others that we can relax. When we accept ourselves the way we are and where we are at the moment in life, we become filled with energy. When we can honestly and genuinely congratulate others, who have achieved what we also wish for ourselves, we focus on what we want in the future instead of retaining a sense of failure. We feel hopeful and get filled with more energy because we put focus on the possibilities.

If, instead of comparing ourselves to others, we see other people as teachers and inspirers, we can encourage ourselves to stick to our intentions to feel better in the long run. There are many people who have come out of very difficult situations in life and who are willing to share some fantastic life experiences and lessons. If we allow ourselves to be inspired and rejoice in how these people have succeeded, we feel hopeful that we too can succeed. If we help each other and share our successes, we get filled with energy.

To please others and to care about what other people think is rooted in the fear of not being accepted and liked by others, and with this I don't mean we shouldn't help out or show consideration for others in a friendly, equal and healthy way. What creates an inner stress is when we try to adapt to others in a way that doesn't match who we are or what we want. We adapt to social interactions, cultures and unwritten rules on how to act and behave together with others because we don't want to stand out and do something that's considered strange or different. We easily hold ourselves back, and we are more concerned of other people's wellbeing instead of making room for ourselves. Many of us don't say what we're actually thinking, and instead keep our needs and desires to ourselves. We are there for others and do things that we might not actually want to do. We don't set boundaries and let fear rule, we please and care more about what other people think than of our own wellbeing.

When we please and / or care about what others think in a way that limits us, we notice it by having energy taken away from us. Sometimes it's very clear that we go against our own needs, but we don't want to acknowledge it because it feels difficult to say no and make someone else disappointed or angry. We sometimes even get a migraine before we do something, because we deep down do not want to. We're being told by the migraine that this is not okay. The question is, what's most important, to please others or to feel good?

If we practice not judging, criticise or to compare ourselves or others, it becomes easier to accept ourselves and others just as we are, equals. When we know our own worth, we don't need the approval of others to feel okay, just as others don't need our approval for them to feel okay. When we know our own worth, we can set boundaries and maintain our integrity. Other people's criticism, judgment or negative opinion is not about us. It's about people who can't handle their own problems and who instead blame others for their own internal struggles. Sometimes we might need feedback from others in order to evolve, which is very different, because constructive feedback is not about deciding on another person's worth.

As we begin to change in our ambition to feel better, we'll encounter challenges. We have to show more courage and love and respect ourselves enough not to fall back when our surroundings begin to react. People in general don't like change and when we start taking more responsibility for our lives and set boundaries, it is more difficult for our surroundings to control and influence us. Some people may react by trying to hold us back or convince us that what we are doing is simply not a good idea. Somehow, they are threatened or afraid of how our decisions will come to affect them. It can involve family members, but it can also apply to care staff. We may well be considered tricky of difficult, because we don't do what's expected. It's important to remember that this is not about us. People who truly genuinely want us to recover will encourage us to take our own responsibility and trust that we ourselves know what is best for us. They will cheer us on, rejoice in every step of the way and be of great support.

Guilt and shame take an enormous amount of energy and are the root to a lot suffering. The difference between guilt and shame is that shame is about "I am wrong", while guilt is about "I have done wrong". In essence, there is a reason for us to feeling guilt and shame because it shows that we can distinguish right from wrong.

It's not uncommon for us who have migraines to often feel guilty about things we aren't in control of, things we could not have known about or things we have chosen in good faith. To feel guilty, we have to be able to take responsibility, but we can't take responsibility for other people or circumstances. We can't take responsibility for things that happened that we could not or can not control. As long as we carry guilt, we carry tensions in the body that causes symptoms that often lead to migraines or tension headaches. Some feelings of guilt are deep, and we may sometimes need professional help to deal with them, while others are often about us making unreasonable demands on ourselves. We must learn to forgive ourselves, not for the things we couldn't control, because we forget that we are valuable and do our best based on what we know and can do. If we act on the basis of good intentions without judging, criticising, comparing and evaluating, we can state that we have done our best based on current circumstances. If we act consciously, we have nothing to regret afterwards and we can minimise the feelings of guilt.

So, what does it mean if we feel guilty because we have migraines? Does it mean we could have done something different? If we feel guilty because we have a migraine, it basically means that we are responsible for the cause of it. We are only to blame for what we have done with the intention of harming others or ourselves and therefore feeling guilty for migraines would mean that we caused migraines to, for example, avoid work, avoid taking care of our children or avoid going out and meeting friends. This sounds unlikely to say the least, so what it is about? In my opinion, there are two options in answer to that question. Either we are not honest with ourselves in the sense that we haven't taken care of ourselves, we have ignored the signals from our body and heart and ignored our own needs, which we know makes us feel worse. When we then have to cancel, we know deep down that it could have been different. Alternative number two is that we have chosen the victim position. For some reason, we don't take responsibility for things being the way they are. I don't mean that we are sick, we don't have that control, but we don't respect or love ourselves enough to take responsibility for our needs. Instead, we hurt ourselves with self-blame and negative thoughts. A good way to avoid feeling guilty for migraines is that we take responsibility *before* we end up in a situation that can evoke those feelings. Most likely, there are many of us who sometimes choose to do the things we know has a high risk of resulting in a migraine as a consequence. If we take responsibility for the consequences, there is no reason to feel guilty. In these cases, we can, for example, ask ourselves "I am aware that this can contribute to a migraine tomorrow (when I already have something planned). Am I willing to take the consequences without blaming myself? Will I think this choice is okay tomorrow?"

Worry - worrying about the next attack is a stress trigger that many people recognise. All worry affects us in a negative way, it's not just the worry for the next attack. We probably all know that worrying about different things takes energy and contributes to us not being able to feel good in the moment, even though what we are worried about has not happened. Many of the things we worry about never happen, but some worries become self-fulfilling prophecies, and migraine attacks are usually included in that cate-gory. In other words, we get migraines more often when we worry about getting it. Because worry is about something that may happen at a later time, we have no power whatsoever to do something about it, because we can't control the future. When we worry, we miss what is happening here and now right in this moment, and in a way, it becomes like a resistance to the life that's ongoing. As long as we worry about getting migraine attacks, or whatever it is that we are worried about, we let fear control our lives. When we focus on being in the now, being present in the moment, it means that we take back the power and authority over our lives. We can't reach into the future and influence it, but what we create here and now can change where we end up tomorrow. If we create a calm here in this moment, enjoy it, immerse yourself in the feeling of just feeling good and appreciate what we have around us right now, we can't worry about anything in the future at the same time. If we work on accepting the present just as it is, we have great opportunities to break the negative thought patterns, and consequently, the vicious circle. There are several good techniques to deal with worry and to focus on here and now. Mindfulness and meditation are well known and very effective. I have personal experience of moving forward in my life when fear and worry ruled for many years. It took 2-3 months of daily meditation to release a lot of the anxiety I have carried for years, and when the anxiety now appears, I know what to do. Letting go of worries and what we can't control, and instead have confidence in life, is a very effective migraine medicine.

Becoming aware of what happens when we're stressed and what impact it has, not only on the body, but also on an emotional level, is an essential for understanding ourselves better, having patience and being able to more easily reverse the downward spiral that we often have ended up in. When we become aware of how stress contributes to our thoughts being limited, and how it in turn can be difficult for us to see opportunities and solutions, we understand how important it is that we learn how to manage our everyday life and relax. When we learn to relax, both our body and mind, we activate the relaxation response. The more we activate it, the greater access we get to positive and creative emotions such as gratitude, love, joy, inspiration, power etc. Positive emotions help us to have more energy, which in turn helps us to look more positively at our own ability to influence our health.

When the relaxation response is activated, the level of stress hormones decreases, and the parasympathetic nervous system is activated. It's only in this rested, relaxed state that the body can heal itself.

THE SUFFERING

Talking about suffering can be a sensitive chapter. In my opinion one of the reasons for this is that you confuse being a victim of / affected by an event with feeling like a victim. Anyone can be affected by tragedies, diseases and crime, and there are many people who are affected by war, torture, starvation and natural disasters. Suffering from something we have no control over induces both physical and mental reactions, and the feeling of powerlessness and fear can be overwhelming. These are completely natural reactions and people can suffer severely under these circumstances. The problems arise when the crisis is over and there is no longer an acute danger, and at the same time you hold on to your suffering by getting caught up in negative thought patters. We are held hostage by our own mind through an eternal negative cycle of thoughts about how powerless we are, about guilt and shame, about self-loathing and about how worthless we really are, that we are punished for something we have done "wrong", that our suffering is due to other people's faults etc. This happens over and over again, and if we don't try to break the pattern, we get stuck in self-pity and nothing ever changes for the better. Sometimes professional help can be absolutely crucial to process trauma and difficult life events, and the help that everyone needs can vary based on the actual event and individual needs.

To stop thinking like we are the victim, we need to become aware of our behavior and thought patterns, and then decide that we want to make a change. This means that many things in life can change, including how our surroundings sees us, reacts and treats us. It can mean changes we need to be prepared to carry out when we decide to take responsibility for our lives. There are no shortcuts to feeling better or having the life we want. Choosing to take responsibility is the only solution, and to do this continuously.

Choosing the victim role means that we give away our power and authority over our lives to people and circumstances around us. If you are a victim, it means that it's the circumstances that control, and when circumstances or people control our lives, the risk that we become like a feather in the wind is great, depending on what's going on around on. Let's say we feel good when people understand us, are kind and positive, and we feel bad if someone is angry at us, rejects us or in other ways express themselves negatively and incomprehensibly. We feel good when the bus arrives as scheduled because we'll then be on time and arrive when we planned to. But when the bus is delayed, we become stressed, irritated and in turn feel unwell. This means that we must try to control the circumstances, and it might work within the family, as our closest ones show consideration and do everything necessary for us to feel good, but in the rest of the world this is completely meaningless. There are people and circumstances everywhere who don't do as we please. If we let circumstances and other people control how we feel, we always lose, we give away our own power of action. In fact, no one can make us feel bad if we ourselves don't allow it through our own negative thoughts that have convinced us that we are powerless. Having a migraine is a difficult circumstance, but it doesn't automatically mean that we have to feel bad emotionally. We are not powerless, on the contrary, we have more power in us than many know.

Getting caught up in the victim role is treacherous. It feels good when we get attention and comfort, people show consideration and take care of us. We may have friends or belong to a group that gives our suffering attention, and we feel safe and seen there. The problem is that we are digging a hole that's getting harder and harder to get out of. Anger, jealousy, condemnation, self-destructiveness and other negative expressions are given free rein and it may even be that we, among our friends and other groups of people, come to the conclusion that we have a common enemy and we thereby confirm the injustices of life. The only thing this leads to is that all energy run out and we don't feel any better, on the contrary, even more internal stress is activated which eats away at the body.

When we wait for the miracle medicine, the cure, the solution to our mood, we find ourselves in the victim role because it's something beyond ourselves, a circumstance that will make us healthy and happy. I don't mean that you shouldn't take medicine that helps, what I mean is that once the medicine is here it may not work as well as we thought it would, or maybe the effect subsides after a while and then we start feeling bad again. When we take active responsibility for our well-being regardless of the circumstances, a miracle cure does not become crucial to our quality of life.

I think we all choose to play the victim role at regular intervals and it's not something we should complain about, on the contrary, we have to be kind to ourselves and realise that we all do our best based on our experiences and our current life situation. The most important thing is that we learn to recognise the signs of when we are heading towards the victim position and immediately change direction.

Something that has helped me a lot that I can warmly recommend is to take part in other people's stories and in this way gain perspective. It's easy for us to paint a pitch-black picture of our lives if we are lonely with our thoughts, or if we meet or in other ways have contact with other victims who confirm that picture. We can't compare suffering, but what we can be inspired by is how other people have gone through very difficult life traumas and illnesses and are happy and grateful for life.

RELATIONSHIPS

One of the areas in life where the minds impact on the body is the greatest, is our relationships. Love doesn't only heal the soul, but also the body. Loneliness, anger and bitterness are like poison to the body. A healthy relationship strengthens the relaxation response in the body. An unhealthy relationship activates the stress response.

To really think about what relationships we have and who gives and takes energy is crucial to how we feel. Being forced to spend time with people who in some way, consciously or unconsciously, try to control us or in another way influence who we are, contributes to inner stress and a feeling that we're not worthy just as we are. It can be about a partner, family members, friends, colleagues, etc. The relationships that give energy and allow us to be ourselves, the relationships where we feel support, encouragement and freedom, are the relationships we must nurture.

To feel good in our relationships, we must set boundaries and stand up for ourselves. We must opt out of the relationships that puts us in the victim role or in another way contribute to destructive thoughts and feelings. Of course, it's not easy, we are many times dependent on people around us and change evoke fear of being alone. It can also regard fear of not getting help when we are sick and etc.

The first step is to become aware of which relationships are not good for us and start there. Making small changes, starting to set boundaries and practicing relating to others in a way that prevents other people's negative energy from destroying us, causes us to slowly phase them out.

For me, the world of yoga has made the importance of relationships so clear. Yoga has led me to people and opportunities that I would never have found in all the stress and activities. I have found new communities in my life full of people who give love, joy and acceptance, where we don't compete, judge, compare or have opinions about one or the other. We wish each other the very best. We take responsibility for our lives. We choose to see the positives in other people, we laugh a lot, we look beyond the surface and attitudes. We are not defined by our illness, our age, our gender or our roles, we are valuable just as we are. We don't have to explain ourselves to anyone because we don't need anyone else's approval to be ourselves. We see our difficulties as challenges and hold each other extra tight when life is turbulent. These moments create a being that means creativity and one's own positive power can emerge. A context that provides positive energy, evokes relaxation and flow, and where tension and pain are absent. To me, these contexts contribute to a meaningful and happy life.

WORK

For us with migraines and other severe headaches, coping with a job can be a challenge. With chronic migraine, it can really feel hopeless, but even if the migraine appears less often, the very fear of having an attack can take a lot of energy. A very important part of our lives is what we do for a living, therefore it's extremely important to us, just like for anyone, to really enjoy our work and feel that we're in the right place to do what we are passionate about, to get stimulation and satisfaction. Employers have a vast responsibility for their staff, and a good boss works hard to create an environment that is surrounded by a minimal amount of stress.

There are several things we can do ourselves to influence the situation in our workplace. Firstly, it is extremely important that we enjoy our work. If we're not happy with our work tasks or our colleagues, we'll suffer even greater difficulties in coping with a functioning working life. Secondly, we need to keep track of our rights and obligations so that the starting point is ready for us. It's always important to know where to begin. When this becomes clear, we get to the next step, which is what we personally need. Common to us who suffer from migraines is the need to work in a, as much as possible, stress-free a work environment. We may need adapted work tools depending on our task assignments, with the aim of reducing the risk of tension and strain on the body. Some people may need to work part-time or otherwise have their working hours adjusted. In other words, we need to start by making sure that the external circumstances are as favorable as possible.

When the external conditions become clear, we get to the part of work that only we ourselves can take responsibility for, namely our attitude and our ability to handle the stress that the job causes. It's about how we handle the situation if there is a lot or little to do, how we relate to our colleagues in day-to-day work, but also in relation to the fact that we may be absent from time to time. We need to take responsibility for having enough energy to work and for how we take care of ourselves, both physically and mentally, to feel good enough to cope with work. If we don't learn to deal with stress and the approach towards our surroundings, it doesn't matter how well-adapted our work conditions are. If we think about it, this is noticed when we're on sick leave and may have the opportunity to rest and recover for several weeks or months without the stress we experience at work, but when it's time to return to work we are soon getting back into old habits, and soon the thoughts that we can't do our job are back and the migraine arrives like a letter in the post.

It's important to not let the migraine control our choice of work. If we do, it's easy for us to end up where we don't thrive (because we limit ourselves when we let migraine control) and when we don't thrive, an internal stress with consequences is induced, such as migraine. The body and the heart strive for balance, and this also applies to mental well-being. This means that we'll receive continuous signals that this is not what we want, signals in the form of negative emotions that lead to pain. At the same time, we have to be realistic and not run ourselves down with performance anxiety and fear of what others might think.

The time we live in is fantastic in the way that more and more jobs become flexible. There are opportunities to work from home or in other ways control your work, and there are many opportunities to thrive and make money despite migraines. The most important thing is to not limit your thinking but to think freely and then gradually start looking at what's possible right now and start from there. There are many examples of people who have ended up not being able to work as they intended due to illness or other circumstances, but who, thanks to being forced to rethink, have found a new, even better meaning in their work. I myself have been a social worker for almost 30 years, and that is where my heart belongs. After working my way to total exhaustion to help others, I have now, after a few years, found an inspiring path with great opportunities that I probably never would have found if I had continued to move forward on the path I was on. Therefore, I am grateful that I was forced to listen to my heart in the end, even though it didn't feel that way when I was right in the middle of all the chaos. Not feeling comfortable or ending up on sick leave due to stress can also, when we start feeling a bit better and calm our thoughts, mean new opportunities and paths to meaningful employment pursue.

CONTROL OR CREATE

Trying to control the circumstances (to control how we feel) means that we have to be allowed to hold on to the thing we want control over, so we know where it's at. To resist, to fight to keep the circumstance in place, can claim all our energy.

What's worst of all, is that having control is an illusion, at least the control that means getting circumstances and other people to behave in a certain way for us to allow ourselves to feel good. The more we try to control the circumstances, the more stiff, rigid and stringent we become. If we don't look up, we end up straight down in the victim role, and then we lose strength and power to do differently.

However, we can train ourselves to control the approach to our surroundings, which means taking control of our mind and thoughts, and by that, in the long run, our emotions and reactions. It's an exercise, just like training the muscles, which needs to be done continuously throughout life, but which gets easier and easier with time. If we stop exercising, we lose focus and it's easy for us to fall back into old patterns. When we practice our inner control, we can make the decision on how to react (as opposed to just reacting), which reduces emotional storms and tensions. We become calmer and more stable, more confident in ourselves and are less often dragged down by feelings of guilt, because we think before we act and by that reduce the risk of us reacting to others. Internal control does not mean that we don't care, on the contrary, we care about how we feel, we are kinder to ourselves and we project a calm energy, a calm and secure impression to our surroundings. In turn, this has a ripple effect and we support other people in a completely different way than otherwise. We make better decisions and trust ourselves. Practicing inner control requires self-awareness, responsibility and courage, because it means staying in the present together with the emotions that awakes in the moment, instead of disappearing into anxiety, the mind frame of a victim or other expressions of fear and powerlessness.

To assent to our creativity is a powerful way to evolve and release the flow and energy that heals us. When we find ways to express our creativity, we are filled with energy and soon find our balance again. When we open up for creation, we open up to the flow of energy that we need to make a change, and grasp the things we need to feel better, which happens when creation requires us to focus here and now. It's in the present that we make the changes we need, it's in the present that all our strength and power exist because we can neither reach into the past and change anything that has been, nor stretch into the future and change anything there. If we make time to create and challenge ourselves in a way we enjoy and fills us with energy, it will become easier to lessen the need for control. We challenge ourselves and at the same time think about why certain things really have to be a certain way. What is the purpose of this? We need to question and move the boundaries of our comfort zone bit by bit. Then we'll grow as human beings and let new opportunities into our lives.

Control and create are two opposites. When we put time and energy into controlling, we miss the opportunities that constantly appear in the moment. By focusing on control, we get caught up in the same old ways of thinking, which guarantees that nothing changes. We can't expect to feel better if we continue to control and have the same thoughts we've had so far. If we look at our lives, we see the result from years of the same thoughts and patterns over and over again. And this will continue into the future if we don't choose differently. When we let go of what we can't control and let creativity in, anything can happen. We leave room for new ideas and we have the courage to try new things and an open mind for new opportunities. If we let go of control we have the courage to do more because we don't feel the need to control the result. If it goes well that's great, if not then at least we have tried, and so, we move on. Letting go of control is really what we need in order to reduce the triggers we have that concern inner stress.

WHAT DOES GOOD HEALTH MEAN, TO BECOME WELL?

I t's very important to really think about what it means to be healthy. We are all different and have different desires and frames of reference, but the absence of migraines does not automatically mean that we are healthy and well. When I felt my worst, I could after all sometimes experience a headache-free day and I appreciated that a lot, but I was still tired, exhausted and un-focused. I used to take the opportunity to do some extra activities those days which resulted in severe attacks the next few days. I told myself for a long time that my migraine had to go away in order for me to feel healthy. When I started thinking about what healthy meant to me, I came to the conclusion that it's to feel joy, vitality, energy, to be creative and focused, have a clear brain and a strong body.

Most of us have at some point been advised by medical staff or by people in our surroundings to keep a migraine diary. In it you should write down how many attacks you have, what degree of dif-ficulty it has and what medications you have taken. Some diaries also imply that you have to write down tension headaches. In addi-tion to this, you should focus on your triggers and what triggered the attack. The point is to have grounds when you see your doctor and discuss which treatment would be suitable. I always think it's good to try being as concrete as possible when describing things to others, especially something as important as health. On the other hand, the question of what will happen if we focus too much on our migraine diary arises. Since it's a diary, it means that we should put focus on it every day, then we can see what the weeks look like, and then the months and years. I kept a migraine diary for a long time, and it was not a fun read because according to my own logic I was healthy when I was headache free. It felt pretty hopeless because I had headaches and migraines pretty much everyday day year after year.

A few years ago, I had enough of my migraine diary. I decided to reverse the reasoning and stop keeping track of which days I had migraines, I really didn't feel better about it. I started applying another strategy which means that when you want to quit something (in this case to focus on the number of days with migraines) you have to focus on what you want instead. It's never a good strategy to remove something first, everyone that tried to stop something unwanted knows that just removing something does not automatically mean that the void that arises is filled with something good.

So, the strategy that works is *first* putting focus on what to fill the upcoming void with, and *then* stop. For the most part, we don't even have to stop, the unwanted is phased out without much effort. In this case, it meant that I started turning the reasoning around and keeping a feel-good diary where I (even today) write down everything that makes me feel good, everything good I do for my health, what I am grateful for, and that allows me to continue to feel good and be happy. There is no focus on migraines. It's a completely different feeling and energy to read the diary and see all the positive factors that actually exist every day and to praise myself when I see how many good things I do for my health. Try writing a success diary where you pay attention to all the positive things you do for yourself and take notes of how your body feels.

LISTEN TO THE BODY

A starting point for feeling better that we can't skip, is that we love and take good care of our bodies. To dislike, or even hate one's body (or a body part) and then expect to feel better, is an equation that doesn't add up. The body gains from what we eat and what we do, but our thoughts also affect the body to a very high degree. Filling the body with negative or hateful thoughts is a self-harming behaviour, and we understand this when we learn more about how extremely great of an impact the thoughts have on the body.

To think of the body with love can be difficult to apply if we have migraines every day and feel desperate and ready to resort to any methods to get relief. But it's not impossible to change a habitual thought pattern. As with much else, we have to decide, take the first step and stick to our intention. The more positive thoughts we have, the more we'll gain, as what we focus on grows stronger. It doesn't matter if we think that we don't want migraines or if we suppress our pain. We can't focus anything away, we can only include what we want more of in our lives.

The next step to feeling better is to listen to the body's signals. As the body strives for balance, it will make you aware when things are not as they should be. Negative feelings and pain are the body's way of getting our attention, to get us to listen. I am convinced that most of us who have chronic migraines didn't just get it from one day to another. The body has for a long time signaled that something is not okay, we've had more and more migraines, nausea, anxiety or maybe other symptoms, but we have often not taken the signals seriously and instead dismissed them. Since the body's task is to strive for balance, it has to do a bit more to reach us. Migraines effectively put us on hold. It literally holds us down. Unfortunately, this doesn't always make us listen anyway. We try different medicines and treatments and sometimes we find the right one, the medicine works, and we feel happy and content. Unfortunately, this also often means that we just push the problem ahead, for example when we take medicine and go to work instead of resting. When the medicine then no longer works, the body continues to signal that something is wrong, but the symptoms are temporarily alleviated by medicine, so we are back to square one or even in a much worse condition because we have gone beyond our limits for what our body can handle. That is when we have "tried everything" and become desperate and depressed.

Listening to the body is not always easy when we have done everything we can for a long time to ignore it. Many of us have also learnt that if we don't feel well, we should go to the doctor and he/she will make it better. Healthcare is fantastic in many ways and listening to the body doesn't mean that we shouldn't seek help if we need it. Nor does it mean that we shouldn't take medicine if we need it. However, we need to take responsibility for our own part in the treatment. As a sufferer of migraines, it's not uncommon for us to be exposed to different types of medication, and both doctors and nurses may well claim that we should continue to take a medication that doesn't work and gives unpleasant side effects. Sometimes, of course, it can be during an escalation period, but it's still important that we really make an active decision about this. In my repeated experience, not all doctors and nurses appreciate that patients listen to their body and have their own opinion, which surely many can relate to. In these situations, it's important to be strong and stay focused. If this is difficult with a throbbing head, we can bring a person we trust as support when we have to convey our messages and opinions. When our entire body knows what's right and wrong, we have to *follow that knowledge*. We should never be persuaded to go against our internal feelings, what we know deep down is right. In this context it's also important to remember that since migraines affect millions of people, there is a market for all kinds of medicines and treatments as well as alternative methods that promise the world, but which are completely ineffective. If we become desperate enough, we can end up both paying for and listening to advice that leads us to overlook the body's signals, and the end result may well be that the head continues to ache in undiminished strength, the hopelessness is even greater, and the money has gone.

If we decide to really listen to the body, it can take time before we actually hear something. We are not used to it and don't really know how it's done, in addition, our mind might tell us that there is no point and a lot of other things that makes us doubt that it's a feasible road.

What's so amazing is that the body always gives us signals. The body doesn't stop signalling to us just because we haven't listened for 20 years, but we can start listening today. Now. Think of your body as your best friend who has the knowledge of your needs to feel better. The body knows what you need. Listen to the body as you listen to the one you love, with focus and attention.

To listen to the body also means that we may hear things we don't want to hear, it may be that we need to make some change that affects others in the long run or something else that requires courage and determination. It's in these situations that we must not forget that if we choose not to listen, life will not change, it will instead continue as usual. All change has consequences, and it means active decisions and choices.

If we don't listen to the signals, it often ends with sick leave. Being on sick leave and resting does not usually mean that we thereafter can return to work full of energy and with the situation under control, but recovery in a conscious way is required on several levels. To live (not merely surviving) with migraines requires being aware of how to replenish energy, how we retain it and where we put its focus, so that our energy is always on the plus side. We need energy to change our lives. We need to calm our mind and put our thoughts on hold in order to let the good energy in.

So, how do you listen to the body? The first requirement is that our thoughts are still enough in order for us to hear. Sensations, feelings and pain are the body's way of communicating with us, but we have to be present enough in the moment to understand what it's all about. We often feel like there are things we "have to" do;

participate in various activities or just general life, but once we begin to perceive the body's signals, we might understand that our body needs to rest and therefore has other plans. This is when we need to be aware that we have a choice in what to prioritise. The body tells us what it is we need *right now*, not what we need later, in just a moment or another day. If we choose to listen, we slowly begin to recover and replenish energy. If we choose to rest *later*, it means that we push the recovery ahead of us, and the result is that it will probably take longer because the activity will take energy away from us, energy that we need for something else or energy that we really don't have. Migraine is a disease that steals a lot of our time. Therefore, it can be difficult to rest when, for once, we may feel a little better. When we have a headache-free day, we want to take the opportunity to do everything we possibly can. A headache-free day is like winning the lottery. We also know that this price has a cost, many times it brings us straight back to the dark. The benefit of listening to the body and also resting on good days is that we produce strength to use when feeling worse, which in the end means that we recover faster.

If we listen to the body it won't let us down, it is my experience and my absolute belief. We betray ourselves by not trusting that our body has an outstanding healing ability. The problem is that many of us lack the patience and knowledge to let the body heal at its own pace. We become desperate for relief and take medication or something else that is ultimately not good for us. It's not our fault that we have migraines, but we are responsible for taking care of ourselves based on our circumstances. We only have one life and it's happening right now. We can't expect to feel good if we ignore the body's signals. We can't expect to recover in a just few weeks if we haven't listened to the body's signals for several years. For most people with chronic migraines, there is no quick fix. Thankfully, there are good medicines that can help us go through the recovery, but as long as we put all our trust in medicine, we'll be dependent on it working. It's not uncommon for the effect to diminish over time. If we have the patience to listen to the body, get to know the signals and to trust it, we will have our own control and knowledge of what we need, and not only be dependent on healthcare and / or other people or circumstances, but instead trust our own judgment of what we need. While we wait for the miracle medicine or something else that will make the migraine disappear, life goes on. Every day is valuable and will never come back. The most important thing of all is to find an approach and tools that allow us to participate in life here and now, regardless of whether we have migraines or not. I am living proof that this works.

Yoga and meditation took me on a journey that made me start listening to my body and heart. I knew nothing about yoga, it was blurry and strange to me, but at least it couldn't get any worse. When I started yoga, everything gave me migraines. It wasn't worthwhile to keep track of triggers, it was easier to keep track of what I didn't get migraines from, for example, breathing or drinking a glass of water. My yoga debut started with a workout called "The Little Back Session", and I couldn't even turn my body before I got cramps, I couldn't bend my head before I got a migraine. I often laid down to just breathe and I called that yoga, it was the only thing I could do. I many times literally crawled to the yoga mat. It was claimed that 40 days was required to feel the effect, and that was my goal. I slowly began to hear what my body was telling me. It didn't take long, but the most difficult thing was to *pursue* that message, because the power of habit is great and breaking thought patterns takes time. But I had no choice, I had no life.

Since I started listening to my body, amazing things have happened. Without any major effort, things I don't feel good about have been phased out and things I need have been added, for example, when it comes to food and exercise. Yoga, meditation and breathing exercises have taught me to listen to my body, and it has given results beyond expectation. When I ran the 5 kilometres Spring Race without stopping, it was a victory bigger than many can understand. From feeling like a powerless, exhausted, depressed zombie with a knife in my head, I ran 5 kilometres. Since that day, I feel an even greater admiration for what my amazing body can accomplish. If we listen, changes naturally happen without struggle, judgement or a bad conscience. I am stronger today than I have been in 20 years!

It's important to point out that listening to the body is not the same as being passive. Listening to the body is not really difficult at all, the biggest challenge and difficulty is to get the mind / thoughts to agree instead of putting sticks in the wheel.

TO ENJOY LIFE

Many of us with chronic migraines and a lot of pain have experience from mental illness. Many have been or are depressed and exhausted. It becomes a vicious circle - the pain triggers depression and depression trigger more pain. At the same time, there are many who witness that when they, for example, changed jobs or ended a relationship, their migraines got much better or even disappeared. Being at a job we don't like, continuing with a relationship that deep inside doesn't feel good, or constantly find ourselves in a place we deep down don't like, creates internal stress, which in turn contributes to tension in the body. We can't deal with these tensions by taking stress-relieving medications, going for a massage, resting or going on holiday. These measures may remove the symptoms for a while, but the basic problem remains. Nor is it always the case that we make the connection to our health. We deny that we don't thrive or feel free and happy in certain situations and relationships, because it would mean big changes that we may not be able to cope with or that frighten us. Big changes often involve other people, people we love and care about. We don't even want to think about the idea of disappointing others and instead choose to stay. We suppress our longing, and the body continues to protest. Eventually, the body becomes like a pressure cooker and the migraine thrives amongst the tension and denial.

There are probably many of us who have been told during a visit to the doctors that we are depressed, that we feel mentally un-well etc. It can often feel provoking because we believe that it's the migraine and the pain that are causing our mental illness, and that can certainly be true, but I think it can be good to sometimes still think about whether it's only the migraines that we can't handle, or if in fact there may be other grounds as well. If we are to change a situation we don't thrive in, we need to be honest with ourselves and have the courage to listen to what we deep down want and don't want.

Most people who, despite all internal resistance, change their lives and break up from a negative situation and feel better, can in retrospect, with perspective, see that there have been times when they realised that the current situation is not what they really wanted. The insight has come at regular intervals but has been ef-fectively pushed away and denied. Personally, I have met many peo-ple who state that they get migraines when they are not happy, and that the changes they have made have been necessary in order to feel better.

LET YOUR HEART LEAD THE WAY

L ove and humour are the hearts way, and really the only way we need to go. I have always strived for simplicity and clarity to understand and to be able to stick to important lessons. I have found a way to easily describe how I have learnt to relate to the environment, to everything that might possibly show up on a daily basis. I have learnt this approach through yoga and meditation, and it helps me to stay calm, to focus, to let go of things, to be kinder to myself and to rejoice and enjoy life. Migraines are taking up less and less space in my life.

For us to feel good, I believe we have to start with what contributes to love, joy, energy, vitality, creativity and curiosity about life. Unconditional love lives in the heart, which means love free from prejudice, judgement, comparisons and criticism. When I use the word love, I mean love in a broader concept, love for our loved ones, but also love for our fellow human beings. Love for our fellow human beings can be to show compassion and support, to listen and be present, a pat on the shoulder when you are sad, etc.

Unconditional love that comes from the heart means a love that's free from the fact that circumstances must be a certain way for us to feel it. A good example of this is by looking at an important loved one who's unconditionally loved simply because he/she exists. The heart knows when we act out of love for ourselves and respect for our own worth. When we act on the basis of self-love and respect for our own worth, we feel good and our entire body feels good, when we go *against* the heart, accuse ourselves, feel ashamed that we have migraines or whatever it may be, our bodies don't feel particularly good and we don't feel well. In this way, the heart leads the way to where we need to go to in order to feel increasingly better. The clever thing is that when we listen to the heart, all the good spreads to our surroundings. I will explain with a couple of examples:

Example:

You're at work and things are going well now that you have a plan for how to cope with a whole working day and keeping the stress in check, and therefore also the migraine. It feels good, you find confidence in the future. One day when arriving to work a bit later, just like you had agreed with the boss, one of the colleagues comes up to you and tells you that you are in fact not the only one at work with a headache, there are several more, so why do you get a free pass?

How do you react to this?

Option 1: You get sad and feel misunderstood and run over, you may think this person is an idiot who should keep quiet, he/she does not understand that there is a difference between a migraine and headache, sigh. Or something like that. You start defending yourself and soon the day is ruined. You feel sad and maybe go to the toilet and cry in secret. You get back into the mind frame of a victim.

Option 2: You consult the heart. The heart that conveys unconditional love tells you that this person may not be well, this person may have had a sleepless night, you know that he/she has small children. The heart shows you that this is not about you, but about the other person's inner struggle. So instead of defending yourself, you say for example, that it was sad that he/she perceived the situation that way. You might say that if he/she has a lot of headaches, the boss is great at giving support, so the work situation should become good for him/her as well.

In option one, you begin to defend and excuse yourself, hence giving your power and dignity to the other. You think negative thoughts about the other, which means that you hurt yourself in the long run, because we now know what negative thoughts do to the body. You increase your inner stress.

In option two, you retain your power over the situation. You show compassion for another person who may need a break at work, which might lay a seed in the other person resulting in him/her changing their situation. You keep your mood at a steady level, you keep calm and the stress under control.

To ask the heart a question doesn't mean that we should become weak and let people walk all over us, absolutely not. Asking the heart means that we should become aware of the times we put ourselves down and gave away our power and dignity. Asking the heart means that we follow the path to feeling better, because when we maintain our power and dignity, we act accordingly and evolve.

When we give up our power and dignity, we become victims and end up staying where we are and instead continue to suffer.

Things happen when we start asking the heart for guidance, both in our body and surroundings. If we listen to the heart, we feel better, which benefits everyone around us. The family will become happy if we feel better, we'll feel calmer because we learn not to get started on things that have nothing to do with us. In the long run, it also means that major changes can take place without anxiety, such as changing jobs or changing other situations we don't like. Asking the heart for guidance is a process that never ends. Asking the heart is a lifelong learning experience, but it's also a great way to evolve and experience life. My heart guided me to the Sahara where my life turned. It has guided me to Puerto Rico to dance and meet strong and amazing women who also listen to their hearts and who gave me lifelong friendships. My heart has guided me to meetings with wise people who have taught me a lot about life, and who in various ways have helped me let go of migraines and suffering. My heart has taught me to listen to my inner creativity, which enriches my life on so many levels, and which has meant that I can choose to work differently and avoid stress.

TO DISTINGUISH BETWEEN EMOTIONS AND PAIN

My whole life turned when I realised that I could distinguish between my emotions and my pain. For a long time, I had been practicing yoga and meditation, I had been resting and listening to my body and feeling much better. I was starting to get more and more energy, but I still had a lot of migraines and tension headaches. One day I realised I was happy! I was happy for no reason, just like that. It was at that moment I realised that I was done letting the migraine control my life and that I had made a choice. I had decided to be happy regardless of the migraines.

From that day on, I began to focus more consciously on what I wanted more of in life and I finally let go of the migraines altogether, something I had talked about many times in CBT therapy, but it was only now that the token fell down. Letting go of the migraine doesn't mean that I *suppressed* that I have one, to suppress something is not the same as letting go because constriction creates tension. I let go of the migraine by *giving up the fight* against it. I had been fighting the migraine for many years and it was pointless. I would never win. I gave up, it could be there if it wanted to.

I realised I was missing out on life while struggling. I wanted to live, I wanted to be happy and enjoy my life.

Focusing on what you want more of in your life and having a positive attitude towards life, despite the headaches, requires training and patience. It takes confidence in life and to let go of the control of things having to be a special way in order to feel good. It requires living consciously by constantly making active choices, several times a day, taking responsibility for your own feelings and reactions and getting to know yourself. It requires living in the present. It also requires acceptance and self-love, not to judge, criticise or beat yourself up when, despite all the insights, you are suddenly back on square one and curse the whole world for the hell of migraines. Once we have experienced the power of focusing, we get back on our feet much faster because we know what works.

To me, there is no reasonable doubt that if we are to achieve what we want, what we want most of all, we must reverse the whole reasoning. Most people who suffer from chronic migraines think, as far as I know, that when the cure comes, you will engage in life, do the things you long to do. You will do it *later*, when times get better. And the days go by, that turn into months and soon into years. In the meantime, life goes by. By reversing the reasoning and focusing on a better feeling, on things you want in your life, you are not dependent on whether the cure comes tomorrow or in 10 years. If you create the feeling that what we want most of all has already happened, you can enjoy life regardless, despite pain. And the migraine and pain end up in the background because the struggle is over.

Distinguishing between emotions and pain is easier said than done if we don't know how it's done. Admittedly, it's only us that control how we should feel, and we do so through our thoughts. Migraines and the pain that it causes often contribute to negative thoughts that contribute to feelings of fear, hopelessness and helplessness, or anger and bitterness, and then the negative spiral continues, and we aggravate our pain, the physical, but also our inner pain. It's not the migraine itself that is the cause of the negative thoughts and feelings, but our thoughts are often the result of years of the same repeated thoughts, and the power that's in these negative thoughts takes time to break.

There are many ways to break negative thoughts and other destructive patterns that cause us harm. From my experience, it can be difficult, even provocative, when someone claims that you can be happy even though your head hurts. Anyone who says that probably doesn't know how awful it is to have a migraine or is stuck in some kind of denial stage. But I claim, with my own experience with the migraines from hell and having tried to cure them with denial, that it works. It actually works beyond all expectations. This is where we need to start really getting our lives and zest for life back. Take back power over our lives.

When something feels difficult, it can be helpful to find another way to approach the subject, a way that is not loaded with questioning and negative perceptions. Believe that your feelings are energy!

EMOTIONS AND ENERGY

I f we think that emotions and energy are the same thing, we can get around the problem of what's possible and not possible to control. When emotions and energy are the same, it's not difficult to understand that when we are happy, we are full of energy and we feel light and absorb our surroundings in a positive way. When we are depressed and sad, we feel powerless, our mind feels heavy and maybe even our body. We have no energy. We may prefer to be alone and we can't cope with people who don't understand how difficult things are for us.

With simple tricks we can raise our energy and thereafter our emotional state, and when practicing this several times a day it will become gradually easier.

There are two things involved here, one is that we train ourselves in a positive approach in the long term, at the same time as we adapt a "quick fix" in the moment. Just like with the negative thoughts that have been built up over a long period of time and become powerful because we've had our focus on them, we are now starting to focus on increasing the energy (to focus more on positive feelings), in a way where we partly have our own power to influence our feelings and being, and partly that joy should have more place in our lives. As these thoughts become more powerful, the negative thoughts increasingly lose their power. The idea of learning to raise our energy, hence our emotional state, is to first become aware of the negative thoughts at the moment and then immediately break them. To be able to do this, we need different tools.

In order for us to raise our energy and positive emotions, *all* means are allowed, i.e., all means subjecting that we are able to look at ourselves in the mirror afterwards and feel proud of how fantastic we are to bring out the power and do good things for ourselves. We can examine which means suit us individually. An easy way to raise energy immediately involves breathing exercises and to move the body. We can do some yoga exercises, dance for a while, stretch, walk, swim, walk in the woods, play, laugh, pet the cat or anything that feels good and that we are able to do. When we move the body, serotonin is stimulated, which contributes to us feeling better. Having a strategy that helps us raise energy, hence the possibility of feeling better, is extremely helpful and this strategy doesn't have to be complicated or difficult.

As with all changes, it's important to start from where we currently stand. It's unlikely that going from feeling depressed, tired and sad, we'll suddenly start feeling a zest for life, joy and happiness, and to soon thereafter wanting all the challenges in the world. However, we need a direction forward, even if that means we have to start by deep breathing on the yoga mat because that's the only thing that works. We simply have to get energy and lift our spirits to be able to feel better in the long run.

Just as there are energy-boosting activities, there are opposites. Things that take our energy away and that ultimately leads to a mood drop, things that make us depressed and feel worse. These are things we do out of old habit or that we think lead to more energy. Again, this is another good time to gauge how we feel on the inside, but also to consider whether it's something we risk regretting afterwards. I'm thinking of eating sweets or something else that contributes to a temporary increase in energy, but which in the long run worsen our mood. How many times have we not eaten something to numb our emotions and in hindsight feel guilty? This also applies to activities such as gossiping, blaming others, judging and generally speaking negatively about ourselves and others. Sure, in the moment it might feel good talking about it, but it's treacherous. It's unlikely that we can look at ourselves in the mirror with pride over the fact that we have gossiped about others or blamed ourselves. Gossip and negative talk create an inner stress. It's extremely important that we stay out of whining and complaints, both our own and others'. It's a safe way to prevent us from running out of energy and becoming exhausted.

We need to be uncompromising with our energy. Migraine itself takes a lot of energy and we have to make do with what we have, be sure that we take more energy in than we give out. We do this by becoming aware of how we bring energy home and where and to whom we give it. We also need to make sure we replenish energy every day in whatever way possible. We many times wait until the weekend, or for when we're free, and that doesn't work because we continuously need new energy to keep our body balanced. Our body doesn't care when there is a free space in the diary, our body is here. Right now.

THE POWER OF THOUGHTS

When people around us say that we have to think positive and other similar things to this, it's easy to feel that this person doesn't understand anything. Unfortunately, positive thinking has become worn out and is used without a thought for anything else. If we let go of the preconceptions against this statement for a while, and think about what it means to think positively, we discover the power in it. When the positive thinking goes deep and becomes a positive attitude, a healthy optimism mixed with self-love and humour, miracles can happen. Then it's powerful! If we train ourselves to focus on positive thinking and attitudes, we are halfway to the goal. Note that this *doesn't* mean that we should repress or deny our situation or the reality we live in, that's when positive thinking becomes the shallow clichés that we can't stand.

So, what is positive thinking that goes deeper and becomes a positive approach? My experience and interpretation are that it's a thought process that needs to be trained until it becomes the obvious in life, but one that also needs to be maintained. We can always fall back into negative thoughts if we don't look out. Therefore, we need to practice taking care of ourselves, and make reasonable demands on what we can handle. We don't have to take everything so seriously, life can be very comical in the midst of all the misery.

Becoming aware of one's attitude requires that we get to know ourselves and our reactions, and that we find the voice of our heart, i.e., the love and care for ourselves. It's only when we listen to our heart, instead of the old negative thoughts that easily can appear when we've done something "wrong", that we can choose. As an example, I have an endless number of times forgotten important things and kicked myself for it, considered myself a bad mother, a bad colleague and all sorts of things. I have become angry and disappointed in myself, which in the end resulted in migraines and suffering. When I've become aware that I can actually choose a different approach, meaning that I see myself as a competent and valuable person that do the best I can, the result is completely different. Even though I still have forgotten what I was supposed to remember, I avoid headaches and feeling guilty, because I know that I have done everything I could, based on current circumstances. This also means that I can let go of mistakes I have made. It's when we feel that we could've done differently or that we hurt someone else that the feelings of guilt thrive, and we dwell on the same thing to try to justify something that has already happened.

A positive attitude is extremely important, even in difficult situations that are not only about dealing with stress and chaos in everyday life, but when we train our thoughts and our attitude, we can also handle situations that are about deep fears, severe pain, anxiety and uncertainty. When we start to become aware of how much difference it actually makes how we relate to different situations, not just intellectually, we discover how much we can influence how we feel. Life is full of situations we can't control, but we can choose how to relate to them. The most important thing is that we make that choice *before* the situation arises. Once we are there, it's much harder to choose.

THE UNDERSTANDING
FROM PEOPLE AROUND US

I t's important to spread knowledge about migraines so that everyone affected has the same opportunities for specialist care, work and rehabilitation. When it comes to the understanding from people around us on a more personal, individual level, such as family, friends and work colleagues, I think like this; first of all, a person that's never had an attack can't understand what it's like to have a migraine, so we can't expect them to actually understand the pain, the feeling or the anxiety. In addition, migraines are not visible, so when we're amongst people we usually look quite okay, which makes it even more difficult for non-sufferers to understand how bad it can actually be. This is not really strange because if we look at another example, people with two healthy legs can't understand what it can be like to live paralysed from the waist down. We can show consideration, we can have compassion and try to support as best we can, but we can never fully understand another person's experience or what it's like to live with one or the other condition.

In our society, there are many diseases, diagnoses, disabilities and conditions that require understanding and compassion. Just like we who are affected by migraines need to spread knowledge, the same applies to, for example, people with diabetes, people with mental illness or people with other diseases and conditions. There are several associations and subjects that require understanding, it's not the knowledge itself that is the problem, there is an endless amount of knowledge available on everything we need to know. The understanding we seek is the understanding and consideration that *everyone* seeks, which deviates from the so-called normal, or actually, from all people really. An understanding that is about avoiding prejudices and condemnations for things people don't understand, which may evoke fear. To avoid people's opinions about things they have nothing to do with. That we are okay however we are. My view is that if we are to create an understanding of migraines, we need to stand up straight and stop being ashamed. There is nothing to be ashamed of, we have not gotten a migraine to avoid working or taking care of our children. We have suffered from migraines the same way others suffer from other things. But if we *act* like victims, apologise for our illness, work even though we should rest, or ignore the signals from the body and heart because we're afraid what others will think, or because others don't understand, then the result we don't want is the result we'll get, we leave our power and our dignity to people and circumstances around us. As long as we wait for someone else to change their behaviour to make us feel better, we make ourselves victims. We can't control other people (luckily), but we can decide how to relate to our surroundings. There will always be people who don't take us into account, but they should not be allowed to control or limit our lives.

I think many people are good at informing their colleagues about what it means to have a migraine, the suffering it gives and how much energy it takes. But what happens if, after all the information, we still go to work even though we are not in a condition to work at all, even though we have by far crossed the line and stay upright only due to painkillers and all the other tricks we usually use? What do we teach our colleagues? We teach them that it's probably not as bad as we claim. We teach them that we may be exaggerating a little when we explain how terrible the pain can be, how we lie in bed and vomit in a dark room and then still show up to work. We ask the impossible of our colleagues if we say one thing and do another. How should those who have never had a migraine understand? It's not possible. What we send out is what we get back, it's a simple basic universal law. If we want to change the view of people affected by migraines, of ourselves, we have to start with us!

Let's think of a workplace. We have a job that we enjoy, but sometimes the impressions become too much, we get tired, stressed and when we get home all our energy is gone and we can't do anything else for the rest of the day because our head hurts. The next morning, we might have a migraine when we wake up, we end up taking medicine and then head to work. The days continue like this until the day we have to call in sick, we can't postpone the migraine anymore. We may stay at home for 1-2 days before returning to work. Then we start from square one again. Does anyone recognise themself? On all the occasions we have to call work and report sick we get a bad feeling in our stomach, bad conscience, feelings of guilt, maybe a little anxiety about staying at home once again, that colleagues get a bigger workload due to our absent.

Let's look at it from another point of view. We figure out what's needed from us to have the energy to work a whole day without it resulting in migraines and time spent in dark rooms during our spare time on weekends and holidays. In this way, we take power over the situation, we take responsibility for listening to the body and we are able to work. We inform the workplace what migraines are about and how it affects us. We tell them what we need to be able to do the job and agree with the boss on how this should best work. There are probably many who have already done this, but the point is that you then just have to stick to the plan without explaining, defending or apologising! We stick to the plan without judging or having a bad conscience because we do what we have to. If we begin to *explain, defend or apologise* for sticking to the plan we have decided on, we become victims. We have already explained. The boss knows. End of. We have to show that our worth does not come from how much we adapt to what others think and feel, but that we are all different, and that it's okay. We don't appreciate our own worth if we start apologising for wanting to look after ourselves so that we can work and have a good life. On the contrary, an illness like migraine, which really requires us to listen to the body, can help us learn other important things about life. Because by sticking to the plan, we can teach our colleagues how important it is to take care of yourself when you have a migraine. We can teach them that it's okay to take a break when it's stressful. We can teach them that our needs are important. By respecting our needs, we teach our fellow human beings that when *they* feel unwell for some reason, it's okay for *them* to take responsibility and to take care of themselves. Most people are kind and wish others well, and by showing that we actually want to be their colleagues, that we take our responsibility to make sure we're able to work together and do our part of the job, we get consideration and respect back. The plan applies even if there now happens to be a colleague that starts whining about us potentially getting an extra day off when he/she still has to work. We need to just let it run off us like water off a duck's back, and then stand up straight because this can be a critical point for us where we could potentially come off track. It's suitable to have a good strategy here (which we have decided on in advance) to encourage ourselves.

If, after all, there are days when we still have to call in sick, it evokes a completely different feeling. The boss and colleagues have a knowledge of migraines and know what is required of us. They know there is a plan. They know we're following the plan. Then they also know that when we call in sick, it's serious. Then we don't have to lie at home with a bad conscience because we "disappoint" our colleagues, we know they are aware we have taken care of ourselves. The rest is not at our disposal. When we take responsibility, we release a lot of our anxiety and fear. When we take responsibility, we regain our strength and our dignity. When we take responsibility, we are not victims.

If we try to make others understand how much we suffer by presenting ourselves as victims of a terrible illness, there is a great risk we'll be perceived as whiny or that we exaggerate. Because a person who doesn't have migraines can't possibly know how terrible the pain can be, they can believe anything. Most people who have an illness or a problem and behave like victims, believe they are suffering the most. We think that having a migraine is one of the biggest sufferings you can have. Others think, for example, that having a stomach ulcer or a man who is unfaithful is the worst suffering you can have. Everyone thinks that the difficulties they go through are the worst suffering you can have. *You can't compare ways of suffering!* Our worth does not lie in how much or how little we suffer. We are all worth equally in whatever disease or circumstance we live with.

Furthermore, I think it's the same starting point that applies in private life. We inform and talk to our loved ones, give them knowledge and describe things as much as we can for them to understand, but I think it's also important to set a limit here. When important and beloved people around us have the knowledge of migraines and we have told them what it means for us, we then shouldn't have to continue to explain ourselves, defend and apologise. I believe that it's devastating for our well-being to put migraines in focus all the time. It doesn't have to be in focus, we won't forget that we have migraines. It's what we want more of in our lives that needs to be in focus. In any case, my point is that there is a big difference between saying that you need to go and rest for a while, to just actually do it (because we know that the others are aware of why), or to start explaining, defending and apologising for the fact that you have to rest and to remind them of migraines. Does it matter, you might be wondering then. Undoubtedly yes, if you ask me. To explain, defend and excuse ourselves because we need to take care of ourselves sends us straight back to the negative thoughts, suffering and ultimately the victim position. We don't have to explain, defend or apologise to *anyone* that we have a migraine and that we need to take care of ourselves because in practice this means that we ask permission from people around us to do what makes us feel good. And we don't need anyone else's permission. Asking for permission means that we give someone else the power to approve and, in this way, we diminish ourselves and give away our power and dignity. We need no one's approval for anything, however, we often need to be kinder to ourselves. I want to emphasise that I don't mean that we should hide having migraines, absolutely not. It's important to spread knowledge and information, but it's also important to think about the purpose of highlighting migraines as a cause of certain behaviours. Is the purpose to inform or to get an approval?

Finally, I would like to emphasise that, of course, it's not easy to change attitudes, it takes time and patience. If we come to the conclusion that we want to change our attitude, we need to surround ourselves with people who support and encourage, and who can provide constructive feedback, so that we don't stand alone against all the unpleasant challenges. Changing one's attitude is challenging and requires courage and determination, but the gain is a wonderful feeling of freedom and victory that leads to energy and better health. Meeting others who suffer from migraines to support each other and feel connected can be very rewarding and enjoyable. However, my most important experience and biggest warning flag is that sometimes these groups can lead us to not move an inch towards our desire to feel better, because when the conversations of comparing suffering and injustice stop, we are undoubtedly stuck in the victim position and there is no energy or power left for changes. I have experienced it many times and it leads to nowhere further than to the confirmation of our suffering. But if you, with the support of the group behind you, have the courage to challenge yourself and make room to grow and evolve, it can be worth its weight in gold. It's like having a big safe hug to come back to and rest in after exploring on unknown territories for some time. People cheer you on and love comes your way, and confirmation of there being hope for a better quality of life and that you can actually influence your life. And success breeds success, by self-development, but also being present when others develop themselves is very rewarding and instructive. Taking back power over life is the only way to feeling better.

MOVE YOUR BODY - THE POWER OF HABIT

We all know by now how important it is to move the body and how difficult it can be for us to find the motivation and get started. During the worst attacks, of course, it's not possible, but as soon as we can stand up, we can move.

Finding the motivation doesn't mean that we can just sit or lie on the couch and wait for it to fall down on us. However, we can kill the motivation by trying too hard so that we instead feel bad, get a bad attack and just hate everything that exercise and workouts are called. It becomes increasingly harder to get to grips with things, we find explanations, we are either too unwell to move, our migraine is too severe, or we get dizzy etc. Breaking habitual patterns is difficult for everyone. There is a security and a predictability in the way things are, even if it's pain and fatigue, depression and a bad conscience. The positive thing is that we have the power to change our lives in many different ways ourselves, and if the life we live on a day to day is not the life we want, we have to start changing ourselves. No one can change our lives for us.

The first thing we have to do is to realise our starting point with self-love. We were perhaps sporty in the past, were fit and could run, cycle and climb trees. Today, we have run out of energy or decreased drastically, but we hold on to the past and plan our workouts according to an unrealistic picture that evokes demands for performance and results. Therefore, it's important to let go of the old image and focus on here and now. Honestly and clearly, lovingly and without paraphrasing, we ask ourselves what we can do right now. Start small, almost too small, it quickly becomes a success and when we make progress, we are encouraged to continue a little longer.

As a goal, start by moving on certain days of the week, let's say five days a week. Make a success diary where everything that is more than nothing is a success. Everything counts and anything beyond the five days is a bonus! Find the way you feel you can move, it doesn't matter what it is, just that it happens. It can be anything from walking three laps around the house, walking the children to school, cycling to the local supermarket, going for a powerwalk, swimming or riding or anything that means you move a little more than usual. A very simple trick can be to use a step-counter. Determine the number of steps you should take per day five times a week. If you walk more steps than you have decided on, or if you do anything else in addition to this, it's a bonus, if you cycle or dance for example. This should also be included in the success diary. All means are allowed for you to be encouraged by the diary and continue. Use crayons, happy stickers and more. Make a summary once a week and when you feel that it's quite easy to reach your goal, you increase it a little more. Remember that this is not a competition. Remember not to put yourself down if you end up on the couch again despite all the good intentions. Observe your thoughts and what triggered the negative spiral, think of it as an experience and thank yourself for learning something new about yourself. Get up and continue the next day. It's important that we pay attention to the success and remind ourselves why we do this and why we have patience. If we've had migraines and been exhausted for a long period of time, it will take a while before things turns around and feel like something we want to do voluntarily. Since this is about changing a (bad) habit and doing something else, both your body and your mind will struggle, sometimes very hard. As long as we move in a conscious, empathetic and realistic way, just keep going. Try not to focus on whether the migraine is getting better or worse, focus on what you want, on the positive effects that will arise.

Anyone who tells themself that the migraine gets better from being still has only fallen into the trap created by the ego to stay in the same familiar state. Migraines will never get better from being still. At the same time, it's a balancing act, on one hand to recover strength by resting and sleeping enough, and on the other hand by moving the body to become stronger. The point is to find a way to move the body that feels good, that feels strengthening and that in fact in the long run can very well mean that we long for movement and based on that feel how the body becomes stronger and more flexible.

I have gone from being totally exhausted with the migraine from hell to longing to run, dance, do yoga and many other things. I have energy and my body feels strong, and I now appreciate my body just as it is. Of course, I have headaches and migraines sometimes, a little pain here and there, but it belongs to everyday life and nowadays it's about not listening properly. It's usually about stress and negative thoughts, but it passes when I listen and focus on my needs.

It has taken several years to get to where I am today. Once I decided to change my life, I tried over and over again to get started with some kind of exercise, but many times ended up in the achievement trap and everything became a big mess. In the end, I let go of the demands, got tired of pushing myself and instead decided on three things; Yoga and meditation every day, if only for 5 minutes, walking at least 30 minutes a day (because I have a dog it was a must), writing in my success diary and throwing the migraine diary away. I sometimes walked and moved a little extra, wrote in the success diary, smothered myself in my successes, encouraged myself, cheered myself on and thought about how strong I was. The walks continued to get longer and one day (after about 2 years) I suddenly wanted to run! I felt like running, I still feel like running. And dance. And swim. And ride. I never force myself to exercise anymore, I want to! I feel good about it. It makes me happy. I'm getting strong. I stand up straight. It's rare that I get a migraine before or after exercise, but if I get one, I take care of myself without putting any thought to it. I know what I need. After exercising, it's wonderful to rest, lie on the couch and read and just enjoy.

Together we are strong. When we find other people who share the same desire and the wish to feel better and have more energy, we can get fantastic support to help break habits on the way. If we support each other's successes together and show love and support for each other, we can more easily get out of the weaknesses we sooner or later get stuck in. A support group where we can be just the way we are, where everything is okay and we evolve at our own pace. In addition to the fact that we can sometimes get a (loving) kick in the butt, we also learn from each other what it means not having to achieve something in any way or to fix something, we are worthy just as we are. It gives a ripple effect on our everyday life. The crucial thing is that we gently but firmly help each other to move away from having the mind frame of a victim and remind each other that we have the power to change our lives. Another great way to spur yourself on is to speak to others. Many of us are good at talking about our limitations (stop that!), but now is the time to reverse the trend. When we speak to people around us and tell them that we've started exercising, we get positive feedback from those who want to see us develop and anyone with doubts gets phased out. The reason why it's good to speak to people is because we then concentrate on our focus and feelings. We feel a bit proud and that means more than we sometimes understand. We change direction on our future, even if we only manage to walk around the house twice a week. Suddenly, the desire will run an extra lap and then we'll smother ourselves in happiness and success! It's important that we find something that feels fun to do, even if it's not the ideal according to common perceptions. The most important thing is to get started. Be curious and try something new.

WHAT DO YOU NEED TO HEAL?

I f we are to be healed in the long run, we need to ask ourselves the question what we are prepared to change in order to be healed. How much do we want it? Do we have the courage? If you had to move to feel good, would you do it? Could you imagine ending certain relationships to feel good? Would you change jobs? Changing one's life requires determination and courage, but also confidence in life. When we change and make new choices, we turn and go a new way towards the unknown. Brave and with a straight back, we have to embrace the unknown and trust ourselves, turn to our inner strength and move forward. We must focus on the way forward, the feeling of already feeling better and letting go of the fear and the familiar, what we leave behind. If we really want a different life, a different future, it's one foot in front of the other. The ego and mind will struggle, probably also the people around you. A good way is to practice doing things we don't really have the courage to do, small things that on the whole may not seem so significant, but which contribute to greater confidence in ourselves.

The body doesn't know the difference between saying no to someone or to go parachuting, it gives the same worrying feeling in the stomach and the same palpitations, sweating and other symptoms. If we thereby practice challenging ourselves little at a time, moving the boundaries of our comfort zone, we'll suddenly realise that we have taken several steps forward onto our new unknown path. Every time we do something we don't actually have the courage to do, we grow stronger, we embrace our own power, we honour our value, we create a new future, we break patterns, we encourage ourselves, we grow as people, we evolve, we become stronger, we increase our self-awareness and our experience by having power over our lives.

It is not always easy to do things we don't have the courage to do, for example, if we say no to someone we used to say yes to and the person in question reacts in a negative way, it can feel as if it wasn't worth it. Or if we challenge ourselves and get migraines. Therefore, it's important that even before we challenge ourselves, we prepare and repeat to ourselves why we do this. If our challenge of wanting to change and take responsibility for our own lives come from a genuine desire from the heart, any negative expressions from the environment will be about other people's fears of change. Remember that we are not responsible for other people's reactions. Our goal and our intention are not to feel better at someone else's expense.

Challenging oneself is not just about doing new things, it's mainly about turning inwards and to listen. Many of us who suffer from migraines are ambitious and active, which in many cases has been a contributing factor for us not stopping ourselves in time. A big challenge can be to do *nothing*, to just be, to sit and breathe and experience what's happening. Challenging yourself by *not* perform-ing, *not* being active, can be the most difficult, but also the absolute best. Activity and performance can often be an escape from some-thing that hurts, something that we don't want to feel, some old fear that we haven't let go of, and that causes inner tension and pain. It can also be a dream, something we long for, but which we don't al-low ourselves to feel because we think we can't get there.

Changing direction in life, moving towards something that is currently the unknown, means that we also have to let go of expec-tations of results and just be. That's the key to healing.

This is also great to practice in a support group. It's easier to re-mind each other to persevere, to have trust, if we do it together. Healing needs space in our lives and it doesn't fit if the space is occu-pied by expectations, impatience, control and performance anxiety.

Taking the step from a well-known everyday life and changing direction requires, as I said, focus, courage and trust. We many times get stuck in thoughts such as "if I do migraine yoga for 40 days *how* will it help me feel better?" We want guarantees, control over how things should help us, preferably in advance. The point of em-bracing the unknown is also about letting go of how things should work out exactly, how the body should heal and so on. Our focus must be on why we want to heal and then we have to focus on the feeling of feeling good, that is, being happy, have a clear head, hav-ing energy, feeling love and joy and everything else amazing that life consists of.

THE ENDING

I hope this book has given you hope that life can be amazing despite migraines and that you have the power to create the life you desire. Start where you are, one thing at a time and make the most of each day. Focus on what you want more of in your life and let go of control as much as you can. I wish you good luck with all my heart.

I end by sharing some diary notes.

Notes from 2011 - 2016

"The Knife"

Waking up early in the morning, it's still dark. The head aches. The knife cuts behind the eye. The pain is sharp and intense. I move and the knife cuts. I feel a pair of warm feet pressed against my thighs. Beloved child, when did you crawl into bed? I feel the warm little body next to mine. I feel an intense moment of the endless love for my child. Please, can I just lie here in the warmth and fall asleep again. Let me get rid of the knife. I have to get up. I stand slowly. Stumble and fumble. The sounds and movements send missiles of pain to the head. Water and tablets. I sit down at the kitchen table and light the candles. All I hear is the wind, the time ticking in seconds and the breathing of loved ones. How many times have I sat like this? I know what to expect. A new day lies ahead of me. What I make of it is what it will turn out to be. What I planned will not come true. The knife holds its grip. I choose to fill my day with silence, without demands and achievements. Just be. That's good enough, that's my life. I don't know how long I sit at the kitchen table. The pain subsides. I crawl into bed again, close to my beloved, with my arms around, the warmth and calm from the child fills me with a peace of mind and happiness.

"A vacation from hell"

We met with relatives, as we often do in the summers. We thrive together, it's usually cosy, we hang out, talk and plan some excursions. Laugh a lot, walk and cook in large quantities. The children love their cousins and are out all day long. But that summer was a nightmare. The migraine didn't want to let go. I barely wanted to go on holiday, I felt that I couldn't cope with many people, at the same time I wanted to go so badly. The family didn't want to go without me. I followed. It was a summer to remember and to forget at the same time. To remember because it should never be repeated. Forget because it was so terribly difficult, and I just felt so bad. I was lying in a dark room with the migraine from hell wanting to die. I cried and cried every day. Tried to get up and talk a little. There was pain, anxiety and nausea in a single chaos. Had to go to bed again. Heard all the sounds from loved ones through the thin wall, who hadn't seen each other for a long time and they talked, joked and laughed. The little girls who had longed for me, who think I am a fantastic and funny aunt, they missed me even though I was there. The little girls who wanted to bake a cake with me which we then would take photographs of. I could not bear them. I was in so much pain, I was restless, the anxiety had an iron grip around my lungs. In the end, I went out in sheer desperation. I walked and walked and walked. Mile after mile, fast, quickly away from it all, I wanted to feel so exhausted that I would fall asleep and get away from every-thing. I was really not to anyone's delight. I didn't know what to do. I was in the prison of hell from pain and anxiety. The only thing I knew was that I never wanted to feel so bad again. Either do every-thing to have a better life or the alternative. Fall asleep. Avoid feel-ing. An option that was not an option. But that was the only conso-lation, that the resort was always there.

"The journey"

I had decided. I give myself another year, if I don't feel better I will choose the only way out. The resort that was the only consolation. I had no life. I couldn't take it anymore. I didn't want to live in the hell of pain and anxiety anymore. I had tried everything, countless medications. Like a guinea pig. I heard about migraine yoga, I had never tried yoga. It could not make my life worse, so I started. Or whatever you might call me doing. The Little Back-Session, the ba-sic workout of migraine yoga. It went so-so. I got migraines when I bowed my head, cramps when I twisted my body and I hated Breath of fire. But I did it. Every day for 40 days. Or not really. Some days I couldn't get out of bed. I crawled to the yoga mat. Breathing. I called it yoga. Slowly I got a little bit better. Yoga helped, not the pain, but the mind. I got a few seconds of peace of mind. So, I continued a little longer. And got a little more peace of mind. I started singing the mantra, the chaos in my head was put on hold. Good. I continued. Some days I wanted to give up, but there was no alternative. Just darkness. I started a course. And one more. One day I received a letter in the post. A card with some people sitting in the desert meditating. In close contact with Mother Earth. A yoga trip to the Sahara. My heart said yes.

Go! I wanted to so badly. But how would I cope with chronic migraine? Some days I couldn't get up. I called and talked to one of the yoga teachers. You were supposed to gather in Marrakesh, the journey to the Sahara crossed the mountains in an off-road car and we would travel in the evening. Sit in the car all night on winding roads and be there in the morning. Rest one day. Hike in the desert and live in tents. Primitive. Without running water, just bring the essentials. It sounded great and challenging, but it wouldn't work. I would not be able to. I would get sick, get a migraine, vomit on the way, get anxiety and miss home. But I wanted to. I felt that this would help me find myself under all layers of illness, pain and hopelessness. I asked myself what the worst thing that could happen was.

That I got a migraine and everything that comes with it. I realised that it didn't matter because I would get it regardless. I got a migraine from everything. If I wanted to follow my heart, I couldn't let the migraine limit me. I was facing a decision. I was terribly scared. The thoughts of disaster took turns. And what would everyone else think? All other healthy people who would join. What if I became a burden? I will never forget what the yoga teacher said.

Words that finally sank into my heart. "Maria, everything is ok just as it is. We deal with what happens. Only you can decide if you should go along". I looked in the mirror. Have I not always seen myself as a brave person? Without fret, I embark on anything and everyone. I'm not scared. But this was different. It was not just a trip to the Sahara, it was a trip to my inner self. Over mountains and through fears. Embrace Mother Earth and let me be held, give up trying to have everything a certain way. I could choose. Dare, or stay in what I didn't want to be in. I closed my eyes, took a deep breath and said yes. I went. It was amazing. I was forced to give up all my attempts to control the circumstances. My life turned. From that day on, life got better. And by day, it continues to get better. Because I found courage and started shifting my focus to opportunities instead of limitations.

"Freedom"

The automatic door slowly closed behind me. I took a few steps to the side, closed my eyes and stretched my arms towards the blue spring sky. Filled the lungs with the crisp spring air. The sun's gentle lukewarm rays dried the remnants of my tears. One more breath. It was as if the healthy clear breath spread throughout the body, from the feet, up to the stomach, the heart and finally the head. I lowered my arms. Opened my eyes in surprise and felt an intense presence. Suddenly everything was clear to me. I had just left the neurologist at the University Hospital and had seen a migraine specialist. I stood amongst the crowd of people walking in and out of the glass doors of the giant building that contains so much knowledge, experience and helping hands. Every now and then the realisation came that this was the last time. The last time anyone would tell me what my life was like. That would demand things of me that I didn't want. That would tell me who I am. Take this medicine. Do this. Don't do that. Do as the specialist say otherwise you will continue to have migraines and a poor quality of life. I decided there and then. Never again will I silence my own will, my knowledge from within and my dignity for someone to call themselves a specialist. Never again will I let anyone take my hope away from me and fill my mind with negative prospects. I slowly started walking towards the city centre. The steps were easy. The headache phased out with each breath. The jacket was unbuttoned at the neck and no longer sat too tight; the feeling of spring could circulate under the collar. I felt a smile spread across my reddish face. I thought of all the experts I have met over the years. It was a mixed crowd that gave me both good and less good experiences. Experiences of hope, despair, humiliation, insight, perspective and envy, but also of joy and confirmation. I thanked them all. Yes, in fact. Everyone had done their best based on their ability. Everyone had contributed to this moment of clarity, insight and inner freedom. I stopped and glanced back at the hospital window and all the life stories that hid behind the scenes. We never know where life will take us. I started walking again. Whatever happens in the future, I would at least enjoy this very day that sparkled, gave me warmth and held me.

simplify your study

Study Skills

Academic Success
Academic Writing Skills for International Students
The Business Student's Phrase Book
Cite Them Right (11th edn)
Critical Thinking and Persuasive Writing for Postgraduates
Critical Thinking Skills (3rd edn)
Dissertations and Project Reports
Doing Projects and Reports in Engineering
The Employability Journal
Essentials of Essay Writing
The Exam Skills Handbook (2nd edn)
Get Sorted
Great Ways to Learn Anatomy and Physiology (2nd edn)
How to Begin Studying English Literature (4th edn)
How to Use Your Reading in Your Essays (3rd edn)
How to Write Better Essays (4th edn)
How to Write Your Undergraduate Dissertation (3rd edn)
Improve Your Grammar (2nd edn)
The Mature Student's Guide to Writing (3rd edn)
The Mature Student's Handbook
Mindfulness for Students
The Macmillan Student Planner
The Personal Tutor's Handbook
Presentation Skills for Students (3rd edn)
The Principles of Writing in Psychology
Professional Writing (4th edn)
Simplify your Study
Skills for Success (3rd edn)
Stand Out from the Crowd
The Student Phrase Book (2nd edn)
The Student's Guide to Writing (3rd edn)
Study Skills Connected
The Study Skills Handbook (5th edn)
Study Skills for International Postgraduates
Studying in English
Studying History (4th edn)
Studying Law (4th edn)
Studying Physics
The Study Success Journal
Success in Academic Writing (2nd edn)
Smart Thinking
Teaching Study Skills and Supporting Learning
The Undergraduate Research Handbook (2nd edn)
The Work-Based Learning Student Handbook (2nd edn)
Writing for Biomedical Sciences Students
Writing for Engineers (4th edn)
Writing History Essays (2nd edn)
Writing for Law
Writing for Nursing and Midwifery Students (3rd edn)
Write it Right (2nd edn)
Writing for Science Students
Writing Skills for Education Students
You2Uni: Decide, Prepare, Apply

Pocket Study Skills

14 Days to Exam Success (2nd edn)
Analyzing a Case Study
Blogs, Wikis, Podcasts and More
Brilliant Writing Tips for Students
Completing Your PhD
Doing Research (2nd edn)
Getting Critical (2nd edn)
Managing Stress
Planning Your Dissertation (2nd edn)
Planning Your Essay (3rd edn)
Planning Your PhD
Posters and Presentations
Reading and Making Notes (2nd edn)
Referencing and Understanding Plagiarism (2nd edn)
Reflective Writing
Report Writing (2nd edn)
Science Study Skills
Studying with Dyslexia (2nd edn)
Success in Groupwork
Successful Applications
Time Management
Using Feedback to Boost Your Grades
Where's Your Argument?
Writing for University (2nd edn)

Research Skills

Authoring a PhD
The Foundations of Research (3rd edn)
Getting to Grips with Doctoral Research
Getting Published
The Good Supervisor (2nd edn)
The Lean PhD
PhD by Published Work
The PhD Viva
The PhD Writing Handbook
Planning Your Postgraduate Research
The Postgraduate's Guide to Research Ethics
The Postgraduate Research Handbook (2nd edn)
The Professional Doctorate
Structuring Your Research Thesis

Career Skills

Excel at Graduate Interviews
Graduate CVs and Covering Letters
Graduate Entrepreneurship
How to Succeed at Assessment Centres
Social Media for Your Student and Graduate Job Search
The Graduate Career Guidebook (2nd edn)
Work Experience, Placements and Internships

simplify
your study

effective strategies
for coursework and exams

peter lia

 macmillan
international
HIGHER EDUCATION

 RED GLOBE
PRESS

First published 2020 by
RED GLOBE PRESS

Red Globe Press in the UK is an imprint of Macmillan Education Limited, registered in England, company number 01755588, of 4 Crinan Street, London, N1 9XW.

Red Globe Press® is a registered trademark in the United States, the United Kingdom, Europe and other countries.

ISBN 978-1-352-00892-0 paperback

This book is printed on paper suitable for recycling and made from fully managed and sustained forest sources. Logging, pulping and manufacturing processes are expected to conform to the environmental regulations of the country of origin.

A catalogue record for this book is available from the British Library.

A catalog record for this book is available from the Library of Congress.

contents

acknowledgements

After 20 years of supporting students in higher education, I have lost count of the number of students I have met, worked with and been inspired by. Without their contribution I could not have developed the ideas and created the strategies that make up this book.

I would also like to thank the following: Katherine Ajibade, Jareer Aldaoud, Maryam Alhilal, Sheila Ali, Oscar Bates, Sheila Blankfield, Janet Chapman, Layla Dahmani, Dr Ranjita Dhital, Dr Iria Giuffrida, Ruari Lane, Lorraine Petel, SanYuMay Tun and Rachel Shaw for giving me permission to use examples from their student work. Jemimah Norman whose inspirational email finally persuaded me to put together a proposal for publication. Sevilay, who showed me that with a lot of hard work and a little bit of the right kind of guidance, a student can become a great teacher (and that is a wonderful thing to be). All the reviewers who read through my drafts, gave me encouragement and made valuable suggestions. Helen Caunce for giving me the opportunity to develop my ideas and turn them into a book and for providing insightful and wide-ranging support. Rosie Maher for answering all my questions with expertise and understanding. Everyone at Red Globe Press who contributed to simplify your study.

This book is dedicated to the Lia family in Japan: Steve, Chiyomi, Chihiro, Anna and Caterina.

introduction

simplify your study

I have worked as a tutor in higher education for twenty years and have never met a student who isn't capable of doing well. But I have met a lot of students who want to do better and many more who simply don't know how to do academic work. In my experience, there are two reasons why students can find it difficult to show their true abilities:

1. they don't really understand what they have been asked to do

2. they haven't found an effective way to work

Simplify your study doesn't mean that studying is easy or that the work is simplistic. It means simplifying the mechanics of study. The mechanics of study are the form of things produced (like an essay or an exam answer) and the steps taken to produce them. I believe the forms can be made explicit and easy to understand and the steps can be made explicit and easy to follow.

> if the mechanics of study can be simplified, the complexity of academic work can be shown where it should be shown: in the final product

the aim of study

This book makes doing well in assessed work the primary aim of study. Not because learning in general terms isn't important, but because learning is more effective when it is focused on a task. Doing coursework and preparing for and sitting exams are the most important tasks. So, in this context, studying with a clear aim means knowing the format and purpose of a coursework assignment or the structure and requirements of an examination.

> look at the end first and know what you are producing

thinking differently

Thinking differently can lead to working better and it may be necessary to think differently about studying. This can mean trying a new strategy or applying a new idea. The strategies and ideas presented in this book can be used as they are, or they can be adapted. Information and ideas are processed in different ways by different people, and strategies for study are more effective when they are designed to suit individual ways of understanding.

> a good strategy is a strategy that works for you

the content of the book

This is a book of ideas presented as 9 units and 65 subunits. The ideas have been developed over many years of working with thousands of university students. Their feedback has been crucial in helping me shape ideas into practical and effective strategies for coursework and exams. Many of the strategies are innovative, others take existing ideas and consider them in new ways. Wherever possible, they encourage a visual approach to working and learning. They have all been tried and tested by many different students. The strategies are designed to be simple to understand and easy to use or modify.

Key strategies are introduced with three headings:

 the aim  why this can help you the strategy

a strategy is a plan of action, but the best plans are flexible, so strategies should be adapted to suit personal preference and need

the value of preparation

This book promotes preparation as part of the process of study. Reading the strategies will provide ideas of how to proceed. Making or using templates will give focus and organisation. There are lots of ideas for preparatory steps and templates in this book. Some of the subunits refer to templates that can be downloaded from the simplify your study companion website: www.macmillanihe.com/lia-sys.

good preparation can simplify your study

how to use the book

If I were a student using this book, I would start by reading subunit 1.1 and make an assessed work overview. This would give me the focus and rationale for all my academic work. However, different students have different needs and the material in this book can be accessed in any order. To encourage this, a spatial layout of contents has been included. This display can also be used to monitor the use and review of material by ticking the boxes next to the subunits. Each subunit can stand alone, but the ideas and strategies they present are transferable to other tasks and so, where appropriate, the subunits have been cross-referenced.

After leaving school, the demands and nature of education change. Despite this, many students think that they should automatically know what they are doing and how they should do it. An unwillingness to ask simple questions can be a barrier to effective working. I hope this book answers some of the questions that should be asked. I hope it helps students to simplify their study, understand what they are doing, work more effectively and reach their potential.

don't be reluctant to ask simple questions, they often provide the most valuable answers

simplify
spatia

This spatial contents is
you to access the conten
You can monitor you
ticking the box nex
If you want to do
the book, you car
this spatia

Instagram:
@simplifyyourstudy

your study

contents

esigned to encourage
·f this book in any order.
·se of the material by
·o each subunit.
·his without marking
·download a copy of
·ayout from

www.macmillanihe.com/lia.sys.

unit 1

organisation and planning

When you organise, you put things into an order that makes sense to you. While some students can get by without explicitly organising their work, most will benefit from effective organisation and planning strategies. This unit presents three strategies for organising and planning academic work. The strategies are simple, easy to implement and personalise and don't take long to complete. The strategies can be used together as a 3 step process:

step 1:   make an assessed work overview to identify and provide focus for all your academic work
step 2:   produce an academic year overview that puts your coursework deadlines into a clear timeframe
step 3:   use a weekly planner to plan and monitor your work

The unit ends with a simple strategy aimed at effective working in timed sessions. Ideally, you should think about organisation as early as possible, but you can implement these strategies at any time during the academic year, especially if you become overwhelmed with the demands of your study. Because these strategies are simple, they can easily be overlooked or dismissed but they will help you identify, focus, prioritise and monitor your work.

1.1 making an assessed work overview

★ the aim

Establishing a clear focus at the start of the academic year is important. This strategy provides an easy to use document that displays all the assessed work (coursework and exams) that you will be required to complete for a particular course. It aims to replace the idea of 'reading around the subject' with a clear task-focused approach to academic work.

ⓘ why this can help you

The work you do for any course should be focused on the assessed work, not simply on the course title or subject or on reading all the books on a reading list. However, when starting a course, many students are uncertain about the amount, type or value of the assessed work they will need to do. This uncertainty can cause unnecessary anxiety.

Making an assessed work overview displays and, importantly, limits the work to be done. This can help you achieve a sense of control. It also identifies the most important work (that which carries the most marks) so that you can allocate and prioritise your time more efficiently. It gives a clear and specific focus, which will be the basis for reading and for other work involved in completing coursework and preparing for exams. The assessed work overview is the first step to effectively organising and planning your work.

⚙ the strategy

From the various sources available (module handbooks, e-learning sites, websites, introductory lectures, tutors etc.) identify, collect and list all the assessed work for each module of your course.

The overview should include:

- the type of assessment (essay, presentation, poster, exam etc.)
- the length of the assessment (word limit, time for a presentation or exam etc.)
- the date of submission or date of exam
- the value of each assessment (as a % of the module)

For this document, you only need this essential detail. Put this information into a table on a single sheet of A4 paper. There is an example of an assessed work overview below and a template for you to adapt is available to download from www.macmillanihe.com/lia-sys.

Once you have made your overview, you can use it to monitor the progress and completion (with grades) of your assessed work.

Making an assessed work overview is the first step in creating focus for your reading (see subunit 2.2). If you want to work effectively, tell yourself that everything you do (read, make notes, write etc.) should help you with a task listed here. If it does not, then it is not essential work.

assessed work overview: term 1

Name: **Jane Smith**   Course: **War Studies**

module: Contemporary Security Issues				
essay	words: 3,000	hand in: Oct 24	40%	
briefing paper	words: 1,000	hand in: Nov 5	20%	
essay	words: 3,000	date: Dec 12	40%	

module: Conduct of War				
essay	words: 2,000	hand in: Oct 30	25%	
exam	time: 2hrs	date: Jan 6	75%	

module: Islam: Later Developments				
essay	words: 2,000	hand in: Oct 30	40%	
exam	time: 3hrs	date:	60%	

module: Religious Truths and Philosophies				
text analysis	words: 500	hand in: Oct 5	–	
essay	words: 3 ,000	hand in: Feb 25	40%	
exam	time: 3hrs	date:	60%	

It is best to make the overview at the start of the academic year or term, or, if possible, even before you start your course. In this way, you will know, at an early stage, what is expected of you.

The information you need (to make the overview) should be available, but you may have to access several sources in order to pull it together. Module handbooks usually contain detailed information for each module of a course, but the onus is on you to find any information that is missing. If some information is not available, creating the overview will help you identify any gaps that can be filled in later.

The assessment types (essay, report, presentation etc.) will identify the kind of tasks you will need to do. For example, if you are expected to write a lot of essays, you will need a good essay production strategy (see subunit 6.2) and, in this case, it would be useful to find and understand a good strategy before you start working on the essays.

If your assessment for a module is wholly by examination, any notes you take in lectures or from reading should be useful for revision and for use in the exams. On the other hand, if a module or course is assessed entirely by coursework, any notes you take should be focused on the specific requirements of the assessed work. There is no point producing endless notes if they are not going to be examined or they are not useful for your work.

The assessments for each module should total 100%. This information is useful because it will show you the most important tasks and allow you to prioritise your planning by allocating more time to them. For this reason, the overview is primarily for summative assignments, but you can include formative work. A summative assignment is an assignment that is marked and contributes to your overall grade. A formative assignment can also be assessed but the mark does not count towards your final grade. However, the feedback you receive for formative work can be valuable especially in practising a skill for subsequent assessed work.

The overview can cover the work for one term or, if you prefer, you can prepare an overview for the whole academic year. If you are feeling anxious, overwhelmed or uncertain about what is expected of you, making an assessed work overview is a useful thing to do at any stage of your course.

making a more detailed overview

Although the simple assessed work overview is sufficient for most courses, some students like to make a more detailed document. This might be especially useful for courses with more than 4 modules per term, where the assessment is primarily or totally by examination or where there are a lot of small tasks that need to be completed (like problem sheets or lab reports). A detailed overview will take longer to produce than a simple assessed work overview, so you should only make one if you can see the benefits of it. For example, it might be mandatory to attend lectures, so adding a list of lecture topics to an assessed work overview will allow you to monitor attendance.

If you want to make a detailed overview, A3 templates for 4, 5 and 6 modules are available at www.macmillanihe.com/lia-sys. These can be adapted to suit individual needs or preferences.

You can change the headings in the template and, by placing a mouse cursor and right clicking in any cell or cells, you can divide or merge cells to list or represent different tasks.

In a detailed overview (as well as your assessed work) you can include things like a list of all the lecture topics, the number of problem sheets or the available past exam papers. Here are two example columns taken from a detailed assessed work overview:

Law of Tort	
module topics	
Duty of Care	
Psychiatric Injury	
Pure Economic Loss	
Omissions	
Public Authorities	
Breach of Duties	
Causation	
Remoteness of Damage	
Product Liability	
Occupier's Liability	
Nuisance	
Trespass to Person	
coursework (10%)	
Essay (formative) 15 Oct	
Essay (formative) 24 Nov	
Essay (summative) 17 Jan	
exams (90%)	
date: 22 May (2pm)	
time: 3 hours	
structure: Part A (2 from 5) Part B (1 from 2)	
question types: problem questions x 2 discussion question	

MS1 Calculus			
coursework (10%)			
test 1			
test 2			
test 3			
test 4			
test 5			
exams (90%)			
date: 17 Jan (10am)			
time: 3 hours			
structure: A: Differential calculus B: Integral calculus C: Multivariable			
problem sheets			
problem sheet 1			
problem sheet 2			
problem sheet 3			
problem sheet 4			
problem sheet 5			
problem sheet 6			
problem sheet 7			
problem sheet 8			
problem sheet 9			
problem sheet 10			
lectures			
1	2	3	4
5	6	7	8
9	10	11	12
13	14	15	16
17	18	19	20
past papers			
2013	2014	2015	
2016	2017	2018	

⭐ the aim

This strategy aims to set all your coursework deadlines (for each module studied on a course) into a clear, visual timeframe.

ⓘ why this can help you

The perception of time is subjective. Some students find it difficult to estimate how long they have for a task or how close a coursework deadline is. The academic year planner will help you prioritise and plan your work. After creating an assessed work overview, you can set out your coursework deadlines and display them in relation to time (dates) and to each other. This will show you how long you have to complete each task and it will allow you to select the order in which you will do the work.

⚙ the strategy

Download and modify the A3 academic year planner template. Go to: www.macmillanihe.com/lia-sys.

Check your term dates and enter the (teaching) week number and week beginning dates in the left-hand columns.

Then shade out any holidays (e.g. Christmas) and reading weeks or half-term breaks.

List the modules of your course in the column headings. Then enter the individual coursework task deadlines next to the appropriate weeks.

Some modules will be completed in one term, others will continue into the second term.

This planner is for coursework. For any exams you have, you can use the revision planner (see subunit 9.3).

week	term 1	Contemporary Issues	Conduct of war	Islam: Foundations	Relig
1	30 Sep				
2	7 Oct				
3	14 Oct	Tue 15 Oct: proposal			
4	21 Oct				Wed 2
5	28 Oct			Wed 30 Oct: essay	
6	4 Oct				
7	11 Nov				
8	18 Nov		Tue 19 Nov: essay		
9	25 Nov				
10	2 Dec			Mon 2 Dec: briefing	
11	9 Dec	Fri 13 Dec: essay			
	16 Dec				
	23 Dec				
	30 Dec				
term 2				Islam: Later Issues	Easter
12	6 Jan	Fri 10 Jan: essay			
13	13 Jan				
14	20 Jan		Tue 21 Jan: essay		
15	27 Jan				
16	3 Feb			Wed 5 Feb: essay	
17	10 Feb				
18	17 Feb				
19	24 Feb		Mon 24 Feb: report		
20	2 Mar				Wed 4

1.3 making and using a weekly planner

⭐ the aim

Knowing your weekly timetable is a good way to start planning your work. This strategy creates a visual display of regular activities over a period of a week in order to show you the time available for academic work. It aims to make explicit the link between available time and workload.

ℹ️ why this can help you

Some students plan in too much detail; others need to plan more. A weekly planner is a simple to use and flexible tool that can help you plan your work:

- it provides a clear, visual timetable of your regular appointments
- it gives a clear, visual idea of the time available for you to do your work
- it keeps a list of the major work that needs attention
- it allows you to plan work in terms of working sessions (see subunit 1.4)
- it helps you to stay organised and focused

⚙️ the strategy

Use a template that shows the days of the week broken down into hourly slots. You can adapt the times on the template to suit your personal routine.

Start making the planner by entering your regular appointments such as lectures, tutorials and seminars. Then add any activities you do every week such as non-academic work or going to the gym. Use colour to indicate the same subjects or the same activities. There are two main ways you can use the planner:

1. You can make the planner on an A4 template and print it out to take with you. Although many students now use a variety of digital planners, an A4 paper copy can give a clearer display of activities and time. It is also faster to access and easier to personalise. In the 'things to do' box, note the assessed work you have to do for that week. During the week, add items to the list and cross off completed tasks. At the end of the week, open the weekly planner file on your computer and, if necessary, adapt it for the week ahead. Print out the planner and transfer any incomplete activities into the new planner's 'things to do' column. Discard the old planner.

2. You can make the planner on an A3 template and print it out to display on your wall. This can act simply as a visual timetable that shows your weekly routine or you can add information to the 'things to do box' in pencil or with sticky notes. Erase the information or replace the notes as required.

You can download an A4 or A3 weekly planner template from www.macmillanihe.com/lia-sys.

If you wake up earlier or want to divide the evening into hours, simply add new rows to the template before entering your activities.

Visualising time broken down into hourly slots can help you see how much work you can realistically do in any one day and week. Although the templates show cells divided into periods of one hour, each slot is made up of two 30 minute cells. This allows you to enter activities that start or end on the half hour. If you want to mark these 30 minute cells, click and drag the mouse cursor over the two parts of an hourly slot and right click. Then, select **Insert Horizontal Border** under the Borders symbol. If you want to divide any cell further (e.g. the 'evening' slot), select a cell with a mouse, right click and select **Split Cells**…

Once you have drawn up your timetable, you may even be encouraged to change your routine, especially if you see that you do not have enough available time for your academic work.
Here is an example of a weekly planner using the template:

date								things to do:
	Monday	Tuesday	Wednesday	Thursday	Friday	Saturday	Sunday	
9				Work, Org and Society Lecture (B 50)	Work, Org and Society Seminar (B 50)			
10								
11	Accounting and Finance Lecture (G1.17)	Communications Lecture (B5)				W O R K		
12				Business Mgt Lecture (B5)				
1			Communications Seminar (B5)	Business Mgt Seminar (B5)			social	
2	Accounting and Finance Seminar (G1.17)							
3								
4			Sport					
5	Gym							
6								
7				Gym				
evening								

You can plan the tasks for each week by deciding when you will do them and enter them into your planner. Alternatively, you can use a more flexible planning approach and decide how many (one-hour) working or study sessions you can do each day and select one task from the things to do for each session. Creating effective study sessions as a strategy is explained next.

If you are likely to procrastinate (put off doing your academic work for many different reasons), it might be better to timetable coursework alongside the regular weekly activities and keep the 'things to do' box for short or easy tasks.

1.4 creating effective study sessions

⭐ the aim

Starting work and maintaining focus and concentration can be hard. This strategy can help you plan, complete and monitor a realistic number of focused work sessions in a single day. It is aimed at addressing lack of focus, distraction, low motivation and procrastination.

ℹ️ why this can help you

Many individuals lose focus on a task after about 45–50 minutes and work after this time is less efficient and sometimes totally ineffective. Some people simply cannot concentrate for long periods or find it difficult to get going at all.

Planning to work in a realistic number of short sessions can:

- help establish and maintain focus on a single task
- improve concentration on an explicit task
- overcome procrastination by setting a realistic, achievable target
- establish a working routine
- measure progress
- create a sense of completion and achievement

⚙️ the strategy

For this strategy, a work session is normally considered to be between 30 and 60 minutes long. However, if you are finding it difficult to motivate yourself or to concentrate, consider a working session to be shorter (e.g. between 10 and 20 minutes). If you start by doing 10 or 15 minute sessions, try to slowly build up the sessions to reach 30 minutes.

Decide how many sessions you can realistically do in one day (usually between 1 and 6). Then plan a realistic start time for the first session. This strategy is flexible and it doesn't state the times when you have to work. However, a scheduled start time for the first session of the day is important. It may be useful to also provisionally plan a time for the second and third session.

Before starting the first session, identify a specific task (e.g. reading a certain chapter, making revision notes on a lecture or writing a part of an essay). This is important as it will establish a clear focus for the session.

If you are finding it difficult to work (e.g., you may be lacking motivation or you may be procrastinating because something is difficult), make your target explicit. In this strategy, your target is not to complete a task, but to work, with focus, for a stated number of minutes. In other words, your aim is to complete the session. Sometimes, getting started is the hardest thing to do. Setting an achievable goal can help you overcome this barrier.

Start the first session. Work until you become aware of losing focus or concentration. If your concentration levels remain high, continue to work. When you lose focus, stop. Set a start time for the second session and take a break. The break can be any length. It is usually at least 30 minutes but can be longer. Taking breaks is an important part of this strategy because breaks give you time to process the information or ideas from the session.

At the start of the next session, quickly review what you did in the previous session. This will help re-establish focus. Continue to work in this way until you complete your target number of sessions for the day. The strategy is summarised visually on the next page.

monitoring your work sessions

It is important that you monitor your progress by marking the completed sessions. This is particularly useful if you are experiencing a lack of motivation, because even small achievements can help you feel better. You can use the weekly planner to plan and monitor the sessions.

Plan to do more sessions at the time of day you find it easier to concentrate. Your energy levels can fluctuate throughout the day, so you should take this into account when you plan and when you take breaks from working. Cross out the sessions as you complete them. If you have a good day, try to do a bonus session. On a bad day, you can carry one or more of the sessions over to the next day. If you think that setting a daily target is not practical or is too rigid, think about setting a weekly target instead.

This strategy can be useful to keep you working at a minimum number of hours a day or week during the term. It will help you set a good routine. It is also useful when you have to revise for exams at a time when you may not have scheduled lectures or seminars that help structure your day. During revision periods, you can monitor the sessions you complete on your revision planner. In the example below, the target was set at 4 to 6 sessions a day, with most of the sessions in the morning and the first session at 10am.

			morning	afternoon	evening
Mon	3	Jan	10am ✖ ✖ ●	●	● ●
Tue	4	Jan	10am ● ●	●	●
Wed	5	Jan	10am ● ● ●		●

Planning can become a form of procrastination, so it is important to make plans that can be implemented. This means being simple, realistic and flexible. Working effectively is the basis of the strategies and ideas contained in this book, and preparation is part of that process. The simple strategies in this unit do not take long to complete. Before you start to make complex, detailed plans, think about whether they will help you work better.

creating effective study sessions (working in sessions):

- working session: 30–60 minutes
- decide on a realistic number of sessions per day
- plan a realistic start time for the first session

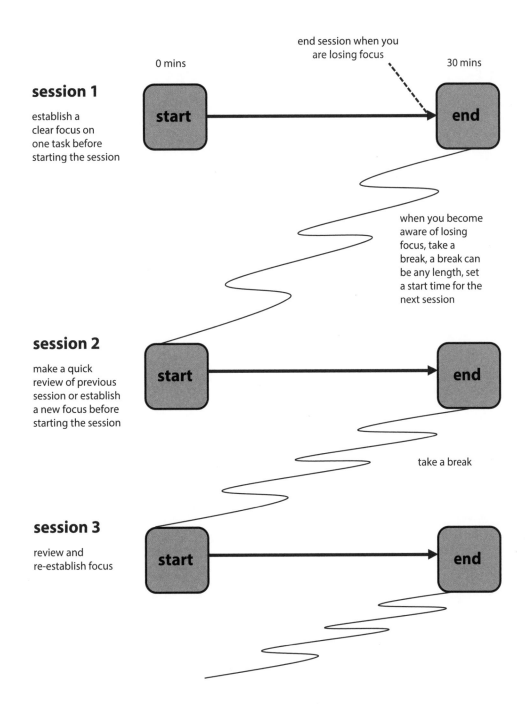

unit 2

reading

You can make your reading more effective by using a good strategy. But you can't do this without focus. Focus tells you why you are reading. When you do academic work, if you don't know why you are reading, you should be thinking, not reading. When you read an academic text, your primary aim is to extract relevant information and ideas and use them in your own work. So, effective reading is also about making good notes. If you want to improve the efficiency of your reading, you need to recognise and make these links:

- reading ←→ understanding a task (focus)
- reading ←→ making effective notes

The ideas presented in this unit are designed to help you think about your approach to reading and how you can start reading in a more strategic way. This leads into unit 3 (making notes) which contains practical strategies designed to make reading active and purposeful.

2.1 reading: getting started

Reading for coursework and exams needs to be efficient. Thinking about how you approach reading is an important first step to make your reading more effective. The table below lists seven things some students think about before they start to read. These thoughts are positive because they show a desire to understand everything. However, if they are all put into practice, they can have a negative impact on reading efficiency. Check how many you do.

I want to do all the reading on the reading list.	
I want to know everything on the subject.	
I want to understand everything on the page.	
I won't accept something if it doesn't make sense, so I'll reread it until it does.	
I need to know the meaning of all the new words I come across.	
I want to read in order (from start to finish) in case I miss something out.	
I sometimes think because I can't finish something, I won't start reading it.	

This table shows 5 things that happen when some students start to read:

I try to process (make sense of) all the information and ideas in the text.	
I try to remember all the information and ideas in the text.	
I have my own ideas when I read so I create a mental dialogue with the text.	
I try to visualise the information and ideas as I read.	
I think about other things when I read and so I get distracted.	

These activities and thoughts burn energy. If you practise most or all of them, reading can lead to extreme tiredness and reading academic texts can be a frustrating experience that provides little benefit. Don't read just because a book is on the reading list or you have been told to or because you think you should. Simply passing your eyes over text and ticking a box that says you have read something is a waste of time.

There are many reasons to read. If you don't have a clear reason, your brain can latch on to any idea or piece of information and try to process it. This can lead to an overload of information, loss of direction, loss of concentration, distraction, slow reading, highlighting the whole text or forgetting what was read.

Before reading, make yourself aware of why you are reading. If you don't know what you are looking for when you read, you should be thinking or asking questions, not reading.

2.2 the importance of focus in reading

If you are asked to read something, the first thing you should do is ask 'why?' Asking 'why?' is the first step to creating a focus for your reading.

Focus tells you what you are looking for when you read.	**Focus** replaces 'reading around the subject' with reading for a purpose.	Reading strategies will not work without **focus**.
Focus allows you to use reading and note making strategies effectively.	The most important factor in effective reading is **focus**.	**Focus** helps you find and select relevant material.
Focus gives your brain a better chance of filtering out irrelevant material.	The more explicit the **focus**, the easier the reading.	If you are struggling to read effectively, stop reading and find your **focus**.

Module handbooks or web pages, essay and exam questions, lectures, seminars and your tutor are all sources of questions that help create focus for reading. But another important source is yourself. You should be able to provide an answer to the question: why am I reading this?

Because the primary reason to read is to help you attain good grades, the assessed work requirements of your course or module should be the first step to creating a focus for your reading. It is useful if you clarify what these are as early as possible. To do this, see making an assessed work overview (subunit 1.1). Effective, focused reading that is based on the requirements of assessed work (essays, reports, exams, etc.) will help you understand and remember a lot more of the subject literature than reading without a defined purpose.

Once you know your assessed work requirements, you can create a more explicit focus by considering individual tasks. The table below shows some key academic tasks for which you will be required to read. It suggests ways of establishing focus before you start to read.

task	how to create focus before reading
essay	Your reading should be focused on a specific question, not just the topic of the essay. See making a spatial breakdown of essay questions (subunit 6.3).
reflective essay	Familiarise yourself with and list the key questions normally asked in reflective writing. See unit 7 reflective writing.
dissertation and report	Establish the type of dissertation or report you have been asked to produce (empirical, systematic review or theoretical) and find a model or template for it. Different sections of a report will address different questions. See unit 8 doing a dissertation.
analysis of a research paper	The questions you need to answer when analysing research papers are usually based on the different methodologies. Check the methodology of the paper you are reading and then analyse it against set questions. For these questions, see analysing research papers with templates (subunit 8.11).
book review or critical review	For questions you will need to address in a critical review of a text, see using a template: doing a critical review (subunit 3.7).
literature review	Define, as clearly as possible, your research question. Familiarise yourself with the purpose of a literature review and the questions it asks of the literature. See doing a literature review (subunit 8.7).
seminar	Prepare an outline template with relevant questions before doing the reading. See using a template: making notes for seminars (subunit 3.5).
examination	Use past exam paper questions to focus your revision. If your course is assessed by exams, try to access past papers as soon as you can. See making an exam overview table (subunit 9.1) and step 2 of the 3 step revision strategy (subunit 9.2).

When you read for these and other academic tasks, focus can help you address three overarching questions:

1. What do I already know?

2. What do I need to know (what is relevant to the task)?

3. What don't I need to know (what is irrelevant to the task)?

If you can answer these questions, your reading and note making will be more productive.

2.3 using indicators to read

When you read for an academic task, your aim should be to find and take out only what is relevant to the task. For this, you need to know how to locate information or ideas in a text. In most cases, you won't need to read the whole book, paper or article and you don't need to read in order (from beginning to end). All academic texts have indicators. The indicators sometimes contain the specific information or ideas you need. More often, the indicators can help you find the most relevant part of a text.

indicators	
conclusion, summary or last paragraph(s)	Always look at the end first. Even if you plan to read a paper or chapter in full, it is worth reading the conclusion first. If there is no formal conclusion or summary, read the last paragraph(s) as writers tend to summarise what they have written.
headings and subheadings	Look through the text. If some of the headings seem relevant to your needs, read these sections first.
first sentences of paragraphs (first words of sentences)	These sentences are a form of indicator because they usually identify what the paragraph contains. You can read many pages quickly by only reading the first sentence of paragraphs. Stop only to read a paragraph in full when you think it may contain something you need. Sometimes, even the first words of sentences can be used as indicators.
abstract	This is typically found at the start of a dissertation, research paper or lab report. It contains a concise summary of the content. Abstract reading is a method used to select the most relevant papers and exclude others.
list of key words	Some academic articles also include a list of key words. These words can help you decide how relevant an article is for your purposes.
introduction	A book introduction will usually be a few pages in length and can often provide the specific information you are looking for. It can also indicate where in a book or paper you are likely to find what you need. The introduction to an article or paper is usually the first paragraph or section.
preface	A good preface will give an overview of a book and can be used to identify the most relevant chapters or sections to read.
table of contents	This can be used to locate relevant chapters or sections within chapters. Read these first to see if they contain the information you need.
index	The index is an alphabetical list of content that appears at the end of a book and directs you to specific pages.
blurb	This is a concise summary or overview that typically appears on the back cover (or inside sleeve) of a book. Although it is generally a short paragraph, the blurb can often contain specific information relevant to your task.

As well as directing you to relevant sections of a text, indicators can be used to determine whether a text is worth reading. Indicators can therefore help select, prioritise and exclude texts.

Skimming and scanning are two well documented reading strategies. They both aim to speed up reading and make it more efficient. However, there is some confusion about the difference between them because they have been defined in different ways.

Some guides describe skimming as a method of obtaining a general overview of a text and scanning as a fast way to detect detail. But when reading for assessed coursework or an exam, it is unlikely that you will be required to gain a general overview of a text. If you do need a general overview, the best approach is to find an existing summary or review online or to simply read the appropriate indicator (the abstract for reports, the preface for books, the conclusion or summary for essays, papers, articles or chapters in books).

Once you have established a focus for your reading, your aim will be to find specific information from texts. Most of your reading will involve looking for relevant details (quotes, facts, figures, opinions, theories etc.). Skimming and scanning can be used to do this, but they do it in different ways. So, it is useful to establish a practical definition of what they are.

skimming	When you skim read, you only read certain sections of a text. You intentionally miss out large chunks of a text.
	Your reading speed can be normal or slightly faster than normal.
	When you find some information relevant to your task, you slow down your reading and extract what you need.

scanning	When you scan read, you look at text quickly. You try not to say or vocalise the words. Vocalisation can be out loud or 'in your head'. When you skim read, you try to suppress vocalisation.
	Your reading speed is much faster than normal.
	When you recognise a key word or phrase, you slow down your reading and read the information around it (the sentences before and after the key word) to check if it is relevant to your needs. If it is, then you extract it.

When reading for academic tasks, skimming and scanning cannot be used to understand a text in its entirety. If you need to fully understand a text, use a different strategy such as drawing an understanding (subunit 3.2). However, you can skim and scan a document before reading it in detail.

skimming

Because skimming means reading selected parts of the text rather than the whole text, you do not need to read a text in the order it is presented. Skimming uses the indicators in a text (see subunit 2.3) and the best place to start is usually at the end, by reading the conclusion, summary or last paragraph. Here are four different academic tasks for which skimming might be a useful strategy:

task	skim reading strategy examples
check to see if a document is relevant for your needs	Establish the focus (the reason for reading) by listing some specific questions. Read the abstract, conclusion, summary or introduction. If none of these indicators is relevant to your questions, find another source to read. You should always aim to read the most relevant source first as this will identify major themes or topics relevant to your question. These topics can then be looked out for and developed in further readings. If you have a number of sources to consult, you can use this approach to put them in order of relevance. Reading the most relevant source first will make subsequent reading easier because it makes the focus clearer.
read a whole book	If you read a whole book from cover to cover, it will be impossible for you to remember and retain all the information and ideas in the book. If you are asked to read a whole book, you can skim read it by reading the preface (or, if there is no preface, the introduction), the blurb and the conclusions or summaries of each of the book's chapters. If there are no conclusions, read the last page(s) of each chapter. If you have more time, read the introductory paragraphs of each chapter. Then, skim the book for headings and subheadings and read the most relevant parts.

read any document to extract relevant information	First, establish the focus (the reason for reading) by listing some specific questions. Read the conclusion, summary or final paragraph(s). Then, paragraph read the document. When skimming, paragraph reading means reading the first sentence of each paragraph. First sentences indicate the content of paragraphs and you should stop to read the whole paragraph only when you think it contains something relevant to your task.
find specific information from a research paper	Different sections of a research paper or empirical dissertation contain different content. Familiarise yourself with the structure of these reports (see unit 8) and go directly to the relevant section (e.g. method, results or discussion) and read it first.

Skim reading is as much about leaving things out as it is about finding relevant information. It can seem an unnatural way of reading because you might be afraid of missing important details. However, skimming is only effective when you intentionally miss out large sections of a text. So, when skim reading, focus on the benefits of the strategy.

scanning

Scanning means reading fast and looking for key words or phrases. Successful scanning requires a high level of focus (an explicit reason to read) and good visual recognition. So, before scan reading something, it is useful to write down, and read out loud, the key words (names, dates, terms or key phrases etc.) that you are looking for. Keep these key words and phrases nearby as you read so that you can refer to them regularly and refresh your focus. Scanning can be tiring. It burns a lot of energy quickly, so it is best done in short bursts.

Because scanning is based on visual recognition, it is sometimes not even considered a form of reading but a form of looking. When you read quickly (scan):

- try not to vocalise (sound out) the words
- try to predict the whole word from the first few letters you see
- don't pronounce words
- don't stop to look up words you don't understand
- don't go back and reread
- stop to read slowly only when you see a word or phrase that is relevant to your needs

aids to scanning

When you read, your eye doesn't move smoothly across a line of text. It fixes on a point on the page and then jumps quickly to another point. When you scan read, you do this, but you do it faster. There are some things you can do to help you scan more effectively:

reading aid	Scanning can be more effective with the use of a reading aid like a coloured ruler, a pencil or your finger, which you run down the page and under the text as you scan it. This will help your eye tracking (moving your eyes across and down a page). It will also increase your 'peripheral vision', which is the number of letters or words (both left and right) you see when your eye fixates on a point on the page. This is sometimes called the 'span of recognition'.
'find' feature	Most software programs that present text in digital form will have a 'find' feature (often accessed with the F3 key). This opens a search window where you can enter key words or phrases you want. The processor will use a form of optical recognition and scan the document for you. You can then quickly scan through all instances of the word as it appears in the text.
flash or speed readers	Some programs (sometimes called 'flash readers') will 'read' text by flashing words at you on the screen. You can select the number of words shown and the speed at which they are shown. You can also select the colours and font type you prefer. You look at the words and sentences as they appear and pause the program when you recognise what you need. One example of a flash reader that is free to use is Spreeder, but there is a growing number of alternative applications.
text readers	Although scanning is a visual (or optical) process, you can use it in combination with a text reader, sometimes called 'text to speech' (TTS). The reader normally highlights text as it reads to you. If this is uncomfortable, then remove the highlighting feature, or simply 'scan' read with your ears by listening to the text as it is read out to you. You can increase the speed of the reading and pause it or slow it down when you hear a key word or phrase. There are numerous TTS programs, some of which are free to download and use. Microsoft Word and Google Docs both have inbuilt TTS. ClaroRead and texthelp's read&write are advanced software packages that include TTS. Free downloads currently include Acapela Group's Virtual Speaker, Audiobookmaker, Balabolka and NaturalReader.

2.5 prereading by using other sources

Before reading a recommended text, a useful strategy is to read other sources that describe or discuss the recommended text. Ideally, these sources will be concise and easier to understand. They don't need to be academic sources or sources you reference in your work. Online dictionaries, encyclopedias, reviews and short articles are all sources that can provide a good overview or relevant detail about a recommended text.

Prereading by using other sources is a form of preparation that makes the main reading more effective. In some cases, prereading other sources is enough to answer all your questions. Here are some academic reading tasks for which prereading by using other sources can be a particularly useful strategy:

task	prereading strategy
doing a book or film review	Look for existing reviews or articles that can identify the main themes, arguments, strengths and weaknesses of a book or film. A non-academic source (like a user review) might provide valuable ideas you can develop and support with evidence from an academic text.
reading a difficult but essential primary text	Most established texts will have reviews or concise summaries online or in published form. Before you read a primary text, read about it. Note the key arguments or aims of the text. Aim to identify and understand key words and definitions, especially if they are new and specific to the subject. A difficult text (like a philosophy paper) can be less intimidating if you know some details about the content in advance.
reading to prepare for a (formative) seminar	Most seminars are formative (they do not count towards your overall grade) but they can be a useful source of ideas for an exam or a piece of coursework. If you don't have time to do all the reading for a seminar, preread other concise sources. Take down the key ideas in a spatial form (subunit 3.1) or use a template for making notes for seminars (subunit 3.5). When you attend the seminar, add details to each of the points as they are introduced and discussed.
reading for a task that requires you to use a specific perspective (e.g. a critical theory like feminism or structuralism)	Before you apply a perspective, you need to understand it. Try to find concise forms of the perspective you have been asked to use. Create questions or identify themes that are relevant to it and refer to these when you do the main reading. For example, ask 'what would a feminist (a Marxist, a postmodernist etc.) look for?'
doing an essay question that asks you to discuss a quote	Essay questions often contain quotes you are asked to discuss. Search for the quote online to find its origin. Find out about the author of the quote and what people have written about this author.

2.6 reading and visual disturbance

Some readers experience a visual disturbance or distortion of text when reading. For some, this can happen almost immediately; for others, it happens only when they have been reading for a long period of time. The disturbance often occurs when the font and background colour are distinctly different (like dark black print on bright white paper). The form of perceptual distortion differs. Text can seem to float from the page, patterns appear between the letters or words and lines might blur and distort.

This kind of perceptual disturbance is not caused by poor eyesight and is not a symptom of ill-health. Some forms of visual disturbance (such as double vision, floaters or flashes in the eye) can cause migraines and be signs of underlying health problems. These symptoms should be acted on immediately.

Perceptual distortion in reading has been associated with different terms, including 'visual perception disorder', 'scotopic sensitivity syndrome', 'Irlen or Meares-Irlen syndrome' and 'visual stress'. Although the causes remain uncertain, there are five simple things you can do to effectively reduce the perceptual distortion of text when you read:

1	**make and use your own coloured overlay or overlay rulers**
	You can buy transparent coloured overlays and reading rulers that sit on top of the text as you read. These colours can have a dramatic effect in 'calming down' or stabilising the text on the page. They can allow you to read for much longer periods before disturbance occurs. In some cases, the overlays will stop text distortion completely.
	Making coloured overlays yourself is easy and much cheaper than buying them. You need an acetate sheet (sometimes called a 'universal transparency film') with at least one matt (non-shiny or non-smooth) side. Draw a rectangle on a word processing document and fill it with your preferred colour. Then print the square onto the sheet. Make sure you print the rectangle onto the matt side.
	The colour that works best for you can change and some readers prefer to use a range of colours. Pastel or light colours tend to be the most popular, but you should experiment with different colours. You can cut your overlays to use as a reading ruler or for different page sizes so that they can fit the books you most often read.
	When sitting exams, you should seek permission to take your coloured overlay into the exam so that you can place it over the question paper to avoid misreading questions and instructions.

2

use a program that can colour or shade the screen

Simply reducing the light level on your laptop, phone or PC can make a big difference to the perception of text.

There are numerous software programs available that can shade, tint or veil your device screen with a variety of colours and different intensities. You can shade all or certain parts of the screen to help you read. Many of these programs (such as ColorVeil) are free to download.

3

personalise your word processing interface

You can change the default settings on your word processor. You can change the page view, the background colour, the line spacing and the type, size and colour of the font. You should do this before you start working and make your preferences your new default settings.

Most people who experience perceptual disturbance prefer to read 'sans serif fonts', which are simple or minimalist font designs that don't have extra strokes on individual letters.

Light or pastel coloured backgrounds are also very effective in reducing disturbance. However, colour preferences differ, and they can change over time.

Personalising your word processing interface will also help you process text when you write and proofread your work.

4

use colour tinted lenses

Coloured lenses act in the same way as overlays. You can buy coloured lenses online or at most opticians, without a prescription. Some optometrists specialise in coloured lenses and use a colorimeter to identify the optimum colour.

If you use prescription lenses for reading, then you can have glasses made in a variety of shades. If you want to try coloured contact lenses, you will need to arrange an eye test from a registered optician.

5

read paper copies rather than on screen

Some people find that perceptual disturbance is lessened when reading on paper than on screen. Printing documents on coloured or lower quality paper can also reduce the distortion. This paper tends to be greyish rather than white and therefore less bright. Some people know their preferred colour and print onto coloured paper.

unit 3

making notes

Good note making is essential for effective academic work. This fact is often overlooked and note making can become a routine process of collecting a lot of information, much of which is not relevant or accessible. Many students continue to take notes in a conventional linear form but there are other, often more effective ways to collect and display information and ideas from research. One flexible approach is to use visual or visuospatial note making strategies and another is to prepare and use templates. If you can make relevant notes in an appropriate format, doing coursework and sitting exams can be easier. The strategies presented here will help you make notes that:

- relate to an explicit task
- are easy to use when applying them to a task

3.1 making notes in spatial form (spatial note making)

⭐ the aim

Spatial note making is an active reading strategy that helps you produce notes in a focused and accessible format. The strategy uses the principle of reformatting information to help understanding, and to make notes relevant to a specific task. Reformatting means putting information and ideas into a different and personalised form. In this case, the form is changed from linear (lines in a book or journal) to spatial (notes, symbols, abbreviations etc. spread over a page):

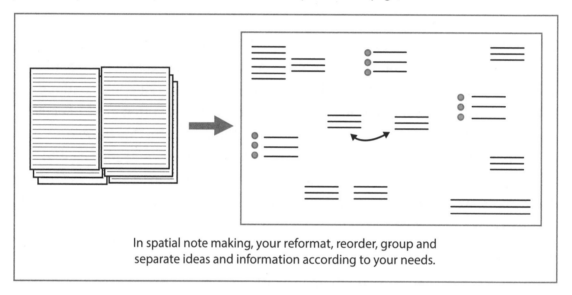

In spatial note making, your reformat, reorder, group and separate ideas and information according to your needs.

ℹ️ why this can help you

Spatial note making is particularly useful when doing research for a specific assignment like an essay or report or for gathering important information for a literature review. Here are seven good reasons why you should try spatial note making:

1	makes notes for your own, explicit purpose

When you make notes in spatial form, you purposely do not reproduce the order in which information appears in the source you are accessing. That order serves the purpose of the author, not yours. When you make spatial notes, you separate, group and order your notes according to your explicit need (e.g. making notes to address an essay question). A spatial representation of information and ideas therefore helps you see how information and ideas can be used by you.

2	**shows relationship of information**

When you make spatial notes, you can see all the information and ideas from your reading on one page. This not only provides detail but shows how the ideas of an author relate to your needs and how the ideas relate to each other.

3	**helps you be selective and reduce the quantity of notes you make**

In this strategy, you use a single sheet of A3 paper. This sets a frame that acts as a limit to the quantity of notes you should take. This encourages you to be selective and not to make too many notes from any single source. If you highlight or underline too much information when you read, make spatial notes of only the key information. Always try to be selective. If you are more selective at the note taking stage, the writing stage will be easier. Some students highlight using two colours, one to indicate highly relevant information (that is noted), and the other to show information that could be relevant (this is not noted, but might be returned to later). Also, because you are required to write by hand, you are less likely to copy large chunks from a text.

4	**makes quick review easy**

Because you are making fewer notes in an abbreviated form and reformatting them to suit your needs, reviewing the notes is much faster than reading lines of text that have been highlighted or copied and pasted.

5	**allows you to compare notes**

When you make spatial notes, you should only use one side of the paper. This allows you to compare notes from different sources. Because you have grouped information and ideas according to your needs and spaced them out over the page, a comparison between different authors (or sources) is easy and can be made quickly.

6	**makes notes accessible**

Because spatial notes are already grouped according to specific categories, they are easier to access (than linear notes) during the writing phase of an essay or report.

7	**allows you to work in sessions**

Spatial note making is an activity that can easily be done in short (manageable) work sessions (see subunit 1.4). When you start to tire or lose focus, stop. When you start your next session, begin by quickly reviewing the spatial notes you have already made.

⚙ the strategy

- Take a sheet of blank (unlined) paper. Turn it on its side (landscape). This emphasises that in spatial note making, the sequence in which you take or display your notes is not important. You will create your own arrangement according to your specific needs. A3 paper (29.7 x 42cm) is the equivalent of two A4 sheets. It is the ideal size for this strategy because it gives enough space to make notes that can be spread out but also limits the notes you take. However, you can make spatial notes on any size of (unlined) paper.

- As you read, highlight or mark in the text what you think is relevant to your task. If you are using a library book that you can't mark, you can use coloured highlighter strips.

- You must be selective. You must know why you are reading before you start. This will help you to highlight only relevant information (see subunit 2.2). Rather than highlighting or noting too much, trust the voice in your head that tells you when something is not what you really need. Highlighting a point in the margin of the text rather than across the page (or over the text) will encourage you to paraphrase when it comes to making your notes.

- At any stage of your reading (after a couple of pages or when you have finished reading the document), stop and go back to the highlights. Transfer them to your blank A3 sheet of paper by making notes. The first note you make can go anywhere on the page. The second note you make should be written in relation to the first. This arrangement will depend on the purpose for making notes.

- If you know your reason for reading (your focus), you will automatically group information or ideas you think should go together.

- As you add notes to your A3 page, spread the notes out over the page. Trust your intuition in separating and grouping different information.

- Use abbreviations, key words and phrases. Use symbols (like arrows), bullet points and numbers. Avoid writing full sentences.

- Make notes on one side of the A3 page only as this will allow you to compare notes from different sources.

- You may want to note down quotes, but don't copy long quotes (more than 3 or 4 lines) or whole paragraphs. Try to keep quotes as short as possible and make sure to include the page number next to a quote.

- If you think a whole paragraph or page is relevant, then just note a key word or phrase and the page number so you can come back to it later if necessary.

- You can also add your own ideas to the information from the source. If you prefer, you can use a different colour when you add your comments.

organising your spatial notes

Some students are reluctant to make spatial notes on individual sheets of paper because they don't want to end up with a pile of unorganised papers. If you make spatial notes for an assignment, you need to keep them together. One idea is to use an A3 or A4 pad of unlined paper. However, this will not allow you to group notes on the same topic and it makes comparison more difficult.

When you make spatial notes, make notes on one side of the paper and write the reference details on the other side. Use an A4 size ring binder folder with punched pockets. You can put each of your spatial notes into individual pockets and reorder them to suit your needs. You can pull the notes out whenever you need to consult or compare them. If you use A3 sheets, fold them over to A4 size before putting them into the pockets. This enables you to immediately see the reference(s) and any other heading(s) you write on the back of your notes.

spatial note making, mind maps and mind mapping software

Spatial notes are not mind maps or spider diagrams. They are simply a spatial arrangement of information and ideas. How they are made and how they appear will depend on individual preferences and purpose. There is no generic look to spatial notes (as there is for mind maps). Spatial notes from one source can look completely different from those from another. This flexibility and personalisation of notes is key to the strategy. When you make spatial notes, you are free to be as creative and original as you want.

There are many software programs that allow you to make spatial notes in digital form. These programs include MindManager, Inspiration, MindView and Microsoft Visio. They are often used by students who prefer not to make handwritten notes or to work with paper. One immediate disadvantage of digital notes is that it is harder to see the relationship of information and ideas, even on a large screen. Making notes by hand is also more likely to prevent you from taking too many notes.

However, if you prefer to make spatial (or linear) notes on a computer, laptop or tablet rather than on paper, you can still reformat and reorder the notes at the note taking stage so that they reflect your needs and make sense to you. Whether you use mind mapping software or a word processing program, you can retain the principles of spatial note making by:

- changing the order of notes from the original source
- grouping information and ideas that go together
- creating headings and categories and moving notes between them
- adding your own thoughts to the notes you make

examples of spatial note making

This strategy is flexible and each time you make spatial notes, the appearance of your notes will be different. They are not simply a display of information (like a mind map or a summary), they are an arrangement of information and ideas made for a specific purpose.

When you make spatial notes, you can use one sheet of A3 paper for each major source or you can use one sheet and combine the notes from several sources. If you do the latter, you will need to keep track of which bit of information came from which source. You can do this with colours, numbers or letters.

You can make spatial notes from any sources, not just written material. For example, you can make them from a video, a film, a lecture or a meeting.

Some students prefer to use coloured A3 sheets (like a pastel blue) because they find it easier to process information when the background is less bright and does not contrast too much with the text (see subunit 2.6).

Here are two examples of spatial notes made by students when doing research and note making for academic assignments.

spatial notes made for an essay in Theology:

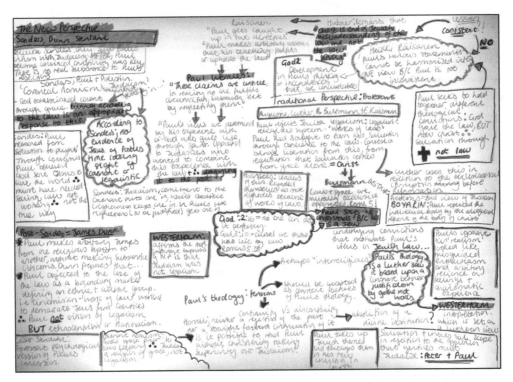

spatial notes made for a report in Genetics and Molecular Medicine:

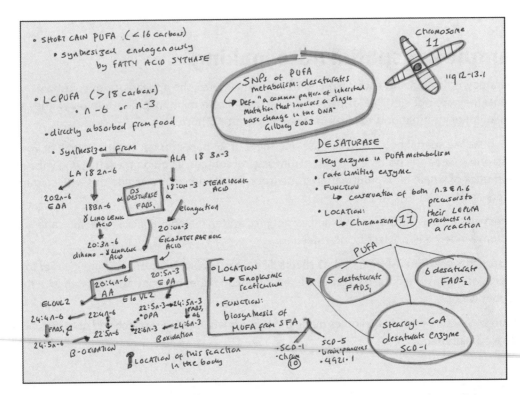

Some students try mind mapping without success and return to making linear notes. The spatial note making strategy is not about making mind maps, it is about trying something new to see if it works for you.

3.2 drawing an understanding

Another strategy that uses the principle of reformatting information to help understanding is called 'drawing an understanding'. It retains some of the aims and advantages of spatial note making in that the process deconstructs information and ideas and rebuilds them into a visuospatial representation of linear text.

However, this strategy has a specific aim: to make a single, integrated diagrammatic or schematic representation of a text or part of a text. The result of 'drawing an understanding' will be an original diagram or schema that shows your understanding of information and the relationships within that information. Many difficult concepts have been represented and simplified as models. This is what you are doing with this strategy.

Drawing an understanding is best used to analyse a core text in detail. It is useful for breaking down difficult concepts that have interlocking elements or for understanding complex processes with different steps. You should use blank paper (either A3 or A4 size). As you take notes, build up the schema step by step by adding different elements. You can use colour to distinguish different parts. Review your diagram regularly so that you understand the process of your note making and of what you are creating. Here is an example made from a reading on Freud's Oedipus complex:

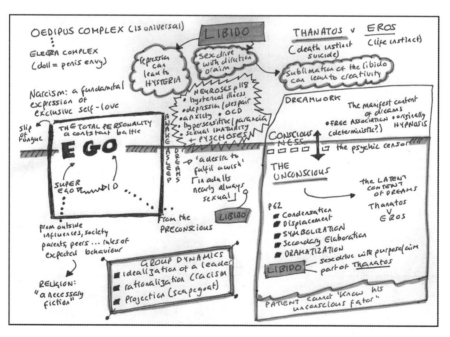

When making notes in this way, the reading rate is likely to be slower than normal and the process can take longer. However, like spatial note making, it can be chunked into short working sessions. Drawing an understanding can take time so it should be used selectively, but it is a powerful way to break down, understand and remember important information. It is also a good way to memorise key information when revising for exams.

3.3 skeleton note making for lectures

It can be difficult to take notes during lectures while also listening to and trying to understand what is being said. As a result, you can end up with scribbled notes of little value, miss important details and lose the flow of the lecture. Some students stop attending lectures and rely solely on lecture recordings (visual or audio) or lecture slides.

However, you can benefit from verbal and visual explanations, original thoughts and questions and information that might not appear on the prepared handouts. More lectures are now being made available in a recorded format and you can use these to revise, review and consolidate the content of lectures.

Skeleton or outline note making is a useful strategy for lectures. The aim is not to write down everything, but, instead, to produce a kind of map or flow chart that highlights the key points covered in the lecture.

This will allow you to listen as well as make notes. It will also allow you to see the flow and order of the content.

You can write down any detail you think is interesting or useful. Although you will produce an overview of the lecture, it's the details (e.g. key terms, themes and questions) that are important.

Also useful are any original thoughts made by the lecturer or thoughts you have in relation to the material being delivered.

The skeleton notes can then be used as a guide when you review the lecture recording and make more detailed notes.

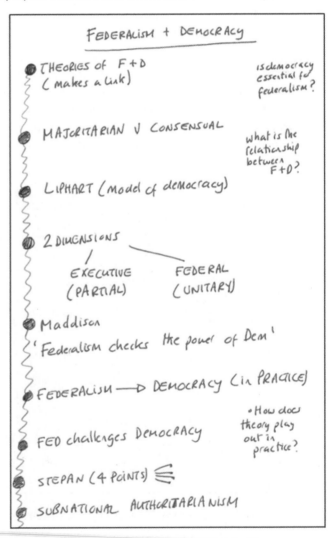

FEDERALISM + DEMOCRACY

- THEORIES of F+D
  (makes a link)

  is democracy essential fo federalism?

- MAJORITARIAN V CONSENSUAL

  what is the relationship between F+D?

- LIPHART (model of democracy)

- 2 DIMENSIONS
  /
  EXECUTIVE   FEDERAL
  (PARTIAL)   (UNITARY)

- Maddison
  'Federalism checks the power of Dem'

- FEDERALISM ─▷ DEMOCRACY (in PRACTICE)

  • How does theory play out in practice?

- FED challenges DEMOCRACY

- STEPAN (4 POINTS)

- SUBNATIONAL AUTHORITARIANISM

example of skeleton notes takes from a lecture on Federalism and Democracy

⭐ the aim

This strategy prepares or makes use of existing, suitable templates for collecting information and ideas from research so that the notes you make can be easily accessed when planning or writing an assignment.

ℹ why this can help you

If you collect notes in a template, you can organise and categorise information in a highly structured way. This makes it much easier for you to use the information for a specific task. For example, you might be asked to make a comparison between two things, to collect information and then identify themes (sometimes called a 'thematic analysis', see subunit 8.11) or to make recommendations on existing practice. Templates can be drawn up for these and other tasks. In fact, you can make a useful template when collecting notes for almost any academic activity. Specific examples are detailed throughout this book. Using templates to make notes can be particularly effective for the following tasks:

- collecting notes for an essay (see below)
- preparing for seminars (see subunit 3.5)
- making notes from verbal communication (see subunit 3.6)
- preparing notes for a critical review, like a book review (see subunit 3.7)
- making notes for reflective writing (see subunits 7.3 and 7.5)
- collecting information for different parts of a dissertation (see unit 8)
- collecting information for a literature review (see subunit 8.7)
- comparing papers in a systematic review (see subunit 8.10)
- analysing research papers (see subunit 8.11)

You can use templates that already exist, or you can make your own. Preparing your own template may require a little time, but the activity can improve the focus of your work by emphasising what you will be looking for when you begin to research. If you prepare your own template (or adapt an existing one), you can design it to match the needs of your task.

You can make templates and print them out to use or you can enter information directly into the template on your electronic device. The advantage of a template used digitally is that you can easily resize it, move the information around (in order to group it under themes, questions or categories) and alter or add to the categories. However, it's important not to simply copy and paste too much information into a template otherwise you will end up with too many notes. One of the aims of using a template is to be selective in your note taking. Some students therefore find it more effective to make notes into a printed template, by hand (as it limits the quantity of note taking) and then transfer the notes to a digital copy of the template.

⚙ the strategy

Read your essay question or assignment brief and think about how you might categorise or group information and ideas to answer the question or address the task you have been given. Break down and brainstorm the question (see subunit 6.3) and see if you can create a table that will allow you to collect relevant information in a structured way. Look (online) for existing templates that can be used or adapted. A good template is easy to use and to understand. A template normally takes the form of a simple table. Here are two examples of templates created to collect research information for essay questions that ask for a comparison:

essay question: Compare the use of supplementary schools in an inner city and a small town.

Supplementary school in Camden (North London)	Supplementary school in Bury St Edmunds

essay question: Compare the conception of human nature of Thomas Hobbes and Jean-Paul Sartre.

Hobbes' conception of human nature	Sartre's conception of human nature

If you prefer to make notes by hand, you will need to make the template boxes large enough to contain the notes. If an A4 sheet is too small, you can print or draw your template on A3 paper. If you prefer to make notes digitally, the boxes will expand as you enter text. But remember, effective note taking means only making notes of information that is relevant to your task.

Making notes with prepared templates is a strategy that can be used alongside any other form of note making. For example, you might decide to use spatial note making (see subunit 3.1) or linear note making as the primary method of collecting information and use a template as a place to group the main findings of your research. This form of template is used as a summary and it can help you develop your main argument, write a thesis statement or write the conclusion of an essay (see subunit 6.7). Alternatively, some students only use templates to collect relevant quotes that can be used in an essay. Below are examples of these templates.

essay question: What practical lessons have been learned from serous case reviews?

example template for summarising major findings from researching the essay

lessons	notes	evidence
lesson 1		
lesson 2		
lesson 3		
lesson 4		

example template for collecting quotes for an essay or written assignment

quote	notes: why it is relevant	reference (including page no.)

You might not be able to find a suitable, existing template for your task or you might not feel prepared enough to create your own template before you start researching. However, you can create a template at any time during the research process. For example, one useful strategy is to identify a core reading and then make a template based on the themes or issues that emerged from this reading. This will give you focus for further research because you will be looking for the same themes or issues in other sources. This kind of template can be useful when you are doing a literature review (see subunit 8.7).

example template for collecting information for a literature review

source	issue 1	issue 2	issue 3	issue 4
Smith et al. (2017)				
Wilson (2014)				
Lee et al. (2011)				
Burgess (2005)				

Thinking about and making a template during your research can also be an effective way of consolidating and categorising your findings and ideas up to that point. This can be especially useful if you are becoming overwhelmed or confused by the amount of information you are collecting.

3.5 using a template: making notes for seminars

what is a seminar?

At university, the word 'seminar' refers to a class where students discuss a specific topic in depth. Typically, students can ask or answer questions, give their opinions on a topic and discuss and share their ideas. The seminar is usually led by a tutor, but students are encouraged to make a contribution to the discussion. Because seminars are meant to be interactive, seminar groups are often smaller than those attending lectures.

Seminars are not usually assessed. Sometimes, participation in seminars can carry a small percentage of the total marks available for a particular module (usually no more than 10%). However, this is not always the case and any marks allocated can often be gained through attendance, not participation.

Some course modules may require you to prepare a seminar paper or short presentation on the discussion topic. These papers may be formative or summative (see subunit 1.1).

what are the aims of seminars?

Seminars are designed to:

- promote student to tutor interaction
- promote student to student interaction
- listen to other points of view
- encourage critical thinking (see subunit 4.1)
- practise debating, making and supporting an argument
- increase knowledge of a subject
- link the lecture topics(s) with the recommended reading

preparing for seminars

For many students, seminars are an enjoyable and informal forum for debate. However, it is sometimes difficult to see the benefit of seminars in terms of assessed work. You can spend a lot of time reading and preparing for a formative seminar, time that you could use for a summative assignment.

Seminars typically discuss a topic presented in a previous lecture and, to prepare for the seminar, the tutor will recommend readings. If the lecture and seminar are in the same week, you may only have a few days in which to complete the preparatory work. Some students simply cannot keep up with the amount of reading required for seminars and either don't attend them or don't benefit when they do.

Reading and preparing for seminars should have two aims. The first is to allow you to participate in the seminar and not feel lost. The second should be to make the seminar relevant to your summative work. The notes you take to a seminar and the notes you make during a seminar can be made useful for assessed work like essays or exams.

The more knowledge and ideas you take to a seminar, the more likely it is that you can participate. But you don't need to arrive at the seminar fully informed. When you read for a seminar, you are not expected to understand everything you read. Some texts can be difficult. Sometimes the quantity of reading is too much to complete. But attending the seminar can still provide a useful opportunity for collecting information, learning more about a topic and about discussion and critical argument.

a strategic approach to reading for seminars

Ideally, you will want to complete all the reading that has been set for a seminar. However, this is not always possible so you might approach the task with a strategy. For example, if you are asked to read a book of 10 chapters, you might take this approach:

- search online for information about the book (like short reviews)
- read the preface of the book
- read the blurb on the back of the book
- read the conclusions, summaries or final paragraphs of each chapter
- skim read part of the book for more detailed information

If you are asked to read a paper or an article, you might:

- search online for relevant information about the author (or the paper)
- read the conclusion, summary or last paragraphs of the paper
- read the abstract
- skim through the paper by paragraph reading (see subunit 2.4)
- read selected parts of the paper for more detailed information

If you take a strategic approach to reading for a seminar, you won't have to complete the reading in order to gain useful knowledge and attending the seminar can still be worthwhile. One effective way to do this is to use a template to collect information. Add as much relevant detail to the template as you can when you read, and then take it to the seminar and add more notes to it during the discussion.

A template (like the one below) can be used for seminar preparation or any recommended reading or research. Sometimes, themes and questions are set for a seminar. This is particularly the case when there are several tutors teaching the same seminar and there is a need for consistency. Any themes or questions given by tutors should be included in the template and referred to during reading.

a template for making notes for seminars and in seminars

This template is made in A3 size so that you have enough room to make relevant notes. You can download it from www.macmillanihe.com/lia-sys and adapt it.

the source

author(s):
Look for some specific and relevant information about the author before you start doing the reading.

audience:
Who is the text written for (author's target audience)?

questions:
Write down any questions from the lecture that relate to or direct the reading for the seminar.
Add any coursework essay questions (or questions for assessed work) that you are doing or planning to do. These questions will give focus to the reading.

thesis:
What is the author's main point or argument?
What is the author's main belief or opinion?
What is the author's main purpose or intention?
Can you write (or find) a thesis statement for this source?

context:
How does the source relate to other work in the field?
Does the source represent something new, build on something that exists or support an existing view?
Does the author present anything controversial?
Is the date of the source relevant?

method, scope and focus:
Does the author use a stated method or perspective?
What does the source cover (focus on)?
Does it have a wide or narrow scope (this can include themes, location or time)?
What is the generalisability of the thesis (see subunit 8.8)?

evidence:
What form of evidence does the author use?
Is the evidence drawn from practice, theory, research or policy?
Is the evidence supporting the theory strong or weak?
List the 3 most important or useful sources or types of evidence used by the author.

conclusion:
Does the author come to a conclusion, and if so, can you sum it up?
How valid is the conclusion and is it logically drawn from the evidence?

quotes:
Make a note of any relevant or useful quotes from the source or written about the source.

notes:
Add any further questions or ideas that you have (or that other students make in the seminar) about the source.

In the 'questions' category, you should add any questions set for the reading (usually from the lecture) because they will provide focus. Any essay questions you will be required to answer should also be added. In this way, you can use the reading and the seminar to collect information for formative work. The notes you make in the template can also be a useful revision source for exams.

Using templates for note making is not restricted to taking notes from written sources. You can take notes while watching a film (if you are doing a film analysis) or when attending a presentation or lecture. You can also use templates to take notes when the information is given verbally as a series of instructions or as answers to a set of questions. This often happens in practical situations, for example when students are on placement, in work experience or doing practical exams. Three examples are presented below to show that, with some thought and planning, you can make and use personalised templates to help you collect and order information from verbal communication.

a nursing student on placement: Maria's table

When Maria was studying Adult Nursing, an important part of her course was spent working on hospital wards. One of her roles was to accompany consultants who assessed the needs of patients. For each patient, consultants would give a lot of verbal instructions directly to the nurses. Maria would have to remember the details and follow the instructions. Because the consultants talked quickly and did not give the information in a regular order, Maria found it difficult to keep up and remember everything that was said. Using a notepad to record the information helped a little. But, usually, Maria couldn't write quickly enough.

After brainstorming all the possible instructions given, Maria found that although there were quite a few, there was a limit to them. Furthermore, she found that most of the instructions were repeated regularly.

Based on this information, Maria made a table (shown here) using abbreviations for the key terms that related to each instruction. She made space to either tick, mark or enter a numerical value against each one.

Maria printed several of the tables and made them into a booklet that she took with her. She used one per patient to note the verbal instructions given to her.

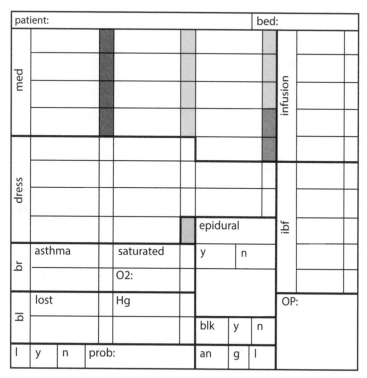

a medical student on placement: Rachel's template

As part of her degree in Medicine, Rachel had to interview or speak to patients and record details of their presenting problems and relevant clinical history. There were key questions to remember and there was also a sequence in which the questions were usually asked. However, patients often gave information at different times, spoke very quickly and gave information that was not relevant. Sometimes, Rachel would forget to ask a certain question. When on placement on a psychiatric ward, Rachel created a template to help her collect information from patients. It is shown below and is a great example of how a template can be created and used to meet a specific need.

presenting complaint		referral status			
mood screen: how are you feeling at the moment?		affect screen			
high/low		blank	flattened	blunted	exaggerated
		congruent/incongruent		responsive/delayed	
		depressed	anxious	angry	elated
risk assessment					
harm from others	do you feel safe?				
harm to others	do you have feelings or thoughts of hurting other people?				
self-harm					
suicide	thoughts				
	attempts				
other risks	financial		self-neglect		promiscuity

physical	details		**social**	details	
sleep			occupation work		
appetite weight			family + friends		
pain			finance		
substance use			forensic		

past psychiatric		**pmh**	**dh**	**fh**
1° care contact 2° care contact prev mha detention				

psychosis screen	details				
delusions	persecutory	reference	grandiose	guilt	nihilistic
	hypochondriacal	jealousy	amorous	religious	control/passivity
hallucinations	auditory 2 person		auditory 3 person	auditory commentary	other

It was easier for Rachel to circle, tick or make brief notes in the template than take notes in a notepad and write them up later. Also, in taking time to create the template, Rachel was able to identify, rationalise, order and understand the information she needed.

meetings with a dissertation supervisor: Chang's agenda template

Chang, a Theology student, had to complete a 12,000-word dissertation in his final year. He was allocated six one hour meetings with his supervisor. In the first meeting, Chang struggled to take in all the information, ideas and guidance given to him and was left uncertain about the focus and direction of his work. Chang knew how important the meetings with his supervisor were, so he decided to prepare for the next one by creating a simple agenda template.

This helped Chang organise his thoughts leading up to the second meeting and allowed him to make better notes during it. It also allowed him to set the agenda and keep a logical order to the discussion.

The remaining meetings followed the same order. Chang started by giving his supervisor a progress report. Chang was keen to establish and maintain the focus of his work, so he then presented and clarified the research question and research aims.

Between meetings, the template was used to list questions or issues that needed to be discussed. Chang made sure to prioritise these so that the most important were dealt with in the time available.

Before the final three meetings, Chang emailed any essential questions to his supervisor one day in advance. Chang needed targets and a deadline to work to, so he finished by agreeing a date for the next meeting and by making a list of new targets. Although Chang was also able to voice record the meetings, making and using the agenda template helped him to prepare and make the most of each session.

date:	meeting number:
progress since last meeting	
• • • •	
research question / aims / objectives / focus	
questions / topics / issues	**notes**
1	
2	
3	
4	
5	
date of next meeting:	**days to next meeting:**
to do	• • • •
other notes	

It is important to do some preparation before you meet your dissertation supervisor. If you want to use or amend Chang's agenda template, you can download it from www.macmillanihe.com/lia-sys.

using a template: doing a critical review

One of the guiding principles behind the strategies in this book is to know what you have been asked to do before you start working. This means spending more time on preparation. Creating your own template for coursework, or adapting an existing template, is a form of preparation. It not only provides a document in which you can note and categorise information, it is a process that can help you clarify a task.

In this example, a template is used to collect notes and to help you write a critical review of an academic (non-fiction) source. A critical review can be made of any paper, article, film, chapter or book. A critical review is not the same as a literature review, which analyses and integrates different sources (see subunit 8.7).

Using a template to do a critical review:

- gives a clear focus on what to consider before reading a text for review
- encourages you to make relevant and concise notes
- allows you to collect notes in any order
- allows you to group information and ideas
- makes it easier to structure (order) your final review

what is a critical review?

A critical review is a form of written academic coursework that consists of information from or about an academic text. A critical review is not just a report or summary. It needs discussion (analysis) as well as description. In fact, the discussion is much more important than description. A critical review analyses an academic text that communicates information and an author's ideas and arguments. The clarity, validity and persuasiveness of ideas and the contribution to a field of study are the most important concerns.

the contents of a non-fiction critical review

There are many things that can be included in this type of review, but they can be categorised under the following 12 headings:

1	details of the text	7	context of the text
2	author of the text	8	scope of the text
3	summary of the text	9	perspective of the author
4	format of the text	10	main thesis of the author
5	style of the writing	11	evidence supporting the main thesis
6	audience for the text	12	conclusion of the author

These categories form the structure of the critical review template detailed on the following pages. You can download the template from www.macmillanihe.com/lia-sys.

taking notes for a critical review using the template

1. Look at the template below. This provides information and useful questions for each of the 12 categories. It will give you a good idea of what to look for and think about when you read the text. Depending on the length of your review and your assignment brief, you can select the most appropriate questions and adapt the template. For example, in a short review, you won't be required to discuss things like format or style, instead you will focus on the thesis and evidence used to support it.

2. Before reading the text, read about the text. Search for existing concise information. For example, if you are doing a book review, try to find short reviews and make notes in the template. This will also prepare you to read the text because you will already know some of the main themes, arguments, criticisms and strengths.

3. Read the text and make relevant, concise notes in the template. These notes should include information about the source and your analysis. If you don't have time to read the whole text, skim read it. For example, if you are asked to do a book review, read the preface, introduction and chapter summaries first. Use all the indicators of the source (see subunit 2.3) to gain as much information as possible. You don't need to read the text or make notes in any particular order.

4. When you have finished reading, look at your notes and decide how many sections your critical review will have and draw up an outline structure.

Although some of the questions in the template suggest descriptions of a text, you should always be analytical in your thinking, so ask questions about the notes you make and write down relevant ideas. If you're not sure what discussion means, or how to make analytical notes, see description and discussion in academic writing (subunit 4.5). Use specific information or examples from the text to support the points you want to make. Your critical review will have a word limit, so it is important to be selective and address only those questions you think are most important.

details	• How does the title relate to its topic? • When was the text published? Is this significant? • Where was the text published? Is this significant? • Who is the publisher? Is this significant?
author	• What is the status of the author in relation to the topic of the text? • What relevant qualifications does the author have? • Is there any relevant background information about the author? • Has the author published any relevant, previous works?

summary	In a short review, you may decide not to include a summary and refer to the contents of a text throughout your review. In a longer review, the summary can give a concise overview of a text (especially if you are doing a book review when the summary can be broken down to reflect the sections or chapters of the book). Avoid long, descriptive summaries and keep this part as short as possible.
format	You can comment on any of the structural elements of a text such as: ● preface ● table of contents ● chapter headings, introductions, conclusions or summaries ● visual displays of information (tables, graphs etc.) ● index However, it is unlikely that most reviews will go into such detail. Only comment on any format elements in order to discuss their value (good and bad). You might consider some of the following questions: ● Does the organisation of the text help the reader understand it? ● Is the organisation logical or confusing? ● Do the visual elements of the text (e.g. maps) help understanding? ● Could the information have been structured or presented in a better way?
style	You might comment on the author's writing style in order to discuss whether the text is well written and easy or difficult to understand. You could ask: Is the writing style: ● formal or informal? ● technical and difficult to understand? ● emotional and persuasive? ● logical or confusing? ● pragmatic (realistic and practical) or abstract (theoretical)? ● dogmatic (follows strict principles) or opinionated? ● descriptive or analytical (if both, what is the balance)?

audience	• Does the text have a clearly defined audience in mind? • Is it written for the general public, students at a specific level, academics, experts in the field or practitioners? • What is the author's main purpose for writing (e.g. a textbook)? • Does the text suit the needs of the intended audience (e.g. if it is a course textbook, will students like it, if it is a book for practitioners, will they find it useful)?
context	• How does the text relate to other works about the same topic? • How does the text relate to other works about related topics? • What kind of contribution does the text aim to make in its field? • Is it about a current debate? • Is it about a non-current or historical debate?
scope	• Does the author aim to provide an overview of a larger topic? • Does the author have a clear focus? • Does the author look at a specific individual, idea, place, time or period? • Does the author make a comparative analysis (e.g. between different places or time periods, between different thinkers or theories)? • Is the scope of the text sufficient to deal with the topic? • Does the author leave anything out that should have been considered? • Does the author acknowledge the text's limitations?
perspective	An academic source may base its ideas on an existing theory such as: liberalism, socialism, Marxism, structuralism, poststructuralism, psychoanalysis, modernism, postmodernism, postcolonialism, feminism or queer theory. You might consider some of the following questions: • Does the author use a theoretical perspective or theoretical framework? • From what point of view is the work written (e.g. economic, political)? • Is the theoretical perspective (or point of view) a strength or weakness? • Is the author biased (subjective) or unbiased (objective)? • Does the author omit facts, ideas and alternative arguments?

main thesis	One essential question in any critical review is: ● **What is the author's main thesis (i.e. main argument)?** For a definition of a thesis statement, see subunit 6.7. The thesis could be: ● cause and effect (e.g. arguing that pollution is causing climatic effects) ● establishing a relationship (e.g. a relationship between poverty and crime) ● a comparison (e.g. one form of society is morally superior to another) ● proposing or supporting an idea or hypothesis (e.g. that humans are predisposed to act in certain ways) ● Does the author begin with the main thesis or work towards it? ● Is the thesis a new idea? ● Is the thesis a confirmation of previous knowledge or does it build on or develop previous knowledge? You can often identify an author's main thesis before reading a text by using a prereading strategy (see subunit 2.5).
evidence	This is one of the most important parts of a nonfiction critical review. By discussing the evidence, you are trying to assess the validity of the author's thesis and, as a result, the authority or value of the text. You might consider some of the following questions: ● What methodology of study does the author use to support the thesis? ● What types of evidence does the author use to support the thesis? ● Does the author use primary or secondary evidence, or both? ● Does the author use a variety of sources or just a few (or rely too much on a single source)? ● Is the evidence clearly referenced and are the sources reliable? ● Does the author manipulate the evidence to make it fit the thesis? ● Is the evidence strong or weak? For example, do you think the evidence 'proves' an argument (strong) or just supports it (less strong)? ● Does the author make assumptions without evidence (weak)? ● Does the author make a strong or weak link between the evidence given and the argument made (i.e. is the argument convincing in an academic sense, not an emotive or persuasive one)? ● Are the sources of evidence used old or new?
conclusion	● Does the author come to any clear conclusions? ● Does the author conclude that the main thesis is validated? ● Does the author discuss the consequences of the main thesis? ● Does the author point to future developments of the topic?

unit 4

critical thinking for academic writing

Critical thinking and critical writing are needed if you want to achieve the highest grades. So, you need to understand what these terms mean before you can use them in your work. This unit establishes a clear definition of critical thinking and emphasises the link between critical thinking and its application in practical terms, especially in academic writing. Critical thinking will change the way you think when you process information. It will improve your powers of reasoning. Becoming a critical thinker will enable you to apply the strategies in this book more effectively. You will ask appropriate questions, make better notes and improve your academic writing. The key strategy in this unit divides academic writing into description and discussion. This practical and easy to use idea will help you incorporate analysis into your work, which will improve your grades.

4.1 what is critical thinking?

There is no single or universally accepted definition of critical thinking. In fact, there are countless definitions that stem from a variety of academic disciplines. But reading some of them shows that they have common features. Here are four short descriptions of critical thinking:

critical thinking is ...	
A cognitive activity associated with using the mind. Cottrell (2017) p. 1	Reasonable reflective thinking focused on deciding what to believe or do. Ennis (1996) p. 166
The deliberate application and assessment of a set of skills and dispositions with a view to reaching a reasoned judgement as a fundamental basis for our beliefs, decisions or, in general, behaviour. Nieto and Saiz (2011) p. 203	The mental processes, strategies, and representations people use to solve problems, make decisions, and learn new concepts. Sternberg (1986) p. 1

Because it is an essential part of academic work, it is useful to see critical thinking as a process you can apply when you are required to do so. From the descriptions above, three essential elements of this process can be highlighted. Critical thinking is:

1. An intellectual or cognitive process that needs conscious effort and motivation.

2. A process that uses skills and strategies.

3. A process that can challenge and change the thinker's theory (ideas and beliefs) and practice (behaviour).

These three elements are expanded upon below.

In the context of academic work, the process of critical thinking should result in stronger academic writing. However, many students are told that their academic writing is not critical (or analytical) enough. To avoid this, critical thinking is something you need to do at each stage of your academic work. You need to think critically when you:

- try to understand an assignment brief or essay question
- carry out research (especially when you read academic texts)
- collect information and make notes
- gather your thoughts about or discuss an assignment
- write up an assignment

critical thinking as a conscious cognitive process

Because critical thinking challenges your knowledge, beliefs and assumptions, you need to choose to do it. In other words, you need to be prepared to accept different points of view and to change your mind. This can be difficult, especially if a long-held belief is challenged by something you see or read. To overcome assumptions when doing academic work, you need to:

- be aware of your thoughts and behaviour (how and why you think or behave in certain ways)

- accept the goal of new learning (to improve your knowledge and skills through addition and change)

- monitor the process of critical thinking (check that you are being open-minded and acknowledging your progress)

Critical thinking does not mean that your assumptions are wrong. But it puts them to the test. A research hypothesis is essentially an assumption. It is a statement based on limited evidence or inadequate knowledge. At the end of a research process, you are in a better position to conclude whether a hypothesis is valid. Your assumptions and beliefs are like hypotheses, and you should be prepared to test them objectively. In academic work, the process of critical thinking replaces your assumptions and beliefs with something else:

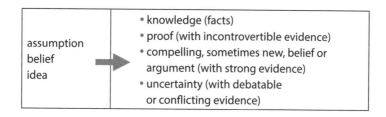

The motivation to learn new things is therefore essential to the process of critical thinking. Its implementation is helped by certain skills and strategies.

critical thinking as a process that uses skills and strategies

The skills you need to actively engage in critical thinking are often described in abstract terms, such as 'reasoning', 'analysing', 'making inferences' and 'evaluating', but these skills are easier to apply when you have a practical tool to use. These tools are available in many forms. The critical appraisal checklists (see subunit 8.11) and the Gibbs' reflective cycle (see subunit 7.5) are only two of many different examples. However, they are all made up of the same things: questions.

> the fundamental skills you need to engage in critical thinking for academic purposes are the facility to ask the right questions and (if possible) to answer them

Critical thinking is critical enquiry. The questions you ask will depend on the requirements of your assignment, but they will also depend on the type of source you are working with. When you carry out research for an academic task, you can consider information and ideas from practice, theory, research and policy. Sources from each of these categories require different focused questions:

	includes	examples of questions asked
practice	observed practice your own practice	• Is the practice effective and efficient? • Does it represent best practice? • Is there a different (better) way of doing something?
theory	academic theory your own ideas	• What is the evidence to support the theory? • Is the theory clear and easy to understand? • Is the theory based on subjective ideas? • Is the theory useful in practical terms?
research	(peer reviewed) research your own research	• Is the research sound in all its aspects? • Is the research peer reviewed? • Is the research up to date? • Does the research have practical value?
policy	policy guidelines legislation	• Is the policy clear and easy to understand? • Is the policy able to be implemented or enforced? • Is the policy outdated or no longer appropriate?

The relationship between these four categories can also be a focus for critical thinking and there are many questions you can ask. For example, you could ask whether:

- a theory is based on practice or research
- practice is in line with policy guidelines
- the results of research have led to policy changes

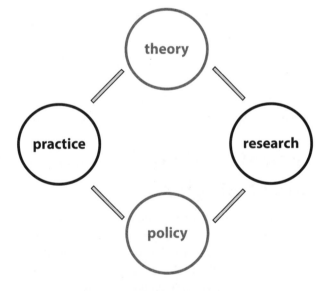

This idea is explained in detail as a critical thinking strategy in subunit 4.2.

If critical thinking for academic purposes is essentially about asking questions, then finding and asking the best questions is important. This requires preparation. You may have to think about and formulate some of the questions yourself, but most of them are already written. When you are given an essay question to answer, you can work on it to generate more specific questions that will help you during your research.

For other tasks, like writing or analysing research papers, you can look for appropriate appraisal tools, checklists or templates before you start the critical thinking process. Some of these are highlighted in subunit 8.11. If one doesn't exist for your specific purpose, think of adapting or making one yourself. This strategy is detailed in making notes with templates (subunit 3.4).

The steps of critical thinking as a process are identified in numerous theoretical models. These steps are usually associated with different skills. Analysis and evaluation are two that are often written about. They are usually described as sequential tasks. First, you analyse something (you break it down to see what it consists of) and then you evaluate it (you recognise its strengths and weaknesses or limitations).

However, the process of critical thinking is theoretical. In practice, it can be difficult to understand and separate these skills because they often occur at the same time. The terms themselves can be confusing because they seem to mean the same thing. Understanding theoretical models of critical thinking is not important (unless it is your topic of study). Recognising the benefits of open-minded critical thinking is important, because the potential outcome of critical thinking is critical writing, which will benefit your coursework or exams. The outcome is also a positive change in you, the thinker.

critical thinking as a process that changes the thinker

When you begin your academic career, it is unlikely that you will be a good critical thinker. You may be a critic who is able to criticise, but critical thinking is not a negative process. It is something that is learned through mindful practice and it has outcomes that are necessary components of many academic tasks. The benefits of critical thinking include:

- recognising and (sometimes) understanding the complexity of something
- recognising the value of something
- recognising the limitations of something
- making a strong argument
- taking a position and supporting it with evidence
- finding the solution to a problem
- improving your knowledge or skill by learning new things

Without critical thinking, there can be no critical writing. Critical writing as an essential part of academic writing is discussed in unit 5 academic writing.

critical thinking: practice, theory, research, policy

⭐ the aim

When you carry out research for an assignment, the information and ideas you collect can come from any of these four sources: practice, theory, research or policy. This strategy defines the four sources and shows how they can interrelate. The aim is to provide a thinking tool that can encourage critical thinking and improve the critical quality of your academic work.

ℹ️ why this can help you

You are often required to discuss the strengths and limitations of the sources of evidence that you reference in your work. This can depend on the nature of the source (e.g., the date and size of a piece of research and the methodology it uses). But the strength and weakness of information can also depend on a wider context: its relationship to other types of information. For example, you may argue that an academic theory based solely on observation is not as strong as one supported by research. This strategy presents this idea as a simple visual model that encourages you to think critically about the wider context of the information and evidence that you read and use in your academic work.

⚙️ the strategy

First, it is useful to clarify the four categories from which you can get information and ideas during research:

	This source can include your own practice as well as any practice that you observe directly or indirectly. Direct observation might be something you observe as part of a team on a placement or in an internship. Indirect observation might be something you see on a video or film, or a practice that you read or hear about. Practice includes things you do (method) in a lab or in fieldwork. It can also include events, like a historical event, a performance or any form of (practical) action.
	Practice examples that you might refer to are usually regulated by policy and often observed by theoreticians or observed by researchers as part of a research methodology.
	This source consists primarily of academic thought, whether it is in the form of a theoretical system, a concept model or simply an expressed idea. It can also include your own, sometimes innovative, thoughts.
	A useful theory is often considered to be something with practical value like a model that helps you to understand something. Some theories are considered valuable even if they don't lead to practical change. While some theories can never be proved, others can be tested and supported through research.

This includes research that is published in academic journals and has been reviewed by experts in the field (peer reviewed research). It can also include non-peer reviewed research, for example the results of surveys that might appear in magazines or newspapers. Your own research is also a potential source.

The value of research is often associated with outcomes that lead to a change in the way things are done (practice) or thought about (theory). Research can often link directly to practice by making recommendations.

This source comprises any (usually written) documents that express a preferred way of doing something. Most policies are linked with official bodies or formal institutions and are in the form of legislation or guidelines. Some policies are not officially recognised, for example an art movement manifesto or even an individual political pamphlet.

Good policy is often derived from strong research. However, legislation or guidelines are not useful unless they can be implemented or enforced in practice.

Because any of these four categories can influence one or more of the others, the model looks like this:

If you have been asked to discuss a source from any one of these categories, asking how that source relates to the other is one way to generate critical thinking.

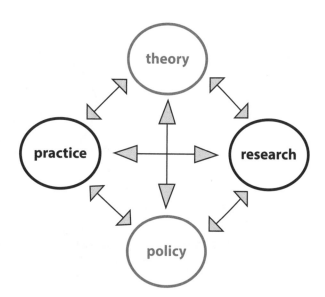

Here are two examples to help you understand how this idea can be used:

In a work placement on a mental health ward, a patient shows aggressive tendencies towards you. You have been asked to write a reflective piece discussing your reactions and behaviour (practice). In thinking about your reflective piece, you could:

- consider the relevant policy guidelines to determine whether you knew them, followed them and, if so, whether they were useful or not

- read the relevant theory on the causes of aggressive behaviour and think whether you would have acted differently had you known more

- consider any relevant research that supports your actions or explains your reactions

For an essay, you have been asked to discuss the national guidelines for promoting best practice in education at primary school level (policy). In thinking about your essay, you could:

- look at the relevant education theories and see whether there is strong, mixed or weak support for the guidelines among academic thinkers
- look at the research on educational best practice, to determine whether the guidelines are supported by strong evidence
- consider examples of teaching practice and ask whether the guidelines work well in the primary school environment or whether they are difficult to implement

Academic assignments often ask you to consider the following associations:

practice ←→ theory   **research ←→ policy**   **policy ←→ practice**

These are the most obvious relationships, but a consideration of the interrelationship of all four categories widens the context and gives you more scope to think critically about the sources of information you use in your work. Even when an assignment brief doesn't directly ask you to consider these associations, you can do so. You can use the model at the start of an assignment to help think about or even display the kind of source material you will need to find and analyse. Here is an example of how an essay question can be applied to the four categories:

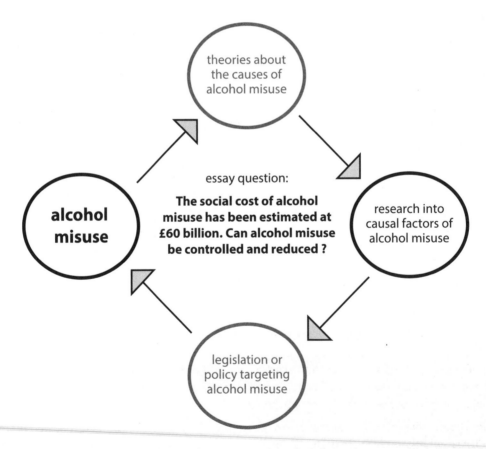

This strategy is primarily designed as a thinking tool. It is a model designed to increase critical thinking. However, it can also be used to display your major findings in each or any of the four categories. If you want to use it in this way, you can download a template from www.macmillanihe.com/lia-sys. At any point during your research, or when your research is complete, the model can be drawn to show the relationships in different ways. Doing this at the end of your research can help you write an important part of your conclusion. Doing it during research can help you generate appropriate questions to consider in your critical writing. Here are three examples:

example 1:

In this example there is a clear relationship between theory and practice but there is no research or policy. You might ask:

- How does practice influence theory?
- How does theory influence practice?
- Does the lack of research and policy make this practice less effective?

example 2:

This shows that research is derived from practice and that it has led to policy changes, but this policy has not been implemented. You might ask:

- Is the lack of a theoretical base the reason why policy has not been implemented?

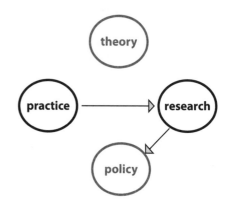

example 3:

Here, practice informs theory, which has changed policy, which, in turn, has influenced practice. However, there is no research that supports these changes. You might ask:

- Can policy, based on ideas, be justified without objective research?

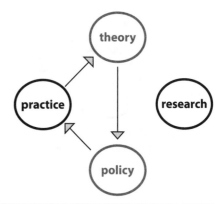

As with all the strategies and ideas in this book, you are encouraged to take and use what you understand and find useful. You are also encouraged to adapt strategies to suit your individual way of thinking and preferred way of working. Critical thinking: practice, research, theory, policy is a strategy with many potential applications, but it is primarily designed to help you think and write critically, especially about the evidence you use to support your academic writing.

4.3 critical thinking and spatial note making

Critical thinking and critical writing are vital to good academic work. The notes you make during research cannot be called academic writing until they are properly written, correctly referenced, logically ordered and formatted (see subunit 5.1). However, if it is approached well, note taking is the step that can make critical writing easier. It allows you to ask questions, focus on your ideas and control the quality and relevance of the information you are collecting. Making notes is not just about getting down the information from reading, it is also about noting down your thoughts and your reactions to the information. It is easy to overlook the freedom and flexibility that note making can give you, but for some students, this step is essential, and its benefits need to be highlighted. For many, spatial note making (see subunit 3.1) is the most effective strategy to use, and it can go hand in hand with critical thinking.

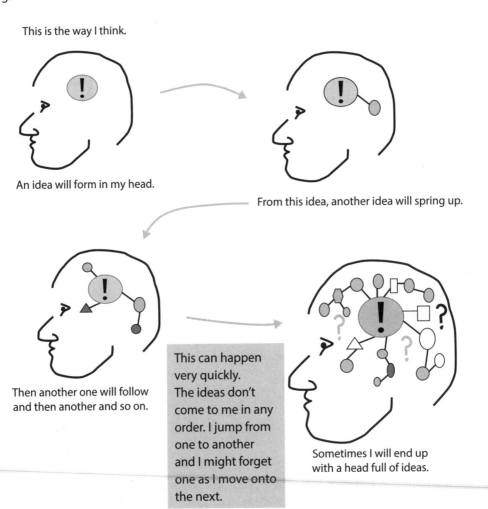

This is the way I think.

An idea will form in my head.

From this idea, another idea will spring up.

Then another one will follow and then another and so on.

This can happen very quickly. The ideas don't come to me in any order. I jump from one to another and I might forget one as I move onto the next.

Sometimes I will end up with a head full of ideas.

When I have to write these ideas down in an essay, I find it hard. I don't know where to start. I don't know what order to put my ideas in. I don't know which ideas to leave out. Sometimes I forget what I want to write. My writing can end up as a jumbled mess.

If I could draw the ideas in my head using symbols, they might look something like this:

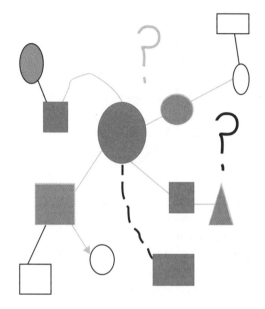

But the ideas in an essay should look more like this:

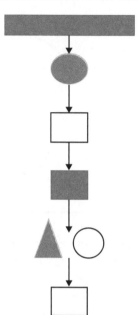

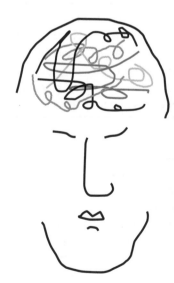

In order to sort out the confusion, I need to get my thoughts out of my head before I try to write the essay.

They are not in my head as complete sentences, so I don't try to write them down as sentences.

They are not in my head in any particular order, so I don't try to sort them out before writing them down.

I can't write in a logical order by just thinking and then writing, so I need a step between the thinking and writing stages.

Making notes lets us get our critical thoughts down on paper without worrying about order or grammar or spelling. All we have to think about is how our ideas are relevant to what we are doing. To other people, our ideas can sometimes appear disconnected. But for us, everything seems connected and it can be difficult to decide what to leave out! Making spatial notes is a good way of sorting out our thoughts and seeing how relevant they are.

Spatial note making uses a large sheet of blank paper. We use unlined paper and turn it to landscape because we want to show that order isn't important. We write our ideas as they come to us. We spread them out anywhere on the page. It doesn't matter how silly the ideas are, they might be valuable later. Spatial note making can be used when we collect information from research. But it can also be used when we are writing sentences or paragraphs.

When we make spatial notes from reading, we group information and ideas that we think go together and separate things that don't. We also ask questions of the information we are collecting and make a note of any relevant answers. For example, if we write down a quote, we also write our thoughts about it. Grouping information and ideas on the page helps us to see what the most important points are. If there are lots of notes about one issue or topic, we know it is significant. If there are only a few, it helps us decide to leave it out or to integrate it into one of the main points.

Making spatial notes from reading allows us to see the information we have collected and our critical thoughts in the same place. When we look at our spatial notes, they can resemble the form of the ideas in our heads. Seeing them on the paper in this way can help us sort them out and put them into an order that other people can understand. If you would like to try spatial note making, go to subunit 3.1.

I also use spatial note making to help me write smaller sections of an essay, a report or an exam answer. It can help me to structure paragraphs and even individual sentences.

When I write, I always have a large, blank sheet of paper next to me. If I am struggling with a paragraph, I note down the subject of the paragraph. Then I add the points I want to make. Remember, when making spatial notes, the order doesn't matter, I can sort that out later.

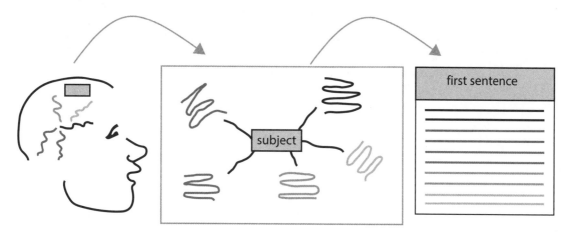

Sometimes I get stuck on a sentence and have to rewrite it several times. So I note down the subject of the sentence (what the sentence is about) and then add notes of all the things I want to say about the subject. Once I see my critical thoughts on the page, I can decide how to order them. I can build them into my paragraph by putting the ideas into one or more sentences.

To help me build my paragraph and make sure that my writing is critical and not just descriptive, I use spatial note making alongside a strategy called building a paragraph with description and discussion (see subunit 5.6). When making and referring to my notes, I try to ask the three discursive questions: 'why?', 'so what?' and 'what if?' (see subunits 4.4 and 4.5).

Another strategy is to record your critical thoughts. Just talk about them, either by yourself or with somebody else who can prompt you by asking questions. Listen to the recording and pause the recording to write down the most relevant ideas. When you discuss your academic task, your ideas won't come out in the order you will write them in your academic work. So, as you make notes of the recording, use the spatial note making idea and spread them out, trying to group similar ideas on the page.

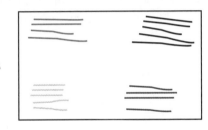

For us, good note taking can be the vital link between critical thinking and academic writing. By gathering our thoughts before we write, we can ensure that critical thinking is part of our working process. We know that when we take notes from our research, we do so for a purpose. Spatial note making allows us to focus on that purpose.

Whatever way you make notes, the principle remains the same: it is easier to sort out, select and order your thoughts once you get them out of your head so that you can see them.

4.4 critical thinking: questions for description and discussion

Critical thinking for academic work combines open-mindedness and enquiry. Asking questions is an essential part of the research process. The questions you ask will depend on the requirements of your assignment. But they can be grouped into 2 categories:

1. questions for description
2. questions for discussion

An essay question, exam question or assignment brief will tell you if you need description, discussion or both. Most coursework tasks require both. Some exam questions, especially multiple choice questions and a lot of short answer questions, require only description (facts). When setting assessed work, tutors use a variety of words to give instructions. These words are sometimes called 'command words' because they tell you what you should do. However, these words can also be grouped into the 2 categories of description and discussion.

describe	discuss
when you describe you might:	when you discuss you might:
• outline	• analyse
• state	• evaluate
• give details	• assess
• illustrate	• examine
• show	• appraise
• define	• explain
	• review

There are distinctions between some of these words. For example, in mathematics, to 'evaluate' something might specifically mean finding a quantitative expression. In theoretical models, like Bloom's taxonomy of learning, some of these words (like 'analyse' and 'evaluate') are given distinct meanings and functions and form different steps in a process.

These subtle distinctions are difficult to define, hard to understand and even harder to remember. Unless you are studying Mathematics or Education Theory or a specialist field in which these words have been purposefully defined, the difference between them does not matter.

> **for most of your academic work, the
> only difference you need to know is the difference
> between description and discussion**

The categorisation of information, ideas and instructions into description or discussion can:

- help you understand what you need to do for an assignment
- help you think about the information and ideas you process during research
- help you when it comes to your writing (academic writing)

understanding what you need to do

> the following (descriptive) instructions are essentially the same:
>
> **Describe** how the hypothalamus controls body temperature
>
> **Detail** how the hypothalamus controls body temperature
>
> **Show** how the hypothalamus controls body temperature
>
> **Illustrate** how the hypothalamus controls body temperature
>
> (even if the last two invite you more clearly to draw something as well as write, the information you provide will be the same for all)

> the following (discursive) essay titles are essentially the same:
>
> **Assess** Arendt's view of human rights
>
> **Discuss** Arendt's view of human rights
>
> **Evaluate** Arendt's view of human rights
>
> **Analyse** Arendt's view of human rights
>
> **Appraise** Arendt's view of human rights
>
> **Critically assess** Arendt's view of human rights
>
> **Critically discuss** Arendt's view of human rights
>
> (even if the last two emphasise that you need to give your own ideas, the information you provide will be the same for all)

Don't waste your time trying to decode all these command words in order to break down and understand an essay question. You will come to the same conclusion: you will need to describe or discuss or, most commonly, do both.

To address the descriptive instructions above, you can ask these questions:

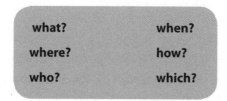

what?   when?

where?   how?

who?   which?

To address the discursive instructions above, you can ask these questions:

why?

so what?

what if?

There are certain tasks that require only description. One example is when you are asked to provide a definition of something. The definition needs to be a clear and precise statement. Another example is when you are writing a research method. The method needs to be accurately described so that it could be replicated. Written work that requires discussion can also include descriptive parts (statements of fact etc.), but the discussion addresses the 3 key discursive questions. These questions are essential to critical thinking and critical writing. They are explained in more detail in subunit 4.5.

thinking about the information and ideas you read during research

The various instructions to describe or discuss in assignment questions refer directly to the type of work you will produce once you have completed your research. This work is usually in the form of academic writing (in an essay or report) but it can also be a visual presentation (see subunit 8.12) or a speech.

But when you research, you will be processing (usually reading) description or discussion. It is useful to be aware of this distinction because when you read well-written academic sources by experts in the field, your tendency might be to simply accept what is stated as fact. Even experts make claims that can be challenged. Critical thinking requires you to ask questions. When you read something, ask yourself:

1. Am I reading description (a clear statement of facts)?

2. Am I reading discussion (the ideas and opinions of the writer)?

Below are two extracts from student's academic work. The first (Dhital, 2015) is a good example of description in academic writing. It is taken from a paper investigating interventions into the consumption of alcohol. The second (Giuffrida, 2009) is a good example of discussion in academic writing. It is taken from a paper examining the concept of accountability.

Example 1 (description):

These theories, which informed the development of alcohol brief intervention (BI), were applied in early studies presented in a review paper by Bien (Bien et al., 1993). One of the BI studies included two sessions with a physician, an approach designed to implement the counselling style of motivational interviewing (MI) in a BI format (Drinker's Check-Up) (Miller et al., 1988). Bien's review also presented the acronym FRAMES (Feedback, Responsibility, Advice, Menu, Empathy, Self-efficacy) to be used as a guide when delivering a brief alcohol intervention (Bien et al., 1993).

Example 2 (discussion):

This vision of accountability recalls the transmission-belt model, with legitimacy moving up the belt and accountability down the belt. The link between involvement and greater responsibility reveals that the Commission maintains a vision of accountability subject to a reinforced separation of powers. Greater participation would lead to greater accountability only to the extent that responsibilities are more clearly allocated among the governance actors. The Commission used this principle to shield its disguised goal of reinforcing the primacy of its executive function from the interference of other bodies, such as comitology committees.

In the first example, the writer is clearly stating facts and references the sources of these facts. In the second, the writer is giving opinions, suggesting outcomes and explanations. Both are potentially the kind of academic source you might read for an assignment. If you were to make notes from them, you would be taking facts (description) from the first and opinions and ideas (discussion) from the second. However, you could critically question both sources.

Recognising the difference between description and discussion can help you develop your own ideas and help you to write. This is explained, as a key strategy, in the next subunit.

description and discussion in academic writing

⭐ the aim

This strategy links the principles of critical thinking with the practical task of academic writing. It does this by dividing all writing into two categories: description and discussion. Its aim is to help you improve the quality of both your descriptive and your discursive (or analytical) writing.

ℹ️ why this can help you

This strategy can help you:

- distinguish between description (descriptive writing) and discussion (discursive or analytical writing)
- recognise good and poor description in your academic writing
- be discursive (or analytical) in your thinking and writing

Some students describe but do not discuss. Some students discuss but don't make it clear what they are discussing. In order to gain the highest grades, you will need to combine description and discussion effectively in your written work. This strategy defines description and discussion and provides a quick and easy way to generate discussion by asking the 3 key discursive questions:

> why?   so what?   what if?

The strategy also introduces the third element of academic writing: evidence. It shows how description, discussion and the use of evidence (that references description and supports discussion) are combined in academic writing.

⚙️ the strategy

When you read something, you are either reading description (facts) or discussion (ideas). When you write something, you can either describe or discuss. This division is the basis for this practical strategy, so it is useful to start by clarifying the difference between description and discussion.

description in academic writing

When you describe something in writing, you provide factual information. This information can be in many forms, including labels of drawings, statistics, dates, quotes, quantities, measurements, ideas, models or definitions. Description in academic writing is at least one of the following:

- it is observable (it can be seen or imagined)
- it is quantifiable (it can be measured)
- it is verifiable (it can be shown, beyond reasonable doubt, to be a fact)

Here are two examples of sentences that describe:

> Zero degrees centigrade is the equivalent of 32 degrees Fahrenheit.
> Tokyo is a complex, bustling metropolis, teeming with life at high speed.

These two statements cannot really be disputed. The first is a simple statement of factual knowledge, the second is a more creative description of what most people would accept to be true. They are both good, grammatically correct sentences. The important difference between them is that the first example gives precise detail, the second does not.

The following two examples describe the same thing:

> When text is read, information is obtained during the very short period in which the eye is fixated on the page. The amount of information that is assimilated will vary, but it has been estimated that an educated adult recognises fewer letters to the left of the central point of fixation than to the right.
>
> ---
>
> When text is read, information is obtained visually during the period in which the eye is fixated, approximately 250 milliseconds (Eysenck, 1993). The amount of information (in the form of single letters or graphemes) that is assimilated will vary, but it has been estimated that an educated adult reader recognises approximately 18 letters, 3 or 4 to the left of the central point of fixation, 15 to the right (Eysenck, 1993; Gaspar and Brown, 1973).

Again, both extracts are written properly. They consist of grammatically correct sentences and use an appropriate level of formal English. However, the second extract is stronger as a piece of academic writing because it gives precise detail. It also includes academic references.

The improvements you can make in your descriptive writing sometimes only happen after you have written a first draft. When you reread your work, you should ask whether more relevant and precise detail can be added or whether the existing writing can be made more accurate and precise.

It is quite common to find poor description in the first sentences of paragraphs. This might be because students have been told that paragraphs move from the general to the specific. This can be true, but if possible, it is better to start an academic paragraph with a specific point and move to even more specific points.

Some first sentences of paragraphs are like superfluous headings or thoughts that have found their way onto the page. In the example below, simply removing the unnecessary first sentence makes the writing stronger.

We should also consider credibility theory because it has an important role to play in effecting defined outcomes. It states that the more committed the principal is to certain policy outcomes, the more likely it is to empower expert agents with greater discretion to achieve the stated outcomes.

Credibility theory states that the more committed the principal is to certain policy outcomes, the more likely it is to empower expert agents with greater discretion to achieve the stated outcomes.

You should bear in mind that some first sentences of paragraphs are intentionally used to introduce the subject of the paragraph (these are sometimes called 'topic sentences') but when you edit your written work, look out for weak first sentences of paragraphs. Look out for sentences that could be made more precise by adding detail. Try to eliminate general words like 'a lot', 'many', 'a few' or 'some' (see subunit 5.2). Try to replace them with more accurate measurements, words or phrases.

As well as being precise, descriptive writing needs to be relevant. Student essays and other written assignments often include too much irrelevant description. Students may feel that they have to establish their knowledge or define all their terms. But, being relevant to the task means answering or addressing a specific question or meeting all the requirements of an assignment brief.

You rarely achieve high grades in academic assessments by writing lengthy descriptions. When you break down an essay question or brief, your aim is to identify the question within the topic (see subunit 6.3). This will help you to determine what is relevant. The greater your subject knowledge, the more likely you are to produce a high level of work. But for most essays, knowledge needs to be applied, not just stated. However, there are many academic tasks that require good description (see table below). For example, some essays explicitly require you to define terms before you answer a question. This is common in disciplines like Law and Philosophy.

Most students find description easier than discussion, but they can also make improvements in their descriptive writing. The instruction 'tighten up your writing' means make it shorter. It means cut out irrelevant detail. It means make it more precise and accurate.

in academic writing good description is:

- **precise and accurate**   - **relevant to the task**

poor description is:

- general and vague   - not relevant to the task

Some academic writing tasks need only, or mostly, good description. This table outlines some common examples and gives references to subunits in this book where you can find more details of how to write them well.

task	descriptive content	unit
abstract	An abstract is a concise report of what you have already written in the body of a paper. It is a precise description of what exists. The abstract might contain a summary of your argument, but it is a statement of your argument, not a discussion of it.	subunit 8.5
reflective writing	Reflective essays contain description and discussion. The descriptive parts give details of an observed event or experience, and descriptions of feelings or thoughts. These descriptions need to be concise as well as accurate because most marks in reflection are given for discussion.	unit 7
method	A research method is written so that it can be replicated. Describing a method therefore requires precise details like accurate measurements and clear processes. A method is usually called a 'methodology' when it includes discursive parts like justifications and limitations. But a method does not discuss what was done, it describes it clearly, step by step, like a recipe.	subunit 8.8
search strategy	Like a research method, a search strategy (a compulsory part of systematic reviews) is written so that it can be replicated. It tells the reader the decisions and steps made in searching for information. Some search strategies may require you to justify the choices you have made (e.g., why a certain database was chosen), this part would be a form of discussion.	subunit 8.10
results	Longer reports tend to separate the results (or findings) from the discussion of results. When displaying results, description can be used to highlight trends or patterns in the results. The causes and consequences of the results are left for the discussion section.	subunit 8.9
(exam) short answer questions	Most short answer questions ask you to list or state or illustrate. These are clear indications that you should describe with precise terms or sufficient detail. Some short answer questions may also require the discussion or application of facts.	subunit 9.5
site survey or study area data	In a research report, a site survey describes relevant details of a location (like a geographical site or an institution) where the research took place. A site survey can also be carried out before research, to assess the suitability of a site. In this case, the information collected is descriptive, the assessment is discursive.	subunit 8.8
There will almost always be a word (or page) limit for descriptive academic tasks such as these, so any detail included must be relevant to the task.		

Descriptive writing still requires critical thinking and questioning, because you need to make sure that the source of information or ideas is reliable. To do this, you will usually need to reference the information you provide (see subunit 5.9). Sometimes, you will be asked to assess the quality of the source you are referencing (see subunit 8.11).

Because many students find description easier to write than discussion, there can be too much descriptive writing (too much irrelevant detail) and little or no analysis. This can lead to tutor comments like 'you need to develop this point' or 'you need to go into more detail here'. These kinds of comments are usually asking for more discussion.

Most academic assignments mix description and discussion, so as well as good description, good discussion is essential. When you are writing a discursive piece, a good rule of thumb is: don't describe what you can't discuss. In other words, don't give the reader information without showing how and why it is relevant to the task. Some students don't really understand what discussion or analysis means. This is explained next.

discussion in academic writing

Discussion consists of ideas. These ideas can be opinions, arguments, theories, models, reasons and concepts. Ideas can be mental representations of any kind. If you were asked to discuss something, how would you do it, how would you produce your own ideas? Ideas don't just form, they form in relation to something else and the best way to generate ideas is to question things. In critical thinking you ask questions about the information and ideas that you read, see or hear. In academic writing, you write down some of your answers.

Here are two statements you might read when researching an essay on Picasso:

Between 1901 and 1904 Picasso predominantly used different shades of blue and green in his paintings. This was described later as his Blue Period.
Picasso's emotional state after the death of his friend Casagemas manifested itself in the paintings of the Blue Period.

The first statement is factual (information). It can't be disputed, so you can't disagree with it. The second is an opinion (idea) and you can either agree or disagree with it. But you can discuss both by asking the 3 simple, key discursive questions: why?, so what? and what if? Asking these questions will generate some ideas and can lead to other useful questions:

Between 1901 and 1904 Picasso predominantly used different shades of blue and green in his paintings. This was subsequently described as his Blue Period.

Why did Picasso use a monochromatic approach to painting in these years?
What was the effect on Picasso (and his critics and reviewers) of his Blue Period?
What if Picasso had painted differently in this period?

Picasso's emotional state after the death of his friend Casagemas manifested itself in the paintings of the Blue Period.

Why does (the author think) Casagemas' death marked the beginning of the Blue Period?
What were the (artistic) consequences of the Blue Period, what did it lead to?
What if Casagemas had not committed suicide, would Picasso have had a Blue Period?

The table below gives more details about the three key discursive questions. Asking them is a quick and easy form of critical thinking. It generates ideas from facts or from the ideas and opinions of others. You don't have to answer all the questions and you don't have to ask them in any order. Sometimes the questions aren't relevant, sometimes there aren't any obvious answers and sometimes the answers overlap. This doesn't matter. What matters is that you ask the questions to generate good ideas and discussion that are relevant to your task.

WHY?

When you ask this question of a fact, you are really asking two questions in one. When you ask why something was done in a certain way or why something exists in a certain form, you can ask:
 	
● What is the **aim** or **purpose** of something?
  (e.g. Why was Gibbs' reflective model designed to include 6 steps?)
 	
● What is the **origin** or **cause** of something?
  (e.g. Why did parliament pass the Prisoners Act in 1913?)
  (e.g. Why was the enzyme catalysis less than expected?)

SO WHAT?
When you ask this question of a fact, you are asking what did or could something lead to. In other words, you consider the: (potential) **consequences**, **implications** or **outcomes** of something. The consequences of a property or an action can be positive or negative, beneficial or harmful, theoretical or practical. Sometimes, there is no significant change, so an action could be inconsequential or ineffective.

WHAT IF?

When you ask this question, you can consider three things. You can think about an **alternative** to something, make a **comparison**, or consider the **absence** of something.
 	
● **alternatives (comparison)**
  (e.g. If we used something else or applied a different method, then what would happen?)
 	
● **absence**
  (e.g. If something hadn't happened, or wasn't available, what would the outcome have been like? Would it have been different?)

You shouldn't treat these questions as a checklist. The aim is to encourage enquiry and to use the useful outcomes of that enquiry in the discursive parts of your academic work.

discussion and evidence in academic writing

When you discuss something, you are not stating facts. Depending on the strength of your argument, people might agree or disagree with you. Your discussion (your ideas) can come from your own observations and thoughts. However, discussion at the academic level is stronger when it uses objective evidence. Evidence supports your discussion. The stronger the evidence, the more compelling your point of view will be. Here is an example of discussion:

The three elements that gave life to the modernist movement in architecture were concrete, steel and glass. Add to these the new construction techniques of the time and we have a matter-of-fact explanation of why buildings changed their shape so dramatically in the United States and in Europe at the beginning of the twentieth century. The underlying philosophies of modernism had evolved as part of the Enlightenment project, but they would have been redundant without these new materials and the innovative methods that had been developed to put them together. Practical engineers, not fanciful architects, made architectural modernism a reality.

The paragraph is well written. The writer makes a lot of statements and claims. The writer's point of view is clear, and it might be a valid one. But there is no evidence to support the position taken. The writing could be described as 'opinionated'. This extract is like a written piece you might find in a newspaper column or a magazine article. It does not meet the highest standards of good discursive academic writing, because it lacks evidence.

Evidence is what you reference in your work. Evidence is factual. In discussion, it can be used to support an argument, show something is true or persuade the reader that your ideas are valid. Evidence comes in many forms, but it is drawn from four sources:

1. **theory**: reliable sources of academic theory

2. **research**: up-to-date, peer reviewed research

3. **policy**: official documents

4. **practice**: examples of practical experience, events, actions

Academic writing can therefore be understood as an interplay between description (information), discussion (ideas) and evidence.

You can use this strategy to help you write academic paragraphs (see subunit 5.6).

The ideas in this subunit have been put together in an easy to reference model of description and discussion in academic writing. The model is a summary designed to help you review and remember these ideas. You can download it from www.macmillanhie.com/lia-sys.

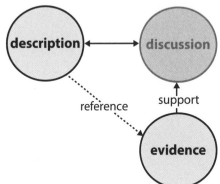

unit 5

academic writing

There can be a barrier between thinking and writing. Because academic writing has a lot of rules and conventions, this barrier can seem more difficult to overcome and some students do not enjoy the process of putting thoughts into writing. If you apply the rules of grammar and punctuation, your academic writing will improve. But much of this work can be done after writing, when you edit or proofread. Although some important conventions are explained, the primary aim of this unit is to help you write by using your own voice and by applying strategies (like the Paragraph Buster!) if you get stuck or don't know how to proceed. The unit presents ideas to help you:

- learn and use good words
- learn to write simple sentences
- understand how to build paragraphs

Your academic writing will only improve with practice, but effective practice needs a goal, and so the unit begins by outlining the requirements and purpose of academic writing.

5.1 what is academic writing?

Academic writing describes the style and form of writing that you are required to produce for academic assignments. A knowledge of academic writing and how it is different from non-academic writing can help you understand and therefore remember some of the rules that are presented later in this unit. Academic writing is writing for:

- a specific audience (your tutor or an examiner)
- a specific goal (usually to answer a question)

Your academic writing should aim to meet these 9 fundamental requirements:

1 structure	Academic writing is arranged in a set structure. There are many different structures. The most commonly used is the essay. But not all written work is in the form of an essay. Lab reports, dissertations and literature reviews all have their own structures. The structure can help you with the order and content, and it is a principle of this book to make sure that you know what you are doing before you start researching or writing. Another thing to know is the word limit (or page limit). Nearly all written academic assignments have a specific word limit and you can be penalised if you exceed it.
2 format	Academic writing should be well presented and correctly formatted. The formatting requirements are often given to you in detail. These instructions are sometimes called 'the terms of reference'. They state things like the required font, the font size and the line spacing. Make sure you know the terms of reference before you start writing. You can use your preferred word processor settings when you write but make sure you format the work correctly before submitting it.
3 grammar, punctuation, spelling	Academic writing applies the rules of grammar. You can lose marks for poor grammar and bad spelling. You don't need to write long sentences and you shouldn't try to mimic an 'academic style' of writing, but you need to proofread your work before submitting it. See step 10 in subunit 6.2 for strategies on proofreading.
4 vocabulary	The words used in academic writing tend to be longer than those in informal writing. But it's not the length of the words that counts, it's the accuracy of meaning. Try to use the correct word rather than a long word. The vocabulary used is formal, so avoid colloquialisms, conversational language, informal or slang words (see subunit 5.2).

5 terminology	The correct use of terminology makes academic writing stronger. 'Terminology' refers to words that have a subject-specific application and meaning. Academic writing makes use of the appropriate terms so that you don't need to keep explaining or defining ideas that both you and your reader understand. At first, some terms can seem quite daunting. But once they are in your long-term memory, they become 'normal' words. Learning and using some key terms is one way to improve your academic writing (see subunit 5.4).
6 explicitness	The aim of academic writing is to set out information or ideas clearly and with no hidden meanings. It can be difficult to decide how much you need to explain, especially if you have a lot of ideas. You might think that the connection between your ideas is obvious, but it may not be obvious in your writing. In solving a maths problem, you normally show the working out, step by step, and you should think about applying this idea to academic writing so that your written thoughts are clear to your reader.
7 objectivity	Apart from reflective or creative writing, academic writing is objective. It is free from personal feelings and emotions. It is unbiased. It is the product of critical thinking (see unit 4). When you are asked to take a stance or present an argument, your academic writing is stronger when it is supported with evidence.
8 referencing	Academic writing requires accurate and consistent referencing. Your work should apply the rules of the referencing system you have been asked to follow. There are numerous referencing systems (see subunit 5.9) and now there are also many freely available referencing software programs to help you reference your work correctly.
9 learning and understanding	One aim of academic writing is to improve your knowledge, so your writing should show the understanding and learning that comes from research. One way of doing this is to apply and reference academic sources. You need to show your reader that you have read or researched widely.

You will not be expected to produce the highest level of academic writing at the beginning of your course. You can only become a good writer through practice. If you understand and address the nine fundamental requirements in the table above, your academic writing will get stronger. Many courses use formative assignments to help you develop your writing. Formative assignments (as opposed to summative assignments) do not count towards your final grade, but they are useful learning tools. They inform you. They allow you to learn through your mistakes without being penalised.

To improve your writing further, there are several conventions you can consider. The table below lists 15 directives. Don't try to memorise them all at once. You can't approach your writing with a head full of rules and many of the weaknesses in your writing will only become apparent when you proofread it or when you get feedback on an assignment.

1	don't use 'I', 'we' or 'you' (unless you are writing a reflective piece)	
2	don't use the apostrophe to abbreviate words	
3	don't repeat yourself by using two words that say the same thing	
4	don't write single sentence paragraphs	
5	don't use too many direct questions	
6	don't use jokes or puns	
7	don't be general when you can be precise	
8	don't use the exclamation mark!	
9	don't use colloquial or conversational language or slang	
10	don't use etc. when the extra information is not obvious	
11	don't use the / symbol to separate words with similar meanings	
12	don't confuse e.g. with i.e.	
13	don't use emotive phrases (except in reflective or creative writing)	
14	don't use acronyms that you haven't spelt out	
15	don't use quotes and repeat what they say in your own words	

These 15 points are explained in more detail (with examples) in subunit 5.2.

caution: the tone of academic writing

The best way to understand tone is to imagine how your writing will 'sound' to your reader. This book, for example, has an informal tone. Tone expresses your attitude in writing, and this is controlled by the words, formats and structures you use. Academic writing has a formal tone. It is not showy and flamboyant in the way creative writing can be. It is controlled and disciplined. It is regulated and well ordered. An important principle that helps you achieve this tone is caution. Compare these statements:

A change in the current policy will **undoubtedly lead** to an increase in infection rates.

A change in the current policy **could** lead to an increase in infection rates.

The first sentence lacks caution. It may be that the writer goes on to support the statement and shows beyond any reasonable doubt that a change in policy will increase infection. In academic writing, an argument is stronger and more persuasive if it is based on reliable sources of evidence and considers alternative positions and viewpoints. However, it is rare that any idea, point of view or argument can be proved beyond doubt.

Caution does not mean that you cannot make strong statements. You can be more certain in your phrasing when the evidence is substantial. However, you would need to provide incontrovertible supporting evidence before writing a sentence like this one:

> The failure of the military campaign **can be directly attributed to** poor intelligence, lack of leadership and inadequate equipment.

Caution in academic writing would favour a sentence like this:

> There is strong evidence to suggest that poor intelligence, lack of leadership and inadequate equipment were major causes of the failed military campaign.

Caution does not mean that you can't take a stance. It means not jumping to conclusions or using the emotionally and personally persuasive language that you might find in a poem, political pamphlet or newspaper editorial.

an example of academic writing with common faults

The paragraph below does not contain any grammar, punctuation or spelling errors. The writer's point of view is clear. A good reference is used as evidence. However, it is not a good example of academic writing. The paragraph could be improved by addressing the 10 issues highlighted:

Annotation	Text
vague language (5.2 point 7)	A lot of children commence education at the age of 4 or younger. In the past, children started school at five but now it is customary to start at an earlier age. This
abbreviation of number 4	
apostrophe: abbreviation of 'it is' (5.2 point 2)	is because mothers need to go back to work and they think it's beneficial for their children to attend school. Can this really have a positive effect on children's
too many direct questions (5.2 point 5)	
colloquial language (5.2 point 9)	learning? Can it be good for parents? Can it be useful for society? According to Jenkins (2005), early schooling can cause kids to become 'removed from the productive source of their basic needs'. Jenkins argues that the lack of close and regular contact with the mother may negatively impact on early language
incorrect reference, a quote needs a page number (see subunit 5.9)	
unclear what etc. refers to (5.2 point 10)	development and the ability to form stable, emotional bonds etc. The results of Jenkins' research proves beyond doubt that children's learning would improve if
lack of caution in writing	
repetition of word with same meaning (tautology) (5.2 point 3)	mothers stayed at home to look after them in these crucial and important, formative years. Jenkins supports the idea that mothers should receive a government subsidy. However, I do not agree.
use of first person 'I' (5.2 point 1)	

academic writing: 15 points to consider

The 15 points detailed here highlight common weaknesses found in some academic writing. They are not described as 'errors' because they are not necessarily addressing mistakes or broken rules. But if you apply these ideas to your writing, it will improve. You don't need to try and memorise these points. If you don't know them already, they will become familiar through practice. Many of the improvements you can make will only happen when you proofread. If you want to review a list of these points, you can use the outline table in subunit 5.1. It may be useful to read this list just before proofreading your written work.

1. don't use 'I', 'we' or 'you' (unless you are writing a reflective piece)

It's easy not to use 'I' in your writing. In an essay, anything you write that isn't referenced to somebody else or isn't common knowledge belongs to you, the writer. Simply take away the part of the sentence that includes 'I'.

> I think Marx was correct when he described capitalism as one step in the process of political change.
>
> **make your statement (and then support it with evidence):**
>
> Marx was correct when he described capitalism as one step in the process of political change.

Some students replace 'I' with 'one' or 'the author'. But these are just other forms of what is called 'the first person'. You would normally use the first person only when you are writing a reflective piece or when you have been specifically instructed to do so. If in doubt, ask the person who set the assessment.

Some writers use 'we' because it connects the writer with the reader. Although it isn't against the rules, it is better to avoid it. It can sound presumptuous (the reader might not agree with you) and too familiar.

> Hence, we can understand that the most important part of the system is stress testing.
>
> **make your statement (and then support it with evidence):**
>
> The most important part of the system is stress testing.

When a sentence contains 'you', it sounds vague. The reader may not understand who 'you' refers to. In academic writing, replace 'you' with specific details of what or who it stands for.

> A graduated pipette can help you measure more accurately.
>
> **specify what 'you' stands for:**
>
> A graduated pipette can help clinicians and clinical researchers measure more accurately.

2. don't use the apostrophe to abbreviate words

In English, words that are shortened with an apostrophe are called 'contractions'. In academic writing, always write the words out in full. For example:

won't = will not	can't = cannot	isn't = is not
didn't = did not	don't = do not	they're = they are

Most contractions end …n't, so you can check for them by using the 'Replace' feature when you proofread. Word processing programs allow you to choose different grammar and spelling options and set them at different levels of formality. If you use a program regularly for your academic writing, change the settings so that contractions are highlighted or replaced automatically.

3. don't repeat yourself by using two words that mean the same thing

When you repeat a word or a phrase that says the same thing, it's called a 'tautology'. You can often write tautologies without realising. Perhaps you feel that you want to emphasise something, or you can't decide which of two words is the best one to use. You should look out for tautologies when you proofread your work and select the most accurate word.

> The BBC corporation was founded in 1922.
> It is useful and beneficial to compare the two approaches.
> Asimov was a highly productive and prolific writer.
>
> **choose the right word or phrase:**
>
> The BBC was founded in 1922.
> It is useful to compare the two approaches.
> Asimov was a prolific writer.

4. don't write single sentence paragraphs

The average length of paragraphs in undergraduate academic writing is 150–200 words. A sentence that stands alone needs to be added to an existing paragraph or made into a paragraph by adding more sentences. If you state a fact, you will usually be expected to add more information to it (inform the reader) or discuss it (develop the idea). See building a paragraph with description and discussion (subunit 5.6).

5. don't use too many direct questions

You can pose questions in your academic writing, but generally you should avoid listing lots of questions one after the other, even if you are going to answer them in the written text that follows.

6. don't use jokes or puns

Even if your lecturers and tutors use humour in lectures and tutorials, you shouldn't replicate this in written assignments.

7. don't be general when you can be precise

Academic writing presents precise information by using accurate language. Words that are used to describe something in general terms (often quantities), can make your writing sound vague. Whenever possible, you should replace vague words with more precise words.

> **reconsider your use of words and phrases like:**
>
> • many • a lot • a great number • a large number
>
> • a considerable amount • big • huge • massive • little • a few
>
> • a small number • not many • a handful of • very • quite

You might be able to replace the general word with a specific quantity or a name, or you might have to scrap or rewrite the sentence.

> In the last decade, the population has grown by a considerable amount.
>
> There was a big difference between the sides in terms of fighting men.
>
> Some academics argue that Freud's seminal work continues to influence thinking today.
>
> **be as specific as you can:**
>
> Since 2009, the UK population has increased by five million.
>
> The British had a quarter of a million troops, the Boers no more than sixty thousand.
>
> Smith (2014) and Jones (2019) argue that Freud's seminal work continues to influence current thinking.

A general statement can appear as the first sentence of a paragraph. This is followed by a sentence with more detail. But paragraphs can often be improved by replacing the first sentence with the second.

> Thousands died in the Somme offensive. Twenty thousand British soldiers …
>
> Research recommends the use of hydroxyapatite for bone implants. Wilson et al. (2017) make recommendations for …
>
> **don't start with a general point when you can start with a specific one:**
>
> Twenty thousand British soldiers were killed on the first day of the Somme offensive.
>
> Wilson et al. (2017) make recommendations for the use of hydroxyapatite for bone implants.

8. don't use the exclamation mark!

The exclamation mark is used in writing to indicate things like exaggeration, emphasis, humour or irony. Unless it is part of a quote, it shouldn't be used in academic writing.

9. don't use colloquial or conversational language or slang

A colloquial or conversational style gives an informal tone to your writing and academic writing should be formal. This principle can be one of the hardest to implement because in trying to make a word or phrase sound more formal, you might replace a good word with an inappropriate one. Formal writing does not mean that sentences have to be complex and that words have to be long. It is always better to be clear in your academic writing than to try and sound formal. You should avoid:

- using words that you don't know the meaning of
- trying to show off or bluff
- imitating the academic style of something you have read

When you write, use your voice to guide you. Writing out exactly what you say or think (transcribing) can help you get ideas on paper. For example, in the first draft of an essay, it is not only acceptable to write informally, it can be an effective strategy.

There are degrees of formality in writing. Some informal language is easy to recognise and change while other instances are less obvious. Trying to think about writing formally can prevent you putting your thoughts on paper. You should avoid highly informal language (like slang) when you write, but other levels of informality can be dealt with when you proofread.

highly informal (slang): I done some research.

Mums and dads rocked up.

informal: Research was done.

Mums and dads came.

The tyre was blown up.

formal: Research was carried out.

Mothers and fathers arrived.

The tyre was inflated.

10. don't use etc. when the extra information is not obvious

The abbreviation 'etc.' (et cetera) means 'and so on' or 'and other things'. It is used to indicate items in a group or list that have intentionally been omitted. It should only be used when these unlisted items are obvious to the reader. The abbreviation should also have a full stop after it (etc.). But if it is the last thing in a sentence, you only need one full stop. Because academic writing should be precise, it might be better to avoid using this abbreviation at all. But if you want to use it, use it correctly.

> **look out for incorrect uses of etc. like these:**
> Research samples were taken from the five great American lakes (Superior, Huron etc.).
> Alcohol abuse has been linked with consequences such as obesity and organ failure etc.

11. don't use the / symbol to separate words with similar meanings

In academic writing, the forward slash (formally known as a 'virgule') can be used to divide two words that are different when you want to show that both or either could apply in the context of a sentence. Here are two examples of it being used correctly:

> Academic writing consists of description and/or discussion.
> The tutor will then give his/her recommendations.

But using this symbol in writing looks clumsy and it sometimes complicates the meaning of a sentence. It is best to avoid it whenever possible and rephrase the sentence. The symbol should never be used for two words that have the same or similar meanings.

> It is useful/beneficial to consider both approaches.
>
> The evidence disproves/invalidates Smith's hypothesis.
>
> **choose the best word:**
>
> It is useful to consider both approaches.
>
> The evidence invalidates Smith's hypothesis.

12. don't confuse e.g. with i.e.

Two abbreviations that are sometimes misused are:

- e.g. = for example
- i.e. = that is, in other words

You can use e.g. as an abbreviation when you provide an example of something but consider using the term 'for example' instead.

> Students should select only one of the recognised clinical skills, e.g. hand-washing, and discuss it with reference to national guidelines.
>
> **usually it's better to avoid the abbreviation:**
>
> Students should select only one of the recognised clinical skills, for example handwashing, and discuss it with reference to national guidelines.

You can use 'i.e.' to clarify or reiterate something but it is better to avoid it wherever possible and write the explanation in sentence form instead.

> Students can choose any of the four gospels (i.e. Matthew, Mark, Luke or John) for the close reading.
>
> **usually it's better to avoid the abbreviation:**
>
> Students can choose Matthew, Mark, Luke or John for the close reading.

13. don't use emotive phrases (except in reflective writing)

Academic writing is objective and should avoid bias and displays of emotion. However, words that carry emotional significance can be powerful. If used appropriately, they can give your writing impact and make it more interesting to read. But you should at least be aware of the emotive words you use.

> Sadly, the unemployment rate has increased in the last twelve months.
>
> **minimise your personal feelings:**
>
> The unemployment rate has increased by 5% in the last twelve months.
>
> **but you can write things like:**
>
> The fourteenth-century plague was given a terrifying name: the Black Death.

14. don't use acronyms that you haven't spelt out

Acronyms are abbreviations that use the initial letters (or some of the letters) from the full form of the word. Strictly speaking, abbreviations are only called 'acronyms' if the abbreviation can be pronounced as a word or words. Otherwise, there is no difference between an acronym and an abbreviation that uses initials. Here are some examples of acronyms and abbreviations:

> NATO (North Atlantic Treaty Organization)
>
> NICE (National Institute for Health and Care Excellence)
>
> USA (United States of America)
>
> NMC (Nursing and Midwifery Council)

The first time you use an acronym or abbreviation in your writing, you should use the full form with the abbreviation in brackets. Subsequently, you can just use the abbreviation. This does not apply to commonly known abbreviations (such as the USA). If in doubt, just follow the rule.

15. don't use quotes and repeat what they say in your own words

If you use a quote in your academic writing, you can clarify it, expand on it or add to it in the sentences that follow. But don't repeat it by putting the same meaning into your own words (paraphrasing).

> **avoid saying the same thing twice:**
>
> According to Stein, 'right hemisphere specialisation evolved for the accurate sequencing of locations in space … not for the purposes of reading' (1991 p. 39). Therefore, the right hemisphere of the brain did not evolve in order to help us read but to enable us to move in space.

5.3 the building blocks of academic writing

There are 4 building blocks of academic writing: words, sentences, paragraphs and thoughts. You need to use the right words, structure proper sentences and build coherent paragraphs but if you have nothing to say, you will have nothing to write. However, there can be a barrier between thinking and writing.

Your thoughts will change. The ideas you have when you start research are likely to be different from those you have when you start writing. Researching and writing are different tasks, so it is useful to separate them and do a period of research and note making before writing. Good note making can be a route to good writing. One way to tackle difficulties with writing is to reconsider the way you make notes. Unit 3 presents some strategies that can ultimately make putting ideas into writing easier.

In this model, the blue shaded boxes show the 4 building blocks of academic writing.

An improvement in any of these will mean an improvement in your academic written work.

The challenge you face is to put your thoughts into good writing and this unit presents strategies designed to help you do this.

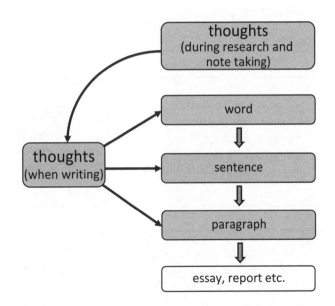

Knowing the principles and aims of academic writing before you start working can help you take better notes and guide your writing. However, many of the rules and conventions can be applied when you edit and proofread. There are numerous programs that can help you with grammar, punctuation and spelling. Some are free or partially free. Some of the best known are Grammarly, MS Word, Reverso, Ginger, Google Docs, WhiteSmoke, Hemingway Editor and Grammar Slammer. These programs have advanced features that will identify your errors and show you how to avoid them.

Seeing, understanding and correcting your own mistakes can be a better way of learning than trying to apply abstract rules. When you write, especially when you make notes and write first drafts, you should focus on getting your ideas down on paper without being afraid of making grammar or spelling mistakes.

Here is some useful advice about writing. This is followed by strategies for working with words, sentences and paragraphs.

The process of putting your thoughts into words is not easy. Everybody has difficulty breaking down the barrier between thinking and writing.

If you're not sure what you're talking about or what you want to say, the only thing that will be clear in your writing is that you are bluffing.

Don't write what you don't understand. Don't use words you don't know the meaning of.

If you understand a question clearly, it will be easier to research and write. Only start a task when you have understood the question.

When you write, keep focused on the question. Focus, focus, focus and then, when you start to lose focus, step back and refocus.

Learn the structure of simple sentences. Practise writing them often.

Don't try to imitate an academic style that is not your own. Instead, use your own voice and write simple and clear sentences.

Don't waffle. Address the question from the start. Don't write anything that doesn't have a clear purpose in answering the question.

Aim to make your point with the fewest number of words. Don't repeat the same point.

If you've made a point, add enough information to make it clear, then move on to the next thing.

5.4 learning words visually

⭐ the aim

All academic disciplines make use of subject specific terminology. Some of these terms can initially appear difficult but most of them can be simply defined. This visual strategy aims to help you improve your vocabulary by learning key words in a creative, imaginative and effective way. It aims to take away the fear of using difficult words in your discussions and in your academic writing.

ℹ️ why this can help you

Difficult words can be defined as words that:

- you don't know the meaning of
- you can't work out the meaning of
- you can't remember the meaning of

One way of showing learning and improving your academic writing is to use appropriate terminology relevant to your field of study. Using images can help you understand and remember these key terms. This simple strategy encourages you to process words differently by reformatting them and associating them with drawn pictures and written examples. It is a strategy regularly used by younger students but is equally effective at any level of education. Once you have mastered (understood and remembered) a key term, not only can you start to use it with confidence in your writing, it can act as a trigger word for other words and for thoughts about your topic. If you can make sense of a word, remember it and use it, it ceases to be a difficult word.

⚙️ the strategy

For this strategy, you need a book of unlined pages (A4 is the best) and some words you want to put into your long-term memory. Select words or terms that will be useful for you to know, such as words you come across regularly in your reading or in lectures. These can be terms specific to your subject area or words used in academic writing generally. Don't try to learn too many at once, select a few to start with. In your notebook, you should use one page per word (or one page for two words with opposite or associated meanings).

This is not a spelling strategy, but it can be helpful to break a word down into syllables (or beats), especially if the word is long:

1. Say the word aloud a few times and tap each beat with your hand (if you can't say the word, listen to it online or by using a text reading program).

2. Write down the number of beats before you write down the word.

3. Write down each bit (beat) of the word on the page in clear letters. Take your time, and work on each segment of the word. Different people will separate words differently. There is no right or wrong way of doing this. Just do what you prefer. Do what makes most sense to you.

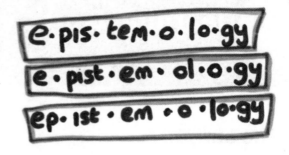

Sounding out a word and breaking it down can help you remember it. For example, the word 'epistemology' (6 beats) can be broken down (sounded out) and written in different ways.

4. If you want to learn the spelling of a word, it is helpful to highlight any unusual features of the word like double letters or silent letters. But only highlight parts of a word you tend to spell incorrectly so you can visually focus on these.

5. Once you have written the word, search for its meaning or definition online or in a dictionary.

6. On a blank sheet of paper, write down the various meanings you come across until you are happy you have found an agreement between them and an understanding of the word. Accessing several concise sources will produce words and phrases commonly used to define the word you are trying to learn.

7. Once you have established the meaning, think how you might link it to the word and represent it in a visual form. It's here that you can use your imagination and creativity. It doesn't matter if you think you can't draw. You are more likely to remember your own images drawn by hand than by using existing pictures. Even if you don't like your handwriting, you should write and draw. This is a personal learning strategy. It is for your eyes only. Once you have mastered a word, you can apply it in your work and show your learning to others.

Here is an example:

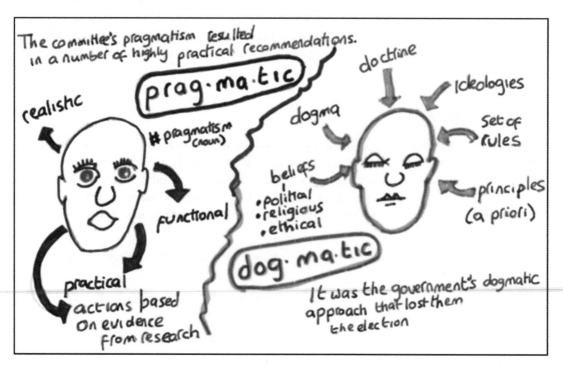

As you add words to your book, don't put them in alphabetical order. Instead, group words that have similar meanings.

Put the words into sentences. Writing your own sentences can also help you learn and remember the word better than using an existing quote. But you can do both. Add these sentences to the page.

Use images. Use colour. Add synonyms (words with similar meanings).

For words that are more difficult to define, you might have to access numerous concise sources before you find a meaning that makes sense. But this will allow you to think about the word and how you are going to represent it visually on the page.

Draw in pencil first so that you can erase anything you don't like.

Some words can be difficult to pin down because they have so many complex associations. Your aim is to identify a basic or fundamental meaning that makes sense to you. This basic understanding is not a general understanding, it should include specific details.

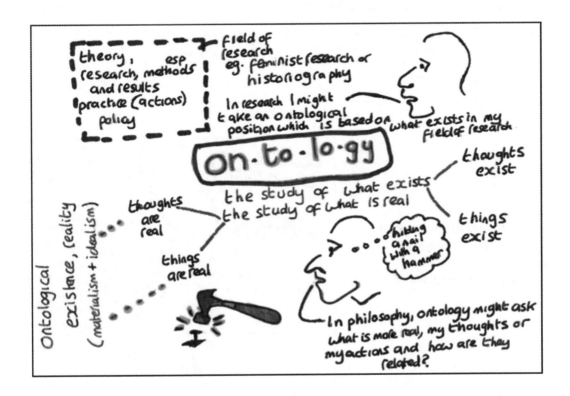

Some people will remember the sound of a word, others will remember the word as a picture.

On some pages, you can put two words. This is especially useful if the words are opposites.

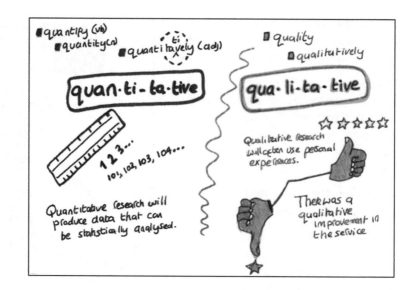

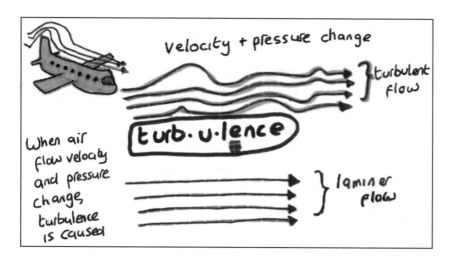

Review the words and consolidate your learning by writing more sentences.

When a word and its fundamental meaning are in your long-term memory, you can use it with confidence in your academic work.

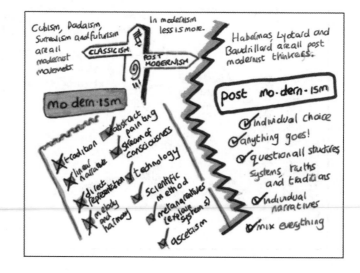

5.5 an easy way to write simple sentences

⭐ the aim

Academic writing can be built by using simple sentence structures. This strategy presents four commonly written sentence structures and aims to show how they can be learned and used without applying the complex rules of English grammar. It is a strategy designed to help students break down the barrier between thinking and writing.

ℹ why this can help you

For some students, learning to write proper sentences can be complicated by having to understand and remember terms like verb, phrasal verb, noun, pronoun, clause, relative clause, indirect object and conjunction. But learning to write sentences can also be made simple. The only terms you need to know for this strategy are ones you already know: subject, capital letter, comma and full stop.

⚙ the strategy

If you look closely at academic writing, you will see that four sentence structures are used regularly to express information and ideas. Identifying, understanding and practising these four structures forms the basis of this strategy. They are presented under the following headings:

1. subject and one thing about the subject

2. subject and two things about the subject

3. adding information at the start of a sentence

4. bracketing information with commas

1. subject and one thing about the subject

The most basic form of the sentence can be called a 'statement sentence'. It states a subject (what the writer is writing about) and one thing about the subject. The subject is written first. The single piece of information about the subject comes next. This can be a fact or an idea. Here are two examples:

Western legal theory has undergone almost three thousand years of development.

Wittgenstein identified sentences as 'atomic' or 'non-atomic'.

This structure can be represented like this:

Subject | one thing about the subject.

91

Here are two more examples of statement sentences:

| Commentators | share the view that constitutional practice weakens ministerial responsibility. |
| Benjamin Bloom | considers evaluation to be the highest representation of learning. |

These sentences make clear and strong statements. They are easy to write. They start with a capital letter and finish with a full stop. They don't need any internal punctuation. You don't even need to worry about whether there is a verb present. If you use your voice and say these kinds of sentences aloud, you will automatically use a verb, even if you don't know what one is.

Sometimes it helps just to get the subject out of your thoughts by writing it down. Then you can think of what you want to say about it. Sometimes, writing a simple, precise statement sentence can help you start a paragraph. If you make a clear statement, the reader is then expecting you to expand on it. If it helps you to get your ideas into writing, you can write a whole series of statement sentences and repeat the subject (or replace it with another word):

The interviews were conducted inside private consultation rooms.

The interviews were conducted in accordance with ethics committee requirements.

The interviews lasted approximately fifteen minutes.

They consisted of ten questions.

You can write a statement sentence, press the return key on your keyboard, move to the next line and write another one. You can leave the sentences like this until you are ready to make them sound better by combining some of them.

In most statement sentences the subject is short and the information about the subject is longer:

| The findings | indicate a preference for an environment with humidity levels at 51 %rh. |

But in some sentences, the subject is longer than the information about it:

| Seven studies undertaken to explore the experience of patients in acute hospital wards | were chosen. |

Sometimes, when writing a basic statement sentence of this type, you might say two things about the subject without realising it. Don't worry. The only thing that matters is that you write the sentence:

| Anxiety | may take the extreme forms of hysteria and the patient can suffer a breakdown. |

If you practise writing basic statement sentences, you will see that most proper sentences only require two things. The first is a subject. The second is some information about the subject. Apart from knowing that you need a capital letter at the start and a full stop at the end, that's it. Sometimes, a statement sentence is all you need and you cannot improve it. If you can master this basic structure, you can begin to build more complex sentences.

2. subject and two things about the subject

The next structure builds on the basic statement sentence by using a joining word or phrase and adding another piece of information about the subject. Here are two examples:

Five researchers piloted the study for two months and then recruited 100 participants.

Modernism rejected the classical form of narrative and called for a new representation.

This structure can be represented like this:

Subject	one thing about the subject	joining word	another thing about the subject.

Here are some more examples:

| Freud | returned to Vienna | and | practised on patients with nervous diseases. |

| Seventy-five per cent of respondents | were male | and | in full-time employment. |

| Intergovernmentalism | emerged as a defence of the role of the nation state |

| in European integration | and | proposed a different vision of Europe. |

| Huxley | considers the premise that each of us is capable of storing every one of our individual experiences | and | that we are able to perceive all events anywhere in the universe. |

Like basic statement sentences, these sentences are easy to construct. Apart from the capital letter and full stop, they don't need any punctuation.

The most common joining words are words like 'and' and 'because'. There are many more, but you don't need to learn a list of these words. Most, if not all of them are already in your long-term memory. Use your voice. Say the sentence aloud and the joining words will come without you having to think about them.

You can use this structure to combine sentences you had previously written as basic statements and left on different lines. For example, these sentences:

> The interviews were conducted inside private consultation rooms.
>
> The interviews were conducted in accordance with ethics committee requirements.
>
> The interviews lasted approximately fifteen minutes.
>
> They consisted of ten questions.

can be put together like this:

> The interviews were conducted inside private consultation rooms and in accordance with ethics committee requirements. They lasted approximately fifteen minutes and consisted of ten questions.

It's easy to see how you can build on this structure by adding a third piece of information about the subject. Here is an example with only the subject and joining words highlighted:

The first Greek written laws were made available for public inspection and the few who could decipher the code now had tangible grounds for appeal while those who could not read would have to depend upon those who could.

This example shows that when you add more information about your subject, other subjects might appear in the sentence. If you were to analyse this sentence grammatically, multiple subjects can be identified ('the first Greek laws', 'the few who could decipher' and 'those who could not read'). So, strictly speaking, you are really adding information about an initial or main subject. But this kind of analysis does not matter. The aim of this strategy is to simplify sentence structure so that you can write proper sentences. State your (initial) subject. Add information about it and don't worry about creating multiple subjects or things like clauses or subclauses.

Don't overload your sentences or give the reader too many things to process at one time. Vary the amount of information you contain in each sentence. Alternate between basic statement sentences and those that say two or (occasionally) three things about the subject.

The two sentence structures presented so far don't contain commas. When you are trying to simplify your writing, don't use commas unless you have a reason to do so. For these two sentence structures you can nearly always get away without using a comma. Word processing or grammar checking software will prompt you when to use commas. This will often be to avoid a misunderstanding when two adjacent words are read without a pause. But don't focus on when to use commas. When you write, focus on getting down the subject and adding one or two pieces of information about the subject.

3. adding information at the start of a sentence

The subject is frequently the first thing that is written at the start of an English sentence. However, sentences often start with extra information about the subject or with a short introductory phrase or word. This extra information is followed by a comma. The subject of the sentence is then stated. Information about the subject is then added. Here are two examples:

In the last fifty years, Europe has experienced unprecedented changes.

When this process was completed, a marking template was developed.

This structure can be represented like this:

Extra information, subject one thing about the subject.

Here are some more examples with just the extra information highlighted:

Once confirmed and corroborated, a hypothesis can only be validated after rigorous testing.

From a theoretical perspective, Smith's work is a form of interpretative analysis.

In the most proficient readers, inner speech helps comprehension.

In many cases, the information that begins the sentence could come at the end of the sentence, so you could move it there if you wanted to:

Inner speech helps comprehension in the most proficient readers.

So, learning this structure provides another way to vary your writing. In many sentences of this type, the extra information is just one or two words:

However, prevention is better than cure.

Not surprisingly, he was in favour of nuclear power.

For example, Picasso used a palette knife whereas Rothko used a brush.

The extra information at the start adds some meaning to the sentence. But, in all cases of sentences with this structure, it could be removed. The sentence would still be correct and make sense although it would be less informative:

In this context, it is impossible to separate patriarchy from culture.

It is impossible to separate patriarchy from culture.

4. bracketing information with commas

The final sentence structure involves the use of two commas to bracket information that is relevant, but not essential, to the meaning of the sentence. Here are three examples:

The cabinet, in its semi-judicial review function, may quash certain decisions.

A scientific law, no matter how well established, is rarely constant.

Theories that point to a more complex distribution of brain functions, across and between hemispheres, give encouragement to readers who rely disproportionately on visual abilities.

In these examples, two commas are used like two brackets placed around some of the text. In fact, you can use brackets instead of commas. An easy way to check that you have used the commas correctly is to block out the text between the commas. The sentence should still be grammatically correct and make sense:

The cabinet , in its semi-judicial review function, may quash certain decisions.

This structure can be represented like this:

Subject, information, one thing about the subject.

The information surrounded by commas can be placed in different parts of the sentence. Sometimes it comes immediately after the subject, sometimes it splits the information that follows the subject. Don't worry about this. If you use your voice and transcribe what you say, most of the time the order of words will be correct. You just need to put the commas in the right place.

Here are some more examples with only the subject highlighted:

The review reported that, despite the intervention of the World Health
Organization, prevalence rates increased in all sites.

Andrew Bonar Law , the only British prime minister not to be born in the British
Isles, was succeeded by Stanley Baldwin.

Recent case law suggests that, in cases of scientific uncertainty, competent authorities
should take responsibility for seeking expert opinion.

This structure allows you to add information to a basic statement sentence already written or to combine two statement sentences into one. For example, these two statement sentences:

The interviews lasted approximately fifteen minutes.

The interviews consisted of ten questions.

can become one sentence:

The interviews, which consisted of ten questions, lasted approximately fifteen minutes.

adding the comma to avoid a misunderstanding

Apart from the comma used to separate information at the start of a sentence and the commas used to bracket information inside the sentence, this strategy aims to minimise the use of punctuation within sentences. But sometimes you may need to add a comma in a sentence to avoid a possible misunderstanding. In the examples below, the sentences are better once a comma is added:

The findings suggest that before 1946 children were more vulnerable.

The findings suggest that before 1946, children were more vulnerable.

The backstreet is necessarily spatially large containing a multitude of characters.

The backstreet is necessarily spatially large, containing a multitude of characters.

When it reached seven results changed.

When it reached seven, results changed.

practising the four sentence structures

Here is a summary of the four sentence structures presented above.

1. Subject | one thing about the subject.

2. Subject | one thing about the subject | joining word | another thing about the subject.

3. Extra information, | subject | one thing about the subject.

4. Subject, | information, | one thing about the subject.

The best way to put this strategy into practice is to write sentences. Work on one structure at a time and practise it before moving on to the next one.

The key to writing these types of sentence is to get the subject down first and add relevant information or ideas to it. Use your voice to guide you by saying the sentence aloud. Don't think about grammatical rules as you write. Good proofreading strategies can be used to correct most errors (see subunit 6.2 step 10).

Of course, there are many more sentence types, but learning and using these four basic structures will help you get your thoughts into writing. You can write extensively and well by just using these four structures.

Here is a paragraph that uses the four sentence structures. Notice how few punctuation marks are used:

The Decision did not solve the underlying problems concerning the allocation of responsibilities in the implementing stage.   ] 1

The issue of accountability had not been addressed and the European Parliament was not even mentioned in the Decision.   ] 2

In this institutional scenario, the European Parliament had scarce knowledge of what matters were dealt with by comitology.   ] 3

The key concern was that, while comitology evolved from a system of control to a mode of governance, there was no corresponding evolution of suitable accountability mechanisms.   ] 4

5.6 building a paragraph with description and discussion

⭐ the aim

When you write, you can either describe or discuss (see subunit 4.5). Description involves giving the reader relevant facts (like a definition). Discussion involves developing ideas, for example by questioning, forming arguments or evaluating evidence. This strategy aims to show that, from a simple descriptive sentence, you can build a paragraph by alternating between description and discussion.

ℹ️ why this can help you

Paragraphs in undergraduate academic texts can vary in length, but on average they are 150 to 200 words long. Sentences also vary in length. But to build a good paragraph, you are unlikely to need more than 10 to 15 sentences (and often less). This strategy builds paragraphs by adding sentences in a step by step process. This process is easy to follow. It invites you to describe and encourages you to discuss.

⚙️ the strategy

Before you prepare to write, format your word processing program. Select a font and background you like (see subunit 2.6) and set the line spacing at 1.5.

1. Write a basic statement sentence that describes or gives a piece of information.

2. Press the return key and move the cursor to the next line.

3. Read the sentence you have just written and ask yourself: Do I need to give the reader more information (more description)? Or do I need to discuss the relevance of what I have written (discussion)?

4. Write a second sentence that provides more information or discusses the information.

5. After each sentence you write, ask: Do I need to give the reader relevant information (add description)? Or do I need to discuss what I have written (discussion)?

6. When you have achieved the aim of your paragraph, stop and move on to the next paragraph.

Description means the addition of facts. When adding more information, it must be relevant to your task. If the relevance of the information you are providing is not obvious, you need to explain it to your reader. Discussion is prompted by the three key discursive questions: why?, so what? and what if? See description and discussion in academic writing (subunit 4.5).

Spacing the sentences out and writing each one on a new line will allow you to check and consider each sentence you write. It will also encourage you to write short sentences. You can write a series of short sentences that build a paragraph and then combine some of them later when you review your writing.

The strategy is summarised in the model below. From each box, you can only follow one of the arrows and only in the direction indicated:

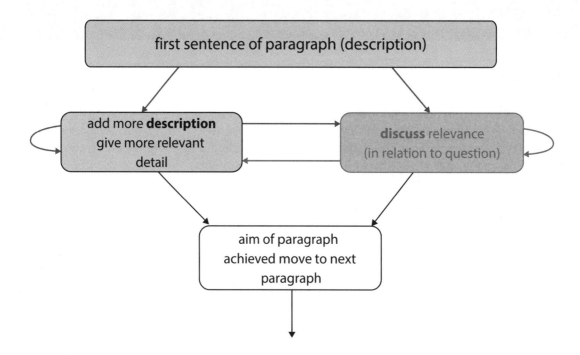

Here is a paragraph that alternates between **description** and **discussion:**

According to Barthes, meaning is open to the interpretation of the individual reader (Perkins, 2014). However, in a hegemonic reading, it can be difficult for the reader to avoid the author's intention. This is the case in *The Refusal of Time* (2012) by William Kentridge. A still image from this work shows a series of human shadows in procession. This procession connotes people with a common purpose, either moving towards a common end or escaping a difficult or dangerous situation. The figures have their heads bowed and some have one arm resting on the back of the person in front. The bowed heads and the arms leaning for support express weariness. Bowed heads also signify oppression. Kentridge grew up in the northern suburbs of Johannesburg, South Africa. He lived there during the apartheid regime of the 1950s and 1960s. As a child, he would have witnessed the daily procession of oppressed black African workers as they moved from areas where they were forced to live (in deprived conditions) to those where they were forced to work. This childhood influence is a tangible feature of his work.

This strategy can be used in any way that might help you write a paragraph. Although most paragraphs in academic writing mix description and discussion, there are a few things to consider:

- some paragraphs can be totally descriptive, for example you might need to provide a definition, a summary or describe a method
- not all paragraphs begin with a statement of fact, some might start with an opinion or idea
- some paragraphs can be totally discursive, for example a paragraph may discuss the facts set out in a preceding paragraph
- some sentences might contain both elements of description (facts) and discussion (ideas)

5.7 the Paragraph Buster!

⭐ the aim

The Paragraph Buster! is intended to help you write and build paragraphs. It is a tool to keep you writing or to help you overcome writer's block.

ℹ️ why this can help you

Some students don't know how to start a paragraph. Some students make strong and relevant points and move on without developing them. Some students simply get stuck and don't know what to write next. This strategy identifies different things you can do when writing a paragraph. Understanding these aims and functions can be useful, both before you write and during writing. By presenting a number of possible options, the Paragraph Buster! provides ideas to help you start and develop paragraphs. The strategy shows you how to expand on relevant points and can be used to generate both description and discussion.

Most paragraphs in academic writing begin with an introductory sentence that states the subject or main idea of the paragraph (often called a 'topic sentence') and some paragraphs end with a concluding sentence. However, this is not always the case and the order of content in paragraphs varies. Some strategies help you write paragraphs by repeating the order of content, but paragraphs can be much more flexible. The only rule to follow is to make sure that anything you write in a paragraph is relevant to the aim of the paragraph. The Paragraph Buster! encourages you to take a flexible approach to building paragraphs.

⚙️ the strategy

A paragraph can do any of these 6 things:

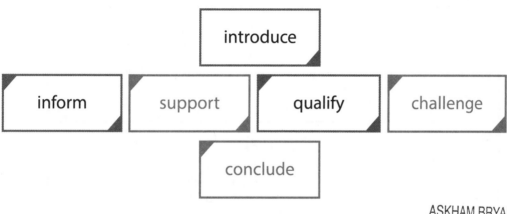

These categories show the aims of sentences in paragraphs. Grey boxes suggest descriptive (factual) writing, blue boxes suggest discursive (analytical) writing, and this division reflects the idea presented in building a paragraph with description and discussion (subunit 5.6). But, in practice, any of these six categories could include descriptive or analytical sentences. So, if you use the Paragraph Buster! focus on writing sentences that have a clear purpose. Here is some detail about 6 things a paragraph can do:

introduce

Paragraphs usually begin with a sentence that states the topic or theme of the paragraph. This is a good way to start writing because it provides a base from which you can develop the topic and also provides a reference that helps you keep on track when writing the paragraph. A good introductory sentence can also help readers understand the order of your ideas.

inform

Sentences that inform add more detail or give more description about what has been stated in the preceding sentence(s). They can also be used to inform the reader of an opinion or argument. Informative sentences can come in any part of the paragraph, but they are often an expansion of the introductory sentence.

support

Support sentences support what has been stated previously in the paragraph. They can explain why something was done in a particular way (rationale or justification for practice) or support a position, theory or argument (evidence for ideas). In academic writing, the best support sentences use evidence referenced to an academic source.

qualify

When you qualify something you have written, you make its focus or range clearer or narrower. You might qualify something to clarify to the reader what the focus is and therefore make it more explicit. You might qualify something by stating its limitations. A lot of qualifying work will happen when you edit your work to make it more precise.

challenge

A sentence can challenge something by questioning its validity or taking an opposing view. A challenge sentence can often come after stating a position you want to criticise or argue against. In academic writing, your challenge is always stronger with evidence.

conclude

When you conclude, you write a consequence or summary of what you have written. Not all paragraphs need to have their own conclusions and some paragraphs are used only to provide conclusions. You are unlikely to summarise in the middle of a paragraph, but you can state or recap outcomes at any time.

Clearly, some sentences fit into more than one category. For example, you can qualify and inform, or support and conclude at the same time. But this doesn't matter. What is important is that this strategy is used to give you clear ideas about building paragraphs. It does this by identifying what you can do and by making you think about what you are doing when you write sentences.

The kind of paragraph you write depends on what you want it to do (the aim of the paragraph). For example, a paragraph that aims to give a definition or describes something could simply consist of:

introduce + inform

A paragraph that aims to provide evidence in support of an idea could consist of:

introduce + inform + support

Paragraph structures can therefore range from the simple to the complex:

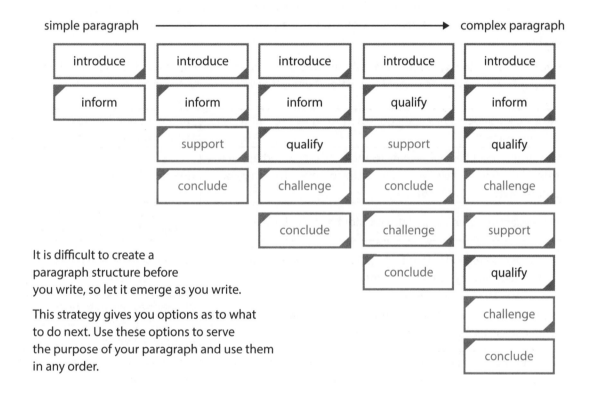

It is difficult to create a paragraph structure before you write, so let it emerge as you write.

This strategy gives you options as to what to do next. Use these options to serve the purpose of your paragraph and use them in any order.

conclusion paragraphs

A conclusion paragraph is placed at the end of an essay (see subunit 6.7). However, you can come to conclusions at any time, especially in longer pieces of writing. This can be done to intermittently tie together the various threads of a discussion. For example, you might provide a definition in one paragraph, describe an alternative definition in the second, and in a third (conclusion) paragraph, summarise how both compare or relate. It can be a lot easier to present or discuss concluding outcomes or comments in a separate paragraph than to try and squeeze a conclusion into a single sentence at the end of a paragraph.

Formal conclusions (that come at the end of an essay or at the end of a chapter) can be made more interesting by using some of the options given by the Paragraph Buster! You would not introduce new ideas into a formal essay conclusion, but you can still discuss rather than simply present information.

the aim of a paragraph

It's easier to write a paragraph if you know what purpose the paragraph is serving. If you have drawn up an essay plan with aims (see subunit 6.6), you will have a good idea of what you are trying to do in each part of an essay. If you are struggling to write or losing focus, make sure you know the purpose of the paragraph and then use the 6 categories of the Paragraph Buster! to help you achieve it.

You will use and reference academic sources in your writing. It doesn't matter whether you are introducing, informing, supporting, qualifying, challenging or concluding, you can always add a reference. In discussion, references support your ideas, whereas in description, references show reliable sources.

Here is a broken down paragraph that shows how the sentences have been used. It is an introductory paragraph and its aim is to present the major themes that will be discussed in an essay:

Western legal theory has undergone almost three thousand years of development.	statement that **introduces** the topic of the paragraph
Its starting point lies somewhere in ancient Greece, perhaps at the time of the famous lawgivers such as Draco (seventh century BC) and Solon (sixth century BC).	**qualifies** (limits) the topic
More exact information on dates has not been established.	gives reader more **information** and **qualifies** (limits) the topic
Alexander (1998) and Schumacher (2006) argue that an earlier form of legal theory in ancient Egypt influenced the west.	**challenges** this and references another point of view
However, Ruben (2005) highlights the progress made in the art of writing in ancient Greece as the key factor.	**challenges** the statement just made (references another point of view)
Scholars agree that writing allowed the inscription of rules that could be understood throughout a considerable part of the Hellenic world.	makes a **concluding** remark (answers the question: so what?)
The first Greek laws derived more from tradition and custom than from sophisticated ideas of justice and morality (Ruben, 2005).	adds more **information** with an academic reference
Nonetheless, the act of committing a set of conventions to stone or to bronze gave legislation a degree of permanency. Agreed rules could no longer be changed arbitrarily. Furthermore, once they became established they could not easily be repealed. The interpretation of written legislation had begun and, then as now, it favoured the controlling forces of the day.	adds **information**, makes **concluding** remarks, shows consequence of previous information

The Paragraph Buster! isn't made for analysing texts. It is a product of text analysis and the example above is given to highlight the fact that when you are writing a paragraph, you can use sentences to do several things and if you explicitly know what you want to do, writing the sentence is easier. Sometimes, you can write without thinking too much about it and your writing can flow. At other times, you might need some help. This strategy presents options you can choose from in order to generate ideas for writing paragraphs. These options can overlap. It may be that you're not sure what the difference between some of them is. But this doesn't matter. The important thing in applying any strategy is that it helps you. Use the Paragraph Buster! in any way that helps you start, write or build paragraphs.

the Paragraph Buster!

pick any card and deal yourself a paragraph!

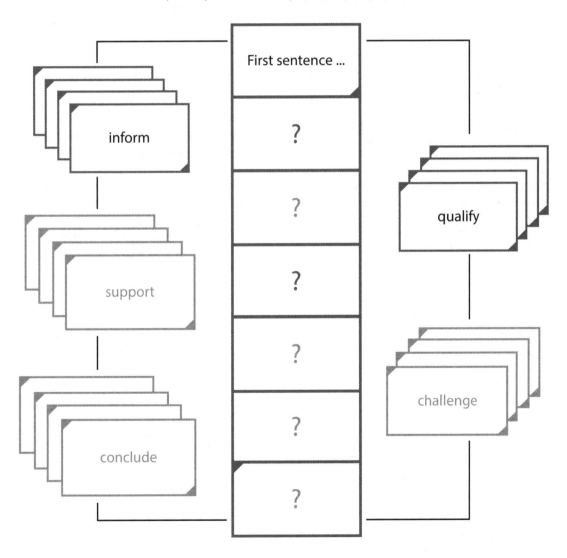

5.8 using quotes in academic writing

The word 'quote' is an abbreviated (but now accepted) form of the word 'quotation'. Using quotes in academic writing can strengthen or weaken it:

good use of quotes ✔	bad use of quotes ✖
The quote is from a reliable academic source like a peer reviewed journal, a published work by an expert in the field or literature from an authoritative body.	The quote is taken from an unreliable source like an internet site that is not monitored for quality control of information or a source that doesn't show the author or organisation from which it came.
You can identify the key words or phrase from the quote and use it to make an impact.	The quote is too long and the essence of the quote is lost.
The quote says something you can't put into your own words without losing or changing its meaning.	The quote doesn't say anything original and could easily be paraphrased.
The quote is relevant to your task and you can show how it is relevant.	The quote is not relevant to your task, or the relevance isn't clear.
The quote is linked to other information and ideas. For example, it is contrasted with another viewpoint.	The quote stands alone and is not related to other information and ideas.

Good use of quotes can:

- show you have read widely
- lend authority to your argument
- show the complexity of a discussion

A quote is a fact. It is a form of descriptive writing because it states precisely what an individual has said or written. You might not agree with what the quote says. It might just be the opinion of the author. But the quote itself is a fact. When you write a quote, you are providing information to be used as evidence. What matters in academic writing is how you apply this evidence.

Relevant quotes can be used in different parts of written assignments. For example, an essay introduction can use a quote to show that you understand the specific focus of the question (see subunit 6.7). If you don't use a quote for a specific purpose, you are just cutting and pasting information. There are various good reasons why you might use a quote (see below). It's worth thinking about these before you start to collect quotes when you research for an assignment.

quotes can be used to:	
provide a definition	If you need to provide a precise definition, you should use a quote. In this case, you must reproduce the exact wording as paraphrasing is not possible. If the definition is too long, you might consider putting it in an appendix or (in a longer document) as a footnote. You can then select the most relevant parts of the definition and quote them in the main body of the text. Definitions should come from authoritative organisations, often associated with a specific discipline, or from academic sources. Some definitions will be generally agreed or accepted by all, whereas others will show a difference in interpretation or thinking. Definitions can therefore be used to show agreement or differences of opinion. Unless you have been specifically asked, you should avoid quoting dictionary definitions.
show disagreement	You can use two quotes (not just definitions) to show contrasting views or emphasise the uncertainty that exists in a debate. This is often done to show the complexity of academic thinking.
give a direct reference for discussion	There may be other occasions when you cannot put things into your own words. For example, you might want to reference a line from a poem or a play, present a short extract from a qualitative interview or quote a legal judgement. When you do this, it is better if the quote comes from a primary source. For example, if you want to quote a line from a policy document, find and reference a copy of the policy. Here you are introducing information with the aim of discussing its relevance to your task. Don't use a quote that you can't integrate into your writing.
support your argument, interpretation or point of view	One of the most common uses of quotes in academic writing is to support your argument or viewpoint by providing evidence from a reliable source (practice, theory, research or policy, see subunit 4.2). However, because a quote is an extract from a larger piece of work, it does not always provide a strong form of evidence. It will not be conclusive evidence that your argument is valid. It is more likely that you can show the reader that your opinion is shared by academics or experts in your field of study.
make an association	You can associate an individual or group with a stance, by quoting what they said or wrote or what was written about them.
sum up	You might find a quote that sums up your core argument or intention. For example, in an essay conclusion you can use a quote to summarise your position.

how to set out a quote in your writing

Any quote you use will need a precise reference. The details required will differ slightly according to the referencing system you have been asked to use (see subunit 5.9). However, you will always need the author's surname, the year of publication of the source and the number of the page containing the quote. When you take notes from a source, make sure you get this information down next to the quote. Despite the differences between referencing systems, some conventions are used in nearly all of them:

1. surround the quote with quotation marks

You can use either double or single quotation marks but be consistent:

> Deaf children can interpret "both spoken and written language visually" (Hart, 1978 p. 6).

> Reading is 'a form of work' (Gaspar and Brown, 1973 p. 82).

2. if a quote you want to use already contains its own quotation marks, use double and single quotation marks

In this example, double quotation marks have been placed around the quote and single quotation marks have been retained from the original text:

> Blankfield has no doubts that the "absurdity of the apartheid era is alive and well in the 'new' South Africa" (2018 p. 7).

3. show when you have omitted parts of the quote by using 3 dots (an ellipsis)

You should only do this if you don't change the fundamental meaning of the quote by leaving words out:

> The White Paper seems 'somewhat ambitious in its aim … by using competing theoretical models' (Giuffrida, 2009 p. 170).

4. use square brackets to show when you have added your own words to the quote

You do this to make the quote shorter but also to ensure it makes sense when read. You can only do this if you don't change the meaning of the quote:

> Reynolds acknowledged that the 'separation of powers model [was useful] in clarifying the legal concept' (2017 p. 88).

5. separate and indent long quotes

Longer quotes are usually considered to be 3 lines or more. They may or may not need quotation marks depending on the referencing system you are using:

In addition, it has been suggested that at least some of the responsibility lies with the reader:

> The linguistic and conceptual content of a piece of writing is likely to be a major cause of poor reading comprehension. Although there are a number of formulae that can be used to calculate the relative difficulty of a text, the reader should be able to recognise the suitability of a book by assessing their own degree of understanding. (Robinson, 2017 p. 55)

introducing the quote

A quote should be part of a sentence and not in a sentence on its own. When you write, you should try to integrate quotes. But you don't always have to directly refer to the author. Both of these are correct:

> One strand of the governance approach maintains that new modes of governance operate 'in the shadow of hierarchy' (Scharpf, 1994 p. 28).

> One strand of the governance approach maintains that new modes of governance operate in what Scharpf (1994 p. 28) describes as 'the shadow of hierarchy'.

It's up to you whether you name the author in the main part of the sentence, put it in brackets or include it as a footnote or endnote. But if you choose to refer to the author, you can change the way you introduce quotes and make your sentences more interesting. You can also indicate whether you agree or disagree with what the quote says. Here are just some examples:

I like Smith!

Smith proves … Smith verifies … Smith knows …	I'm completely in agreement with Smith.
Smith confirms … Smith reveals … Smith teaches us … Smith informs us … Smith tells us …	I'm using Smith to support my argument.
Smith provides evidence for … Smith draws our attention to …	I'm starting to show how Smith supports my argument.
Smith demonstrates … Smith shows … Smith illustrates … Smith states … Smith writes … To quote Smith, …	I'm not agreeing or disagreeing with Smith, I am being objective.
According to Smith … Smith hypothesises … Smith indicates … Smith argues that …	I may disagree with Smith, but I am giving him some credit.
Smith maintains … Smith implies … Smith believes …	I am distancing myself from Smith's views.
Smith suggests … Smith claims … Smith alleges …	I'm not crazy about Smith.
Smith inaccurately … Smith incorrectly states … Smith misunderstands …	I don't agree with Smith at all.

I don't like Smith!

5.9 plagiarism and how to avoid it

There are two things you must do to avoid plagiarism:

1. find out exactly what plagiarism means
2. reference your work correctly

what is plagiarism?

Most people know that if you use or copy somebody else's work and pretend that it is your own, you commit plagiarism. However, there is no single, accepted definition, and different institutions define it in different ways. Students, especially international students, might have an alternative understanding of what constitutes plagiarism. Because it can carry strict penalties, you need to find, read and understand the specific rules of plagiarism provided by your educational institution. Here are some things to consider that should encourage you to do this:

ideas	Plagiarism isn't confined to taking an author's writing or images. You can also plagiarise by using somebody's ideas and passing them off as your own.
paraphrasing	If you paraphrase, you put something into your own words. But if you don't acknowledge (cite) the source, you can still paraphrase and plagiarise.
unintentional plagiarism	You can be guilty of plagiarism even if you weren't aware of doing it. Unintentional plagiarism can occur when you forget to reference, or you reference incorrectly. It may carry a less severe penalty, but it is a form of plagiarism. However, if you have an idea that you believe to be original but it already exists, then it is not plagiarism.
self-plagiarism	You can plagiarise yourself by submitting the same piece of your original work for different assignments.
group work	In a joint (group work) report, plagiarism by one member of the group can affect the grade for the whole group.
collusion	Like plagiarism, collusion is defined in different ways. In most cases, if two or more people work on an assignment, but the work is presented as that of an individual, you can be guilty of collusion. Collusion also includes allowing or offering your work to be presented as the work of another person.
outside help	Outside help can include substantial help with the ideas or information for a piece of coursework, not just the writing. If somebody edits your work and makes substantial changes to the content and form and you do not acknowledge or seek permission for this, it is plagiarism (or a form of collusion). However, having your written work proofread for errors (like spelling and grammar) by somebody else is not considered plagiarism.
common knowledge	Common knowledge can be understood as something that most (or a substantial number of) people believe or know to be true. Common knowledge is knowledge that doesn't belong to any person or group, therefore it can't be plagiarised. Sometimes, it is not obvious whether something can be defined as common knowledge, so, when in doubt, the best thing to do is to include a reference.

what is common knowledge?

It is difficult to define common knowledge because it can mean different things to different people in different contexts. However, for most academic purposes, common knowledge can be understood as:

> something known by a significant number of people either in the general population or in a specific field of academic study

Compare the following sentences:

- In 2017, the population of the United Kingdom was already approaching 70 million people.
- In 2017, the population of the United Kingdom was recorded as 66,040,200 (Office for National Statistics, 2018).

Enough people would know the first statement for it to be considered common knowledge, but few would know the precise detail given in the second.

Compare these two sentences:

- Japan's surrender in 1945 marked the end of the Second World War.
- Japan's surrender on 2 September 1945 marked the end of the Second World War.

If you were a student of Modern History, you could assume that enough people in your field of study (historians, History academics or students) would know both these facts to be true and you would therefore not need to reference them. When you decide whether enough people know what you assume to be common knowledge, you should take into account the context in which you work. However, the general rule still applies: if in doubt, provide a reference.

plagiarism and discussion

Throughout this book, academic writing is categorised as either a form of description or discussion (see subunit 4.5). When you describe, you provide facts. Some of these facts will be your own observations and measurements (e.g., a description of the method in a research paper). Some of the facts you provide will be common knowledge, as in the examples above. Other, less well known or contentious facts will need to be referenced to their sources.

When you discuss, you ask questions of and think critically about the facts. Sometimes, it is unclear whether your opinion (as a student) is valued or even required. But to achieve the highest grades in most written work, your own analysis is important. You should not be afraid of plagiarism when you come up with ideas, but you should let the academic literature guide your opinions.

> any original discussion derived from facts cannot be plagiarising, even if your ideas already exist elsewhere (which they probably do) you are not plagiarising, however, your discussion will always be stronger if it is supported by evidence you can reference

plagiarism detection software (PDS)

Although this term is widely used, plagiarism detectors or checkers do not detect plagiarism. PDS only highlights the possibility of plagiarism in a written document. It does this by comparing new work against a database of existing literature. These programs produce a report (sometimes called a 'similarity report') with a score or percentage mark that shows the level of content that is similar to, or the same as, existing material.

Written coursework is now routinely checked in this way before or when it is submitted for assessment. Unless instructed otherwise, PDS checks all the text in a document. This includes correctly referenced quotes, the list of references or bibliography and even your own name. Therefore, a lot of the highlighted text in a similarity report is not plagiarism, but it does count towards the percentage score.

checking for plagiarism before you submit your work

PDS gives you the opportunity to check your work before you submit it. Most education institutions now use a recommended program (like Turnitin), which you may or may not be able to access before submission. If the program used by your institution does not allow you to check your work prior to the hand in date, there are many affordable or free PDS downloads available. These include programs like Unicheck, PlagScan, Quetext, Grammarly and WhiteSmoke Plagiarism Checker. Free programs may access smaller databases, but they can still identify potential problems. When checking your work before submission, it is a good idea to exclude the reference list or bibliography but not to remove quotes from the main body. PDS can help you understand plagiarism and improve your work by showing, for example, if you have too many quotes.

paraphrasing: using your own syntax

In the context of academic writing, 'syntax' simply means the order of words in a sentence and it is good practice to use your own, original syntax when you write. This means paraphrasing. If you paraphrase, you are less likely to get a high percentage score on a PDS report and using too many quotes is not good practice.

The way you make notes can help you paraphrase. If, when you research, you cut and paste too much original work into a word processor, you will find it almost impossible to change the original text (which has probably been professionally edited and proofread) into your own words. Spatial note making (subunit 3.1) encourages you to change the order of information and to make abbreviated notes and add your own ideas at the time of note taking. The good use of quotes (subunit 5.8) encourages you to take only the essence of a quote and use it for an explicit purpose.

> paraphrasing is made easier if you prepare for
> it by making good notes during research

referencing your work

Understanding plagiarism will help you decide when to reference. But you must also know how to reference. Any work that is not your own and is not common knowledge will require a reference. This includes commonly used sources like books and research papers as well as less obvious sources like presentations, lectures, emails and online blogs. To reference your work correctly, you should:

- find out which referencing system is used on your course (or module)
- learn to use a referencing software program

There are two ways you will reference work:

1. reference something in the body of your text (sometimes called a 'citation')
2. produce a reference list or bibliography

The way you set out these references is dictated by the referencing system you have been asked to use. Writing references correctly will not only help you avoid plagiarism, it is often part of the assessment criteria. Make sure you know which system you are using before you start researching. The most commonly used referencing systems include:

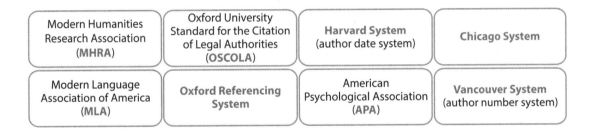

Modern Humanities Research Association (MHRA)	Oxford University Standard for the Citation of Legal Authorities (OSCOLA)	Harvard System (author date system)	Chicago System
Modern Language Association of America (MLA)	Oxford Referencing System	American Psychological Association (APA)	Vancouver System (author number system)

You can check online for details of how to set out references for the system you use. For a typical undergraduate essay, you will provide 10–20 different references. This can vary, so if you are not sure, ask your tutor before you start researching. Unless you know the referencing system well, it is probably better to enter a small number of references into your reference list manually. In this way, you will learn how to set them out properly and identify and correct any mistakes. If you are creating your reference list, start making it when you start researching so that you are only entering (and ordering) one or two references at a time. Don't wait until the end of the process to make your reference list as it can take longer than you think.

Using a referencing software program can save a lot of time, especially when you are required to produce longer pieces of work like extended essays or dissertations. These programs (sometimes called 'reference or bibliographic managers') will automatically generate a reference list or bibliography as well as help you insert citations into the body of your work. Even if you use a referencing software program, you should still know the basics of how to set out a correct reference and be aware of what you put into the software.

Each of the referencing systems shown above has its own online reference list generator. Just search the name of the referencing system followed by the word 'generator'. Most of these programs are free to use. There are also a number of sophisticated reference software programs. Some of them are free and they all include the commonly used referencing systems. Examples include Zotero, Mendeley, Microsoft Word, EndNote and RefWorks.

the bibliography and the reference list

These terms are sometimes confused. A bibliography is an extensive list of all sources used for a piece of academic work and is usually only required for extended essays or dissertations. Some dissertations might even have a separate reference list and bibliography. For most undergraduate coursework assignments, you will be asked to produce a reference list. This is a list of all the sources referred to in the body of the work.

footnotes and endnotes

Some referencing systems use footnotes or endnotes:

- a footnote is text placed at the bottom (foot) of a page
- an endnote is text placed at the end of an essay, or section of a dissertation

A superscript number (a number placed slightly above the main text, like so, [10]) is inserted in the relevant point of the main body of the text. Word processing software will allow you to automatically insert footnotes and endnotes. When you do this in the main body, the same number appears, under a line, at the foot of the page or at the end of the document and this is where you add your footnote or endnote reference or text.

There is no fixed rule as to where you insert a superscript number, but some referencing systems prefer it at the end of a sentence as it is less distracting to the reader. Both footnotes and endnotes are usually numbered sequentially throughout the whole text and not at the start of each page, section or chapter.

A lot of referencing systems use footnotes or endnotes to reference (cite) sources used in the main body. These references may or may not be included in the word count, so you need to check.

In longer essays and dissertations, footnotes or endnotes can be used for extra (but non-essential) information that the author has decided to remove from the main body of the text. Footnotes tend to be used as an alternative to in-text referencing. Endnotes tend to be used to add supplementary details when in-text referencing is used. You might want to do this to:

- point the reader to sources that expand on a point
- provide (more) examples to illustrate a point
- give a definition
- give more details of something (like an event or a document)

These kinds of footnotes and endnotes are more likely to be part of the word count, so you should use them sparingly.

unit 6

producing essays

Before starting work on an essay, you need to know what you have been asked to produce. This unit begins by explaining what an essay is and how it is organised. It then presents an innovative key strategy for producing essays. This strategy divides the essay production process into 10 steps. Each step is explained, and you are encouraged to follow the strategy, adapt it or simply use any of the ideas to help you. A visual overview of the strategy is provided for quick reference. Some of the ideas are then applied to other sections of the unit. This includes guidance on setting out the order of content in an essay, making an effective essay plan and writing introductions and conclusions. The unit ends by highlighting the elements tutors look for when they evaluate academic essays. This will allow you to identify the strengths and weaknesses of your own essays and take steps to improve them.

the structure of essays

Most students have a pretty good idea of what an essay is, but it is always more useful to know something explicitly, and an essay can be clearly defined:

- an essay is a written piece of work with a set structure
- it has three main parts: an introduction, a main body and a conclusion
- an essay is made up of sentences put together to form paragraphs
- the written content of an essay addresses a specific subject that is stated as a question or a title
- an essay contains writing that is descriptive or discursive (analytical), most essays have both
- an essay contains information and ideas
- the information in an essay comes from research
- the ideas in an essay can come from the writer or from researching other sources, most essays include both the writer's ideas and existing ideas
- a list of the references used in an essay is placed after the conclusion

This diagram shows the standard form of an essay. All essays have this basic structure.

Each paragraph (or group of paragraphs) introduces and then expands on a specific point that is related to the essay question or title.

The paragraphs are put in a specific order. This order should lead towards and justify the conclusion of the essay.

The order of the paragraphs depends on the essay question and how the writer wants to address the question.

The difference between essays is in:

- the length (the number of words)
- the content (the information and ideas)
- the order of the content
- the type of language used

The difference is also, of course, in the quality and value of the finished essay.

Question or Title

| introduction |

main body
| paragraph |
| paragraph |
| paragraph |
| paragraph |
| paragraph |
| paragraph |

| conclusion |

Reference List

the length of essays

The length of an essay varies:

- short essay: 1,000 words
- essay: 1,500 to 3,500 words
- extended essay: 4,000 words or over

Making sure you know the word limit before you start is important. If you know the word limit, you will also know, roughly, how many pages you will need to produce. You will also know how many words you should allocate to each of the three sections. The main body of an essay is usually around 84% of the word count. The introduction and conclusion are usually around 8% each. Use the table below to see the approximate length of your essay.

word limit	introduction (8%)	main body (84%)	conclusion (8%)	no. of pages (font size 12, 1.5 line spacing)	no. of pages (font size 12, 2.0 line spacing)
1,000	80	840	80	2–3	3–4
1,500	120	1,260	120	4–5	5–6
2,000	160	1,680	160	5–6	7–8
2,500	200	2,100	200	6–7	8–9
3,000	240	2,520	240	8–9	10–11
3,500	280	2,940	280	9–10	12–13
4,000	320	3,360	320	10–11	14–15

the content of essays: sentences and paragraphs

Essays are made up of information and ideas written in proper sentences that build to form paragraphs. There is no rule to say how long a paragraph should be. However, most paragraphs in undergraduate academic essays are 150–200 words long.

The first sentence of a paragraph (sometimes called the 'topic sentence') introduces a specific point, theme or issue. The rest of the paragraph expands on this point by describing or discussing it. Sometimes, two or three paragraphs can be used to expand on an important point. Therefore, not all paragraphs have to have a sentence that introduces a new topic.

The number of paragraphs in an essay will vary depending on the length of the essay and the amount of information or ideas in each paragraph. Paragraphs are the large building blocks of essays. If you can learn how to write paragraphs, you can build an essay.

If you find it difficult to get your ideas down into structured sentences, see the strategy an easy way to write simple sentences (subunit 5.5). If you want some help in writing or building paragraphs, see building a paragraph with description and discussion (subunit 5.6) and the Paragraph Buster! (subunit 5.7).

6.2 producing essays: a 10 step strategy

⭐ the aim

Producing essays involves more than just writing. It involves thinking, preparing, researching, note making, structuring, planning, writing, editing and proofreading. These different tasks can be organised into a 10 step process. The aim of this strategy is to make the steps involved in essay production explicit so that they can be easily understood and followed. It is important that when you are given an essay to do, you should have a clear plan of how you will tackle the task, step by step.

ℹ️ why this can help you

This structured approach breaks essay production into a series of activities that makes producing essays easier to understand and carry out. It means that you can think about one task at a time and each step of the strategy is designed to make the next step easier. Having a structured, ordered approach will make it easier for you to plan and monitor each step of the essay production process.

⚙️ the strategy

This strategy can be summarised under five headings. The strategy can be used for essays of all lengths and adapted to suit different timescales.

The 10 steps are shown in the table below and more details are given for each of the steps on the following pages. They contain a lot of different ideas, so it may be worth reading through the strategy a couple of times to make sure you understand the process.

Not all the ideas will be relevant to you. You are encouraged to use this strategy or to adapt it to suit your personal approach to essay production.

You can photocopy the table below and use it to plan and monitor your progress for each essay you produce. Alternatively, you can download a copy from www.macmillanihe.com/lia-sys.

A visual overview of the strategy is provided at the end of this subunit.

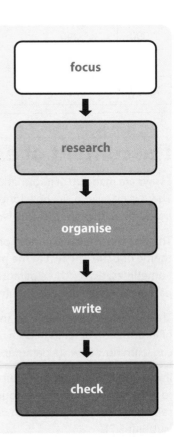

essay no.	word limit:		hand in date:

essay question:

step	activity	time	
1	Work on the essay question. Break it down on A3 unlined paper. Reformat it from linear to spatial form. Use the elements, links and parts (ELP) strategy (see subunit 6.3).	10 mins	
2	Brainstorm the question. Get down initial ideas or knowledge. If you don't understand the question, ask the person who set it.	20 mins	
3	Before starting the main research phase: go small! Do some brief, initial research. Look at concise sources like lecture notes.	1 day	
4	When you have more focus, start the main research phase. Make notes using your preferred method(s). Start your reference list.	varies	
5	During research, try to identify the information and ideas relevant to your essay. Order does not matter at this stage.	–	
6	Draw up an essay plan. If you have noted the conclusion, use it to order the plan. Write an aim for each main section of the plan.	30 mins	
7	Before writing, allocate your notes (information and ideas) to the appropriate sections of the essay plan.	30 mins	
8	Using your essay plan as a guide, write the first draft. Your aim is to get your ideas down in the right place and in the right order.	varies	
9	Write the second draft of the essay.	varies	
10	Edit and proofread the essay.	1–2 days	

step 1

break down the essay question by reformatting it into a spatial form

The essay question is different from the essay topic. Don't do anything until you have understood the essay question. An effective way to do this is to reformat the question from a linear to a spatial form. Don't just break down the question by highlighting or underlining 'key words', break it apart.

When you reformat a question, you are looking for:

- the elements of the question (what the question is about)
- the links or relationship between these elements
- any information that limits or focuses the question
- whether there is more than one part to a question

essay question:

Discuss the role of the Roman Catholic Church in the society and politics of Brazil since the year 2000.

Here is an example of the question above reformatted spatially:

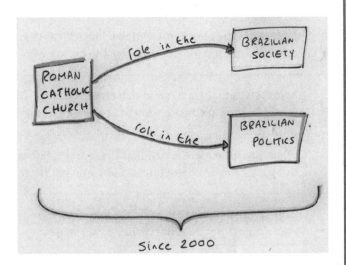

The spatial breakdown shows clearly that there are 3 elements to the question:

- the Roman Catholic Church
- the society of Brazil
- the politics of Brazil

You would need to know something about these things to answer this question. But these elements are not the question. The question is made by the links between them (shown by the arrows). A good answer to this question will lie in focusing on and discussing this relationship.

Breaking down an essay question and reformatting it to a spatial form:

- helps you understand the essay question, not just the essay topic
- gives focus to your reading and research
- encourages you to think critically and to discuss rather than just describe
- helps you form an argument or perspective and form a conclusion
- helps you identify parts of the question that need to be clarified

For a full explanation of breaking down essay questions in this way, see making a spatial breakdown of essay questions (subunit 6.3).

brainstorm the question

The best way to brainstorm an essay question is on A3 unlined paper turned landscape. This gives you more space to write and spread out your thoughts.

Brainstorming means getting any ideas or information you already have, out of your head and onto paper. Order does not matter. You can spread out the notes you make in any way you want.

Use the spatial breakdown from step 1 to help you think more about the essay question.

This step can be useful even though you haven't started the research phase because it helps you to focus on what you will need in order to answer the essay question.

Brainstorming a question with other students can be a useful way of exploring initial ideas.

When you brainstorm a question, you are looking for relevant information and ideas. You may not know details at this stage, but general themes, issues and ideas can be usefully identified. You may also be thinking about definitions or highlighting parts of the question that aren't clear.

steps 2 and 3 can be combined

go small!

Go small! means consulting concise sources before the main research begins. It means not rushing off to the library to take out every book on the essay topic. The aim of this step is to continue to develop a clear focus on the essay question.

There are several things you can do before you start the main research. You can:

- look at notes from relevant lectures (this connects your answer to the essay question with what was taught on the module)
- if appropriate, read the relevant sections of a module handbook and see how the stated aims of the module can be reflected in your essay
- use the internet to get any basic or background information like definitions, or short biographies, search for any quotes from the question to see where they came from (these may be useful, non-academic sources you would not include in your reference list)
- look up any words or terminology you are not clear about (but look them up in concise sources)

After steps 1, 2 and 3, if you are still unclear about any part of the question, clarify it with the person who set it, but ask them specific, not general, questions.

start your main research

Steps 1, 2 and 3 are designed to give your main reading and research a clearer focus. If you start reading and making notes for your essay, but get lost or confused, go back and review steps 1 to 3.

There are many ways to make notes from reading and different students have their preferred methods. You can make handwritten notes, digital notes or both.

Spatial note making is a flexible and highly effective way of displaying information and ideas from reading. Many students have found this strategy useful in making notes for essays. If you want to try spatial note making, see making notes in spatial form (spatial note making) (subunit 3.1).

It is in this step that you can apply effective reading and note making strategies. See unit 2 reading and unit 3 making notes.

order does not matter during the research phase, only relevance does

This step is still part of the research phase and is included to highlight some ideas that might be useful during research and note making.

Order does not matter during this phase, only relevance (to the question) matters, so try not to make too many notes. Try to identify the key ideas, themes, arguments, issues and information you need in your essay. You can put them in order later.

If you want to write something during the research phase, then write, but at this stage, you don't need to allocate the writing to any part of the essay.

If possible, start to get down some ideas for your conclusion. You can write a draft of your conclusion at any time and adapt it as you research. Having a rough conclusion in place will help you make an essay plan (step 6).

A useful activity during the research phase is to make a spatial overview of the essay content. Even students who don't like to make handwritten notes have found this strategy useful. If you want to try it, see using a spatial overview during the research phase (subunit 6.4).

Most students spend about 70% of essay production on research. So, if you have 10 days to do an essay, about 7 will be taken up with research and note making. To avoid research going on too long (especially when you have more time), it can be useful to set a date for the end of the main research phase.

step 6 — make an essay plan with aims

At the end of the research phase, you should know roughly how many sections (or main points) the essay will have. This can be clearer if you have made a spatial overview of the essay during research. Now it's time to draw up an essay plan, but instead of having just a list of headings, the essay plan should have aims.

For each main section (heading) of the essay, write a short aim. The aims can be written informally, as they are for your personal use and will be deleted later. An aim answers questions like: 'what do I want to state or argue in this part of the essay?' or 'what do I want the reader to get from this part?'

A list of aims is more useful than a list of headings. Aims will help you:

- see whether the order of your information and ideas is logical

- make your argument or perspective clearer

- allocate information and ideas to the appropriate sections of the essay

- write each section of the essay

For more details on this strategy, see making an essay plan with aims (subunit 6.6). For some ideas on how to order the content of your essay, see subunit 6.5.

Once you have your essay plan, it can be helpful to allocate an approximate number of words to each section so that you don't write too much.

step 7 — allocate your notes (information and ideas) to sections of the essay plan

It is very useful to allocate your notes to the appropriate section of the essay plan before you start writing.

The best way to do this is to give each main section in your essay plan a different colour (or, if you prefer, a number). Then, scan your notes and allocate them to a section in the essay by highlighting them with the same colour. You should allocate notes (information and ideas) according to the aim of each main section.

Reviewing your notes might take time, but if you can allocate your notes to sections of the essay plan, writing the essay will be a lot easier. This is because when you start to write the essay, you will only be dealing with a smaller quantity of notes that are relevant for each section.

write your first draft

Use your essay plan as a guide and write the first draft. Some students struggle at the writing phase. Don't think of your first draft as your first version of the essay. The only aim of writing the first draft should be to get all your information and ideas in the right place and in the right order.

Don't worry about writing perfect sentences at this stage. Don't worry about writing formally or accurately. If you can't express certain ideas in sentences, write them as bullet points or lists or even as intentions. If you are an international student, you can even write bits of the first draft in your first language. Try to get through the whole essay without worrying too much about the writing style or stopping to correct every line.

If you can write most of the essay in first draft form, any subsequent redrafting of the essay (to make it read better and to make it more academic in style) will be much easier.

write your second draft

When you have finished your first draft and have all the information and ideas in more or less the right order, you can start to write the second draft. The aim of the second and any subsequent draft is to make your writing precise and formal. As you write each section or paragraph, refer to the aims in your plan to help you and look at your thesis statement or conclusion.

After writing the second (or first) draft, you may identify the need for more information or more ideas. For example, you might need some evidence to back up one of your arguments or you might want to use a quote in your conclusion. However, any further research carried out at this stage will be highly focused and much easier because you will know specifically what you are looking for when you search for it.

Most of the essays you write will require critical writing, not just descriptive writing. For a strategy to help you generate critical writing, see description and discussion in academic writing (subunit 4.5). For more ideas and guidance on producing good academic writing, see unit 4 critical thinking for academic writing and unit 5 academic writing.

step 10 · editing and proofreading

When you have finished writing your essay, you will need to edit and proofread it. Although they are often done at the same time, editing and proofreading are different.

Editing

Editing involves rewriting, reordering or deleting words, sentences or even paragraphs so that the writing makes more sense and has a better quality and order. A major part of editing will be cutting things out, especially irrelevant material. However, you may also need to add or elaborate on certain points to make them clearer or stronger. Be cautious about asking other people to edit or help you edit your essay. First, they may not know your subject area and, second, you could be guilty of collusion (see subunit 5.9).

Proofreading

When you proofread, you are looking for errors in spelling, punctuation, grammar, tense, use of vocabulary and so on. It is easier to proofread your essay once you have finished editing it.

Here are some ideas that might help you edit and proofread your essay:

- If you have a good essay plan (with aims for each section), you should use it when you edit your essay. Edit one paragraph or section at a time and make sure that the writing achieves the aims stated in the essay plan.

- If possible, leave time between writing the final draft and editing or proofreading. If you start proofreading immediately after writing the essay, you will miss a lot of errors because you will be 'reading' what you think you have written and not what is on the page.

- If possible, ask somebody to proofread your essay. This should not be somebody doing the same assignment as you. If you ask two people to proofread your work, only ask them one at a time so that you can pass the proofread essay to the second reader. Make sure that you tell them to proofread and not to edit the essay.

- If you proofread your essay continuously from start to finish, you are less likely to spot your mistakes. One useful strategy is to read the essay paragraphs in a random order. Colour the essay text red, choose a paragraph at random, proofread it and when you have finished, turn it black. Then take a break. Choose another paragraph to proofread and continue in this way until you have proofread the whole essay. This approach also allows you to chunk proofreading into small units of work.

- Use TTS (text to speech) to read the essay to you. Using a text reader is a great way of identifying errors because you are more likely to hear mistakes than to see them. Again, do this one paragraph at a time and take breaks.

- Some students prefer to read their essays aloud as this can also help to identify mistakes.

- Some students prefer to read a hardcopy. If you are reading on screen, you can change the background colour and enlarge and change the font (subunit 2.6).

- Use a grammar or spell checker. These programs are built into your word processing software, but more dedicated programs can be downloaded separately.

- Keep a list of 'regular errors'. These are the mistakes you often repeat.

producing essays (a 10 step strategy): a visual overview of the strategy

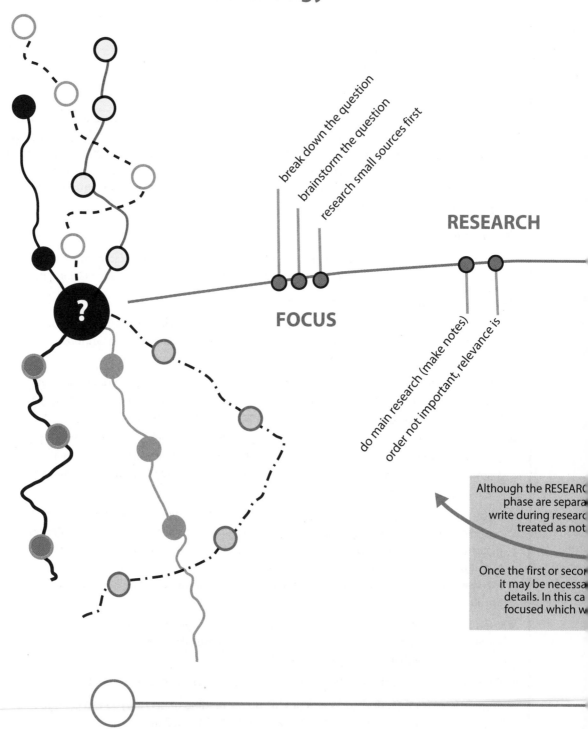

break down the question

brainstorm the question

research small sources first

RESEARCH

FOCUS

do main research (make notes)

order not important, relevance is

Although the RESEARC
phase are separa
write during researc
treated as not

Once the first or secor
it may be necessa
details. In this ca
focused which w

unstructured
ideas & information

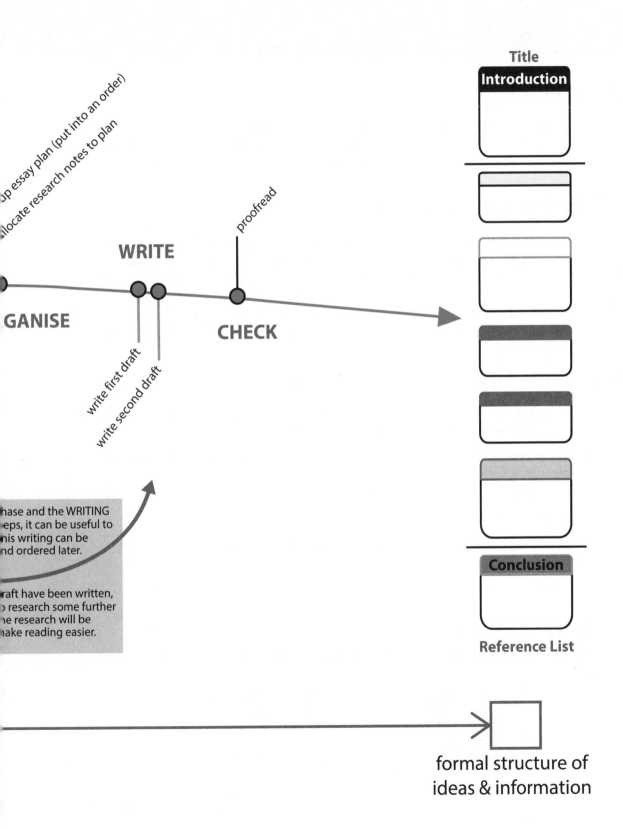

Title

Introduction

proofread

WRITE

GANISE

CHECK

up essay plan (put into an order)

llocate research notes to plan

write first draft

write second draft

hase and the WRITING
eps, it can be useful to
nis writing can be
nd ordered later.

raft have been written,
research some further
e research will be
ake reading easier.

Conclusion

Reference List

formal structure of
ideas & information

making a spatial breakdown of essay questions

⭐ the aim

When you read an essay question, you might immediately think about the topic or subject that relates to the question. The aim of this strategy is to make sure that you highlight, understand and focus on the specific requirements of the essay question, not the topic.

ⓘ why this can help you

This approach uses the principle of reformatting something so that it makes more sense to you. It reformats information from a linear to a spatial layout. Breaking a question apart, bit by bit, and redrafting it will help you identify the different elements of the question and the link(s) between these elements. Identifying and emphasising the link between elements will help you see the question within the topic. This means that when you research and make notes for your essay, it will be easier for you to identify relevant information because your research will have a clearer focus.

⚙ the strategy

This strategy is called the 'elements, links and parts' (ELP) strategy, because you look specifically for these three things when breaking down an essay question.

Take a blank sheet of A3 paper and turn it landscape. Read the essay question. Identify the elements of the question and write them on the sheet. The elements are:

- what the question is about (the topics, subjects, issues, themes, authors, events, works etc.)
- the things you will need to know about to answer the question

Separate and give different colours to the elements on your sheet so that they can be seen individually.

essay question:

Examine the power of the police in the United Kingdom to control assemblies by racist groups.

This question has two elements, but these elements are not the question, they are what the question is about. Next, look for what links the elements. Look for the relationship between them. For example:

- questions often ask you how one thing might contribute to, affect or lead to another
- questions can ask you to apply one thing (e.g. a framework) to another
- some questions ask you to compare or contrast two or more things

Draw this link between the relevant elements by using an arrow or a line and write the linking instruction ('leads to', 'contributes to', 'compares with' etc.) on the link. It is the link that reveals the question.

Examine the power of the police in the United Kingdom to control assemblies by racist groups.

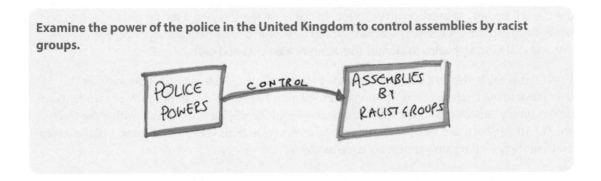

Read the essay question again and see if it has more than one part. Most essay questions have only one part, but some have two or three. Some questions are in fact two or three different questions rolled into one. If the question has more than one part, identify and separate the parts on your sheet and identify the elements and links for each part.

Finally, read the question again and see if it has any other instructions that might limit or focus your answer. For example, the question might refer to a certain period of time, a specific place or a particular writer or thinker. Add this information to your spatial breakdown.

Examine the power of the police in the United Kingdom to control assemblies by racist groups.

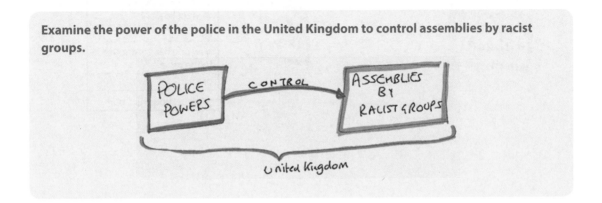

A step by step spatial breakdown will also help you to see which parts of the question are still unclear. These should be clarified with the person who set the question before you start the essay. Once you have made your spatial breakdown of the question, it is useful to refer to it throughout the essay production process as this will help to keep you focused on the question. The relationship between the elements (the link) is really where your thinking should be as you research, collect and develop ideas about the essay question. The link will be the focus for your thesis statement and your final conclusion.

As well as breaking down short questions or titles, this approach can be applied to long assignment briefs. Breaking down complex assignment briefs is particularly useful as there are often many different elements, links and parts you are required to consider.

Some questions provide a quote and instruct you to discuss the quote. For these questions, you can use the ELP strategy to break down the quote to clarify what it is saying. Even for questions that do not have an explicit link between elements, it can be useful to reformat questions and instructions into a spatial form as it helps to identify the different elements and parts.

The ELP strategy is step 1 of producing essays: a 10 step strategy (subunit 6.2). It presents an alternative to the strategy of highlighting or underlining 'key words' in a question. Many students who do this simply underline all or most of the words without identifying the question within the topic. The ELP strategy can also be used for doing long answer questions in exams. See step 1 of the 4 step exam strategy for long answer questions (subunit 9.6).

Below are more examples of essay questions set out in a spatial form after using the ELP strategy. Looking through them will help you understand the strategy and give you a good idea of how to break down your own essay questions in the same way. Practise using the strategy and you will be able to break down essay questions quickly. If you have to choose from a list of essay questions, you can use the ELP strategy to help you decide which question to select.

What has been the most important contribution of feminist thought to legal theory?

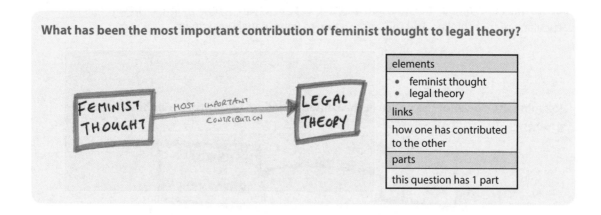

How can midwives improve care for women who are experiencing domestic abuse?

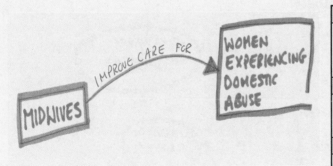

elements
• midwives • women who experience domestic abuse
links
how one group can improve care for another
parts
this question has 1 part

How have diet and behaviour contributed to teenage obesity in the United Kingdom in the last ten years?

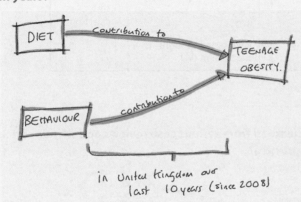

elements
• diet • behaviour • teenage obesity
links
how two elements have contributed to the third
parts
this question has 1 part

Compare the conception of human nature of Thomas Hobbes and Jean-Paul Sartre.

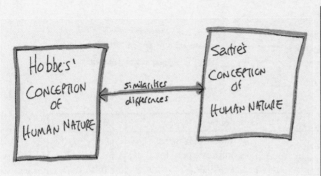

elements
• Hobbes' conception of human nature • Sartre's conception of human nature
links
the similarities and differences between them
parts
this question has 1 part

In what ways did the work of R.D. Laing present a challenge to orthodox psychiatry and are any of his criticisms still valid today?

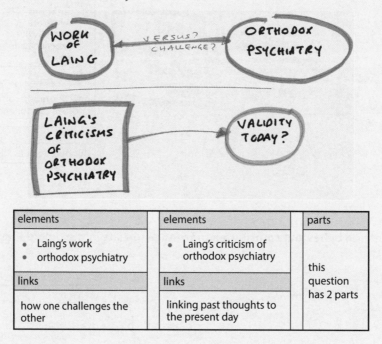

elements	elements	parts
• Laing's work • orthodox psychiatry	• Laing's criticism of orthodox psychiatry	
links	links	this question has 2 parts
how one challenges the other	linking past thoughts to the present day	

What practical lessons have been learned from serious case reviews and why does it appear difficult to put these lessons into practice?

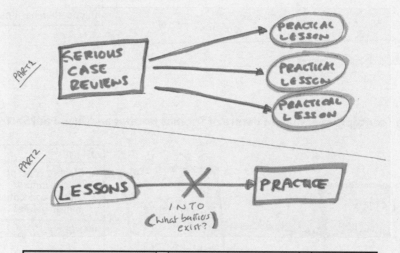

elements	elements	parts
• serious case reviews • practical differences	• practical lessons • improvement in practice	
links	links	this question has 2 parts
how are SCRs the source of lessons, or how are lessons derived from SCRs	barriers in putting what has been learned into practice	

⭐ the aim

A spatial overview is a visual representation of the main research findings and ongoing ideas about the content of an essay. The spatial overview is made during the research phase and aims to identify the key topics that will form the main body of an essay.

ℹ️ why this can help you

A spatial overview is simple to create, easy to modify and always accessible. It highlights and collects main findings in one place so that you can see the key topics that are emerging during research. A spatial (as opposed to a linear) arrangement of key topics makes it easier for you to see the relationship between the topics. This will help when it comes to creating an order for your essay.

If you discuss your essay with a tutor, it is useful to use your spatial overview. It will be easier for you to explain and show your essay ideas and it will be easier for the tutor to see whether you are on the right track or whether you have deviated from the essay question.

⚙️ the strategy

At the start of the research phase, take a sheet of A3 paper and turn it landscape. You know that your essay will have an introduction (I) and a conclusion (C), so you can draw those first. As you find and decide on key topics for the essay, add them to the overview. These key topics will potentially become the paragraphs or the main sections of your essay.

The order doesn't really matter at this stage as it can be changed during the research phase and finalised later. What is most important is that all the topics are relevant to answering the essay question. You can add some detail to the overview by indicating specific content for each major topic, but keep these brief as the intention is to create a concise overview.

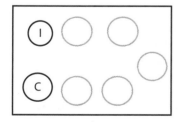

introduction
& conclusion

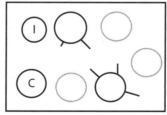

introduction, conclusion
& 2 key topics

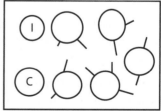

introduction, conclusion
& 5 key topics

As you research, you will start to collect a lot of information and ideas. Try not to list too many key topics. You can remove, combine or divide the topics as you research more and have different ideas about the essay.

Here is an example of a completed spatial overview. It shows the introduction, conclusion and the 5 main topics that were identified during the research phase. The main topics will be developed as paragraphs or sections of the essay. The spatial overview also shows some concise details added to the main topics. These can help in developing the content of each section or paragraph.

essay question:

There has been a decline in turnout at general elections. Identify and discuss why this has happened.

Making a spatial overview on paper means that it is portable and always accessible. But you can create a spatial overview in other ways. You can use a whiteboard to keep track of your main topics, or, if you prefer not to handwrite or draw, you can use a spatial mapping program.

If you make a spatial overview for a longer written assignment like a dissertation, the main topics can represent different chapters or sections (see subunit 8.4). Each chapter can then be given a separate spatial overview with its own introduction, conclusion and main topics.

For most essays, the order of content is up to you. The order of content is important because it can be used to show the information and ideas in a logical way. An essay is easier to read when the order of paragraphs makes sense. However, for some students, putting the information and ideas into a good order can be the hardest part of essay production.

All the ideas in an essay are linked. They are connected because they are relevant to the question. Separating these ideas into different paragraphs can seem almost unnatural and some students find it difficult to decide where something should go in the essay. This can result in a lot of confusion or repetition.

The 10 step strategy for producing essays encourages you to work spatially and not to worry about order until you are ready to write. But at some stage, you will have to decide on an order and make a plan. It is useful to make a plan with aims (see subunit 6.6) because all the information and ideas you have about a question need to be placed in the right paragraphs and the paragraphs need to be placed in the best order.

One of the main challenges in writing essays is to recognise the complexity of an argument or debate and to be able to communicate your ideas by presenting them in a logical sequence that your reader can understand.

There should be a clear rationale to the order you choose, so it is worth thinking about it before making the essay plan. The most important factor when deciding on an order for your essay is the essay question. The most logical order is the one that answers the question in the best way and justifies the conclusion.

in an essay, complex ideas are placed in a logical order

The information and ideas in an essay can be presented and discussed in many ways. The table below is not a prescriptive guide. It is intended to help you think about an order you could use for your essay.

to present an argument or take a position on something			
weakest evidence first ↓ **build up to the strongest** – (your argument will gather force)	**strongest evidence first** ↓ **weakest evidence last** – (your argument will make an immediate impression)	**strong evidence first** ↓ **weakest evidence in the middle** ↓ **finish with strong evidence** – (your essay can seem more balanced)	**present an argument** ↓ **present the counterargument** ↓ **refute the counterargument (i.e. present and discuss your evidence to support the argument)**

to present a balanced discussion or examination of something without taking a position	
supporting evidence (argument) in first part of essay ↓ **evidence against (counterargument) in second part (or vice versa)**	**present the most relevant themes or topics in order of importance and discuss the argument and counterargument under each theme**

to compare or contrast two (or more) things		
present the most relevant themes or topics in order of importance and discuss the similarities and/or differences under each theme	**present and discuss similarities** ↓ **present and discuss differences (or vice versa)** – (good for making a comparison)	**present the first thing** ↓ **present the second** ↓ **discuss the similarities and/or differences between them** – (better for showing differences)

show the development of something or discuss a process	
present and discuss main topics chronologically – (can show change or development over time or cause and effect)	**present and discuss main topics as steps** – (logical way to discuss a method or model)

the essay plan

It is difficult to make an essay plan at the start of the essay production process. You may know some of the content, but a logical order of the content is easier to achieve once you have finished researching the essay. However, making an essay plan before you start writing is very useful. An essay plan should show you the main topics of the essay in the order they will appear. The plan should also help you allocate the information and ideas (that you collected during the research phase) to the relevant sections of the essay.

An essay plan is better if it is not too detailed. You don't have to number and label each subsection of the essay, just each of the main topics, themes or issues you want to discuss. Allocating the number of words to the sections can be helpful as a guide but these are best used as estimates. Here is an example of a typical essay plan:

There has been a decline in turnout at general elections. Identify and discuss why this has happened. (2,000 words)
introduction   (160 words)
partisanship and party politics   (500)
socioeconomic factors   (400)
the political system   (300)
loss of interest, lack of motivation   (200–300)
the media   (200–300)
conclusion   (160)

In this plan, the 5 main topics (reasons) have been placed in order of importance. Because a typical academic paragraph is about 150 to 200 words long, this essay will have around 9 to 11 paragraphs, so some of the topics will be dealt with in more than one paragraph.

An essay plan is more useful if it has aims, instead of just a series of headings. An aim in an essay plan is a statement, written by you, that identifies the intention or purpose of a section of the essay. The aim answers questions like: 'what's this bit for?', 'what do I want to say or argue here?' or 'what do I want the reader to get from this part?'

The aims should be short and specific. They are like mini thesis statements written for each of the main sections of the essay. They are only written to help you, so don't worry about writing them informally, you will remove them once the essay is finished. Here is an example of an essay plan with aims:

There has been a decline in turnout at general elections. Identify and discuss why this has happened. (2,000 words)
introduction (160 words)
partisanship and party politics (500 words)
Here I want to show that research backs that voters are put off voting in safe seats because they know their MP will get in, or that their candidate is a hopeless case.
socioeconomic factors (400)
In this part, I want to argue that the rich or the well-off are voting for the status quo and that poorer people are losing more and more motivation and voting less, especially disadvantaged young people.
the political system (300)
The 2 party system is well established in Britain and it means that smaller parties don't have influence, so people don't vote for them.
loss of interest, lack of motivation (200–300)
Recent corruption scandals have reduced motivation, people have come to trust politicians less and less over time, this has been backed up by research done by Smith (2018).
the media (200–300)
I want to show here that the media, especially television and social media, have become more 'aggressive' and critical towards politicians and lots of people either don't trust the media or aren't sure any more and therefore don't bother voting.
conclusion (160)

An essay plan with aims will make it easier for you to allocate the information and ideas collected from research to the appropriate section of the essay. This is because you will be allocating information according to an explicit aim.

writing introductions and conclusions for essays

It can be difficult to differentiate between the purpose of the introduction and the conclusion of an essay. One approach to writing effective introductions and conclusions is to focus on the thesis statement and build the two paragraphs around it. The thesis statement appears to be required in both, which means that the introduction and the conclusion can end up being the same. Before looking at how to write introductions and conclusions for essays, it is useful to understand what a thesis statement is.

what is a thesis statement?

In an essay introduction, a thesis statement is a short, written statement that is usually one or two sentences long. The type of thesis statement you write will depend on the requirements of the essay question. The thesis statement will directly address (or answer) the essay question. It will be a statement describing one or more of the following:

- your main point or central idea
- your main argument
- your main belief, opinion or point of view
- your position or stance
- your focus or research question
- your judgement

A good thesis statement can be difficult to write because, although it is short, it needs to be specific and capture your main message. Here are three examples of thesis statements written for essay introductions:

essay question	thesis statement for the introduction
According to the Office of National Statistics, households are now four times less likely to be a victim of burglary than in 1995. What are the main reasons for this?	The increasingly sophisticated and affordable technology now available to householders has had an impact on reducing domestic burglaries. However, the main reason for the decline is that the relative monetary value of household goods has reduced considerably.
What will university students lose if continuous coursework replaces traditional examinations?	Examinations, especially in the first year of a degree, are more likely to ensure that students increase their knowledge of their academic subject. This will decrease if exams are replaced by continuous coursework.
Why did the population of the Aboriginal people fall by 90% between 1780 and 1990?	British colonial rule meant that the Aboriginal people lost land and people through displacement and direct conflict. However, the major reason for the population decline was disease, especially smallpox, against which the Aborigines had no immunity.

The thesis statement reads like a conclusion because it is something you formulate by researching the essay question. However, a concise thesis statement should be in the introduction. The thesis statement will also appear in the conclusion, but in a different form. This is discussed later.

It is easier to write the full introduction once the essay has been written, but it is useful to write and develop a draft version of the thesis statement during the research phase of essay production. A thesis statement gives your research and your writing focus and direction. It is also useful to have it in front of you when you decide on the order of your main topics and draw up your essay plan.

A thesis statement requires evidence to support it (in fact, it is derived from the evidence). This evidence will be an important part of the main body of the essay. In an introduction, the thesis statement can be expanded to include a list of the main points that will be discussed in the essay. This allows you to signpost or map out the main content of an essay so that the reader knows what is coming. A concise thesis statement and the main points covered in an essay are therefore two of the important parts of an essay introduction.

writing an essay introduction

Most essay introductions are one paragraph in length. Extended essays can have longer introductions. The content of an introduction depends on its length (usually around 8% of the word limit) and the requirements of the question. But it also depends on choices that you, the writer, make. The content and order of essay introductions are not fixed or regulated. However, there are certain things that an introduction can do. Some are important, some are useful and some are only appropriate for longer introductions.

You can use the introduction to do any of the following:

- show that you understand the essay question
- show that you understand the importance of the essay question
- give some relevant background or contextual information on the question
- show how you are going to address the question (methodology, perspective)
- write your thesis statement
- state how you will support your thesis statement by outlining the main topics
- state any limitations of your essay
- define any relevant terms
- write a sentence that leads into the first paragraph

These items are outlined in the following table. They are presented in the order in which they usually appear in essay introductions. They have been labelled as 'important' (will often appear in essay introductions), 'useful' (you can decide if this will add something useful to your introduction) or 'for longer introductions' (will generally appear in the introductions for extended essays).

a guide for writing an essay introduction	
understanding the essay question (useful)	A good way to start an introduction is to show your reader that you have understood the essay question. You could do this in your first sentence(s) by making a specific point. This will make an immediate impact. For example, you can use a quote from a relevant source, describe an event or use a statistic. **Avoid starting the introduction:** • **with a general point** • **by repeating the question** • **with the phrase 'this essay will …'**
importance of the question (useful)	You can expand your understanding of the question by showing why it is an important question. For example, is it a current issue, an unresolved debate or something that can have major consequences?
background or contextual information (longer intros)	In most introductions, you won't have space to include too much background information. Therefore, only include essential information or essential context. Most, if not all, of the relevant background information will be presented and discussed in the main body.
how you are going to address the question (important)	If you have adopted a specific approach in answering the question, you need to tell your reader what it is. Are you applying a perspective or a theoretical framework (e.g. a feminist, postmodernist or structuralist approach)? Have you used a method (e.g. a case study, a comparative analysis of two texts or a close reading)? You may also want to justify why you used a specific approach.
thesis statement (important)	The thesis statement is a one or two sentence statement of your main argument, position, belief and so on.
outline the main topics (important)	Extend (or break up) the thesis statement by stating what major topics you will cover. Introduce the topics in the same order in which they will appear in the essay. You could write a sentence for each one. Avoid using the phrases: 'this essay will …' and 'then it will …'.
limitations of the essay (longer intros)	You may want to give more detail on the focus of the essay and identify some points that the essay will not cover and state why they have been omitted.
define essential terms (longer intros)	You may need to clarify some essential terms or give definitions that your reader needs to know. This requirement is more likely in technical papers, or in essays for subjects like Law and Philosophy. However, if the explanations are complex, the introduction can be used to introduce the terms, which can then be defined in more detail in the first paragraph(s) of the essay. Avoid using simple dictionary definitions.
linking sentence (useful)	If possible, try to link the last sentence of the introduction with the topic of the first paragraph. This is not essential, and you should only do it if you think it is necessary or useful.

writing an essay conclusion

The conclusion can be written at any time. Ideas for the conclusion can come during the research phase and it is useful to make a note of them. Be prepared to adapt your conclusion as you do more research. Knowing your conclusion before you start writing the essay can help you make a logical plan.

A conclusion can:

- summarise your main points, evidence or findings
- highlight the (possible) consequences of your findings
- indicate areas of uncertainty or disagreement that remain
- highlight the need for possible future research or debate

You can do all these things by rephrasing, expanding and questioning the short thesis statement that is part of your introduction. In fact, the conclusion to most essays is an expanded thesis statement. When writing the conclusion, you should validate your thesis statement by detailing the main information or ideas you have used to support it. Here is an example of rephrasing the thesis statement to write a conclusion:

According to the Office of National Statistics, households are now four times less likely to be a victim of burglary than in 1995. What are the main reasons for this?

thesis statement in the introduction

The increasingly sophisticated and affordable technology now available to householders has had an impact on reducing domestic burglaries. However, the main reason for the decline is that the relative monetary value of household goods has reduced considerably.

thesis statement rephrased for the conclusion

Studies by Goldring (2018) conclude that modern security systems have prevented and reduced domestic burglaries, but it is difficult to quantify this figure. Interviews with convicted burglars show only a small percentage were deterred by the presence of alarms or security surveillance. The effect of technology in reducing break-ins remains uncertain and more research is needed to support the claims made by the UK home security sector. However, Wilson (2018) puts forward strong evidence to show that the relative value of domestic goods like mobile phones, tablets and televisions has reduced to the extent that 'skilled thieves' are turning their attention away from domestic burglaries to non-domestic targets where the monetary rewards are, potentially, much greater. The link between a reduction in burglaries and an increase in digital and online theft was an issue that came to light, but a direct relationship has not been found. A new pattern of criminal activity has emerged in the last 15 years and it differs considerably from the one established in the last decades of the twentieth century. A reduction in domestic burglary is one characteristic of that pattern.

When writing the conclusion:

- try not to use expressions like 'in summary' or 'to sum things up'
- don't repeat the thesis statement word for word
- don't introduce new ideas or new evidence
- try not to write too much (the conclusion is about 8% of the word count)

★ the aim

This tool identifies the elements that tutors consider when assessing essays. It is primarily designed to help you recognise which aspects of your essay are strong and which parts need to be improved.

ⓘ why this can help you

The 10 essential elements of academic essays are clearly presented so that you can easily check that you have addressed all of them. You can use this tool to check your essay once it is finished. However, it can also be useful to read through the elements before you begin working on your essay so that you know what is expected of you.

⚙ the strategy

In the chart below, each of the 10 elements is listed with a different potential score and a worst and best case scenario. Photocopy the template, which you can find on the last page of this subunit (or download a copy from www.macmillanihe.com/lia-sys), and grade your essay according to how closely you feel it reflects the worst and best case scenario for each of the 10 elements. Total the scores in the table for a percentage grade.

The first 4 of the 10 elements are largely structural, in that they adhere to conventions, guidelines or rules. You should be able to improve some of these elements by knowing and applying the terms of reference (subunit 5.1) and by presenting your work well. Academic English also follows rules and conventions (subunit 5.2) and your writing can be improved when you proofread your work.

Although they don't carry the most marks, the introduction and conclusion have specific purposes (subunit 6.7) and need to be well written. A strong, relevant introduction can make an immediate positive impression on a reader.

The 10 elements are relevant to most types of written assignments. However, this tool is designed primarily for formal, academic essays. These essays require you to show good knowledge of a subject, but they also ask for analysis (discussion).

10 elements of a good essay	
1	presentation
2	referencing
3	English
4	order
5	introduction
6	conclusion
7	evidence
8	analysis
9	argument (perspective)
10	answer the question!

For an academic essay you will have to carry out extensive research and formulate and set out an argument or point of view, before reaching a valid conclusion. That is why a lot of marks are given for areas that reflect this type of work. This is included in three of the elements: evidence, analysis and argument. For more ideas on critical thinking, see unit 4 critical thinking for academic writing.

worst-case scenario	best-case scenario

presentation

worst-case scenario
- the presentation does not meet the stated requirements (sometimes called the 'terms of reference') in terms of line spacing, font style or word limit
- the work is inconsistently or poorly presented

best-case scenario
- the presentation meets all the terms of reference
- the formatting is consistent
- the presentation is of a high standard throughout

1	2	3	4	5

referencing

worst-case scenario
- the referencing is poor, incomplete, inconsistently formatted or absent
- some of the sources cited in the essay do not appear in the reference list

best-case scenario
- all references (in the essay and in the reference list or bibliography) are set out correctly and use the required referencing system (e.g. Chicago, Harvard or MLA)

1	2	3	4	5	6	7	8

English

worst-case scenario
- poor sentence structure
- poor spelling
- many grammar and punctuation errors
- use of colloquial (non-academic) English
- no use or misuse of subject specifc terminology

best-case scenario
- high standard of academic English (in sentence structure, vocabulary etc.)
- no errors in spelling, punctuation or grammar
- appropriate use of precise terminology relevant to the essay question

1	2	3	4	5	6	7	8	9	10	11	12	13	14	15

order

worst-case scenario
- there is no clear order to the paragraphs or to the sentences within paragraphs, so the points being made do not follow a logical sequence (writing 'wanders' from the initial point)
- there is a lot of repetition

best-case scenario
- the paragraphs are in a logical order and this order is clear to the reader
- (if required) the essay develops an argument
- points are not repeated

1	2	3	4	5	6

worst-case scenario			best-case scenario	

		introduction		
• there is no clear introduction • the introduction simply repeats the essay question • the introduction is boring and does not inspire the reader to read further • the introduction is too long • the introduction is too short • the introduction is the same as the conclusion			• the introduction is immediately specific to the question but does not repeat the question word for word • the introduction is clear, original and interesting • the introduction makes the reader want to read on • the introduction is the right length • the introduction is different from the conclusion	
1	2	3	4	5

		conclusion		
• there is no clear conclusion • the conclusion simply repeats what is written in the essay (sometimes word for word) • the conclusion introduces new ideas that are not in the body of the essay • the conclusion is the same as the introduction • the conclusion is too long • the conclusion is too short			• the conclusion is logically and clearly derived from the evidence presented in the body of the essay • the conclusion does not introduce new ideas • the conclusion is different from the introduction • the conclusion is the right length	
1	2	3	4	5

		evidence		
• there is no evidence used, so any point of view is just based on the writer's opinion or shows signs of plagiarism • the evidence comes only from a single source which is repeated throughout the essay • the evidence comes from non-academic or unreliable sources • the evidence is not used for any purpose but just placed in the essay without a clear reason • the evidence is too old or out of date			• the evidence is taken from a wide range of reliable sources • if relevant, the evidence is taken from the key readings prescribed by the tutor • the evidence is used for a specific reason (e.g. to support an argument or discuss an issue) • the reason for using the evidence is made clear to the reader	

1	2	3	4	5	6	7	8	9	10	11	12	13	14

worst-case scenario		best-case scenario

	analysis (discussion)	
• the essay is just descriptive and does not discuss, so there is no analysis (i.e. the essay consists of stated information that is not developed)		• information is fully discussed and not simply described • paragraphs are used to introduce a point and then develop a discussion • the essay shows how the main points interrelate and therefore shows an understanding of the complexity of the answer in relation to a question

1	2	3	4	5	6	7	8	9	10	11	12

	argument (perspective position viewpoint)	
• the essay is one-sided and does not consider or acknowledge other points of view or (counter) arguments • any point of view stated is little more than a subjective opinion so there is no argument • arguments are started but not developed or brought to a logical outcome		• the essay takes into consideration alternative points of view that are relevant to the question • the argument (point of view) is derived from the evidence and formed on the basis of the most compelling evidence • the argument is made clear to the reader, it may take one side against another, or it may show the relative validity of both (or different) arguments

1	2	3	4	5	6	7	8	9	10

	answer the question!	
• the essay has too much background information that was not asked for • the essay contains irrelevant information on the topic that does not address the question • there is no link between what is written and how this relates to the essay question (or this link is not made clear)		• everything in the essay (information and ideas) is relevant to addressing the question • the link between what is written in the essay and the essay question is clear or is made clear to the reader

1	2	3	4	5	6	7	8	9	10	11	12	13	14	15	16	17	18	19	20

The best advice you can give to anybody who is doing an essay is to answer the question. That is why this element contains most marks. It is therefore essential that you understand the essay question right at the start of the essay production process (see subunit 6.3).

grade your own essay template

essay question or title

element	score	action required
presentation	5	
referencing	8	
English	15	
order	6	
introduction	5	
conclusion	5	
evidence	14	
analysis	12	
argument	10	
answer the question!	20	
total grade	%	

unit 7

reflective writing

Reflective writing is a specific type of academic writing that is required for some coursework assignments. In order to produce good reflective writing, it is necessary to understand the aims and potential benefits of reflective writing and reflective practice. This unit begins by explaining why reflective writing is useful and how it can help you improve your knowledge and skills. Using evidence to support your reflection will make your writing stronger, so advice is also given on the different sources of evidence you can include. Assignments that require reflective writing (sometimes called 'reflective essays') have specific content and are presented in a conventional order and set structure. Content, order and structure are set out in a new reflective writing model and template you can use or adapt. A visual overview is provided of five well-known reflective practice models so that you can compare different approaches and gain a better understanding of the value of reflective work. The unit ends with a detailed guide and template to help you apply one of the most widely used models: Gibbs' reflective cycle.

what is reflective writing?

Reflective writing is an academic form of writing that comes from thinking about an experience. It is therefore the product of reflective thinking. Reflective writing is one part of a bigger process called 'reflective practice'. Here is how reflective writing fits into that process:

the essential elements (steps) of reflective practice

Although it is a form of academic writing, reflective writing has different conventions. It uses the first person ('I'), it contains emotive descriptions and you can give personal opinions without the use of supporting evidence. Reflective writing is required for some academic assessments, so it is useful to understand it as a practical tool. For most academic purposes, reflection requires you to think and write about:

- why you did something (or reacted to something) in a certain way

- the consequences (good, bad and neutral) of your actions or feelings

- things you can do to improve your knowledge and skill

You can be asked to reflect on:

- an activity or event in which you were involved

- an activity or event you observed

- the presentation of information or ideas for which you were the recipient

Examples of things you may have to reflect on include being part of a team for a group project, your experience in an internship or work placement, or your attendance at a conference, training event or other learning activity.

Reflective writing is usually required on courses that include an element of work-based practice or what has been termed 'work-based learning'. This simply means learning through practical work experiences (in the workplace) as opposed to learning by yourself or in a classroom or lecture theatre. Reflective writing is therefore mostly associated with vocational qualifications, which are courses that educate and train students for specific professions.

Most reflective writing assignments are in the form of a structured written document. The reflective piece (sometimes called a 'reflective essay') is usually around 1,000 to 2,000 words long. In some courses, students are asked to keep a reflective diary that covers the duration of an experience. Reflective writing can also form a single part of a longer piece of written work, like a section in a report or one part of a portfolio of work.

what is the aim of reflective practice and reflective writing?

The aim of reflective practice is to increase your knowledge and skill in a specific discipline. Knowledge can improve with experience, learning and training. Skill can improve with experience, ability and practice. Thinking and writing about your experiences in a constructive way are designed to accelerate your improvement and make you better at what you do (potentially, your profession after you graduate). If you reflect and write about your experiences regularly, you can measure your progress over time. In work, reflective practice is a form of what is often called 'continuing professional development'.

how can reflective writing help you improve your knowledge and skills?

When you do or hear something, you behave or respond in a certain way. Your actions and thoughts are influenced by many things, most of which you will probably not be aware of until you think and write about an experience. Here are some influencing factors to consider when reflecting:

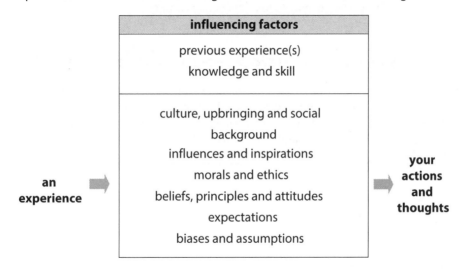

You might know the policy guidelines for doing something (like taking blood pressure) but if you think deeper about how you do it, you will find that your actions and thoughts are influenced by many factors (not just knowledge, skill and experience). An important aim of reflective thinking is to reveal these factors. Reflective writing makes them explicit and discusses how they affect you. An experience can then become a learning opportunity that can lead to better knowledge and practice.

reflective writing and revealing weakness

Good reflective writing requires you to be open and honest. You may be reluctant to reveal weaknesses (e.g., a lack of knowledge) to yourself and especially to your marker. To overcome this, you need to recognise the benefits of reflective practice as a learning tool. You are not expected to know everything or have all the skills. You do not need to write about anything that is not relevant to your practice and you can reflect on your strengths as well as your weaknesses. But, reflecting on a weakness allows you to then identify specific actions you can take to address it.

reflective writing and group work failures

When reflecting on a group project or a team activity, you should never apportion blame to other members of a group in your reflective writing. Reflective writing is not an opportunity to let off steam when things have gone wrong. A group of individuals often fail to work effectively as a team. If this is your experience, reflect on your role. Think about how your behaviour played a part in the actions of the group. Ask what contribution you could have made or what you could have done differently. Keep the focus on yourself and never directly criticise other individuals. Learning from negative experiences in group work is an important part of reflective practice, especially when you are part of a multidisciplinary team where everyone has a different contribution to make but where interdependency is also important.

using academic references in reflective writing

Reflective writing discusses personal actions, thoughts and feelings. However, many tutors will also ask you to include academic references in your reflection. Evidence is not needed for your opinions or ideas, but it can be used to support what you have written. For example, you might want to justify why you did something in a certain way or why you might have done something differently. Here are two examples of using academic evidence to support reflective writing:

academic evidence used to justify or explain an action
I made time to have a conversation with Mr J and his family before prescribing any medication. Mr J is an elderly patient with some communication problems. I wanted to make sure that any decision making was a shared activity and that the patient's own preferences were clear to me. Schuling et al. (2012) have argued that prior assumptions can be a barrier to recognising individual patient preferences, especially in elderly patients, and that clinicians need to be aware of this and take explicit action to avoid it.

academic evidence used to support a different approach
I felt that all the members of our team were highly proficient but there was a lack of awareness of our individual strengths. In retrospect, it would have been useful for the team to have completed a short team training exercise before beginning the project. Team training can improve the performance of a team by up to 20% (Salas and Rosen, 2013). Team training can also improve what is sometimes called 'relational coordination'. I understand this term to mean that a team has better communication when it understands and shares the purpose of a task and is in a better position to decide how to plan for that task as a team. I think this was lacking in our initial approach to the project.

sources of evidence used in reflective writing

Not all the evidence you provide will be from academic sources. In reflective writing you can justify an action or thought by referring to your own practice and thinking. For example, you might use a previous experience or state a personal preference to explain why you did something. The evidence you use in your reflective writing can come from any of these 4 sources:

- **practice**: your own actions or observed actions of others
- **theory**: your own thoughts as well as theory from academic sources
- **peer reviewed research**: usually not more than 5–10 years old
- **policy**: policy guidelines and legislation from institutions or professional bodies at local, national or international level

practice and theory

Reflective writing commonly explores the relationship between practice and theory (doing and thinking) and you are often asked to focus on this relationship in your writing. These elements also share a relationship with research and policy, which you can reflect on.

A simple model combining these 4 elements is presented in the strategy: critical thinking: practice, theory, research, policy (see subunit 4.2).

The version shown here could be described as the ideal model:

- practice influences theory
- theory generates research
- research informs policy
- policy changes practice

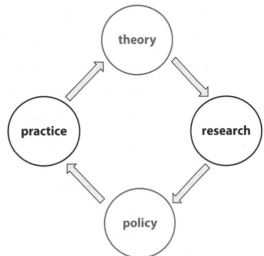

7.2 reflective writing: style and structure

writing style of reflective writing

Reflective writing has a less formal tone than other kinds of academic writing.

It is different in several ways:

- it uses the first person throughout
- it describes feelings and can therefore be emotive
- it is subjective and states opinions without the need for academic evidence
- it can relax some of the style rules of academic writing

For example, you might write:

> I was shocked by my overreaction. Looking back, it's clear that my lack
> of knowledge made me feel insecure. Instead of pretending that I knew what to do,
> I should have asked for guidance from the team leader.

However, reflective writing is still a form of academic writing and you should avoid colloquial phrases and use appropriate terminology when necessary. Your writing should be presented in a logical order, with proper sentences and paragraphs, and any supporting evidence used needs to be referenced correctly.

the structure of reflective writing assignments

Most reflective pieces will be structured more like a report than an essay. The structure can include headings for each section or just follow a set order without headings. Writing a reflective assignment is made easier if you know the order of content before you start writing or making notes of your experience. There are several reflective models (see subunit 7.4 for some examples). Most of them contain 4 essential tasks set out in the following order:

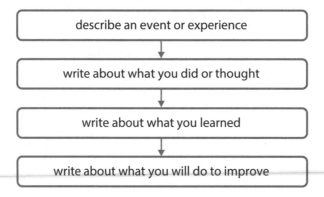

If you haven't been asked to apply an existing reflective model to your work, you can use one as a guide. Alternatively, you can draw up your own simple model. This is a form of preparation and a great way of really understanding the task of reflection. Making your own model can also allow you to adapt it to the specific needs of your assignment brief. An example of a model created for reflective writing is presented next.

Reflective writing tasks are easier if you understand the aims of reflective practice. So, before starting a reflective assignment, it is a good idea to read through and familiarise yourself with the types of questions you will be answering. Look at existing models (subunit 7.4) and use or adapt them to make your own. Here is an overview example of a simple model for reflective writing:

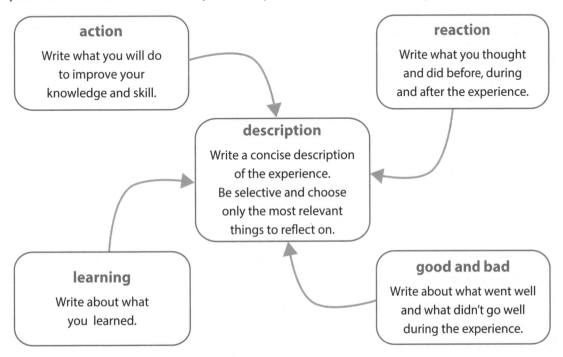

action

Write what you will do to improve your knowledge and skill.

reaction

Write what you thought and did before, during and after the experience.

description

Write a concise description of the experience. Be selective and choose only the most relevant things to reflect on.

learning

Write about what you learned.

good and bad

Write about what went well and what didn't go well during the experience.

In this model, the arrows emphasise that all reflection is made in relation to the experience you are reflecting on (description). The order in which you think or make notes about your experience doesn't matter, but the order in which you present your finished reflective piece does. This is set out as a linear template shown below. It includes key questions regularly addressed in reflective writing. You can use this template or adapt it for your specific needs.

Three important points to aid good reflective writing are:

1	**reflect early**	Write your thoughts down soon after, or during, the experience. Don't wait and try to catch up later by relying on memory.
2	**be specific, not general**	Give details and specific examples. Avoid making general statements.
3	**show the value of reflection**	Emphasise the link between what you did and thought and what you learned. Explain how this new learning can be useful in your specific area of study or (future) work.

a template for reflective writing

The questions given here should be used to guide you. You don't need to answer them all. This template can be used for short, reflective essays and reflective practice diaries. If you want more questions to work with, read through the template for using Gibbs' reflective cycle (subunit 7.5).

---

description: provide a concise description of the experience

Don't describe everything.

Be selective and, if necessary, choose the most relevant things from the experience.

In assessed work, this part carries the fewest marks.

---

reaction: write about what you did and thought
good and bad: write about what went well and what didn't

How did I feel about the experience?

What did I do or think?

Why did I act or think in a certain way? (Is there any evidence to explain this?)

What influencing factors (subunit 7.1) may have influenced my actions and thoughts?

What did I find easy to do or understand, what went well? (Is there any evidence to explain this?)

What did I find difficult to understand, what went badly? (Is there any evidence to explain this?)

What were the consequences of my actions or thoughts, for me and for any relevant others?

---

learning: write about what you learned from the experience

What could I have done better (and is there any evidence to support another approach)?

What did I learn that was new to me?

Do I now understand something that I didn't understand before?

What insights did this new learning give me about myself?

Will this experience change the way I think or act?

How do I think this experience will be useful in my future practice?

---

action: write about what you will do to improve

Do I need to plug gaps in my knowledge? (If so, what do I need to learn?)

Do I need to improve my skills? (If so, what do I need to be able to do better?)

How and when will I do these things?

You can download this template from www.macmillanihe.com/lia-sys.

Here, 5 models for reflective practice are outlined, with references to their original sources, which give more details about the models. Even if you are not using a specific framework for your reflection, reading these overviews will help you think and write your reflective coursework.

Rolfe (1993): a framework for reflective practice

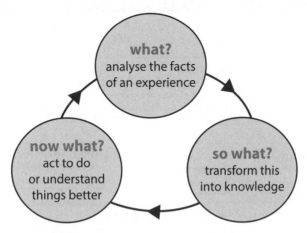

diagram inspired by Rolfe (2014) p. 489

Borton (1970) used the terms 'sensing', 'transforming' and 'acting' to describe three steps of a learning process. To each of these steps, Borton added a key question: 'what?', 'so what?' and 'now what?' Rolfe (1993) recognised how this approach could be effectively applied to learning through reflective practice and created a framework for reflection with further cue questions for each stage of the model. Borton's 3 questions have become important elements of all the reflective practice models presented in this unit.

To read more about this model and see a list of Rolfe's cue questions, see Rolfe, G., Jasper, M. and Freshwater, D. (2011) *Critical Reflection in Practice* p. 46.

Kolb (1984): an experiential learning model (after Lewin)

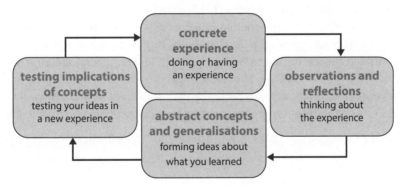

inspired by Kolb and Fry (1975) p. 33 and Kolb (1984) p. 321

In Kolb's model (which built on the work of psychologist Kurt Lewin), 'experiential' simply means learning through experience and Kolb emphasises the importance of subjective experience and conflict as a way of learning and forming new ideas about learning. Kolb also stresses the importance of the process of reflective learning, not just the outcome. The model is in the form of a cycle, so learning can occur by relearning things in different environments and at different times. Kolb links learning, growth and change, especially behavioural change. New experiences can therefore be the testing ground for different behaviour (actions and reactions) and, in this way, experiential learning becomes a continuous process of change.

To read more about this model, see Kolb, D.A. (1984) *Experiential Learning: Experience as the Source of Learning and Development*.

Atkins and Murphy (1994): a framework for reflection

awareness
Identify any uncertainties or insecurities that you felt about your knowledge in relation to the experience.

describe
Describe the experience and discuss any relevant feelings.

action
Detail any action you can take that will perpare you for the next experience.

analyse
Discuss your feelings and highlight your knowledge in examining how you were affected by the experience.

identify
Write about any new learning you gained from the experience.

evaluate
Write about how you used your knowledge and whether it was enough to explain feelings, thoughts, actions and reactions during the experience.

inspired by Atkins and Murphy (1994) p. 51

Atkins and Murphy's framework was made as a reflective practice tool for nurses. It incorporates the ideas of Schön (1991) and Boyd and Fales (1983) to introduce a stage of reflection (awareness), in which you can think about the experience in terms of any uncomfortable feelings you might have about your insufficient knowledge and inability to explain your actions. The relevance of knowledge is central in this model, but knowledge is not just factual knowledge about nursing. It includes the knowledge you bring to an experience (personal knowledge). Atkins and Murphy also emphasise reflection as a constructive experience that considers what went well (achievements) and one that makes a commitment to positive action that can prepare you for the next experience.

To read more about this model, see Atkins, S. and Murphy, K. (1994) Reflective practice pp. 49–54.

Johns (1995): a model of structured reflection

description	aesthetics	personal	ethics	empirics	reflexivity
Write a concise description of the experience.	Write about your aims, feelings, actions, reactions and the consequences of your actions.	Write about your feelings and the factors that influenced them.	Write about how you think your beliefs made you act in certain ways.	Write about existing and potential knowledge.	Write about how the experience makes you feel now, how it has changed you and how you can use it in future experiences.

inspired by Johns (1995) p. 227

Johns' model is based on work by Carper (1978). It sets out a framework with 6 parts. Each part contains cue questions. Johns describes his framework as a heuristic. A heuristic is simply a specific tool, strategy or process that is designed to help you achieve something, in this case, self-improvement through reflective practice. Johns and Carper both emphasise that understanding or 'knowing' the self through reflection is as important as gaining knowledge or skill.

To read more about this model and see a list of Johns' cue questions, see Johns, C. (1995) Framing learning through reflection within Carper's fundamental ways of knowing pp. 226–34.

Driscoll (2007): a model of structured reflection

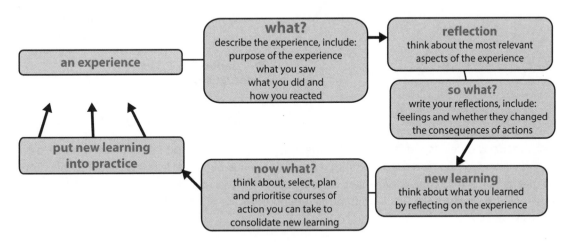

inspired by Driscoll (2007) p. 44

Driscoll's model is sometimes called 'the what? model' because it is structured around the 3 key 'what' questions that were presented by Borton (1970). Driscoll adds several trigger questions to guide reflective thoughts. The model emphasises the importance of transforming new learning (from reflecting on experiences) into practical benefits. This is helped by identifying various but specific courses of action after reflection and before the next experience.

To read more about this model and see a list of Driscoll's trigger questions, see Driscoll, J. (2007) *Practising Clinical Supervision* pp. 44–5.

ASKHAM BRYAN
COLLEGE
LEARNING RESOURC

Gibbs' reflective cycle (or Gibbs' reflective model)

Gibbs' reflective cycle is a theoretical model often used by students as a framework in coursework assignments that require reflective writing. The model was created by Professor Graham Gibbs and appeared in *Learning by Doing* (1988). Gibbs describes the stages of reflection as a kind of debriefing that happens after an experience. The model looks like this:

Gibbs' reflective cycle has 6 stages. They are usually given the following headings:

1. description
2. feelings
3. evaluation
4. analysis
5. conclusion
6. action plan

inspired by Gibbs (1988) pp. 49–50

Gibbs' model was developed from an earlier theoretical model: David Kolb's 4 stage experiential learning cycle (1984). Kolb's model is sometimes referred to as an 'experiential learning model' (which simply means learning through experience), while Gibbs' model is sometimes referred to as an 'iterative model' (which simply means learning through repetition). But both models can be correctly described in these ways.

using analysis in Gibbs' model

In theory, the reflective process follows the 6 steps of the model so that each step informs the next. In practice, students often confuse the evaluation, analysis and conclusion stages. These parts seem to ask similar questions and, as a result, there can be a lot of repetition. Analytical writing is only required in the analysis stage. The other 5 steps are made up of statements of description, statements of value (whether something was good or bad), statements of summation or statements of justification (why something was done).

the aims of using Gibbs' reflective cycle

In common with other models of reflection, Gibbs' reflective cycle can help you:

- challenge your assumptions

- explore different or new ideas and approaches towards doing or thinking about things

- promote self-improvement (by identifying strengths and weaknesses and taking action to address them)

- link practice and theory (by combining doing or observing with thinking or applying knowledge)

a template for using Gibbs' model

Use the questions and guidelines in the template below to help you write each stage of the model. You do not have to answer all the questions. Try to select those that are relevant. You can download this template from www.macmillanihe.com/lia-sys.

description

- Using specific and relevant detail, give a concise description of your experience (what you are reflecting on).

this part is not analytical, it is descriptive, it describes an experience

feelings

Answer any of the following questions you think are relevant to the experience:

- How did you feel and what did you think prior to the experience?

- How did you feel and what did you think during the experience?

- How did you react during the experience?

- How did you feel and what did you think after the experience?

this part is not analytical, it is descriptive, it describes personal feelings and thoughts and actions (reactions)

evaluation

Answer any of the following questions you think are relevant to the experience:

- What went well during the experience (what worked)?
- What went badly during the experience (what didn't work)?
- How did the experience end?
- Was the experience complete (was there a resolution?) or incomplete?

this part is not analytical, it makes positive and/or negative judgements about an experience

if a lot of different things happened during the experience, focus on one or two, try to choose the things that are most important, most relevant or most representative of the experience

analysis

Do any of the following you think are relevant:

- Reconsider the things that went badly and write why you think they went badly (causes of action).
- Reconsider the things that went badly and write what you think this led to (consequences of action).
- Think about what could have been done to have avoided these negative consequences.

- Reconsider the things that went well and write why you think they went well (causes of action).
- Reconsider the things that went well and write what you think this led to (consequences of action).
- Think about how this positive action could have been further improved.

- Think about your contribution to the experience and say how useful it was and why it was useful. (Did a previous experience help you? Can you compare it to a previous experience?)
- If you were unable to contribute to the experience, say why.

- Think about other people present during the experience and try to assess whether their reactions were similar or different from yours.
- Try to say why they were the same or different.

*this part **is** analytical, it does not describe, it tries to explain the causes and consequences of things that happened, it tries to answer the three discursive questions: why?, so what? and what if? (see subunit 4.5)*

conclusion

Reconsider the experience and answer any of the following questions you think are relevant:

- What should, or could, I have done differently?
- What stopped me from doing this?
- What did I learn about myself during the experience (positive and/or negative)?
- What did I learn about my current knowledge or level of skill (practice)?
- What were my main strengths and weaknesses?
- Did the experience achieve any of my learning goals or meet any of my required competencies?

this part sums up what you learned from the experience

try to be specific about what you learned or realised about yourself, give specific details (avoid making general statements like 'I didn't have the adequate knowledge')

action plan

Answer any of the following questions you think are relevant to making a plan:

- What do I need to do to be better prepared to face this experience in future?
- Even if the experience was positive and I did well, which areas can I improve?
- What are the priority areas that need to be developed?
- What specific steps do I need to take to achieve these improvements?

this part is not analytical, it states actions designed to improve knowledge, ability, experience etc. You can include the justification for and value of actions in the action plan (i.e. why you plan to do something)

try to be precise about what you plan to do (e.g. state specific training you may need to undergo, books or policy guidelines you will need to read, resources or software programs you may need to use or become proficient in)

the structure of a reflective coursework assignment using Gibbs' model

With an introduction and conclusion, your assignment will have this structure:

introduction description feelings evaluation analysis conclusion action plan conclusion	The introduction should: • State what the experience was, when and where it took place, and how long it lasted. • State that Gibbs' model is being used (a diagram can be included immediately after the introduction or in the appendix).
	The conclusion should not be a repetition of the conclusion in stage 5 of the model. Instead, it could briefly address any of the following questions: • How valuable was the reflective tool in identifying your strengths and weaknesses and improving your practice or knowledge? • Was Gibbs' model easy to use? • Do you now understand the value of reflective learning and using a reflective learning model like Gibbs' 6 stage model?
	unless told otherwise, keep the introduction and conclusion short

using a word count

It may be useful to use a word count for each step of the cycle to avoid overwriting. Use the table below as a general guide. Remember to adjust the word count if you need to include an introduction and conclusion as part of your assignment.

	steps	%	1,000 words	1,500 words	2,000 words	2,500 words
1	description	20%*	200*	300*	400*	500*
2	feeling	10–20%	150	225	300	375
3	evaluation	20%	200	300	400	500
4	analysis	30%	300	450	600	750
5	conclusion	5–10%	75	112	150	187
6	action plan	5–10%	75	112	150	187

* try to keep the description step as short as possible; it carries the least marks in terms of assessment

including academic references in your reflective writing

If you are asked to include references in your reflection, you can use research (recent studies are best), policy documents (from relevant bodies) or theory (from academic sources) to support your reflections. You might use references:

- to show why something is done in a certain way
  (e.g. by referring to a policy guideline)

- to explain what brought about certain feelings or reactions
  (e.g. by quoting a theory)

- to explain what went well or what went badly
  (e.g. a policy guideline, a piece of research or a theory could be used to explain why a certain action had a positive or a negative outcome)

- to discuss what could have been done differently
  (e.g. policy, research or theory could be used to support your reflection that doing things differently could have had a better outcome)

- to justify why you plan to do something
  (e.g. a research paper might be used to show the value of developing a specific skill or acquiring relevant knowledge)

unit 8

doing a dissertation

A dissertation is likely to be the biggest and most complex piece of academic work you will be asked to complete. So, before starting work on a dissertation, you need to know what you are planning for and working to produce. This unit defines the three main types of dissertation and shows how they can be organised. Making a spatial overview of your dissertation will help you break the dissertation into smaller, manageable tasks that can be understood and tackled separately. A spatial overview will also show you how different sections of a dissertation relate to each other and to the research question. A series of templates are used to detail the typical order and content of the major sections. You should use them to guide you and, when necessary, alter them to suit your specific needs. As you are often required to present your dissertation, a 4 step strategy for preparing a presentation is included in this unit.

what is a dissertation?

A dissertation is a written document produced from a research project. It presents an in-depth investigation or analysis of a chosen topic. A dissertation is required in the final year of many undergraduate degree courses and for most postgraduate qualifications. In the UK, the term 'thesis' is commonly used to refer to the final dissertation produced at PhD or Masters level. But this is not always the case and the terms 'thesis' and 'dissertation' are interchangeable. It is important that before you start work on your dissertation, you know:

- the type of dissertation you are doing
- the structure of the dissertation
- the word (or page) limit
- the hand-in date and the length of time you have

You can normally choose the topic and research question for your dissertation. Sometimes, this choice is restricted to a list of topics that match the available expertise of academics at an institution. But before you decide on a research topic, you should know what type of dissertation you will be doing. Dissertations can be divided into three types: empirical dissertations, systematic literature reviews and theoretical dissertations.

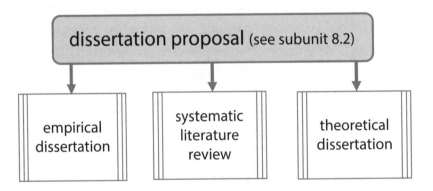

empirical dissertation

Empirical dissertations are sometimes referred to as 'practical' or 'empirical research dissertations'. For an empirical dissertation, you will have to carry out some original research and collect your own data. This might come from work you do in a laboratory (lab work) or outside a laboratory (fieldwork).

You can collect or generate research data in many ways. For example, you might carry out a lab experiment and record the results, you might interview people and record their views, or you might send out questionnaires or surveys and collect the responses.

Empirical dissertations follow a conventional structure. There can be some variations in layout and the wording used for the section or chapter headings (shown below). But if you are doing an empirical dissertation, it will consist of some or all of the sections contained in these three example structures:

example 1:	example 2:	example 3:
This shows the most common structure and order for an empirical dissertation.	The review of literature is part of the introduction and there is no appendix.	The findings and discussion are placed together. The conclusion contains recommendations.
Title Page	Title Page	Title Page
Abstract	Abstract	Abstract
Acknowledgements	Acknowledgements	Acknowledgements
Contents	Contents	Contents
List of Abbreviations	Definition of Key Terms	List of Figures
List of Tables and Figures		
Chapter 1 Introduction	1. Introduction	Chapter 1 Introduction
Chapter 2 Literature Review	2. Methodology	Chapter 2 A Review of the Literature
Chapter 3 Methodology	3. Results	Chapter 3 Methodology
Chapter 4 Results	4. Discussion of Results	Chapter 4 Findings, Analysis and Discussion
Chapter 5 Discussion of Results	5. Conclusion	Chapter 5 Conclusion and Recommendations
Chapter 6 Conclusion		
References	Reference List	Reference List and Bibliography
Appendices		Appendices

Details on the order and content of each section of an empirical research dissertation are provided later in this unit.

systematic literature review

For a systematic literature review (usually abbreviated to systematic review), you do not produce or collect your own, new data. Instead, you search specialised databases for existing research data in relation to a clear research question. These dissertations are sometimes called 'evidence-based dissertations' because they regularly investigate the link between research evidence and (clinical) practice. They are often required on courses like Adult Nursing and Medicine.

All dissertations review relevant literature. However, a systematic review is a specific type of literature review. It is called 'systematic' because it searches for research (literature) by following a meticulous, step by step process. The process is designed to ensure that, as far as possible, the best and most relevant research evidence is found and analysed precisely.

Following the procedure accurately is key to producing a good systematic review and this will be reflected in your grade. The process is also reflected in the overall structure of the dissertation. For a more detailed breakdown of systematic reviews, see subunit 8.10.

the structure and order of a systematic review
Title Page
Abstract
Acknowledgements
Contents Page
1 Introduction/Background
2 Search Strategy
3 Findings
4 Discussion of Findings
5 Conclusion
References
Appendices

theoretical dissertation

This type of dissertation has been referred to as 'non-empirical', 'non-systematic', 'narrative', 'textual' and 'desk based'. It is different from an empirical dissertation because you do not have to produce your own original data. It is different from a systematic review because you won't necessarily have to produce a detailed strategy before searching and reviewing the existing literature. Theoretical dissertations are found in science subjects but are more widespread in humanities courses like History, Literature, Cultural Studies and Philosophy.

The structure of theoretical dissertations can vary. All will have an abstract, introduction and conclusion. Many will follow the typical structure of an empirical dissertation (introduction, methodology, findings, discussion of findings, and conclusion), although some of these sections can have different subheadings to reflect the specific approach or findings.

Some theoretical dissertations will use the review of literature throughout the dissertation and apply it to different themes or issues discussed in different chapters. These chapters can be ordered in different ways. For example, they can be chronological, by subject or by theme. These types of dissertation are best thought of as a form of extended essay. However, they investigate a question in much more depth than essays and you will have more time to research and write the dissertation.

Dissertations in the arts and humanities often don't have a methodology section. Some clinical-based theoretical dissertations will include a methodology that describes and discusses a search strategy similar to, but not as detailed as, that found in a systematic review. In the humanities or social sciences, the methodology can contain a theoretical discussion of:

- the chosen methodology (e.g., qualitative, quantitative or mixed methods, interpretivist or positivist)

- the perspective used by the author (e.g., feminist, Freudian, Marxist or postmodern perspective)

- the approach used to analyse the literature (e.g., textual analysis, discourse analysis, visual or semiotic analysis)

Therefore, the structure, order and content headings of a theoretical dissertation depend on how you have decided to address the research question. But, whether the review of literature is placed in the introduction, in a separate section or discussed throughout the dissertation, the main purpose of doing a literature review remains the same. This is explained in subunit 8.7.

the length of dissertations

There is a wide variation in the length of dissertations required by different institutions in different countries and for different courses. However, the length changes according to the level of study:

- undergraduate dissertation: 4,000–15,000 words

- Masters dissertation: 10,000–50,000 words

- PhD dissertation: 50,000–100,000 words

It is useful to know (as early as possible) the approximate number of words you will be expected to produce for each section of your dissertation.

In a dissertation in the arts and humanities, the length of chapters or sections can vary. However, each chapter plays a significant part, so none of the chapters can be too short. For example, in an undergraduate dissertation of 10,000 words, you are unlikely to have a main body chapter of less than 2,000 words. Typically, a theoretical dissertation (that does not follow the empirical structure) will reflect the percentage word counts found in academic essays:

- introduction: 8–10%

- conclusion: 8–10%

- main body: 84–90% (spread between chapters or sections)

The table below shows the word counts and percentages for sections of dissertations that follow the conventional empirical dissertation structure. The figures are based on a study of Masters and undergraduate level dissertations from social science degrees. However, they can be applied as a useful guide for all empirical and many theoretical dissertations.

total words	Introduction	Literature Review	Methodology	Results or Findings	Discussion of Results	Conclusion
10,000	700	2,500	1,950	2,000	2,150	450
12,000	840	3,000	2,340	2,400	2,580	540
14,000	980	3,500	2,730	2,800	3,010	630
16,000	1,120	4,000	3,120	3,200	3,440	720
18,000	1,260	4,500	3,510	3,600	3,870	810
20,000	1,400	5,000	3,900	4,000	4,300	900
%	7%	25%	19.5%	20%	21.5%	4.5%

average length of Abstract (see subunit 8.5)
278

notes:

- The figures and percentages are median values (the midpoint value in a sequential range of numbers).

- The 'total words' represents the dissertation word limit, not the actual word count. You will be given a word limit you cannot exceed, so make sure you know what it is before you start.

- Here, the word counts do not include the abstract, bibliography, references, text in tables or labels for figures and tables. However, they do include additional text as footnotes and endnotes (see subunit 5.9). Make sure you know precisely what elements are relevant to the word count.

The table shows that the largest sections of a dissertation are the literature review and the discussion of results. This is nearly always the case in dissertations that follow the empirical structure. The results or findings section is the one most likely to vary in word count, and results are often included as part of the discussion of results. Results can sometimes be placed in an appendix, especially if they are not relevant to the research question or hypothesis. If you plan to combine the results and discussion sections, or to have significantly fewer words in the results section, spread the remaining words between the literature review, methodology and discussion.

the research proposal

Before you can start your dissertation, you will be required to submit a research proposal or plan. Your supervisor will consider the proposal and accept it or advise you to make changes. The proposal contains concise, but specific, details about your dissertation and is sometimes part of the dissertation assessment (often 10% but this can vary). If you are not given a framework for your proposal, you can use the template and guidelines on the next page. Not all sections of this template will be relevant to your type of dissertation.

the research question and hypothesis, aims and objectives

Trying to differentiate between these terms can be confusing and there is conflicting advice as to their precise meanings. The only difference between a research aim, question and hypothesis is how something is phrased:

aim: To explore how alcohol intervention can benefit health service users.
question: How does alcohol intervention benefit health service users?
hypothesis: Alcohol intervention reduces drinking in health service users.

aim: To understand American loneliness through the lens of punk identity.
question: Can American loneliness be understood through the lens of punk identity?
hypothesis: Punk identity is a manifestation of American loneliness.

All these aims, questions and statements define studies that investigate the relationship between two things (sometimes called 'variables'). Because a hypothesis is sometimes more precise than a question or aim, it is often found in quantitative studies (research that generates a lot of data that can be statistically analysed). But this is not always the case. Sometimes, the research aim is considered to be a more general statement than the question.

One thing that is consistent is the definition of 'objectives'. These are identified as smaller, specific things you will do to answer or address the aim, question or hypothesis. But showing a clear line of thinking between the research topic and the methodology is more important than the terms you choose (or are asked) to use. In refining your research topic for your reader, you are likely to follow one of these sequences:

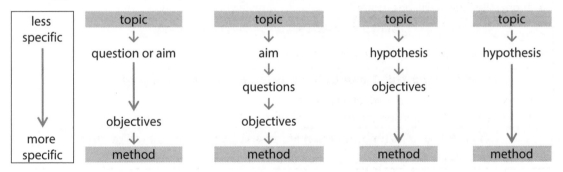

the order and content of a dissertation proposal

1 proposed title

- a working title made as explicit as possible (which can be modified later) (subunit 8.4)

2 research question

- research question (research aim) or research hypothesis
- research objectives
- the range and limits of the research

For clarification on the use of these terms, see previous page.

3 background and context

- brief background (but specific) information on the research topic
- briefly state how your research question relates to the larger topic (context)

Include any of the following that are relevant to your research question:

- the major problem you are addressing
- current knowledge and lack of knowledge about your research question
- current debates about your topic (e.g. agreements and disagreements)
- definitions of key terms
- any theoretical perspective you are using (e.g. structuralism, feminism)

4 justification or rationale

- the value, importance or significance of your research (why it is worth doing)
- what specifically could it add to existing theory, understanding or practice?

5 method and methodology (subunit 8.8)

- if relevant, location and brief site survey of where the research will take place
- general type of research (lab work or fieldwork, qualitative or quantitative etc.)
- participants or sample group (how they will be selected, who they are, how many, what they will be required to do, how they will be contacted)
- type of research tools used (e.g. questionnaires, surveys, interviews etc.)
- how the data will be collected (and what form it will be in)
- how the data will be analysed (e.g. thematic review, statistical analysis)
- briefly state why the proposed method is appropriate for the research question
- highlight any potential barriers, problems or risks and how you will address them

6 ethical considerations (not always applicable)

- level of ethical approval needed
- informed consent (how it will be obtained)
- participation consent form
- confidentiality (how it will be ensured)
- anonymity (how it will be ensured)

There are minimal, low and high levels of ethical approval (often called 'risk categories'). Most research institutions have their own guidelines and an ethics committee that reviews applications.

7 list of proposed section or chapter headings

- relevant for dissertations that do not follow the conventional empirical structure

8 short bibliography of key texts (annotated if required)

- list usually 5–10 important and relevant texts
- annotated means adding key information about the relevance and value of sources

9 schedule or plan for completion of research (with Gantt chart if required)

- a time schedule showing major dissertation targets and completion dates

annotated reference list or annotated bibliography

As part of your research proposal, you will be asked to identify some major sources you will use. Try to list 5 to 10 references. You need to present full reference details in accordance with the reference system you will be using for the dissertation. You may be asked to provide an annotated bibliography. This means that you will have to add a few notes to each source explaining why it is relevant to your study and what you will use the sources for. You don't have to read all the books or papers to write a (short) annotated bibliography, just find the details you need by skim reading or searching online.

making a time schedule (using a Gantt chart)

In the last section of the proposal you may need to present a time schedule showing when you intend to do the dissertation. This is best done in a visual chart like the Gantt chart. A Gantt chart is a simple, visual display of the estimated time it will take to complete a series of tasks that make up a project.

Keep the display simple. Start by listing or brainstorming the tasks. This can be easier if you have made a spatial overview of your dissertation (subunit 8.3). Then number, order and put the tasks in the task column (task 1 is the first thing you will do). Show an estimated start time and finish time for each task by shading the appropriate cells. Here is an example schedule for a dissertation planned over a 10-month period (January to October) and broken down into 15 tasks:

	Task	Jan	Feb	Mar	Apr	May	Jun	Jul	Aug	Sep	Oct
1	finalise research question and objectives	▓									
2	design methodology for research	█	█								
3	literature review research	▒	▒	▒	▒	▒					
4	ethical approval		█								
5	select and contact participants		▒								
6	data collection			█	█	█	█				
7	collate results				▒						
8	analyse results						█	█			
9	write literature review						▒	▒			
10	write introduction							▒			
11	write methodology								▒		
12	write discussion of results								█	█	
13	write recommendations									▒	
14	write conclusion									█	
15	submit final dissertation										▒

You can download a template for making a Gantt chart from www.macmillanihe.com/lia-sys.

doing a dissertation: making a spatial overview

✪ the aim

A dissertation will probably be the longest and most complex piece of academic work you are required to produce. The aim of making a clear, visual representation of your ideas and intentions is to establish focus and control from the start of your work and to maintain them throughout the dissertation process.

ⓘ why this can help you

Making a spatial overview at an early stage will:

- break down the work into individual, manageable tasks
- show you the relationship between each section and task
- allow you to tackle the work in any order
- provide a document you can refer to when you discuss your dissertation
- show you that all sections of a dissertation relate to the research question

⚙ the strategy

For empirical and many theoretical dissertations, you will know the outline structure and content aims of each main section of the dissertation before you start working on them. When you have your research question, you can create a spatial overview. Use a sheet of A3 paper turned landscape. Put the research question in the centre and surround it with the sections. Refer to the content aims for the introduction, methodology and conclusion (given in this unit), and add any relevant content headings to the main sections. Your spatial overview will look like this:

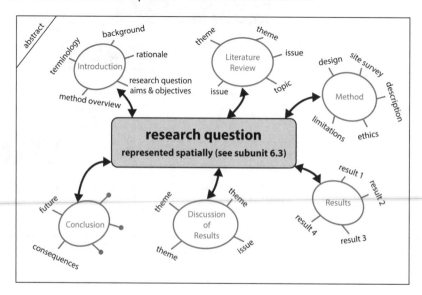

This visual representation shows how the dissertation is made up of smaller units of work, each one with a different purpose. It also shows how the contents come together and relate. In this example, the spatial overview identifies 13 tasks that you already know about:

- writing the abstract
- 5 tasks for the introduction
- 5 for the methodology
- 2 for the conclusion

You can then allocate an approximate number of words to each of the main sections and, if you like, break that down further for each of the tasks.

At this initial stage you will not know the precise content of the literature review, results, discussion of results or conclusion. But you know that each of these sections will consist of different themes, issues, topics, results, conclusions or recommendations. You can add subheadings to indicate the content of these sections as they become known. The spatial overview therefore evolves as you work on your dissertation. It allows you to see and monitor your progress.

For a PhD dissertation, a spatial overview like this can be used to represent an individual chapter. However, even for a PhD, it is useful to make an overall spatial overview by arranging chapters around the central research question(s).

Your final dissertation will be presented in a conventional linear structure like the ones shown in subunit 8.1, but you do not have to work on it in any particular order. For example, you can often write a description and discussion of method or methodology before you complete your introduction and you might have an idea of the themes or issues you want to discuss before you finish analysing your results. The spatial overview shows that a dissertation is like a jigsaw and you can piece it together in any order that suits you.

working with a supervisor

Although you will be able to choose your own research topic and work independently, you will be guided by a dissertation supervisor (for a PhD, you will probably have two supervisors). You will be allocated a number of key meetings that can be used for advice, clarification, direction or setting targets. These meetings can be invaluable and you should, with permission, record them and take notes (see subunit 3.6). Take your spatial overview to these meetings. Show it to your supervisor. This form of visual representation is a great way of communicating your ideas and discussing your intentions with other people.

the research question

Everything you write or display (in all sections of your dissertation) has a relationship to the research question. In the example spatial overview (above), this is emphasised by the two-headed black arrows. When you research, you need to be aware of this link. You need to know the relevance of the information and ideas you collect. When you write, if this relevance isn't obvious, you need to make it clear to the reader.

The table below shows how the main sections of empirical dissertations can relate to the research question:

Introduction	• gives context, relevant to the research question • states the research question (and any related objectives) • justifies the research question (why it is worth addressing)
Literature Review	• identifies current knowledge and ideas relevant to the research question or relevant for addressing the research question
Methodology	• states why the selected method is the best method for the research question and why other methods are less suitable
Results	• displays the results that best address the research question
Discussion	• identifies and discusses themes relevant to the research question
Conclusion	• states to what extent the research question was answered

Making the link between the research question and the literature review is sometimes harder, especially if your study is original. When there is no existing research directly related to a topic or question, some students struggle to know what to include in the review of literature. The answer is to look for any information that is relevant to the key elements of the research question. One way to identify this is to break down your research question and represent it spatially. This can be done by using the elements, links and parts strategy introduced for breaking down essay questions (subunit 6.3). Here is an example:

research question:
What is the impact of data sharing on migrants' access to healthcare in the UK?

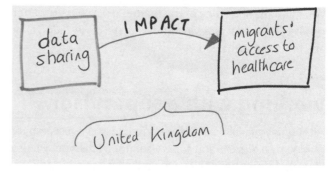

The author researched and wrote about:

• data sharing

• migrants

• healthcare in the UK

But, most importantly, the author only collected information on these topics that was relevant to the research question. For example, information on migrants that could affect their use and need of healthcare and their understanding of data sharing was crucial to the research question. In writing the literature review, the author made this relevance explicit.

> the most useful thing you can do when starting a dissertation is to identify the research question as soon as possible

A spatial representation of the research question can keep you focused. It can help you research, design and discuss an appropriate methodology, select the significant results and identify and discuss the most relevant themes.

8.4 the dissertation title and title page

Your dissertation needs a good title. Ultimately, the precise title is up to you. But here are some guidelines. A good title should:

- give a precise description of what the dissertation is about
- contain specific (accurate) words and appropriate terminology
- be searchable in a database (so it should contain searchable terms)
- use capital letters for the first word and all the key words or use capital letters throughout

The title should not:

- be general or just about the topic
- include phrases like 'a study on …' or 'an investigation into …'
- include abbreviations or acronyms (unless they are common knowledge)
- try to be humorous
- end with a full stop (but use a question mark if it is phrased as a question)

Here are some before and after titles that show poor and good examples:

before (poor)	after (good)
An investigation into whether the drug compound Y/348 inhibits the amount of succinate produced in the fatty deposits of rat livers (too wordy)	The inhibitory effects of Y/348 on succinate in fatty rat liver
Does daycare make happy children? (not accurate enough)	The effects of daycare on the social development of children in the southeast London boroughs of Bexley and Lewisham
More pressure for oxygen? (too informal and 'catchy')	The oxidation levels of polychlorinated biphenyls at different pressures
Peering at the arts profession through Bourdieu's eyes (unclear, trying to be too 'clever')	Inequalities in arts professions: exploring a participatory youth project through a Bourdieuian lens

If you need or prefer a longer title, you can use a colon to separate the main point and any supplementary details:

Social media and its relation to the higher education curriculum:
How students use Facebook, Twitter and Instagram to shape their learning experience

Fulfilling a new obligation: teaching and learning of sustainable healthcare in the medical education curriculum

The title page of your final dissertation should include:

- the full title of the dissertation
- your full name (and if requested, your student number)
- the qualification
- the name of your institution
- the date of submission (usually the month and year)

what is an abstract?

An abstract is a short summary of a dissertation or research paper. It is called an 'abstract' because, in this context, 'to abstract' means to remove something. This is what you do when you write an abstract. You remove (abstract) information from the body of the dissertation and put it together to form a concise and accurate summary. Because it takes some information from each of the completed sections of a dissertation, the abstract is best written last. In a dissertation, it is placed after the title page and before the acknowledgements and contents page. In a research or lab report, it is placed after the title and the list of authors.

the order and content of a dissertation abstract	
research focus	In providing a concise summary, the abstract should inform a reader (a researcher) whether the paper is relevant to their needs. It is a key indicator for reading (see subunit 2.3).
any relevant context or perspective	
value of the research (rationale)	
research question, aim or hypothesis	Like your dissertation title, your abstract should be searchable on a database. Therefore, you need to include key words in the form of precise and relevant terminology.
methodology	
findings or results	In writing your abstract, you can use existing text (sentences) from the main body of the dissertation.
conclusion	The abstract should not contain anything that is not in the dissertation.
implication of findings	

In a short research report or lab report, the abstract will be shorter, and the order will be **hypothesis** (research question or aim), **method, results, conclusion**.

There are no fixed rules, but in a dissertation, the abstract is usually:

- 250–300 words long, rarely over 500 words
- written without headings, but some do have them, especially longer ones
- one paragraph, although some longer ones can have two, some with headings can be separated under each heading
- written in the present tense (e.g. the research investigates …, the aim of the study is …), but some references to method will be in the past tense (e.g. data was triangulated …, semi-structured interviews were conducted …) and reference to findings can be in either (e.g. the findings suggest …, the findings suggested …)
- written without references or quotes, although there are some exceptions

the introduction

A dissertation introduction is different from an essay introduction. It is much longer and forms the first, separate chapter or section. It can be broken down into parts and completed in any order. Your dissertation introduction can include any of the following 7 parts that are relevant to your study:

1. background of the research

2. context of the research

3. rationale for the research

4. research question, hypothesis or aim and objectives

5. site survey

6. overview of method

7. terminology and definitions

the order and content of a dissertation introduction
background aim: to introduce and describe your research topic

In describing your research topic, you should be as specific and relevant as possible to your study. Your topic is broader than your research question or aim (subunit 8.2) but you don't need to present basic knowledge. Don't move from the general to the specific. Start with the specific and move to the more specific.

The information you include here will come from researching the literature. But the background is different from the literature review. In the background, you describe, present details and make statements about your topic, whereas in the literature review, you are discussing things like the strengths and weaknesses of the literature.

context of the research aim: to show the link between your research and existing knowledge or theory

You can put your research into context by relating it to relevant problems, issues, themes, theory, knowledge, practice or research. Your research may be investigating a:

- gap in knowledge (what is the specific gap?)
- topic for which there is little research (what is current theory or practice based on?)
- technology or practice that needs more testing (what is currently known or done?)
- topic with a new perspective or methodology (what is currently done?)
- previous experiment (what did the previous experiment conclude?)
- part of a larger study (how does your study relate to the main study?)

Most of the information you put here will also come from your review of the literature.

Because they can overlap, the background and context are
often combined in the same section of the introduction.

rationale for the research
aim: to state why your research is worth doing

You can state the value of your research by highlighting the potential benefits of the research findings or its contribution to a field or area of knowledge. For example, your research might:

- lead to cost savings
- lead to health benefits
- improve a process or change a practice
- provide research support for an existing process or practice
- create new insights or knowledge
- identify new problems or issues
- make an important contribution to a larger study

If your study is unique, or tackling a current or urgent issue, it is worth stating this.

research question
aim: to refine your research topic for your reader

Refining your research topic means giving focus to the research. You do this by stating one or some of the following:

- a research question(s)
- a hypothesis (or hypotheses)
- research aim(s)
- research objectives

See subunit 8.2 for a clarification of these terms

site survey
aim: to give relevant details of the location(s) of the research

If appropriate (not relevant for a lab study or many dissertations in the arts and humanities), you can give details of where the research took place (e.g., a school or a specific geographical location). This should include relevant details about the location (e.g., the multicultural mix of a school or the biodiversity of an area of land). Alternatively, you can place a detailed site survey in the methodology section and give only a concise overview in the introduction.

overview of method or methodology (subunit 8.8)
aim: to give a concise but specific description of the methodology

The method is described and discussed in detail in the methods section but the introduction can be used to give an overview of the main methodological approach, including any frameworks or perspectives used. In an arts and humanities theoretical dissertation that does not have a method, you can give and explain the outline and order of your chapters or sections.

terminology and definitions
aim: to identify and clarify any important terms or abbreviations used in the dissertation

If extensive, this section can be separated and placed after the introduction and before the literature review. A list of abbreviations can also be placed after the contents page.

When you write your introduction, you can follow this order of content or you can adapt it and combine some of the sections. The important thing is to address any of the relevant points highlighted above.

In shorter reports (like a lab report), the introduction includes a brief discussion of previous research. In a dissertation, the existing literature is usually discussed in its own section or chapter (for doing a literature review see subunit 8.7). However, you will still refer to the existing literature throughout your introduction.

the conclusion

The conclusion should emphasise the link between the research findings and the research question. There is no fixed order for the conclusion, but you can use the four headings in the table below as a guide:

the order and content of a dissertation conclusion
reiteration of main findings
• select the most important findings and restate them concisely
support for the research question or hypothesis
• state to what extent the findings supported the research question or validated the hypothesis (fully, partially, not at all)
• explain how the strongest evidence supports the research question
• state what remains unresolved (unanswered questions, limits of the findings)
research objectives and method
• state whether all the objectives of the research were met
• if yes, explain which was the most important in reaching the findings
• if no, state which were not met, explain why and how this affected the findings
outcomes of the research
• state whether the findings added something new to the existing literature
• state whether the research raised any new questions
• give the (potential) consequences or implications of the research findings and explain whether the findings could influence current practice, theory, research or policy
• propose any future studies that may be needed to take the research further
In a longer dissertation, each chapter or section may have its own conclusion. These conclusions sometimes end by stating how they relate to, or lead to, the next chapter.

making recommendations

If you are required to make recommendations, they are normally added to the final section of the dissertation under the heading: conclusion and recommendations. For each recommendation you make, you should:

- provide evidence (from your research findings) to support it
- state the potential benefits
- explain how (process) and when (timescale) it might be implemented
- highlight any barriers or problems regarding its implementation or use

what is a literature review?

In a dissertation that follows the empirical structure (subunit 8.1), a literature review is an essential and separate section. It is a written summary and discussion of information and ideas that relate to a specific subject (or preferably, a specific research question). The information and ideas are drawn from what is termed the 'literature'. The literature can be in the form of:

- practice: events and accounts of how things are done or were done
- theory: ideas, models etc.
- research: evidence-based information and ideas
- policy: sources that outline how things should be done

The literature can come in many forms:

- published books
- journal articles and peer reviewed research papers (or reliable newspaper articles)
- reliable internet sources, such as government statistics
- policy documents, guidelines and legislation
- dissertations, theses and conference papers
- films, paintings, photos, speeches or any other form of relevant non-text format

In a short paper or research report, the literature review can be included in the introduction. In an empirical dissertation, it is a separate chapter or section (chapter 2) and is placed after the introduction. In a theoretical dissertation, the literature review may be a separate chapter, or the information collected from the literature can be used throughout the dissertation in different chapters. When it forms a separate chapter or section, the literature review is usually the longest part of a dissertation and can account for more than 25% of the total word limit (see subunit 8.1). But whether it has its own section or is disseminated throughout a dissertation, the aims of reviewing the literature are the same.

preparing for a literature review

Students often start reading for a literature review without knowing its purpose, what it should consist of and how it can be structured. Before you start researching and writing a review, you should do 3 things:

1. clarify the purpose of a literature review

2. refine (as much as possible) the research question

3. prepare an appropriate note taking strategy

what is the purpose of a literature review?

The aim of a literature review is to show what is known about a specific subject and to highlight what is not known or what is uncertain. Before you research the literature for the literature review, think about the questions below and highlight those that are specific to your needs.

You can add any questions of your own. When you research the literature, try to find answers that are relevant to your specific field of study or, preferably, your specific research question.

	key questions to ask when researching for a literature review
1	Who are the key researchers or theorists?
2	What are the key texts (or sources)?
3	Is the key literature from practice, theory, research or policy?
4	What form do the key texts take (research reports, visual images, speeches etc.)?
5	What are the main issues or themes highlighted in the key texts?
6	What does the most recent research state, establish or suggest?
7	What are the current theories?
8	What is the current policy?
9	What is the current practice?
10	How do practice, theory, research and policy link? (see subunit 4.2)
11	What are the major areas of agreement in the literature?
12	What are the major areas of disagreement in the literature?
13	Have there been any significant (recent) developments in the topic?
14	Is there any controversy in the literature?
15	What are the main gaps in knowledge on the topic?
16	Which methodologies have been used in researching or discussing the topic?
17	What is the subject-specific terminology used in the literature?

your research question and the literature review

There should be an explicit link between the information you collect for your literature review and your research question, research aim or hypothesis.

When you write the literature review, you should make clear why and how the literature relates to your own study. This means that you need to define your research question before you start researching. The more explicit the research question, the easier it is to identify and collect relevant information. If you have a research question, work on the question in the way you would work on an essay question. Break it down, represent it spatially and create a focus for your research (see subunit 6.3).

A review of existing literature can sometimes be carried out in order to identify a research topic or question. In this case, the aim of researching the literature is to find what is sometimes called a 'gap in knowledge' so that you can propose research to address it. This is often carried out in the first year of a PhD where the initial research is used to create or refine the focus of the study. At undergraduate or

Masters level, students only have a limited period in which to produce a dissertation. So, in practice, it is important to start with a research question or generate one as soon as possible. If you start researching without the focus of a question, you will waste a lot of time. If you don't have a clear question, it is better to propose a few questions to your supervisor, refine them as you access the literature and select one as soon as you can.

> if you are struggling to research for your literature review, you should take a step back and clarify your research question or research aim

taking notes for a literature review

Two highly effective ways of taking notes for a literature review are:

1. taking notes with prepared templates (subunit 3.4)

2. making spatial notes (subunit 3.1)

In order to identify and collect relevant information and ideas, it can be useful to draw up questions, themes, issues and so on and enter them into a prepared template like the one in subunit 3.4. This can be done before the main research or after accessing one or two key sources. This strategy will help you select, restrict, control, categorise and process the information you collect. You should periodically review these questions or themes during the research.

Another useful way to collect information and ideas for a literature review is to make spatial notes (subunit 3.1). One A3 sheet can be used for each of the main literature sources. This strategy can work especially well in the initial stages of research when you are trying to identify the relevant content of key sources. Your spatial notes can become a form of visuospatial index. You don't have to transfer all the information you need from a key source, instead you can simply reference the content on your spatial notes by entering a theme or topic and a page number. In this case, spatial note making will allow you to group all the pages that refer to a specific topic, theme, issue or idea. The notes will then help you when you return to the key source for further reading.

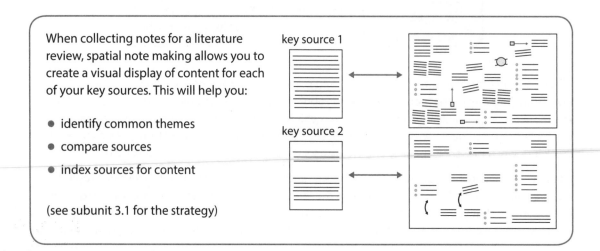

When collecting notes for a literature review, spatial note making allows you to create a visual display of content for each of your key sources. This will help you:

- identify common themes
- compare sources
- index sources for content

(see subunit 3.1 for the strategy)

key source 1

key source 2

the structure of a literature review

A literature review consists of an introduction, a main body and a conclusion:

the order and content of a dissertation literature review

introduction (8–10% of the word count)

Include any of the following you think are relevant to your dissertation:

- a clear restatement of the research topic or question
- a definition of any specific terms used in the literature review
- the time period covered by the literature
- the location covered by the literature (e.g. country, region, city or institution)
- how the literature was chosen (e.g. inclusion and exclusion criteria)
- why certain literature is not included
- how the literature was analysed (e.g. appraisal tool or theoretical framework)
- how the literature review is organised

Although you should restate your research question, don't repeat the background and context of the topic if you have already included it in the main dissertation introduction.

main body (80–90% of the word count)

This section consists of outlining and discussing the sources you have selected for inclusion. Once you have collected the information and ideas, you can order the material in several ways:

- chronologically: can show how knowledge has developed over time
- by theme: sources are discussed in relation to themes or issues
- by method: use this only if methodology is an important aspect of your own study
- by individual source: each source is considered separately

A literature review should not be a descriptive list of sources, so the most common approach is to order the information in the main body by theme. This means that certain sources (key sources) can be referred to in more than one part of the review. If it is not obvious, make it clear why the information is relevant to your own study.

conclusion (8–10% of the word count)

The conclusion of a literature review (especially a long one) is mainly a summary and restatement of how your study fits in with the existing literature. You can include any of the following you think are relevant:

- the major contributors and sources (and what knowledge they established)
- the main themes that emerged
- the most important trends (e.g. how knowledge has changed or progressed)
- the gaps that exist in the research (what is not known, or what is uncertain)
- any major disagreements or current debates
- how your own study fits into the existing knowledge
- the potential contribution of your study (in relation to what you have discussed)
- a link to the next chapter (especially if you're doing a theoretical dissertation)

epistemology and ontology

You may be asked for an epistemological and ontological consideration of the literature. These can be difficult terms to understand. When you research for a literature review, the primary aim is to determine what is currently known. In this context, the terms can be more easily defined and applied. This is what they mean:

epistemological knowledge (quality of knowing):

- the source of the knowledge (how it came about and who formulated it)
- the quality of the evidence (e.g. empirical or non-empirical, rational or subjective)
- the range and limits of the knowledge
- the use of the knowledge (e.g. practice, theory, policy or research)

ontological knowledge (quality of being):

- how the existing knowledge is categorised (e.g. is it put into certain groups?)
- the terminology used to categorise or describe the knowledge
- the relationship between existing knowledge
- what similarities exist in the knowledge (e.g. agreements, similar research methods)
- what differences exist in the knowledge (e.g. different opinions or interpretations)

the literature review and other parts of the dissertation

The literature review can be the hardest part of a dissertation, but if you prepare for it and do it early, it can make the rest of the dissertation a lot easier to write. The literature review informs other parts of the dissertation in several ways:

introduction	background and context are derived from the literature search
method	method design is influenced by the research (e.g. themes identified by the literature will inform questions in interviews or surveys)
results	your choice of how you analyse your results or findings can be based on the form of information you find in the literature
discussion of results	themes identified by the literature are revisited in the light of your own research, this is the basis of the discussion, you discuss how your findings relate to previous practice, theory, research or policy

It is useful to be aware of these links before you start. Making a spatial overview (subunit 8.3) shows that you can piece the dissertation together in any order but starting with the literature review (and refining your research question) is a good idea.

some criticisms to avoid

- the literature review is simply an annotated list of sources (or list of summaries)
- the literature is simply described, not discussed
- there is no discussion on how the literature compares
- there is too much material that is not relevant to your study
- the link between the literature and your research is not clear
- it doesn't include sufficient recent literature (if required)
- only one view is considered, and the literature review is biased or incomplete
- some key sources are missing

8.8 writing a methodology

methodology and method

These terms can be easily differentiated and understood:

methodology describes and discusses, it can:	
• discuss the theory behind the chosen method	**method only describes, it can:**
• justify the method you have chosen by explaining why the method is the most appropriate for your study	• describe the steps you took
	• describe the tools you used (e.g. a survey, a statistical analysis tool, a program)
• explain why other methods were not chosen	
• identify and discuss the strengths and limitations of the chosen method	• describe the materials you used (e.g. a piece of lab equipment)

Because methodology can contain method, you don't need to use both titles. In a short research report or lab report, you will usually only be required to describe the method (so that your experiment could be replicated). In a dissertation, you will usually need to describe and discuss your method, that's why dissertations should have a methodology (and not a method) chapter.

the order and content of a dissertation methodology
methodology
aim: to discuss the theory behind the chosen method and justify it for your study
Research is often categorised as quantitative (generates data that can be statistically tested) or qualitative (generates opinions and ideas that can give insights). There is a vast range of research methods under each of these categories. They include historical, ethnographic, correlational, descriptive, experimental, longitudinal and survey research.
All methods have an underlying theory and aim. In this part, you explain and justify your choice of research method by showing that both its theory and aim(s) are relevant to and appropriate for your research question.
The level of discussion about your chosen method will depend on the type of dissertation you are doing. Again, there is a range of methodological terms that might be relevant to your discussion. They include basic research, applied research, interpretive research, grounded theory, constructivist and positivist theory. Unless you are doing a theoretical dissertation, you should aim to keep the methodology discussion as simple as possible.
You may also want to explain which alternative methods were considered but rejected.

design of method
aim: to discuss the tools used to implement the methodology

This discussion can be combined with the methodology or follow it in a separate paragraph or section. While the methodology discusses the overall theoretical approach, this part looks specifically at the way(s) the methodology was put into practice. It may, for example, discuss details about the use of:

- a case study (or case studies)
- interviews (with open or closed questions)
- surveys or questionnaires
- focus groups
- observation, video recording or photography
- data collection from existing sources (e.g. a specialist database or an archive)
- experimentation (e.g. in a lab or in the field)
- a specific type of analysis (e.g. a semiotic analysis, a framework analysis)

You should consider the strengths and limitations of each tool or process used and, again, justify why it is appropriate for your study.

site survey or study area data
aim: to place the research and discussion of findings in the context of a location

A site survey collects information from a site to assess whether it is appropriate for a task. In research, if your study is based at a specific location, the location will have an influence on your findings, the discussion of findings and the validity of your conclusion. It is important therefore that you include relevant data of the site. For example, you might be required to provide biodiversity data for an area of land or the socioeconomic characteristics of a school or inner-city area.

As well as considering how the location affects your study, you can discuss why the site is appropriate for the research, how it was chosen and whether any other sites were considered.

It's up to you where you put your site survey. It can be included in the introduction, as part of the literature review or in a separate section in the methodology. If you are unsure, discuss it with your supervisor.

description of method
aim: to provide a clear description of the method process so that it could be repeated

This section provides a precise step by step description of what you did to carry out your research. It is written in the past tense and, if possible, presented in chronological order.

The description usually consists of, at least, the following 3 steps:

1. sample or population
2. data collection
3. data analysis

If needed, a materials section is added to give details of any specialist equipment or software used.

Although most of the methodological discussion precedes the description of method, you can include further justification (i.e. why something was done) if required.

The sample or **population** used for your research is either randomly selected or purposefully selected. You can include details on:

- the sample size
- the selection criteria
- the selection process
- any other relevant information about the sample

Data collection can include details on:

- when (and over what period) the data was collected
- how the data was collected (and how it was categorised or grouped)
- the type and format of the collected data

Data analysis includes details of how the data was analysed. For example, applying a:

- thematic analysis (give details of any framework used) (see subunit 8.11)
- statistical analysis (give the name of programs used)

ethics
aim: to show how you have considered and dealt with ethical issues of research

This details ethical issues relevant to your research and the steps you took to ensure the interests of your participants. It can include:

- confidentiality
- anonymity
- safeguarding issues (when working with vulnerable groups)
- any ethical issues that emerged during your research

Your research may require ethical clearance from your educational institution, or, in some cases, from an external body (e.g. the Health Research Authority).

You may need to provide your participants with:

- a participant information sheet
- a consent form

You can search online for templates and guidance on these forms.

limitations of study
aim: to discuss aspects of methodology or method that affect validity or generalisability

The limitations of study is not a criticism of your research. You should identify only limitations that affect your research findings in terms of:

- validity: the relationship between your method and findings (and conclusion)
- generalisability: the extent to which your findings and conclusion are applicable beyond your own study (e.g. beyond your research population or location)

Sometimes, the limitations of study are discussed in the discussion of results. But more commonly, it is part of the methodology. Any issues highlighted here can then be used in the discussion of results (e.g. a small sample size or an inaccurate form of measurement might help to explain an unexpected finding).

Where appropriate, you should include academic references throughout the methodology to support your discussion.

8.9 findings and the discussion of findings

results or findings?

These terms are interchangeable. They describe the outcome(s) of your method. The term 'results' tends to be used more in science-based dissertations, quantitative studies or lab reports. The term 'findings' is used more in humanities (or qualitative) dissertations. But the choice is usually up to you.

You don't always need a separate section for your findings:

- qualitative research: findings and discussion of findings are often combined in the same section, or in two or more sections that discuss different themes or issues
- where there is a display of results: the results and discussion of results are separate, common in quantitative studies where a lot of graphs or tables are generated
- systematic review: the findings and discussion are separate (see subunit 8.10)
- appendix: you can use appendices for findings and refer to them in your discussion

findings: presentation and description

If you include a separate chapter for your findings, it should present and describe but not discuss the findings. Presenting the findings means showing them in the most appropriate way. Describing the findings means highlighting relevant outcomes, trends, anomalies, similarities and differences. Before organising and writing the findings section, there are 3 questions to consider:

> **1. Do you want to show all your findings or only major findings?**
> It is better to show only the findings that are most relevant to your research. These will be discussed in the discussion section. Select the findings you want to display and make sure you know why they are relevant to your research question. You may not have space (or enough word count) to include all your findings. In a longer dissertation you can put other findings in the appendix.

> **2. How do you want to order the findings section?**
> For example, the findings could be:
> - ordered chronologically (in the order they emerged)
> - grouped under certain categories or themes
> - placed in order of importance or significance, beginning with the most significant (i.e. the most relevant to the research question)
> - grouped to show certain trends or patterns
> - displayed to show comparison between groups
> - shown together in a table of findings

3. How do you want to display your results?

Try to choose the most appropriate format. You can use tables, graphs, charts, diagrams, photographs, maps or written descriptions:

• Label all tables: Table 1 …, Table 2 …, Table 3 etc.
• Label all graphs, charts, photographs etc.: Figure 1 …, Figure 2 … etc.

The display of findings is important and useful. Don't wait until you have your findings before choosing formats for display. Think about it earlier so that it is easier for you to collect and process the results. The best method of display is one that allows you and your readers to see important relationships between different findings and (the key relationship) between your findings and your research question. A clear display of findings will make the discussion of findings easier to write.

the discussion of findings

In this section or chapter, you will discuss how the findings relate to the research question, aim or hypothesis. You will also reference the knowledge, ideas, themes and issues you wrote about in the literature review. Before writing the discussion of findings, there are 3 questions to consider:

1. Which findings or results do you need to discuss?

It is unlikely that you will discuss all your findings (unless it is a small study or a short experiment). Select the findings that are most relevant to your research question. This could reflect the display of findings in the previous section (which displays only the most relevant findings) or it could select specific details from these findings.

2. How do you want to structure your discussion?
Once you have identified the findings you want to discuss, think about the best structure to use for the discussion. You can:

• discuss each result individually
• group or categorise the results according to themes, issues or outcomes
• use a structure that highlights some individual results and some themes

If you have done a thematic analysis as part of your method, your discussion section will be structured thematically.

> **3. How do you want to order your discussion?**
> The discussion of findings is a bit like an essay, so the order of content is up to you. This might be:
>
> • chronological, by result obtained
> • most significant result first
> • by theme or issue (e.g. most important theme first)
>
> For more ideas on how to order your discussion, see the table in subunit 6.5. Once you have chosen your order, put it into a plan (like an essay plan) and consider writing an aim for each section (subunit 6.6). This preparation step will help you write the discussion.

asking questions for discussion

When you write the discussion section, you are asking and trying to answer questions about your findings. Below is a list of 15 useful questions. You don't have to answer all these questions. Some of them won't be relevant to your study, so choose the ones that are. For each question you ask, you can enquire further by applying the three key discursive questions (why?, so what? and what if?). This is explained in description and discussion in academic writing (subunit 4.5).

Your discussion will have a short introduction. It may have a conclusion. However, in most dissertations the conclusion is a separate section (subunit 8.6).

introduction

finding, result, theme, issue, topic etc.
discussion

finding, result, theme, issue, topic etc.
discussion

finding, result, theme, issue, topic etc.
discussion

finding, result, theme, issue, topic etc.
discussion

finding, result, theme, issue, topic etc.
discussion

limitations of research
This discussion can appear in this section oras part of the methodology (see unit 8.8).

	key questions to ask when writing a discussion
1	Can you explain why the finding is like this?
2	Is the finding what you expected?
3	Is this finding an anomaly or unusual?
4	Does this finding support the research question?
5	Does this finding refute the research question?
6	Is this finding part of a pattern or trend?
7	Does the finding relate to other findings in your research?
8	How does this finding compare with existing theory?
9	How does this finding compare with existing knowledge?
10	How does this finding compare with existing practice?
11	Is the finding relevant beyond the limits of your research?
12	Has anything new been established?
13	What are the practical consequences or implications?
14	Are there any theoretical consequences or implications?
15	Does this finding suggest the need for further research?

what is a systematic review?

A systematic review is a specific type of literature review. It aims to identify and analyse the most up to date research evidence in relation to a specific research or review question. It does this by designing and implementing a search strategy. This strategy is used to find and select relevant research papers. For an undergraduate assignment, the number of papers you need to identify is usually known before you start. Systematic reviews are most often used to research questions in a medical, clinical or healthcare context. What differentiates a systematic review from other literature reviews is the meticulous process it follows. Following this process is part of the assessment so it is important to understand it. Shown below is the typical structure, content and order of a systematic review:

research protocol

A research protocol is a detailed and complete description of a study procedure. At postgraduate level, a protocol is usually submitted for approval before a systematic review is undertaken. You are unlikely to do this at undergraduate level but, when putting together a systematic review, the order and content are important because the process is highly regulated. Knowing what is expected for a protocol can therefore be useful as a guide. Two websites that give details of systematic review protocols are:

- www.prisma-statement.org: PRISMA (preferred reporting items for systematic reviews and meta-analyses)

- www.cochranelibrary.com: Cochrane Reviews, a database of systematic reviews

using research databases

An essential part of systematic reviews is being able to use research databases proficiently. For many students, this is the hardest part of doing systematic reviews. Before you start working on your review, familiarise yourself with the database(s) you will use. If possible, do some relevant training. If you practise using the relevant databases, you will save a lot of time and effort.

title page
Abstract
Acknowledgements
Contents Page
1. Introduction or Background
background (research topic or question)
definition of key terms or key topics
importance of review topic or question
incidence and prevalence of the topic
refining (framing) the research question
facet analysis (PCIOS, PICO, PIO)
2. Search Strategy
type of studies
type of data (data extraction)
databases used
use of Boolean operators
inclusion and exclusion criteria
critical appraisal tools used
search of databases and study selection
3. Findings
narrative or data synthesis table
written analysis of findings
4. Discussion of Findings
5. Conclusion
Reference List
Appendices

breaking the systematic review into smaller tasks

There are a lot of different parts to a systematic review. The example structure (above) identifies the possible contents of the introduction, search strategy and findings sections. This overview structure helps you to understand the logical order (process) of systematic reviews. It also shows that these three sections of a systematic review can be broken down into 15 different tasks. Considered individually, these tasks are more manageable as each one has a specific purpose. You will also be limited in the number of words you can allocate to each one. Knowing this before you start will help you. Guidance on completing each of these tasks is given in the tables below:

the order and content of an introduction of a systematic review
background (research topic and question)
Start with some relevant background information on the research topic and state the research question. You won't have too many words to spare, so you need to be concise and select the most relevant, current information. You can include information from practice, theory, research or policy but it must be relevant to your research.   At this stage, the question can be more generally stated but it is always best to have a focused research (or review) question as early as possible.   Example: • topic: the self-care of diabetic patients   • general question: what role does diabetes education play in the self-care of diabetic patients?
definition of key terms or key topics
Example: • provide concise but accurate and referenced definitions of diabetes and self-care
importance of the review topic or question
State why your topic or question is important and worth reviewing. This is the rationale for your systematic review. For example, you can refer to a current problem that is growing and having negative socioeconomic or health effects. The rationale is often linked with the growing or significant incidence and prevalence of something.   Example: • the increasing cost of diabetes to the NHS
incidence and prevalence of the topic
Incidence: this shows how often something occurs, especially new cases of a disease measured over a specified period. Incidence is normally given in relation to a total population.   Example: • In the UK, 2.5 people per 100,000 are diagnosed with type 1 diabetes   **Prevalence**: this is the numerical amount of something, especially the total number of people with a disease or condition at a given date.   Example: • In the UK, 3.7 million people are diagnosed with a form of diabetes

refining (framing) the research question

This is when you begin to narrow your research question. The term 'framing the question' is sometimes used to describe this step. Framing a question simply means finding the best way to phrase a research question. Your aim is to create the most effective question from your topic or your initial general question. An effective research question is one that can be addressed and searched for in a database, therefore it must be focused.

For example, the initial (general) question is now rephrased as a more focused question:

• What role does diabetes education play in the self-care of diabetic patients?

• Does diabetes education increase the level of self-care in adults with diabetes?

facet analysis (PICOS, PICO, PIO)

Once the question is phrased effectively, you can carry out a facet analysis. Doing a facet analysis means breaking down the research question into different elements (or facets) and listing the elements separately. This is done in order to provide key words and phrases that can be searched for in a database.

A framework tool is often used to perform a facet analysis. The PICOS, PICO or PIO frameworks are commonly used for clinical research. Depending on which one you choose, the question is broken down into:

P: population, patient or problem: i.e. the group or sample you are investigating

I: intervention(s): e.g. a treatment or action you are measuring the effect of

C: comparison or control: this is used to compare your intervention with an alternative

O: outcome(s): e.g. an improvement in health, an increase in uptake, cutting costs

S: study design: used to restrict or select the type of study to include in your search

Here is a simple example of a PIO analysis for the research question: Does diabetes education increase the level of self-care in adults with diabetes?

population	intervention	outcome
adult*	diabet* training	self-care
diabet*	diabet* awareness	self-management
diabetes mellitus	diabet* education	level
type 1 diabet*	diabet* learning	uptake
type 2 diabet*		increase
gestational diabet*		management of diabet*

The aim is to consider and list all viable search options that cover any of the PICO(S) categories used. As well as entering the precise term, you can also add any relevant synonyms (words or phrases with similar meanings).

In database searching, the asterisk (*) is called a 'wild card'. It is usually placed at the end of a word (but not always) and stands in place of any other letters. For example: diabet* would search for diabetes, diabetic and diabetically. Using wild cards means that one search entry can be used to search several different words.

the order and content of a search strategy of a systematic review

study types

You can begin your search strategy by discussing which type(s) of study you want to focus on. For example, you might think it more appropriate for your research question to include only qualitative or quantitative studies. You may also decide to exclude any existing systematic reviews from your search. The type of studies you select will influence the form of data analysis you will carry out later.

information or data (data extraction)

Here you can state what specific information or data you will be looking for and extracting from the selected papers. If appropriate, state why this information is relevant to your review question. At undergraduate level, you will probably extract information like author, aims of the study, study design, details of participants, methods used for analysis of results and main findings. At postgraduate level you may also need to extract detailed numerical data. This information is presented in a table placed in the findings section.

databases used

The academic research databases you choose will depend on your field of study. You will probably be required to use at least 2 or 3. In this section you need to state why they are appropriate for your study. Some of the major databases used in clinical research are:

PubMed, CINAHL, Embase, PsycINFO, Web of Science, Scopus and the Cochrane Central Register of Controlled Trials (CENTRAL).

use of Boolean operators

You need to state how you will use Boolean operators in your search. Boolean operators are short words that are used to combine words or phrases when carrying out a search on a database. The three Boolean operators you are most likely to use are:

AND: combines 2 (or more) words so that a source must contain them both

OR: combines 2 (or more) words so that a source contains either one or the other or both

NOT: combines 2 (or more) words so that a source contains one but not the other

For example, if you used the Boolean operators and searched this phrase in a database:

self-care **OR** self-management **AND** diabetes

it would show sources that contain one (or both) of the first 2 terms as well as 'diabetes'.

inclusion and exclusion criteria

Inclusion criteria: the characteristics of a research paper that show it is relevant to your research question, they are used to include the paper as part of your search

Exclusion criteria: the characteristics of a research paper that show it is not relevant to your research question, they are used to exclude the paper from your search

These criteria can include language (e.g. include English language, exclude non-English language papers), dates of research, types of research method, the availability of the paper, a detail of the subject of the study or the location of the study. You will need to justify the application of these criteria in relation to your study.

critical appraisal tools used

In this section you can detail the method(s) of analysis you will apply to:

- select the papers
- analyse the selected papers

For systematic reviews at undergraduate level, you are unlikely to be required to perform a sophisticated statistical analysis. Instead, you might use existing templates to assess the quality, validity and potential bias of papers and apply a thematic analysis to your selected papers (see subunit 8.11).

At postgraduate (and especially at PhD) level, you will use more rigorous analytical tools. You may need to perform what is called a 'meta-analysis'. This requires you to extract numerical data from the studies and apply a statistical calculation that will give quantitative values for each study. Studies can then be compared numerically.

search of databases and study selection

When you have finished detailing your search strategy, you apply it to each of the databases you are using. At each step of the search process, you record the number of papers found. As you search, your aim is to reduce the number of papers. You exclude and include papers according to the criteria you set. You exclude any duplicate papers (the same paper is likely to appear in more than one database).

Initially, you will read only titles and abstracts. When you have a manageable number of papers, you can read the full text to select only the most appropriate. Although you have set your search strategy, it may be that, in order to reduce your selection to fit the number of papers required, you will have to make some alterations to the criteria (e.g., narrow the year of publication or redefine the inclusion criteria). For most undergraduate assignments, you know, before you start, approximately how many papers you need to find and analyse.

Your search steps and number of papers found need to be recorded. This is usually done in a table or flow chart. You can search online if you want to see or generate a PRISMA flow chart.

the order and content of the findings of a systematic review

narrative or data synthesis table

Synthesis, in this context, simply means putting the results together so that they can be further analysed and compared. A **narrative synthesis** is the information extracted from the papers (e.g. sample, study design) in written form and put into a table like this:

study	sample	sample size	intervention	design	analysis of results	strengths & limitations
Lee (2018)	gestational diabetics	100	Johnston diabetic training programme	RCT	statistical	• reduced researcher bias • small sample • includes only one type of diabetes
Wilson (2018)	type 1 & type 2 diabetics	20	NPL diabetes self-care model	qualitative	thematic	• low level of generalisability

A **data synthesis** is the collation of numerical values extracted from the papers. This is only needed if a quantitative statistical analysis (like a meta-analysis) is applied.

The primary aim of putting your selected papers in a table is to show the differences and similarities between them. This can include a comparison of any of the chosen headings (e.g. sample size, method design and findings). Once you have tabulated your selected papers, you can analyse them for:

- quality (using an appraisal checklist, subunit 8.11): to identify strengths and limitations
- themes (doing a thematic analysis): to identify themes relevant to your question

written analysis of papers

As well as tabulating the information from selected papers, you may also be asked to provide a written presentation of them. This is sometimes called a 'narrative review'. It usually comes after a thematic analysis has identified the main themes in the selected papers. In a narrative review, the papers are not normally presented individually but under each of the main themes. This part, if required, is different from the discussion of findings, but it can be difficult to distinguish it (see below for an explanation).

when do I analyse the papers?

It seems that a systematic review requires you to continually analyse papers. This can be confusing. Here are the parts of the process in which you need to consider the contents of the papers you search for and find. Each one has a different purpose and they may not all be required for your assignment:

selecting papers during the search	You select papers based on your inclusion and exclusion criteria. For most undergraduate systematic literature reviews, you won't be expected to carry out a detailed analysis at this stage.
the summary (synthesis) table	Once you have tabulated your selected papers, you can analyse them for quality and risk of bias. You can use an existing appraisal tool for this (see subunit 8.11). The outcome is usually presented as a list of strengths and limitations for each study. This heading can be added to your summary table in a separate column. You may also be required to do a thematic analysis where you identify the major themes or issues from the findings of the selected papers.
the written (narrative) review	In the findings section, you may also be required to present an analysis of the selected papers in written form. To distinguish this step from your discussion of findings, you can discuss the strengths and limitations of the selected papers, and/or how the selected papers relate to themes. At this stage, you **do not** discuss the papers in relation to your research question.
the discussion of findings	In this section, the discussion will focus on how the findings (the main themes and issues) of the selected papers are relevant to addressing or answering your research question.

using academic references

You need to use academic references throughout the systematic review. These are often used to justify a method (e.g., the value of a PICO framework or the strengths of a certain database). Many of these references have become standard and you can access them by reading existing systematic reviews.

analysing research papers with templates

using existing templates

Effectively analysing research papers is necessary for producing literature reviews, systematic reviews, reports and presentations. The strategy for making notes with templates (subunit 3.4) can be applied to all these tasks. It puts the emphasis on preparation before reading and provides a template for making effective notes. This can help you:

- identify the strengths and weaknesses of research studies
- make a comparison between studies
- carry out a thematic analysis (the identification, grouping and labelling of key, often recurrent, information relevant to a research question: information grouped under each labelled theme is considered to have a relationship or a related meaning)

Analysing research papers is usually done in relation to a research topic or a specific research question, aim or hypothesis. For a template to be effective, the questions that appear on it should be selective and relate as closely as possible to your specific requirements.

There are three useful websites that provide free, downloadable checklists to use with different types of research methodologies:

CASP Critical Appraisal Skills Programme (https://casp-uk.net/casp-tools-checklists)	CASP provides the following checklists: • systematic review checklist • qualitative checklist • randomised control trial checklist • case control study checklist • diagnostic study checklist • cohort study checklist • economic evaluation checklist • clinical prediction rule checklist
STROBE Strengthening the Reporting of Observational Studies in Epidemiology (www.strobe-statement.org/index.php?id=available-checklists)	STROBE provides the following checklists: • checklist for cohort studies • checklist for case-control studies • checklist for cross-sectional studies • STROBE checklist for conference abstracts
CONSORT Consolidated Standards of Reporting Trials (www.consort-statement.org)	CONSORT provides: • the CONSORT statement for reporting randomised trials

making your own template

Although the academic checklists highlighted above are intended for specific types of method design, there is a lot of overlap in the questions they ask. This means that they can be used as references for making your own template. You might want to make a template to fit a coursework task and if you read through existing templates, you can extract and adapt questions for your own purpose. Here is an example of a template for analysing research papers:

Hypothesis	Is the hypothesis or research question well formulated? (a good hypothesis is one that can be tested practically and effectively in the time allocated for a study)	
	Was the sample big enough? Was its range or focus appropriate (in terms of gender, age, culture, race, etc.)?	
Method	Was the research period long enough?	
	Was the research period too long? (some variables may have changed over the period of the research)	
	If the method used was qualitative, is this appropriate to the hypothesis, research question or aim?	
	If the method used was quantitative, is this appropriate to the hypothesis, research question or aim?	
	If the method used a mixed method approach, is this appropriate to the hypothesis, research question or aim?	
	Is there any possibility of human error or bias in carrying out the research or experiment (e.g. collecting or recording data, preparing samples)?	
	How accurate is the analysis of results? Is there a statistical analysis and is it appropriate? Is there a thematic analysis and is it appropriate? Is there a risk of researcher bias in analysing the results?	

Results	Are the results as expected?	
	Do the results contradict or agree with findings from previous research?	
	Are there any 'rogue' results or anomalies and, if so, are they explained?	
	Are the results well displayed and clearly ordered and grouped?	
	Is there any possibility of human error or bias in calculating or interpreting the results?	
Discussion of results	Does the discussion include all the results or a selected few? What is the basis of selection and is this made clear?	
	Is the generalisability of the results discussed? If the experiment was repeated under different conditions (e.g. different sample group, temperature, materials, gender, location or environment), would the results be the same?	
	Does the discussion relate to previous research?	
	Does the discussion include the limitations of method and how this might affect results?	
	Does the discussion explain the implications of the results for practice, theory, future research or policy?	
Conclusion	Is the conclusion clear and clearly drawn from the research?	
	Does it address the hypothesis, research question or aim?	

You can download this template from www.macmillanihe.com/lia-sys and adapt it to your needs.

If you want to understand what it means to analyse research papers, spend some time reading through existing critical appraisal templates and create one of your own. In this way, you will become familiar with the type of enquiry needed. You will start to read studies with focus and a critical approach.

8.12 presenting your dissertation: a 4 step strategy

⭐ the aim

You may be required to present your dissertation or your dissertation proposal. This strategy provides you with an easy to use visual aid that shows your presentation as a logically ordered sequence of information and ideas. This visual aid can be used and adapted for all types of presentation.

ℹ️ why this can help you

This strategy replaces the use of cue cards or printed notes with a one-page visual display made by hand. The strategy uses spatial working throughout, and requires some A3 unlined sheets of paper. You can work digitally to create a presentation but, for many people, working by hand is a faster, easier and more intuitive process. Making a visual overview in this way can help you:

- select the content of a presentation
- separate and highlight important details you want to deliver
- create a flow (direction) for a presentation
- see how the elements of a presentation link and build
- memorise and deliver the content

⚙️ the strategy

The strategy follows 4 steps:

step 1 establish the presentation focus, purpose and time

- If you are presenting your dissertation, your focus will clearly be the content of the dissertation. But you should also establish the purpose of the presentation (e.g. to give a summary, present only one part of the dissertation such as the methodology, show progress, or show intended future work).
- If your presentation is a coursework assignment, break down the assignment instructions (the assignment brief). You can do this spatially by using the ELP (elements, links and parts) strategy (subunit 6.3).
- Find out how long the presentation is. If it is a group presentation, find out how long you will have for your part.
- You should do these preparatory steps before you think about content. They will create focus and help you select and limit what you want to present.

step 2   brainstorm the presentation content

- Take the contents page of your dissertation, or the breakdown of the presentation brief, and refer to it as you brainstorm the possible content of the presentation. Brainstorming should be done on a large sheet of unlined paper turned landscape.

- At this stage, order is not important. This is a free thinking step and the only thing that matters is that the ideas you put down are relevant to the focus and purpose of the presentation.

- Don't be afraid to make changes when you brainstorm. One of the advantages of working with pen and paper is that your crossings out are always visible so you can see your changing thought processes. Brainstorming for a group presentation can be a highly creative (and learning) process as there will be more ideas and different points of view.

step 3   plan the order of content on a template

- For this step you need a template of squares set out on A3 paper. You can download one from www. macmillanihe.com/lia-sys. The template of squares helps you to identify the main points of your presentation and to start to structure it.

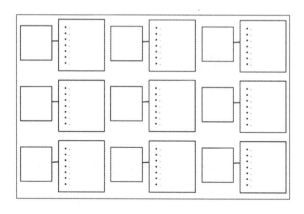

- One square is used to note a main topic, theme or issue, and a connected square is for noting information or ideas related to that point.

- From your brainstorm, prioritise the main points and transfer them to the template squares as headings. Then add relevant details as bullet points in the connected square.

- In this step, try to focus on identifying the most important points. You can leave some blank squares between the main points and finalise the order in the next step.

- Base the number of squares you use on the amount of time you have. If, for example, you have 10 minutes to present, you are likely to be limited to selecting no more than five main points.

step 4 transfer your main headings to make the visual overview

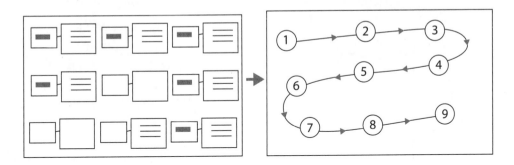

- The visual overview is a flow of main points spread across the page, connected by directional arrows (as in the diagram above and in the example below).

- In this step, you transfer the main headings from your template of squares onto a new sheet of A3 paper and create a visual flow from the introduction of the presentation to the conclusion.

- Once you have the visual flow of main headings, for each heading select the most important things you want to highlight in your presentation. Add them to your overview by using a key word, phrase or a symbol (see example below). This will help you remember what to say when you present.

- If you are using accompanying slides in the presentation, each main heading can be used to represent one (or more) slides.

- The connecting arrows represent your communication to the audience as you move between your main points. You can connect them with phrases like: 'now I would like to move on to', 'having established this' or 'another important point that I would like to highlight is'.

- If you are presenting an empirical dissertation, it is likely that your sequence of main headings will follow the conventional structure from introduction to conclusion. If you are presenting a theoretical dissertation or doing a piece of coursework, you can choose any order suitable for your purpose. The order of content must be logical and make sense to your audience, so it needs to make sense to you. For ideas on ordering information in coursework, see the table in subunit 6.5.

Here is an example of a presentation visual overview made from a dissertation on how to integrate students in teaching dance. Once you have created the overview, practise with it in front of you. Take it with you to the presentation as a visual aid. If you are using a digital presentation program, you will have much more detail on slides than you deliver, verbally, in your presentation, but the overview will help you focus on what you want to highlight about your topic. Also, by seeing everything together on one page, it will be easy to keep track of your place in the presentation (even if you are interrupted). At a glance, you can see what has been delivered and what is to come.

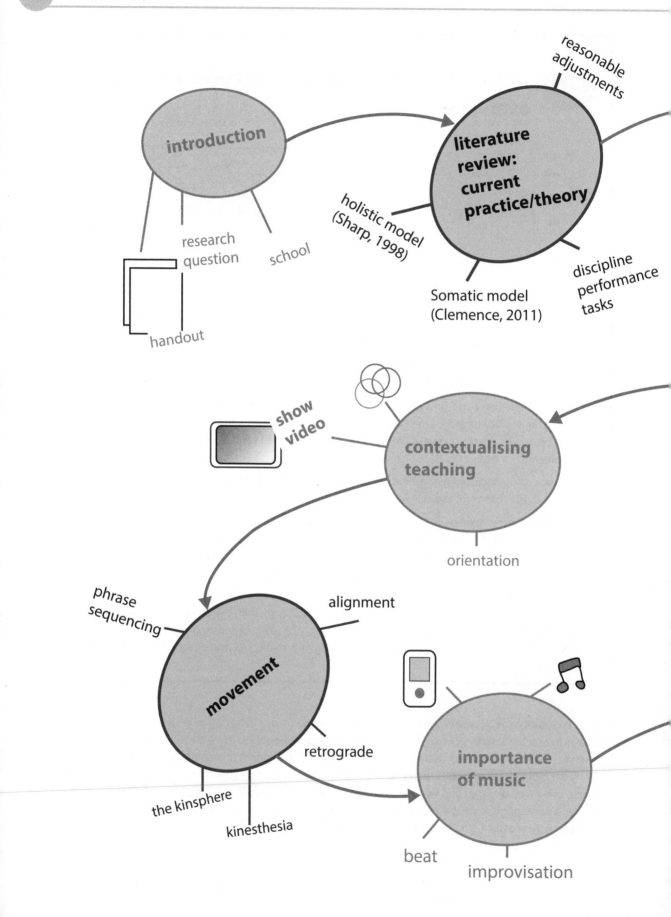

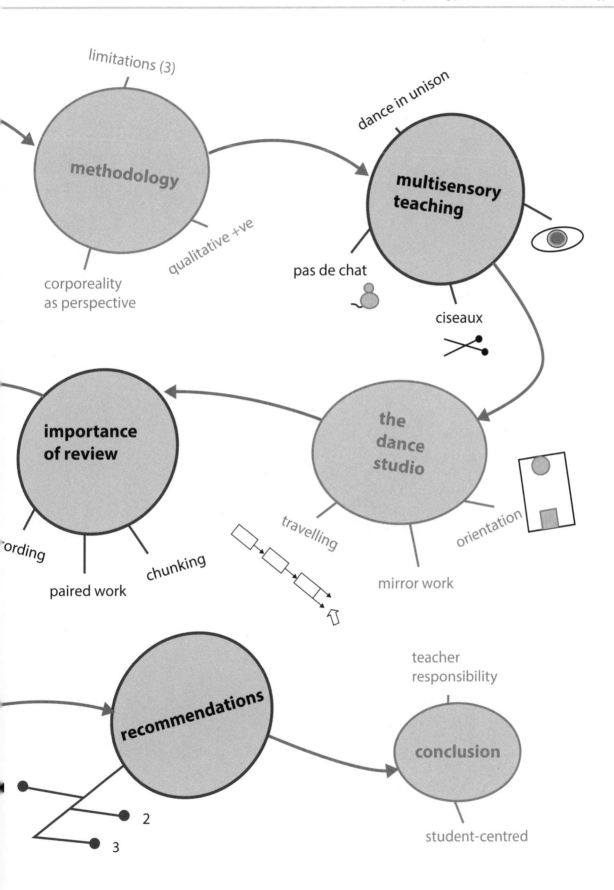

limitations (3)

methodology

dance in unison

multisensory teaching

qualitative +ve

corporeality as perspective

pas de chat

ciseaux

importance of review

the dance studio

travelling

orientation

...ording

chunking

paired work

mirror work

recommendations

teacher responsibility

conclusion

2

3

student-centred

unit 9

revision and examinations

Good preparation and the use of effective strategies will help you do well in exams. This unit presents several clear strategies that incorporate many of the fundamental principles of good revision and good exam technique:

- preparation
- organisation
- focus
- planning and time management
- note making
- memorisation
- monitoring

At university, there is traditionally a revision period when students start to review course content, but you can effectively prepare for revision and exams at any point during the academic year. Knowing the type of exam and questions you are working towards can guide your approach to reading, note making and thinking. Making an exam overview table is therefore a valuable form of preparation and the unit begins with this strategy.

9.1 making an exam overview table

⭐ the aim

The exam overview table is intended to provide a clearly set out display of essential information that will help you prepare for your examinations.

ⓘ why this can help you

Although most exams are taken at the end of the academic year (or term), it is useful to know the details of your exams as early as possible. This is especially important if you are studying a course that is assessed wholly or mainly by examinations.

If possible, look at past papers at the start of the academic year. You won't be expected to answer the exam questions at this early stage, but the information you collect about your exams can guide your work until you start thinking and planning for revision. Any notes you take before revision can be made with the exam requirements in mind and in view. The exam overview table can also help you choose the most appropriate revision and exam strategies.

⚙ the strategy

You can download an exam overview table template from www.macmillanihe.com/lia-sys, or you can make your own. For each of your exams, complete the details as follows:

past papers	The year (and period) of all the past papers available to you.
time	Length of the exam (add any extra time you may have been given), so you will then be able to work out how much time you have for each question.
exam type	Is the exam open book or closed book? Is it an oral or take home exam? You can also add details about any texts you can take in or formulas you will be provided with. If you are using a computer or have a reader for your exam, you can add that here.
structure	Structure and requirements of the exam, for example, note the number of sections or parts, number of questions and number of choices you have.
question types	Multiple choice questions (MCQs), short answer questions (SAQs), long answer questions (LAQs), calculations, problem-based questions, data or text analysis etc.
exam needs	Does the exam require facts, discussion or both? Identify the main types of information needed (e.g. theories, formulas, quotes, references, case law, research, models, diagrams).
revision sources	Main source for your revision (e.g. lecture slides, a core textbook, problem sheets, past exam papers, your own notes, online videos).
revision strategy	Decide on an appropriate revision strategy, read through the 3 step revision strategy (subunit 9.2).
date and time	As soon as you know them, enter the dates and times of each exam.

Here is an example of the kind of information you can put into the exam overview table. Any detail you add should be specific to the exam.

exams	CAUSES OF WAR	NUTRITION
past papers	2016, 2017, 2018, 2019	2019
time	3 hours	2 hours + 30 mins extra time
exam type	closed book	closed book, use computer for MCQs nutritional values table provided
structure	answer 3 questions: **+ 1** **PART A:** 1 from 5 from A **PART B:** 1 from 5 or B	**PART A:** MCQs answer all 30 (30%) **PART B:** SAQs answer all 5 (30%) **PART C:** treatment plan (long answer) 1 of 3 (40%)
question type(s)	3 long answer questions (essay-type questions)	multiple choice short answer questions logical treatment plan (process and reasons why)
exam needs	facts (dates, key events) discussion (why? so what? what if?) theories: esp. Kahneman/Rensho, Levy, Fukuyama, Tuchman, Howard, Boulding	facts: application of nutritional values, interpretation of graphs practice rationales (why do something) know some policy guidelines
revision source(s)	lecture notes, lecture capture key text: Robert Jervis: International Politics	lecture slides keys: nutrition and metabolism
revision strategy	make spatial notes of 4/5 topics make spatial notes of Jervis's theories and ideas	summarise key facts in spatial note form flash cards for nutritional value applications draw and interpret graphs
date & time:	6 May 10 am	10 May 2 pm

For some modules or courses, past exam papers are not released until later in the academic year. You should ask your tutors to provide at least one example past paper. For new courses, there won't be any available past papers. However, it is still useful to gather as much information about your exams as you can. Look for details in module or course books, ask students who have already sat exams and ask your tutors about the structure and type of exam they will be setting. Completing an exam overview table is not revision, but it will help you prepare for your revision when it is time to do so.

9.2 the 3 step revision strategy

★ the aim

The aim of this strategy is to provide an effective, explicit and simple to follow approach to revision that can be adapted for different subjects and courses.

ⓘ why this can help you

Revision for exams presents 3 main challenges:

1. dealing with the large quantity of material you need to cover

2. knowing which material to cover

3. remembering the material

This 3 step strategy addresses each of these points. It presents a way to organise, focus and deal with the information and ideas you will need to know for your exams. The strategy is based on three principles. If these principles are applied in a specific order, they can provide a powerful approach to learning.

1 organisation	If you can recognise the logical order and structure of something, you are in a better position to learn it.
2 focus	If you can approach your work with a clear focus, it will be more efficient and effective.
3 reformatting	Changing the form of information into a format you understand will increase your chances of remembering it.

⚙ the strategy

These 3 principles are reflected in the 3 steps of the revision strategy:

step 1: make and use a module table

sorts information and ideas into a clear, logical order

↓

step 2: get some focus

makes use of various sources to establish focus before revision

↓

step 3: reformat your notes

reformats information to help selection, understanding and memory

make and use a module table

You might feel overwhelmed or confused by the quantity of material that needs to be covered and memorised for exams. The first thing to do is to get organised. Making an overview of a course module (the course content) will allow you to clarify the content and, more importantly, identify the logical order of the content. You should make a separate table for each module on your course. This simple task will put a limit on what needs to be learned. Also, organising and understanding the logical structure of a module or course is an important first step in memorising information. The best way to do this is to complete your own module table. You can download a template from www.macmillanihe.com/lia-sys.

Here is an example of a module table. It shows 12 topics from a module for a degree in Law. The columns on the right can be used for any purpose you think is useful. For example, you can tick a topic that has been revised and then reviewed, mark a topic as a priority, cross off a topic you want to exclude or number the topics to show the order in which you will revise them.

module: The Law of Tort							
1	Duty of Care						
2	Psychiatric Injury						
3	Pure Economic Loss						
4	Omissions						
5	Public Authority						
6	Breach of Duty						
7	Causation						
8	Remoteness of Damage						
9	Product Liability						
10	Occupier's Liability						
11	Nuisance						
12	Trespass to Person						

For each module of your course for which you have an exam, refer to the module handbook, your online platform or your lecture notes and find a list of all the topics (or lectures) for that module.

Transfer the topics into the module table. As you do this, take time to understand the logical order of the topics. For example, you might recognise a chronological sequence or a thematic order. You might find that one topic leads into the next or that the topics can be grouped into categories. Modules and courses are deliberately designed so that content is ordered in a certain way. During the academic year, when you have so much information to process from numerous modules, you may not consciously recognise the logical structure of your module or course.

In the module table, you should write only the main headings and, if necessary, selected subheadings. The aim is to create an overview and not to include other details.

The module table has several columns. You will be able to use these columns to monitor your revision. You can tick topics that have been covered and reviewed. You can indicate topics that are a priority or those you intend to omit.

Keep each table you make on one side of A4 paper.

It is important that you make your own table rather than copying or printing the existing list of topics. In this way you can remove any superfluous details (like room numbers or the dates of lectures). The active process of rebuilding the order of topics will also help you understand how the module is constructed.

When you have made module tables for all your examined modules, you will have put a limit on the material that needs to be revised. Even if there is a lot of information, there is always a limit to it. Defining and seeing this will help the revision process in several ways.

You will now be able to see how the topics within a module relate to each other and even how some topics from one module relate to, or overlap with, topics from other modules. The order in which you revise topics is up to you. For example, you might revise your favourite topic first or, if two topics from different modules overlap, you might revise them one after the other. The module table gives you a simple tool to plan, check and monitor this activity.

Finally, the module table will help you in step 2 of the revision strategy. Exams are often designed to reflect the order of content in the modules they test. When you make an analysis of past paper questions, you are now more able to decide which topics to focus on and how to prioritise your revision.

alternative step 1: make and use a spatial module overview

Many traditional degree modules at university are designed to be delivered in weekly lectures. Each lecture covers one topic and in a term around 12 will be presented. This is typical in subjects like Law, War Studies, History and Philosophy. The module overview table is useful for course modules that consist of 12 to 25 topics. However, some courses are not delivered in this modular format and the content is therefore not easy to represent in a module table. There is no benefit in making a long list of topics that will cover more than one page, because the contextual overview is lost.

For these courses, it is better to create a spatial overview drawn on one sheet of A3 (or even A2) paper. This will take longer than making a module table, but the aim remains the same: to create a personal overview of a course that can be used to understand the logical structure and order of the course and to plan and monitor revision. Here is an example of a spatial overview for Foundations in Medical Science:

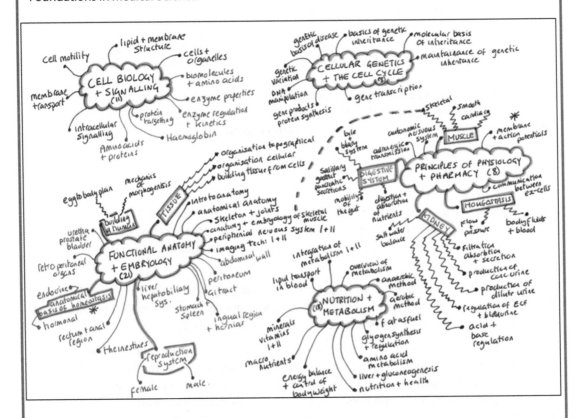

You can create a module table or a module overview at any time during the academic year and it's good to start doing this early. Even if you haven't covered the material, it can be useful to see what is coming. If you have already started to revise but are feeling overwhelmed by the quantity of material, this step can help you gain a sense of control.

One of the difficulties that you may face when revising is to know which topics should be given priority and what information is the most important to learn. There are two ways to determine which topics to revise. The first is to ask your tutor. Some tutors will let you know the topic areas that will be covered in exams, others will not, but you should always ask for some indication. The second is to analyse past exam papers.

step 2

get some focus

analysing past exam papers

An analysis of past papers is much easier if you have made the module table(s) in step 1. When you analyse past papers, you are looking for:

● topics that are regularly examined

● questions that are regularly asked

Try to get as many past papers as possible (especially recent ones) and don't wait until the start of the examination period to analyse them. As you go through the papers, use different colours to indicate different topics and check the topics against the list in your module table. If a topic is repeated regularly, then use one of the columns in the table to indicate it as a priority for revision.

If there are several questions covering the same topic, it is useful to see and read them together. This will give you the focus and range of knowledge you will need in order to provide answers in the exam. So, cut and paste, or copy questions for the same topic and list them so that you can see them together.

The examination and the module (or course) are usually designed together. So, another thing to look out for when you read through past papers is the relationship between the module and the exam. For example, see if the order of questions in the exam follows the order of topics taught on the module or whether certain topics are regularly combined in the same question.

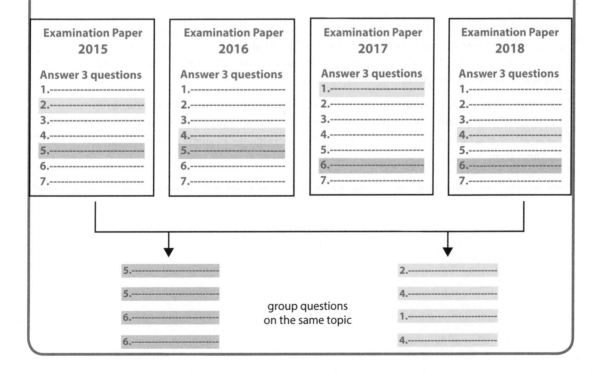

group questions
on the same topic

Analysing past papers is a practical way of familiarising yourself with exam papers. Try to print out (on white paper) at least one hardcopy of a past exam so that you can get used to handling it. Read the instructions and rules on the front and get to know the structure and layout. Some students have a real fear of exams, so addressing this issue early is one way of tackling this fear. When you look at an exam paper at the start of your course, you cannot expect to answer the questions, so it is important to recognise that the aim of this step is to prepare yourself for revision and to take away any surprises.

other sources of focus

Getting focus from past papers is not possible on all courses. There may be no past papers available. Sometimes, the tutor simply tells you to learn everything. Also, your course might be new or not previously tested by an exam. In subjects assessed with multiple choice questions (MCQs), it is difficult to prioritise revision, even with past papers, as the questions will usually cover the whole range of course content.

However, even without past papers or the support of your tutor, it is still possible to get some focus before you begin reading and making notes for revision. There are several sources you can access to try and understand the types of questions that will be asked in your exams:

- questions in the module handbook
- questions asked and discussed in seminars (see subunit 3.5)
- coursework questions, especially essay questions that relate to a specific topic
- questions or aims included as part of lecture notes
- the learning objectives for a module (if they are specific enough)
- problem sheets (these usually reproduce the type of questions in exams)

This step of the revision strategy can help you decide which topics to revise or which topics to revise first. Even if your intention is to cover and learn all the material, you have to start somewhere. Starting at lecture one and going in order to the end might not be the best approach for all examinations.

This step can also help you identify the core knowledge or the most important things to understand or memorise. When you make your revision notes, you will be in a better position to be selective and not to make notes of everything. This step is designed to make things easier for the next step.

step 3

reformat your notes: make spatial notes

Spatial notes are made by creatively reformatting core material from one source (usually lecture notes) to another (an A3 sheet of paper). Here is an example of spatial notes made for revision for a topic in Biochemistry. This layout of information was drawn on one sheet of A3 paper and represents concise notes made from a lecture containing 40 slides:

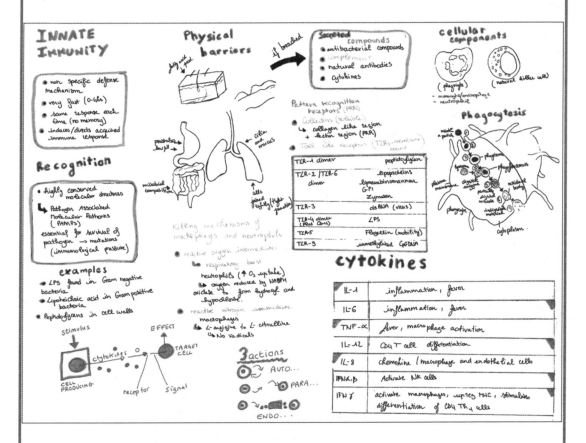

Spatial note making for revision is similar to spatial note making for reading (see subunit 3.1). But when making spatial notes for revision, you are more likely to follow the order in which the material was delivered in a lecture. This assumes, of course, that the lecture, the lecture slides or notes and the lecturer's approach were logical. If the order did not make sense to you, spatial note making allows you to create your own order. In most cases, your notes are likely to start from the top left of a page, down and across the page. This is not a rule, and you can change the order if you wish.

Before making spatial notes, choose a topic from your module table or spatial overview (step 1). If you have them, read through the focus questions you collected (step 2) and keep these questions in view. Refer to them as you make notes. The spatial notes should be made relevant to this focus. A guide to making spatial notes for revision is set out below.

making spatial notes for revision	
Take a sheet of blank (non-lined) paper and turn it to landscape.	• A3 sized paper is ideal as it gives enough working space but sets a realistic limit on how many notes you should aim to make.
Read through your lecture notes and highlight what you think is essential or relevant.	• You should try to be selective. • Your aim is to identify core knowledge and specific details and not to make notes of everything. • These details can trigger memory of other things. • Use your focus questions to guide you and help you to select what is most important. • There is no point reproducing all the information on a topic, even if you have the time. • You can read through the original lecture notes (or watch the lecture video) at any time during the academic year and make spatial notes in preparation for revision.
At any point, stop reading and make notes of the highlighted information. If your source of revision is a video of the lecture, pause the video to take notes of important and relevant information.	• Don't write full sentences. Use abbreviations, key words and bullet points. • Reformat the information as much as possible. Reformat it so that it makes more sense to you. • Be creative. Draw processes as flow diagrams, simplify pictures, use symbols, images and diagrams, use boxes, use labels and numbers. • Use colours, but for a clear purpose (e.g. to identify categories or highlight the same information used in different contexts). • Don't make notes of what you already know (what is already in your long-term memory). • Your aim is not to create a summary of a lecture. You want specific and relevant detail that will trigger your memory of other things. • Make your notes on one side of the page only.

lecture notes   spatial notes

the benefits of making spatial notes for revision

Like making spatial notes from reading, this is an active strategy. You are thinking about the notes you make because you are reformatting them and adding your own comments. When you reformat information, you put it into a form that you understand. Your finished notes will therefore look different from standard (linear) notes and each set of spatial notes will also look different.

Once they are made, spatial notes are easy to review and they will be reviewed regularly when you revise, especially in the days running up to the exam. They should also be reviewed while they are being made and this strategy allows you to work in short sessions (see subunit 1.4). After taking a break, you can restart your next work session with a review of the notes before adding to them.

You can make spatial notes from any source, not just lecture notes. For subjects like English, Classics and Philosophy, lecture notes are only an introduction to a topic and students are required to read texts and commentaries in order to collect more information and ideas. In subjects like Archaeology, Art History or Film Studies, you might have to annotate or analyse an image. You could draw or print the image in the centre of your A3 page and spread your notes around it.

Spatial notes for revision that are based solely or primarily on the contents of a lecture will tend to follow the order of the lecture. You might only need to access other sources in order to clarify something. Notes that combine lectures and supplementary research will be more like spatial notes for reading (subunit 3.1), and the order in which you display and group the information is up to you.

Here is an example of spatial notes made for a topic in Philosophy:

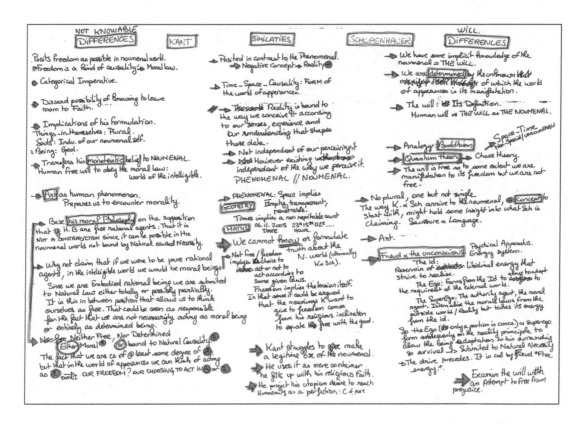

You can start making spatial notes of lecture topics as early in the academic year as you want. It may be too early to start revising, but this is a good way to prepare for revision. If you spread out revisiting the notes, rather than just revising before the exam, you are more likely to remember them.

Use the module table or the spatial overview (drawn up in step 1) and record what you do. For example, mark a topic for which you have made notes and tick it again each time you review the notes. In this way, you can monitor your revision. You don't have to make spatial notes for all the topics in each module. Be selective and start with the most important. Don't let note making become a task you have to complete simply to tick boxes.

By keeping your spatial notes on one side of the paper, you can compare topics from different modules and revise them one after the other. Your spatial notes are like posters, so you can put them on your wall and refer to them regularly. This can be useful especially in the days before an exam.

Some students prefer to make spatial notes on coloured A3 paper. A light, pastel colour seems to help some students process and even memorise the information better than when using white paper (see subunit 2.6).

Here is an example of spatial notes made for a topic in Anatomy:

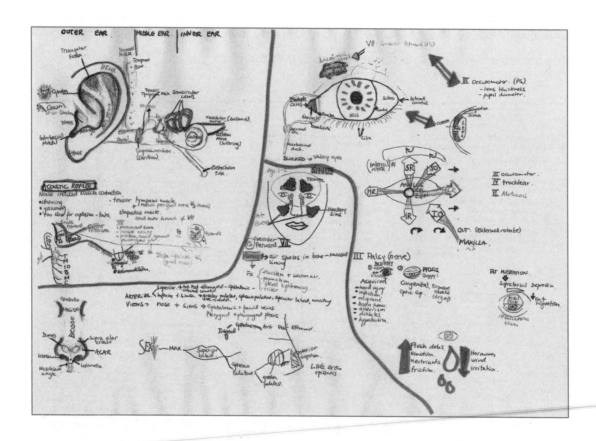

You can combine spatial notes for revision with any other approach. Some students like to make flash cards. Spatial notes are like a poster of flash cards laid out together. The immediate advantage of a spatial layout is that the relationship between information from the same topic is clearer and this can also help memory.

Some students like to make spatial notes in digital form. There are numerous programs that allow you to do this (e.g., Microsoft OneNote and Evernote). One advantage is that you can add multimedia content. The main disadvantage is that you are not using your hand to write or draw the information, which for many students helps memory.

Once you have made spatial notes, reading or watching the relevant lectures again becomes easier and more effective. In the last few days before the exam, you will be reading through the spatial notes quickly. You can test your (visual) memory of them by redrawing some of the information on blank paper.

Here is an example of spatial notes made for a lecture on feminism:

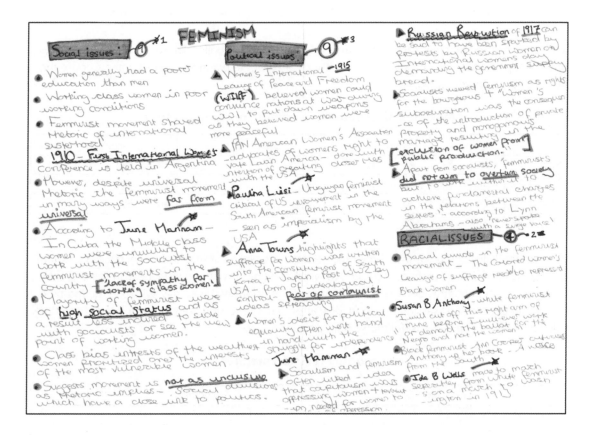

a note on mind maps

Spatial notes for revision are not mind maps or spider diagrams. Mind maps made for revision transform one structure (lecture notes) into another (a mind map). Mind maps consist of a central idea with connected information and ideas radiating from it. Spatial notes don't have a set structure. They are more like posters. Each time you make spatial notes, you will create something with an original and different form. This difference will help memory. If you want to include the name of the topic, don't waste space by putting it in the middle of the page, write it on the back. You don't need to connect the information on the page with lines to show that it is related. Information on the same page already has a relationship to the topic. If mind maps work for you, then continue to use them. If you have tried mind maps or spider diagrams without success, try spatial note making. It is a different approach.

9.3 making and using a revision planner

If you have exams at the end of the term or academic year, you can prepare for revision at any time by making all your notes 'revision friendly'. If you are doing continuous assessment (like completing problem sheets for maths), you are already revising. However, most students start to plan their revision about six weeks before the first exam. An effective revision planner needs to be:

● visible   ● flexible   ● easy to use   ● realistic

Many students find that vertical planners are easier to use and visualise. These planners display days from the top of a page downwards. There are two main types of planners you can make. Choose the one that best suits your needs.

morning, afternoon and evening revision planner

			morning			afternoon	evening	
Mon	21	Mar	●	●	●	●	●	●
Tue	22	Mar	●	●	●	●	●	●
Wed	23	Mar	●	●	●	●	●	●
Thu	24	Mar	●	●	●	●	●	●

This planner divides each day into three time periods. Allocate a realistic number of revision sessions for each day and distribute them according to which time of the day you work best. In the example above, the student has decided to set a minimum of 6 revision sessions a day, with 3 in the morning. A starting time for the first session is a good idea; after that, the sessions can be completed at any time. A flexible plan can be more useful than a rigid time schedule.

module revision planner

			Module 1	Module 2	Module 3	Module 4
Mon	21	Mar				
Tue	22	Mar				
Wed	23	Mar				
Thu	24	Mar				

This planner is divided by module so that you can allocate different days to revising different modules. If you prefer, you can work on more than one module in the same day. Work out how much time you will need for each module (some will require more than others) and allocate the days accordingly.

Both of these 11 week revision planners are available to download from www.macmillanihe.com/lia-sys. Once you have entered the dates and times of your exams, you will know exactly how much time you have and you can start to plan your revision. Unless you are certain about your intentions, it is best not to complete the whole planner at the beginning. It may be better to plan a week at a time so that you can use the planner in a more flexible way.

9.4 multiple choice questions (MCQs)

MCQs are made up of a question (or questions) and a list of options from which you choose the answer(s). The most common form of MCQ is called 'single response' or 'single best answer'. The question is short, and you are instructed to choose only 1 of the 4 or 5 options listed. Here is an example:

> **Q: Which ONE of the following statements is TRUE?**
>
> A: in apoptosis, apoptotic bodies are removed by phagocytes
>
> B: in apoptosis, the intrinsic pathway involves extracellular binding
>
> C: in apoptosis, cell fragmentation occurs only in the extrinsic pathway
>
> D: apoptosis can cause blebbing but NOT mRNA decay
>
> E: in apoptosis, caspases acts as an enzyme inhibitor
>
> In this example, only A will get you a mark.

By looking closely at this example, you can see that short words in the question (in this case 'ONE') make all the difference. Sometimes, MCQs require more than one answer. These kinds of MCQs are usually called 'multiple response questions'. Here is an example:

> **Q: Which of the following statements is TRUE?**
>
> A: in apoptosis, apoptotic bodies are removed by phagocytes
>
> B: in apoptosis, the intrinsic pathway involves extracellular binding
>
> C: in apoptosis, cell fragmentation occurs only in the extrinsic pathway
>
> D: apoptosis can cause blebbing
>
> E: apoptosis can cause mRNA decay
>
> In this example, you would need to state A, D and E to get full marks.

More detailed instructions will appear on the exam paper, but don't assume that all MCQs have the same format. It is important that you know, before the exam, the form of MCQs you will be answering. This will make you familiar with the question types and reduce the risk of misunderstanding instructions when you are under pressure in the exam. There are two other types of widely used MCQs:

- **matching questions**: These are sometimes called 'extended matching questions' or EMQs. A list of options is given, and you are asked several questions that relate to the options. For each question, you must choose one (or sometimes more than one) option.

- **true or false questions**: For most true or false questions, you are given a series of statements and are required to indicate whether each one is true (T) or false (F).

There is a lot of dubious advice about how to approach MCQs in exams. Much of it involves looking for clues or 'tricks' in the wording of the question and answer options. But if you think in this way in the exam, you are likely to waste a lot of time. To do well in MCQ exams you need:

- to prepare and revise effectively
- a good examination strategy
- a bit of luck

preparing and revising for MCQ exams

Most MCQs ask you to recall facts. Some question types might require you to apply factual knowledge to a scenario, use it to do a calculation or make a judgement. However, the basis of doing well for most MCQs is a good recall of factual detail.

Before you start your revision for an MCQ exam, do some preparation work. After you have established what type(s) of MCQs will be in your exam, find out:

- how many option answers there are in the MCQs (usually 4 or 5)
- how many MCQs you will have to answer
- how much time you will have for the exam (or the MCQ section of an exam)
- how much time you will have for each question

The next thing to do is to answer MCQs. This is a form of revision, but it also allows you to get used to the kinds of questions you will be asked. It is also useful to go over MCQs you have already completed because this helps you focus on and get used to the way they are phrased. Familiarise yourself with the words and phrases used (often capitalised or in bold for emphasis). One simple thing you can do with past papers is read the MCQs and highlight these small, key words. You will notice how many similar words there are and how many opposite phrases are used. It is essential that you see and read these key words when you are in the exam, so get used to seeing and reading them before the exam.

typical instructions for MCQs:

NOT	Does NOT	TRUE	is not TRUE
FALSE	only	all of the above	none of the above
All of the following EXCEPT			

When you make revision notes for MCQ exams, you will have to be selective. You don't want (or you won't have time) to make notes of everything from a lecture. Practising lots of MCQs can help you decide which information to make notes of. It can even help you choose an appropriate format for your notes. The best approach to use for MCQ revision is the same as that used for short answer questions (see subunit 9.5). Your aim is the same: to remember as much relevant factual detail as you can in the time you have allocated for your revision.

an examination strategy for MCQ exams

You won't have much time to consider and answer MCQs in an exam. To avoid confusion, you need to decide on a clear strategy. There are two main approaches you can take. The first is to go through all the questions and answer them the best you can. The second is to leave questions you don't know and come back to them later. Either approach can work, the important thing is to prepare a clear strategy.

One thing to consider before you decide on your strategy is whether the MCQ exam has negative marking. Negative marking is designed to reduce random guessing by deducting points for each incorrect answer. The amount deducted can vary, so try to find out what this is for your exam.

The flow chart below shows an example of a step by step strategy for answering MCQs. It is based on answering traditional, single best answer MCQs.

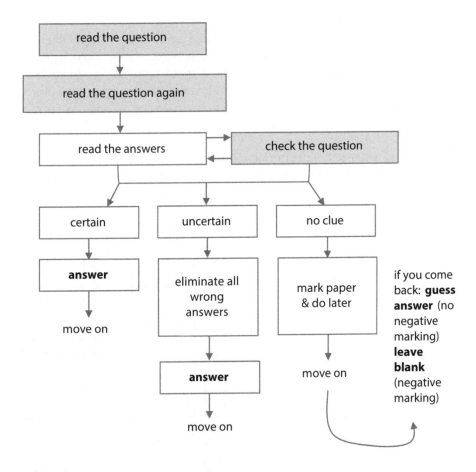

In this strategy, you read the question three times. You only skip a question if you really don't have a clue about it (so that you don't waste time). You mark these questions and come back to them and try them again. If you still don't know, guess. If there is negative marking, leave the question unanswered.

Once you have the details you need, create your own explicit strategy for MCQ exams. Draw the strategy out as a flow chart if it helps. When you start the exam, you should know exactly what your strategy is going to be.

For some exams, you will answer MCQs on a computer. For others, you have to transfer your answers, by hand, to a sheet that can be digitally scanned. This is something else you should know before you sit the exam. In the exam, you can transfer the answers one at a time, in small groups (e.g. 5 at a time) or all together when you have finished answering the questions. The choice is yours, but make sure you decide your approach before you start the exam. Make it part of your exam strategy.

One thing to bear in mind is that even in single best answer questions, more than one of the options can be correct (under certain circumstances) or partly correct. You can waste time trying to look for the 'perfect' answer. The answer you want to identify is the best or 'most correct' answer to the question.

MCQs and visual disturbance

People who experience visual disturbance of text when reading can be disadvantaged when attempting MCQs. There are many short, key words that can be misread, and the sheet used for recording the answers can be visually difficult to work with. If you think that visual disturbance could cause you difficulties, request permission to take coloured overlays into the exam. You can cut the overlays to any size and use one for reading the questions and another when transferring the answers. For more details on this, see subunit 2.6.

When you have answered a question, write the letter (or letters) in a large font next to the question on the exam paper and circle it. This means that when you transfer the answer, you will be reading something clear. It also means that, if necessary, your paper can be checked to see if your answers match those on the answer sheet.

It's a good idea to transfer your answers in groups of 5 or 6, rather than all at once. This means that if you make a mistake, only some of the answers will be entered wrongly. You can enter answers individually, but this can be time-consuming. Whatever you do, decide on your strategy before the exam.

Slide the coloured overlay down the answer sheet as you enter each answer. Use it to help you track each line. If you want to practise using an overlay to transfer answers, ask for a replica of the answer sheet. Alternatively, you can download a mock answer sheet from www.macmillanihe.com/lia-sys.

1	A	B	C	D	E
2	A	B	C	D	E
3	A	B	C	D	E
4	A	B	C	D	E
5	A	B	C	D	E
6	A	B	C	D	E
7	A	B	C	D	E
8	A	B	C	D	E
9	A	B	C	D	E
10	A	B	C	D	E
11	A	B	C	D	E
12	A	B	C	D	E
13	A	B	C	D	E
14	A	B	C	D	E
15	A	B	C	D	E
16	A	B	C	D	E
17	A	B	C	D	E
18	A	B	C	D	E
19	A	B	C	D	E
20	A	B	C	D	E
21	A	B	C	D	E
22	A	B	C	D	E
23	A	B	C	D	E
24	A	B	C	D	E
25	A	B	C	D	E
26	A	B	C	D	E

typical form used for entering MCQ answers by hand

Like MCQs, most SAQs in exams require you to recall facts. SAQs can usually be answered with a single word, a phrase or one or two simple sentences. Sometimes, the answers can be longer. For example, you might be asked to write a definition, give a brief account or explain the meaning of something. However, the answers are concise, and you are often given only a restricted space in which to write.

The mark available for each SAQ is usually given next to the question. This should be used as a clear indication of how many points or key words you need to provide. Here is an example:

> **Q: What are the 3 basic processes of urine production? (3)**
>
> Answer:
>
> glomerular filtration
>
> tubular reabsorption
>
> tubular secretion

In this example, it is clear that you would only need 3 correct terms. You would not need to write anything else about the production of urine. However, the way some questions are worded means that the amount and type of information you need to provide is not as clear. Here is another typical SAQ:

> **Q: What is hyperplasia? (3)**
>
> All these answers will get at least some of the 3 marks available:
>
> Hyperplasia is an increase in the number of cells produced.
> Hyperplasia is an increase in the number of cells produced in an organ or tissue.
>
> Hyperplasia is an increase in the number of cells produced in an organ or tissue. This increase happens at an abnormal rate.
>
> Hyperplasia is an increase in the number of cells produced in an organ or tissue. This increase happens at an abnormal rate and the organ or tissue can enlarge.
>
> Hyperplasia is an increase in the number of cells produced in an organ or tissue. This increase happens at an abnormal rate and the organ or tissue can enlarge. Hyperplasia is a type of hypertrophy and can be an early sign of cancer.

In this example, the 3 marks available suggests that you should make 3 points. One of the blue highlighted answers would probably be enough to get you all the marks. The last answer would also get full marks. It probably adds more information than is needed, but this is concise and relevant detail. You won't lose marks for extra information as long as it is factually correct and doesn't contradict or confuse the rest of your answer.

So, when answering SAQs:

> if the question is not totally clear, you should include any extra information that is relevant and correct but keep it concise and always write short sentences

For SAQs, you need to know key terms and associated key facts. Well written SAQs should be unambiguous and your answers should also be clear. Even for longer answers, you don't need to reproduce definitions or meanings, word for word. For all SAQs, write short, simple statement sentences where you make one point at a time (see an easy way to write simple sentences subunit 5.5). This makes it easier for you to see that you have provided the required information and it makes it easier for the marker to read.

making revision notes for SAQs

As with MCQs, it is good practice to precede your revision by familiarising yourself with the instructions and words used. If you are revising for exams with SAQs, look at past papers and identify the most frequently used commands. To emphasise this, you can make a list of them and mark them every time they reoccur. You will find that the same instructions are repeated often.

typical instructions for SAQs that require facts:

- List the properties of
- Draw a diagram
- Give the steps of
- Give a brief definition of

- Name
- Complete the table
- Give the values of
- Give FOUR properties of

- Label the diagram
- Describe the process
- Give a concise meaning of
- Provide 2 examples of

A familiarity with SAQs will help you make the most effective type of revision notes. It will help you be more selective and reduce your notes to key facts. This is a crucial aim of making spatial notes for revision. This is step 3 of the 3 step revision strategy (subunit 9.2) and can be used for any exam that requires the memorisation of a large quantity of detailed facts.

Whatever your strategy, if you are making revision notes for SAQ (or MCQ) exams, there are some useful ideas to be aware of and implement:

- break the information down into key words and key facts
- reformat your notes so that they are easier to remember
- simplify your notes as much as possible
- use numbers, symbols, schema, drawings and colours
- build up information by learning a few facts at a time
- be creative, use your imagination and make the notes personal and different
- don't waste time or space noting facts you already know
- review your notes regularly (while you make them and after making them)

Creativity and individuality are often overlooked when trying to memorise information for exams. You can:

- create original mnemonics (see Becker, 2018 p. 18)

- make personalised flash cards (use online apps, e.g. Brainscape or Quizlet)

- use text readers to listen to your notes (see subunit 2.4)

- use a memory peg system to associate facts you want to learn with something already in your long-term memory (see Buzan, 2010 pp. 45–83; O'Brien, 2007 pp. 63–70)

Here are some more simple revision ideas for displaying and learning facts. They can be used as part of the spatial note making strategy for revision and they should encourage you to be creative and come up with your own ideas:

- Making numbered or bullet point lists can be helpful. But there are other ways to display and remember a precise number of related facts. Using shapes can help you remember the right number of terms:

- Simplify detailed drawings and photographs as much as possible to leave only the key components. If you want to learn a more complex diagram, start by learning a few components first and add more gradually. You can draw more than one version of the diagram. Draw a version without the names and practise labelling it from memory.

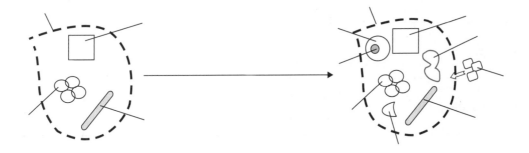

- Simplify processes and draw them out as flow diagrams. Include only the major steps, add more detail later, if required.

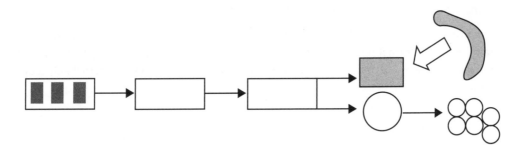

- Extract key words from longer definitions and see if you can reconstruct a good definition from these words. Don't try to reproduce the original definition word for word.

- When revising for SAQs or MCQs, you don't need to make notes of what you already know. This information is already in your long-term memory and you will be able to retrieve it when you are questioned. When making revision notes for SAQs, you don't want to produce summaries or make your notes 'complete'. You should pick out relevant and important detail. This detail will trigger memory of associated facts.

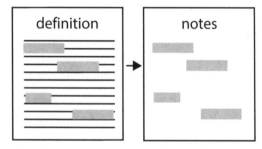

a template for descriptive questions

When an SAQ asks you to 'give an account' or 'give a description' of something, it can be useful to have a trigger for your memory. The 5 headings in this template are designed to help you do this. Simply remembering and noting down these 5 key headings can prompt you in an exam.

O	origins	What causes it? (What caused it?)	give examples
F	function	Why is it made? (Why was it made?) What is its purpose?	
F	form	What does it look like? What is its structure? What is it made of? What form(s) does it take? What are its features?	
P	process	How does it work? What is its sequence?	use diagrams
L	location	Where does it operate (place)? When does it operate (time)?	

The template can be used for making revision notes for exams. It can help you identify, collect, arrange and remember key facts about a topic. The template's 5 headings can be easily interpreted and adapted for science and arts and humanities subjects. Although the template is based on the requirements of SAQs, it can be used to learn detailed information that will form the basis of discussion and argument in a long answer question (subunit 9.6)

Two examples of revision notes made using the template for descriptive questions are shown below. They contain selected information and focus on the key terms and processes likely to be required for SAQs. If you want to use or adapt this template, you can download it from www.macmillanihe.com/lia-sys.

apoptosis (key notes)	
Origins	DNA instruction → cell stress, signals between cells → production of caspases (enzyme)
function	kill cells (programmed cell death), change cells (cell morphology)
form	blebbing (membrane bulge) nuclear condensation DNA fragmentation cell shrinks mRNA decay chromatic condensation

process	INTRINSIC PATH (own cell) mitochondrial protein EXTRINSIC PATH (other cells) binding on outer cell	initiator caspases ↓ executioner caspases ↓ cell fragmentation (apoptotic bodies) ↑ (removed by) phagocytic cells
location	cells of all multicellular animals (plants too, but process differs)	

e.gs: digit formation in foetus, destruction of (potential cancerous) DNA-damaged cells

Yihetuan (Boxer) uprising (key notes)	
Origins	anticolonialism, anti-Christian, drought/famine/floods (northern China), Chinese gvt weak, increase in Chinese nationalism
function	remove colonial presence, reduce colonial powers, increase Chinese autonomy
form	series of battles, skirmishes, summary killings (esp Christian missionaries), revenge attacks, siege, guerrilla tactics, foreign alliances (8 nations), failed diplomacy

process	exile of Guangxu (Empress Dowager Cixi) ↓ attack on Liyuantun village ↓ Cixi support for Yihetuan ↓ killing of missionaries ↓ 400 foreign troops land in Beijing ↓ killing of 'Boxer' boy and revenge attacks	Siege of the Legations (Yihetuan/Chinese army) ↓ Cixi (and Guangxu) declare war ↓ Battle of Tianjin (foreign forces) ↓ foreign force lifts siege of Legations ↓ Cixi (and Guangxu) escape forbidden city ↓ signing of Boxer Protocol
location	China, Qing dynasty, 1899–1901	

notes might include a map showing major areas of conflict

In addition to stating facts, some SAQs require you to discuss. They may ask you to explain something or apply knowledge to a practical situation (a scenario is sometimes provided). Some SAQs are a series of short, related questions based on the same topic and some of these questions may include instructions that ask for discussion. The revision ideas described above are applicable to learning facts. But discussion (analysis) can be generated from facts by asking key questions. See description and discussion in academic writing (subunit 4.5).

9.6 the 4 step exam strategy for long answer questions (LAQs)

⭐ the aim

In exams, long answer questions (LAQs) are usually in the form of essay or essay type questions. This strategy aims to provide an easy to remember and easy to use method for answering exam LAQs.

ℹ️ why this can help you

The strategy breaks the process of doing LAQs into 4 explicit steps and each step of the strategy is designed to make the next one easier:

Having a simple and clear strategy means that you can focus on one step or task at a time. This will reduce your anxiety and, as a result, you will be able to remember and then apply your knowledge more effectively.

When answering an LAQ, the length of your answer will depend on the time you have been given. This strategy can help you use your time efficiently and the approach can be easily adapted to exams and questions of different length.

⚙️ the strategy

Before the exam, make sure you know how many LAQs you need to answer and the length of the exam. If you have completed an exam overview table (subunit 9.1), this will be easy. Calculate how much time you will have for each question. If you are required to select questions from a list of options, allocate some time for this part of your exam strategy.

You should aim to spend roughly an equal amount of time on all questions that carry the same value. Another thing you can do before the exam is to decide the order in which you are going to answer the questions. You can answer them in number order (as they appear on the exam), but a better approach is to answer your best question first as this will give you more confidence.

For each LAQ, you follow the 4 steps of the strategy in sequence and then move on to the next question. You can allocate an approximate number of minutes to each step. If you have 60 minutes per question, you might spend:

It can be difficult to be aware of time when you are in an exam, so you should think about and plan your strategy before the exam. The strategy is set out below, but, first, there are a few useful things to consider about doing LAQs.

preparing for and doing LAQs

LAQs are the most common type of exam question in subjects like History, Classics, Law and Philosophy. Unlike MCQs and SAQs, they nearly always require you to discuss (analyse), as well as recall facts. When you revise and make notes, you may want to add some commentary to the facts you are trying to memorise. If you don't want to add too many ideas to your notes, you need to make sure that you question the facts because, in the exam, you will not simply restate them, you will discuss them in relation to the exam question. The key discursive questions detailed in subunit 4.5 (why?, so what?, what if?) are therefore essential during revision and during the exam.

Examiner's reports can give a useful insight into the content and approach required for LAQs in your subject. These are short summaries, usually made by the module tutor, of past exams. They state the most popular questions and the average or range of marks. More importantly, they summarise the strengths and weaknesses of past answers. Check to see if your department produces examiner's reports and if so, read them and make a list of what is required to get the best marks for LAQs. Here are examples of weaknesses pooled from several examiners' reports for LAQ exams in Philosophy:

- **argumentation:** superficial, not present, not ordered, not set out logically
- **description:** too descriptive, only summaries offered, good definitions but no development into analysis
- **references:** did not go beyond lecture notes, not enough secondary texts used, no evidence of independent research
- **question:** deviated from the question, did not answer all questions required, started but did not complete question

In step 2 of this 4 step strategy, you prepare your answer by getting down all the relevant information and ideas you can remember. This information is unlikely to come to you in the right order, so you can space it out like a brainstorm. However, before you write (step 3), you will need to think about and plan a structure (order) for your answer.

Although LAQs are usually in the form of essay questions, the front page of most exam papers will ask you to do something like 'answer 3 questions'. Your answer doesn't need a complete reference list, nor does it require an essay type introduction or conclusion. Don't become anxious about trying to produce a formal essay. However, your complete answer will look and read a lot like an essay and tutors often refer to 'writing an essay' in your exam.

Your written answer needs to be a logically ordered response to the question. In LAQs, you are often required to put forward an argument that builds towards a conclusion. Once you have got down all the information you can remember, spend a few minutes to think about your overall argument (your thesis) and then number the points you have noted down to show the order in which you will discuss them. A useful way to think is like a lawyer who is preparing a case to present in court.

Here is the 4 step strategy laid out visually. Think of this strategy as a step by step process that allows you to produce an exam answer in a logical way. Each step has a clear purpose. Complete one step before moving to the next one. When you have completed the 4 steps for your first question, move on to the next question and repeat the 4 steps.

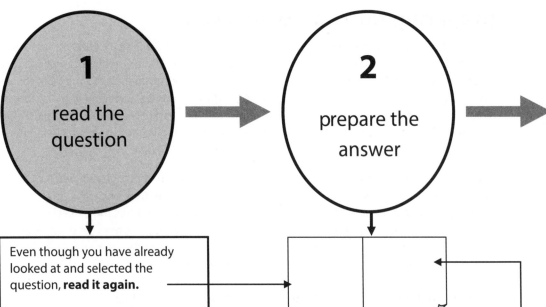

1

read the question

2

prepare the answer

Even though you have already looked at and selected the question, **read it again.**

Make sure you **identify the focus of the question**, not just the topic the question refers to.

Look for a relationship or link between two or more elements (i.e. what the question is about). See **making a spatial breakdown of essay questions** (subunit 6.3) Practise doing this with past questions so that you can do it quickly in the exam.

Does the question require description or discussion or both?

Break down the question to see if there are different parts to it. Often a question asks you to do 2 or 3 different things. In fact, some questions are really 2 or 3 different questions.

Use a separate book for making notes and preparing the answer. This will let you refer to your notes more easily than if you make them on the same booklet as your answer (if you do not have a second book, ask for one before you start the exam or check that one will be provided before you sit the exam). Open the book so that you can spread your ideas over 2 pages (equivalent of one A3 sheet).

Note down **relevant** information and ideas as you recall or think of them. Spread them across the paper and group ideas and information that go together. If you made spatial revision notes (subunit 9.2), you will have a good spatial recall of the information you formatted.

Use the breakdown of the question (step 1) to guide you. At this stage, don't write sentences, just make notes.

When you have finished, you can number the main points in the order you are going to write them in your answer.

Refer to these notes as you write. Tick or cross out what you have covered. Even when writing, you can add new things to your prepared notes as you remember more.

You might spend more time on this stage for your weakest question.

One of the most common reasons for doing badly in exams is not answering the set question, so step 1 is essential. A badly organised answer can lose you marks, so step 2 is also crucial. Another reason for poor marks is not attempting the full number of questions or leaving questions unfinished, so it is important to use the time efficiently.

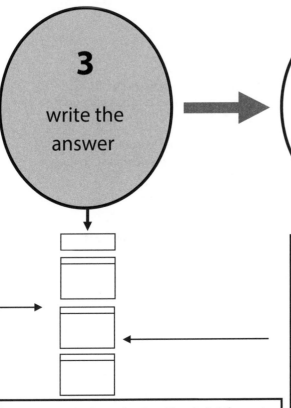

3

write the answer

4

check the answer

Write a concise introduction. Simply list the main points in the order in which you are going to deal with them. For example:
To answer this question, four factors will be discussed. These are A, B, C and D.

Refer to and work with your prepared notes and deal with one point at a time.

If required by the question, don't forget to fully discuss the points. Jot down and use the discursive questions: why?, so what? and what if? See **a model for description and discussion in academic writing** (subunit 4.5).

Use block paragraphs and leave two lines between them. Write clear topic sentences at the start of paragraphs or use headings.

If you forget something, use an asterisk and add the information further down the page.

In proofreading something that you have just written, you are unlikely to detect many errors. You will tend to read what you think you have written.

Focus this step on checking topic sentences or important paragraphs which you can scan in any order.

Check your prepared notes (step 2) to see if you have included everything.

If you realise that you have forgotten some information, but are running short of time, add it to your answer with bullet points.

Don't forget to submit your notes along with your exam script. Examiners will look at plans and notes and can give you some marks for them.

what is a gobbet?

In higher education, a gobbet is a written form of assessment usually found in subjects like History, Philosophy, Theology or Classics. A gobbet is a concise, written commentary based on an extract from a larger piece of work. The length of gobbets varies but they are usually around 500–800 words long.

Gobbets can be part of coursework, but they are usually assessed by examination. In examinations, writing two or three gobbets is often given as an alternative to writing one long answer question (or essay-type question).

the extract

The extract provided for the gobbet is typically taken from a primary source. It can take different forms, for example it can be an extract from:

- a diary
- a speech
- a letter
- a political pamphlet
- a poem
- a novel
- a biography
- an autobiography

The extract is usually in the form of a short, written text but it can also be a visual image like a photograph or a satirical cartoon.

a gobbet is not a close reading

A close reading analyses a text in detail and may relate it to the larger work from which it comes. The aim of a gobbet is to understand and discuss how the ideas in an extract, or the events described by an extract, relate to a wider context. The wider context might mean, for example, the social, historical, artistic or thematic context. A good gobbet doesn't just comment on the detailed content of an extract, it discusses the extract in relation to the period it is from and the ideas it is associated with.

templates for writing a gobbet

If you are only doing assessed gobbets for exams and not coursework or seminars, you should take the opportunity to practise them before the exam.

Below are two templates for writing gobbets. The first gives an outline and the second uses the same structure but adds questions and examples. They are designed to help you think how you might approach the task of writing a gobbet in an exam. You don't have to remember or answer all the questions in template 2, but you can use them if you want to write or practise writing a gobbet. Select the questions you can answer or that are most relevant to your task. You can download the gobbet template from www.macmillanihe.com/lia-sys.

1	template for writing a gobbet: outline template
extract	Comment on the form of the extract.
author	Write something about the author.
audience	Comment on the intended audience.
theme(s)	Identify and comment on the theme(s) in the extract.
context	Relate the extract to other significant events or ideas of the period.
aim	Identify and comment on the aim(s) stated in the extract.
importance (impact)	Assess the impact of events or ideas in the extract.
language	You can refer to the linguistic form (style and content) of the extract to support the discussion in your gobbet.

2	template for writing a gobbet: template with questions and details
extract	<ul><li>What form or genre is the extract (e.g. a speech, a diary entry, a photograph, a political manifesto)?</li><li>What (larger work) is the extract taken from (e.g. lines from an epic poem or part of a speech)?</li><li>What is the date of the extract?</li><li>Does the extract refer to a specific place (e.g. where a speech was made, or a photograph taken)?</li><li>How unique is the extract (e.g. a rare photograph of an event or an entry from a private diary)?</li></ul>
author	<ul><li>Who is the author?</li><li>What is the author's background?</li><li>Is the author associated with any ideologies, theories, artistic movements, literary or musical styles?</li><li>What is the author's status (e.g. military leader, monarch, slave, musician, politician or cleric)?</li><li>Is the extract representative of the author's other work?</li></ul>
audience	<ul><li>Who is the intended audience (e.g. the British government, Western politicians, political activists, the general public, women, musicians, academics or historians)?</li><li>Who is likely to have had access to the extract at the time (e.g. was it a private letter, or, if it was a speech, who was present and was it televised)?</li></ul>

	Some information (e.g. author, date or location) will be given with the extract. Don't just repeat it, discuss its relevance.
theme(s)	The subject of the extract is usually clear, but most extracts will address an overriding theme(s). Extracts are selected because they are good representations of important themes. Associating larger themes with the subject is useful in writing the gobbet, as the commentary can then relate to ideas and events beyond the content of the extract. Here are some examples: **subject:** Emily Davison jumping in front of King George V's horse at the Epsom Derby in 1913 **themes:** women's rights and the fight for universal suffrage **subject:** Les Demoiselles d'Avignon by Pablo Picasso painted in 1907 **themes:** modernism in painting and a radical break from past traditions **subject:** The Jarrow March of 1936 **themes:** unemployment and the rights of workers **subject:** The Declaration of Independence of 1776 **themes:** independence and the right to self-governance, self-rule or national sovereignty ● What is the subject of the extract? ● What is the theme of the extract? ● Was the theme highly relevant at the time of the extract? ● Is the theme as relevant today?
context	Gobbets can comment on how an extract relates to the larger piece of work from which it is taken (e.g. how a stanza reflects other themes in a poem or how an event fits into a story). However, context mostly means discussing the ideas and events in an extract in relation to ideas and events of the period it is from. This can be historical context (e.g. the social or political situation at the time a speech was made) or thematic context (e.g. ideas about music in a particular period). Relate the ideas and events in the extract to those of the period: ● What were the significant events before, during and after the date of the extract? ● How does the extract relate to other works, events or ideas of the period? ● Is the extract representative of works, events or ideas of the period? ● Is the extract unrepresentative of works, events or ideas of the period? ● Does the extract relate to a debate that was relevant at the time? One useful way to learn context is to make a timeline of major events and use it for revision.

aim	• What was the author trying to achieve (e.g. drum up political support, highlight an inequality or injustice, promote a different way of doing things, celebrate a great life, show support for an existing idea or criticise a rival or an institution)? • Does the form of the extract help the author put forward this message? • Is the author's message or aim clear or is it ambiguous?
importance (impact)	Gobbets can comment on the importance of an extract in relation to the larger piece of work from which it is taken (e.g. an essential event in a story or a key theme in a poem). However, in assessing the importance of an extract (the contribution it made), you are usually looking for a change or consequence that came about as a result of the ideas or the information in the extract. • What was the reaction to the ideas or information in the extract? • Did this change or influence the understanding of something? • Did this change or influence how people thought (theory)? • Did this change or influence what people did or how they did things (practice)? • Was this influence immediate or gradual? • In what ways has the extract been used or referenced since its time? • Why was it so influential? • Is it still relevant today? • Why did it have no impact or influence?
language	The form (style and content) of the language used in the extract can be referred to throughout the gobbet. There are many ways to describe the language used. For example, the language can be: • formal or informal • authoritative and technical • inflammatory and confrontational • subjective and biased • objective, fair and rational • unambiguous and clear • ambiguous, containing symbols, metaphors, similes and other hidden meanings However, a good gobbet will not just describe the form of language used, it will discuss it. • How is the style or content of the language used in the extract relevant to its audience, theme, context, aim or impact? You can use examples of key words and key phrases from the extract in writing your gobbet. Look out for specific names (of people and places), titles (forms of address), terminology or movements (e.g. structuralism or futurism). These specific words can be clues to trigger ideas for your gobbet.

what is an open book exam?

An open book exam allows you to consult sources in order to help you answer the questions. The sources are usually textbooks or prepared notes, but for some exams, you will have access to online material. Open book exams require you to understand and apply relevant information but do not usually require you to memorise it before the exam.

There are different rules that govern open book exams. If your course is tested in this way, you should establish the exam details as early as possible and enter them into your exam overview table (subunit 9.1). Here are the questions you need to answer:

- Will the exam be invigilated and on campus or will it be unsupervised and off campus (often called 'take home' exams)?
- How much time will I have for the exam? The time you have to complete take home exams varies, but it is usually between 24 hours and 4 days.
- For invigilated exams, is there a restriction on the amount and type of material I can take into the exam?
- For take home exams, is there a limit to the number of words I can write for each answer?
- Do I need to provide references and a reference list?
- Will I be given the questions (or topics) prior to the exam?

If memorising information is not your strength, an open book exam gives you an opportunity to do well. But to excel, you need to understand the course material and prepare thoroughly. Here are some ideas to help you do this.

create an alphabetic and thematic index

You are usually allowed to take a core text (or texts) as well as your own notes into an invigilated open book exam (sometimes notes have to be approved). You will benefit from preparing the text and making effective notes. One way to do this is to scan a core textbook for the most relevant information and mark the appropriate point in the text with numbered labels that stick out from the body of the book. You can also highlight the key information on each of the pages.

As you insert the numbered labels, make an index of them in a table on your word processor. Make sure that the index table has separate columns for the key topic word(s), the number of the label it corresponds to and any other concise information you think is important and relevant to the key topic.

Once you have completed your index table, select the key topic word column and alphabetise it so that the key topics are in A–Z order. Transferring your table onto one side of an A3 sheet, before printing, will help you locate key topics in the index faster. The numbered labels will help you quickly find the appropriate page in your textbook when you are in the exam.

In addition to the alphabetic index, you can make a thematic index in which you group key information under different themes. For example, if you are studying for an open book exam in Law, you may want to group points under different cases, whereas if you are preparing for a History exam, you may group information under events or theoretical perspectives. You can number the information to correspond with the labels in your core text. Making an alphabetic index will help you identify the key points. Making a thematic index will help you think about how you might apply the information in relation to a question.

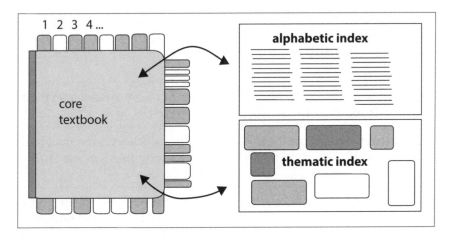

Although the alphabetic index needs to be done digitally, some students prefer to make the thematic index by hand and spread it over one side of an A3 sheet of paper (like spatial revision notes in subunit 9.1). Memorisation isn't crucial in an unrestricted open book exam, but hand writing notes can help you remember things and you are likely to make fewer notes. A thematic index is like a concise set of notes on a particular topic and can be made without the alphabetic index.

During open book exams, you should not spend most of the time consulting your sources, especially if you already know the information. Select only the most relevant notes for your indexes. You can identify these by analysing past paper questions, looking at your lecture notes or slides, or asking your tutor. The texts and notes you take into an open book exam are there when you need to reference, support or clarify a point. The key to doing well in all exams is understanding and answering the question. In open book exams, the emphasis will be on critical thinking, building arguments or solving problems.

off campus or take home exams

Because these exams are unsupervised and you have longer to answer the questions, they can be less stressful. However, you should not be complacent about take home exams. The work needs to be your own and you should be aware of potential plagiarism and collusion (see subunit 5.9). Before the exam, find out:

- when you will receive the questions and when to submit your answers
- how many questions you will have to answer (and whether there is a choice)
- the word limit (if there is one)
- the number of references and reference system to be used
- how you will submit your answers (usually online via plagiarism detection software, see subunit 5.9)

Tabulate this information, so that it is clearly set out. Here is an example:

start of exam	time	questions	word limit	references	submission
9am Friday 5 June	3 days	3 questions from 8	1,000 words each	4–6 references + a ref list for each (Harvard)	10am Monday 7 June via Turnitin

Although you are not under strict time pressure, your time is still limited. You should prepare a strategy and start the exam as soon as you get the questions. Here is a clear 7 step strategy for doing take home exams, which brings together some of the ideas in other parts of this book:

1	Choose the questions you are going to answer and put them in order from the one you like best to the one you like least. Do your best question first.
2	On a blank sheet of paper, use the ELP method to break down the first question (subunit 6.3). You can tackle one question at a time and move on to step 3, or you can break down all the questions you are going to answer and then move on.
3	Once you have understood the question, take a sheet of A3 paper and use the spatial note making strategy to collect and group the information and ideas for the answer (subunit 3.1). Keep the question in view as you research. One sheet of A3 will be enough for each question (know your word limit). You can use non-academic sources to help you clarify things, but make sure you use academic references to support your answer. You should calculate roughly how much time you will spend for each question. Set a strict time limit on this step.
4	Once you have enough material (or you have reached your time limit for researching), think about the order of your answer. Draw up an outline plan of the main sections, and write a short aim for each one (subunit 6.6).
5	Write the first draft of your answer.

At this point, you can research and write the other questions and get them to a first draft form before proofreading your work.

6	Proofread your answers (see step 10 in subunit 6.2) and check that your reference lists are set out correctly and contain the required number of references.
7	Submit your work at least two hours before the deadline. **Never wait until the last minute to submit work online.** Unforeseen technical problems are common.

when you know the question or topic before the exam

For some open book exams, you are given a question (or sometimes a topic) prior to the exam. You are allowed to access any source in order to prepare an answer, but you cannot take anything into the exam. In this form of exam, your preparation can be focused on a question or topic but some memorisation and recall are also required.

When given a specific question, some students research and write an answer and then try to memorise it, word for word, so that they can reproduce it in the exam. This might work if you have a good memory, if the question in the exam is exactly the same and if you have only one or two answers to remember. Remembering answers verbatim (word for word) is not likely to be an effective strategy for many students.

An alternative strategy is to remember a sequence of key words, reproduce these in the exam and then build the answer around them. Adding a visuospatial element to this approach can help you with memory. A spatial layout will also help you understand how the information has been ordered and how your argument has been put together.

When you receive your question, research and write an answer to it. Then, break down and separate your answer into a number of key sections. Each key section should have a heading and 2–4 main points. The headings and points should be words or short phrases taken from your long answer. Take an A3 sheet of paper and transfer the sections onto it starting from the top left, moving around clockwise to the bottom left. Count the number of sections and the total number of main points and write these numbers in the middle of your A3 sheet.

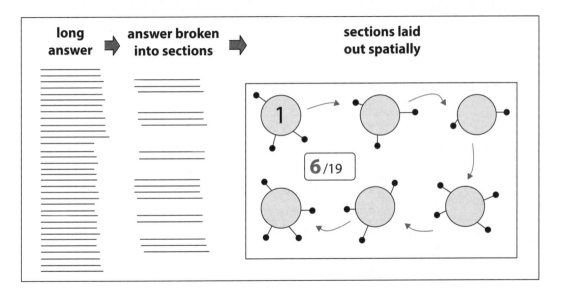

When you are in the exam, try to reproduce your spatial layout in a separate answer book (see step 3 of subunit 9.6) or on a spare sheet of paper before writing the answer. If you can remember the number of sections and key points, write this down so you can check that you have noted all of them. The key words will trigger memory of what you need to write. In the exam, you should refer to the question regularly, as this will also help you remember.

If you are only given a topic and not a question prior to the exam, don't try to predict the question. Instead, use past paper questions to identify the key points, make spatial revision notes (subunit 9.1) of the important points relevant to the topic. This would be similar to the thematic index described above. You can reproduce this in the exam before applying it to the specific question.

oral exams and dissertations

what is an oral examination?

An oral examination is an exam that requires students to answer questions verbally rather than in writing. It is most commonly used in foreign language degrees but it can also be used as a partial assessment in courses like Art and Design, Music and Medicine. An oral examination is a compulsory requirement for most postgraduate qualifications, when it is called a 'viva' (or 'viva voce'). It can also be a significant form of assessment for undergraduate dissertations.

preparing for an oral exam of your dissertation

Most questions asked in this kind of exam address points under 5 categories:

1	your research topic	• what your dissertation is about • why you chose this subject • why it was worth doing (rationale)
2	your approach	• any theoretical framework(s) used • the main literature used • method and methodology (or approach) used
3	your findings	• your main findings, conclusions, recommendations • your (original) contribution to the area of study
4	main limitations and strengths	• these can be related to any of the above, but it is worth identifying and listing them separately
5	the future	• your plans or potential future use of your research (usually only relevant to postgraduate research)

Because you know your dissertation better than anyone else and because you will have read it many times, simply rereading it before the oral exam has limited value. Reviewing your dissertation in different ways can be more effective. Here are four ideas that use visual strategies explained in other parts of this book. They can be used to help you prepare for an oral examination:

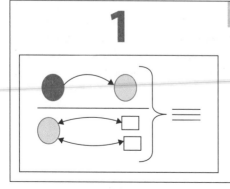

reformat your research question or hypothesis

Everything in your dissertation (all the chapters or sections, the literature, methodology, display and discussion of results and your conclusion) has a connection with your research question.

If you didn't do this at the start of your research, use the ELP (elements, links and parts) strategy (see subunit 6.3) to make a spatial representation of your research question or hypothesis. This will help you to see the major elements of your dissertation and show the relationship between them.

2

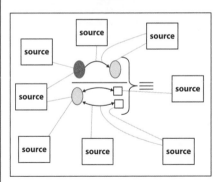

link the literature and the research question

You will need to know how your dissertation relates to other work in the field (the context of your work) and how the literature has been used by you.

Identify your 5–10 major sources (theories, studies etc.) and note down how each one has influenced or helped your work. If appropriate, you can also add whether your dissertation agrees or disagrees with each source. Some of this information may come from the annotated bibliography created as part of the initial dissertation proposal (subunit 8.2).

If the oral examiners' own work is relevant to your own study, make sure you include it. If it wasn't part of your dissertation, then note down how it relates to it and say why it wasn't included.

You can combine strategy **1** and **2** by putting the spatial layout of your research question in the centre of an A3 sheet and arrange the main literature around it. You can show directly (with arrows) how the main sources relate to different elements of the dissertation.

3

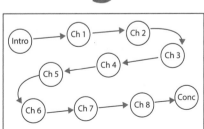

make a spatial overview of your dissertation

This uses the same strategy as that used for producing a spatial layout for presentations (see subunit 8.12). Draw out a map of your dissertation as a narrative that flows from the introduction, through each chapter, to your conclusion.

Your aim is to create an overview that shows the logical order of your work (why one chapter or section follows another) and the main function of each chapter.

In an oral exam, you may be asked to summarise your dissertation in a few minutes. A spatial overview will help you prepare for this.

4

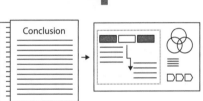

draw an understanding of your conclusion

Using the **drawing an understanding** strategy (subunit 3.2), read through your conclusion chapter and make a one page schema of it. Your aim is to create a visual model of the main points in your conclusion. This can be an effective way to review and display your concluding thoughts and, if appropriate, any recommendations.

Here are some key questions you should be able to answer in preparation for an oral examination of your research dissertation. Not all the questions will be relevant to you, so prepare answers for those that are.

1. your research topic
• Can you summarise your dissertation (in a few minutes)?
• What is your research question?
• What were your aims at the start of the dissertation (research), did they change?
• Why did you choose this topic or this research topic?
• Why do you think this topic or research is important or valuable?

2. your approach
• Why did you use this theoretical framework (methodology)?
• What advantages and disadvantages did this framework (methodology) provide?
• Did you consider using any alternative methodologies?
• What was your major influence(s)?
• Were there any problems with the literature search and, if so, how did you overcome them?
• Did the literature influence your choice of methodology and method?
• Why did you use this method or approach?
• Did you consider any alternative method?
• What were the main problems in carrying out the method?
• What are the limitations of the method?
• Did you have to consider any ethical issues?

3. your findings
• Can you summarise the most important findings or conclusion?
• How do your findings compare with previous research or existing theory?
• If they differ, why do you think they are different?
• Have your (research) findings established anything new or original?
• Do your findings have an external validity or generalisability? (see subunit 8.8)
• What are the practical implications of your findings?
• What are the theoretical implications of your findings?
• How are your findings most useful and who will find them useful?

4. limitations and strengths
• Identify and list your 3 main limitations.
• Identify and list your 3 main strengths.

5. the future (usually only applicable to postgraduate vivas)
• If you did the research again, how would you do it and why?
• Has there been any research in the field since you finished your research?
• How do you think research in this area is likely to develop and how can your research contribute to it?
• Do you have any plans to develop your research further?

list of resources available to download

The simplify your study companion website contains a range of templates, checklists and models you can download, adapt and use. These resources are designed to help you implement some of the strategies and ideas detailed in the book. The list below is given with the relevant subunit. To access the resources, go to www.macmillanihe.com/lia-sys.

simplify your study spatial contents page (A3 size)

- subunit 1.1: assessed work overview
- subunit 1.1: detailed assessed work overview 4, 5, and 6 modules (A3)
- subunit 1.2: academic year or 2 term module planner (A3)
- subunit 1.3: weekly planner (A4 and A3)
- subunit 3.5: making notes for seminars or from reading (A3)
- subunit 3.6: agenda template for meeting dissertation supervisor
- subunit 3.7: collecting information for a critical review
- subunit 4.2: collecting information: practice, theory, research, policy (A3)
- subunit 4.5: model of description and discussion in academic writing (A3)
- subunit 6.2: essay production in 10 steps: a checklist
- subunit 6.8: grade your own essay
- subunit 7.3: template for reflective writing
- subunit 7.5: template for using Gibbs' reflective model
- subunit 8.2: Gantt chart
- subunit 8.11: analysing a research paper
- subunit 8.12: framework for planning the order and content of a presentation (A3)
- subunit 9.1: exam overview table, 4, 5 and 6 exams (A3)
- subunit 9.2: module overview table
- subunit 9.3: 11 week morning, afternoon, evening revision planner (A3)
- subunit 9.3: 11 week module revision planner (A3)
- subunit 9.4: mock MCQ answer sheet
- subunit 9.5: making key revision notes
- subunit 9.7: writing a gobbet

bibliography

Arnheim, R. (2004) *Art and Visual Perception: A Psychology of the Creative Eye* (2nd edn). Oakland, CA: University of California Press

Arnheim, R. (2004) *Visual Thinking*. Oakland, CA: University of California Press

Atkins, S. and Murphy, K. (1994) 'Reflective practice', *Nursing Standard*, 8(39): 49–56

Bassham, G. Irwin, W. Nardone, H. and Wallace, J.M. (2008) *Critical Thinking: A Student's Introduction* (4th edn). New York: McGraw-Hill

Becker, L. (2018) *14 Days to Exam Success* (2nd edn). London: Red Globe Press

Bolton, G. and Delderfield, R. (2018) *Reflective Practice: Writing and Professional Development*. London: Sage

Borton, T. (1970) *Reach, Touch, and Teach: Student Concerns and Process Education*. New York: McGraw-Hill

Boyd, E.M. and Fales A.W. (1983) 'Reflective learning: key to learning from experience', *Journal of Humanistic Psychology*, 23(2): 99–117

Bulman, C. and Schutz, S. (eds) (2013) *Reflective Practice in Nursing* (5th edn). Chichester: Wiley-Blackwell

Buzan, T. (2010) *The Memory Book: How to Remember Anything You Want*. Harlow: Pearson

Carper, B. (1978) 'Fundamental patterns of knowing', *Advances in Nursing Science*, 1(1): 13–24

Cohen, L. Manion, L. and Morrison, K. (2017) *Research Methods in Education* (8th edn). London: Routledge

Cottrell, S. (2012) *The Exam Skills Handbook: Achieving Peak Performance*. London: Red Globe Press

Cottrell, S. (2017) *Critical Thinking Skills: Effective Analysis, Argument and Reflection*. London: Red Globe Press

Dhital, R. (2015) Development and assessment of the effectiveness of alcohol brief intervention delivered in pharmacies by community pharmacists. PhD thesis. King's College London

Driscoll, J. (1994) 'Reflective practice for practise', *Senior Nurse*, 14(1): 47–50

Driscoll, J. (2007) *Practising Clinical Supervision: A Reflective Approach for Healthcare Professionals* (2nd edn). Edinburgh: Baillière Tindall Elsevier

Ennis, R.H. (1996) 'Critical thinking dispositions: their nature and assessability', *Informal Logic*, 18(2 & 3): 165–82

Eysenck, W.M. (1993) *Principles of Cognitive Psychology*. Hove: LEA

Gaspar, R. and Brown, D. (1973) *Perceptual Processes in Reading*. London: Hutchinson Educational

Gibbs, G. (1988) *Learning by Doing: A Guide to Teaching and Learning Methods*. Oxford: Oxford Centre for Staff and Learning Development

Giuffrida, I. (2009) Accountability and the reform of European governance: comitology and agencies in the regulation of GM-food and chemicals. PhD thesis. Queen Mary University of London

Godfrey, J. (2018) *How to Use Your Reading in Your Essays* (3rd edn). London: Red Globe Press

Greetham, B. (2014) *How to Write Your Undergraduate Dissertation*. London: Red Globe Press

Hart, B.O. (1978) *Teaching Reading to Deaf Children*. Washington: AGBAD

Jasper, M. (2003) *Beginning Reflective Practice*. Cheltenham: Nelson Thornes

Johns, C. (1995) 'Framing learning through reflection within Carper's fundamental ways of knowing', *Journal of Advanced Nursing*, 22(2): 226–34

Johns, C. (2000) *Becoming a Reflective Practitioner*. Oxford: Blackwell

Kolb, D.A. (1984) *Experiential Learning: Experience as the Source of Learning and Development*. Englewood Cliffs, NJ: Prentice Hall

Kolb, D.A. and Fry, R.E. (1975) Towards an applied theory of experiential learning. In Cooper, C.L. (ed.) *Theories of Group Processes*. New York: John Wiley

Martyn, H. (ed.) (2000) *Developing Reflective Practice: Making Sense of Social Work in a World of Change*. Bristol: Bristol University Press

National Council for Excellence in Critical Thinking (1992) *Proceedings of The Twelfth Annual International Conference on Critical Thinking and Educational Reform*. Center for Critical Thinking and Moral Critique, Sonoma State University

Neville, C. (2010) *Complete Guide to Referencing and Avoiding Plagiarism*. New York: McGraw-Hill

Nieto, A.M. and Saiz, S. (2011) 'Skills and dispositions of critical thinking: Are they sufficient?', *Anales de Psicología*, 27(1): 202–9

O'Brien, D. (2007) *How to Pass Exams* (3rd edn). London: Duncan Baird

Office for National Statistics (n.d.) *Population estimates*. Available from: www.ons.gov.uk/peoplepopulationandcommunity/populationandmigration/populationestimates (accessed 17 January 2019)

Pears, R. and Shields, G. (2016) *Cite Them Right: The Essential Referencing Guide* (10th edn). London: Red Globe Press.

Pecorari, D. (2016) *Academic Writing and Plagiarism: A Linguistic Analysis*. London: Continuum International

Rolfe, G. (1993) 'Towards a theory of student-centred nurse education: overcoming the constraints of a professional curriculum', *Nurse Education Today,* 13(2): 149–54.

Rolfe, G. (2014) 'Big Ideas: Reach, touch and teach: Terry Borton', *Nurse Education Today*, 34(4): 488–9

Rolfe, G. and Jasper, M. (1993) 'Some strategies for curriculum development in nurse education', *Higher Education*, 17(3): 105–11

Rolfe, G. Jasper, M. and Freshwater, D. (2011) *Critical Reflection in Practice: Generating Knowledge for Care*. London: Red Globe Press

Salas, E. and Rosen, M.A. (2013) 'Building high reliability teams: progress and some reflections on teamwork training', *BMJ Quality and Safety*, 22(5): 369–73

Schön, D.A. (1991) *The Reflective Practitioner*. Farnham: Ashgate

Smith, K. Todd, M. and Waldman, J. (2004) *Doing Your Undergraduate Social Science Dissertation: A Practical Guide for Undergraduates*. London: Routledge

Software Engineering Group School of Computer Science and Mathematics Keele University and Department of Computer Science University of Durham (2007) 'Guidelines for Performing Systematic Literature Reviews in Software Engineering', version 2.3, *EBSE Technical Report EBSE-2007-01*

Sternberg, R.J. (1986) *Critical Thinking: Its Nature, Measurement, and Improvement*. Washington, DC: National Institute of Education

Walliman, N. (2013) *Your Undergraduate Dissertation: The Essential Guide for Success*. London: Sage

Winstanley, C. (2009) *Writing a Dissertation for Dummies*. Chichester: John Wiley & Sons

Wisker, G. (2009) *The Undergraduate Research Handbook*. London: Red Globe Press

index